Implementing the National Dance Education Standards

National Dance Association

Fran Anthony Meyer, PhD, CHES

Editor

Human Kinetics

Library of Congress Cataloging-in-Publication Data

National Dance Association.
  Implementing the national dance education standards / National Dance Association.
    p. cm.
  Includes bibliographical references.
  ISBN-13: 978-0-7360-5788-2 (soft cover)
  ISBN-10: 0-7360-5788-9 (soft cover)
  1. Dance--Study and teaching--United States.   2. Dance--Curricula--United States.   I. Title.
  GV1589.N378   2010
  792.8072--dc22

                                      2009028336

ISBN-10: 0-7360-5788-9 (print)
ISBN-13: 978-0-7360-5788-2 (print)

The Web addresses cited in this text were current as of November 14, 2009 unless otherwise noted.

Acquisitions Editor: Judy Patterson Wright, PhD; **Developmental Editor:** Bethany J. Bentley; **Assistant Editors:** Anne Rumery, Steven Calderwood, and Elizabeth Evans; **Copyeditor:** Ann Prisland; **Permission Manager:** Dalene Reeder; **Graphic Designer:** Nancy Rasmus; **Graphic Artist:** Yvonne Griffith; **Cover Designer:** Bob Reuther; **Photographs (interior):** © Human Kinetics, unless otherwise noted; **Photo Asset Manager:** Laura Fitch; **Photo Production Manager:** Jason Allen; **Art Manager and Illustrator:** Kelly Hendren; **Associate Art Manager:** Alan L. Wilborn; **Printer:** United Graphics

Printed in the United States of America   10 9 8 7 6 5 4 3 2 1

The paper in this book is certified under a sustainable forestry program.

Human Kinetics
Web site: www.HumanKinetics.com

United States: Human Kinetics
P.O. Box 5076
Champaign, IL 61825-5076
800-747-4457
e-mail: humank@hkusa.com

Canada: Human Kinetics
475 Devonshire Road Unit 100
Windsor, ON N8Y 2L5
800-465-7301 (in Canada only)
e-mail: info@hkcanada.com

Europe: Human Kinetics
107 Bradford Road
Stanningley
Leeds LS28 6AT, United Kingdom
+44 (0) 113 255 5665
e-mail: hk@hkeurope.com

Australia: Human Kinetics
57A Price Avenue
Lower Mitcham, South Australia 5062
08 8372 0999
e-mail: info@hkaustralia.com

New Zealand: Human Kinetics
P.O. Box 80
Torrens Park, South Australia 5062
0800 222 062
e-mail: info@hknewzealand.com

E3383

contents

learning experience finder

 All the learning experiences are included in part II of the book and are also on the accompanying CD-ROM for easy printing.

Learning experience title	Page number	Grades	General time requirements*	Accompanying handouts
African and African Diaspora Dance	281	9 to 12	300 to 360 minutes	Rubric for Hip-Hop Combination
Art and Artifacts	135	3 to 5	120 to 165 minutes	Assessment Rubric
Ballet and the Early Ballerinas and Dancing Masters	258	9 to 12	300 to 360 minutes	Ballet Dance Culmination Project Rubric
Bound and Free: Verbs Lead the Way	126	3 to 5	25 to 35 minutes	
Comparative Study of Percussive Footwork Dances	252	9 to 12	300 to 360 minutes	Tap Combination Rubric
Creating New Folk Dances: Linking to the Traditional	159	3 to 5	35 to 60 minutes	Creating a Folk Dance: Understanding and Feelings
Dancing a Story	98	Kindergarten to 2	60 to 95 minutes	
Dancing Balloons	102	Kindergarten to 2	60 to 90 minutes	
Dancing Books	106	Pre-K to 2	20 to 40 minutes	
Dancing With Scarves	143	3 to 5	25 to 35 minutes	
Dancing Words	128	3 to 5	70 to 100 minutes	
Flying Lindy Hop Swing Dance	291	9 to 12	300 to 360 minutes	Teacher Evaluation Sheet: Flying Lindy Hop Swing Dance
Graffiti and Hip-Hop: Exploring Modern Mosaics	266	9 to 12	300 to 360 minutes	Rubric for the Hip Hop Mosaic Assessment Check: Graffiti and Hip-Hop Worksheet
The Influence of African-American Culture and History on Modern Dance	272	9 to 12	240 to 300 minutes	Modern Dance Culmination Project Rubric Choreographic Video Worksheet Elements of Dance Handout
Interdisciplinary Experience: Moving to Written Text	247	9 to 12	80 to 90 minutes	Assessment Check: Teacher Composition Evaluation Assessment Check: Cumulative Self-Evaluation Worksheet
Introduction to Ballet Technique	189	6 to 8	50 to 65 minutes	

*The general time requirements provide a range of minutes for specific learning experiences that can be used in a variety of program scheduling situations.

preface

Dance and a National Education Agenda

If young people are to be fully educated, they need a well-rounded instructional program that promotes development of the whole person so that students are physically and emotionally healthy, knowledgeable in many areas, fully engaged in learning, and motivated to achieve. Over the years, the dance curriculum has fostered these elements and much more. A comprehensive dance curriculum supports students' desires to create and enjoy the works of others, past and present. A comprehensive curriculum helps students build multiple connections among their classmates and the community; learn about and appreciate a multicultural society (within and outside the United States), and practice cooperation, collaboration, and respect. The curriculum uses many teaching styles and learning experiences to help students communicate effectively with others, think critically, solve problems, and make wise decisions. The dance curriculum, further, helps young people develop self-discipline.

Professionals teaching dance should work effectively to make dance an established subject in every school system and encourage student participation from prekindergarten to grade 12. Professionals need to inform key decision makers in schools, the community, and the legislature about the benefits of dance during any discussion about educational reform. Schools that include a dance program within the overall curriculum find that educational experiences for all learners and staff members are enriched. Students today need every opportunity to develop their creative abilities and practice skills desired for work beyond school. A comprehensive dance curriculum is well suited for the task.

To stay on the cutting edge, dance educators need to remain current regarding educational trends and their impact on dance education at the national, state, and local levels. Any changes in educational policy that affect funding, philosophy, and methods of educational delivery can have consequences for dance education, either positive or negative. Awareness is essential for creating opportunities to include or expand dance education in more schools. The National Dance Association, along with other dance and arts organizations, is a strong voice at the national level for initiating, maintaining, and strengthening dance education in the schools. Other educators and advocates also can influence decision makers. They, too, can educate about the benefits of dance, especially highlighting programs based on educational content standards with stringent benchmarks for achievement.

Revised Dance Standards and New Benchmarks

The National Dance Association (NDA) board of directors convened a re-visioning committee, later named the Central Steering Committee (CSC), to review the *National Standards for Dance Education* to determine any needed changes. Without adding to or eliminating any of the standards developed in 1994, the committee reworded the seven standards to be more action oriented and outcomes based. The revised standards are noted in several sections throughout this book.

To complement the revised standards, the CSC developed benchmarks that reflect the student outcomes expected at specific exit grades along the prekindergarten to grade 12 continuum: grades 2, 5, 8, and 12. The revised National Dance Education Standards and exit-grade benchmarks serve as a framework for revising or developing state standards and local curriculum.

Target Audience

Implementing the National Dance Education Standards is written for several audiences: students who are preparing to teach dance in a variety of settings; curriculum administrators responsible for designing policy, developing guidelines, and planning a curriculum; and professionals teaching dance. The professionals in the classroom may be public or private school dance or physical educators teaching dance at any level of the pre-kindergarten to grade 12 spectrum. Professionals also include those in higher education teacher preparation programs, specifically those for dance and physical education.

This book also can be a resource for teachers in community-based parks and recreation programs, before- or after-school clubs, daycare centers, or dance studios. Music teachers who also teach dance may find segments of the book helpful.

Preservice students, young professionals, and those new to teaching dance will find this book useful in all aspects of planning and implementing a dance curriculum and assessing student outcomes. The revised dance standards and new benchmarks will help professionals experienced in dance education assess and revise their current programs.

Administrators at the state, school district, and school levels can use this book. The book provides information state-level leaders can use to revise or develop state standards and learner outcomes for dance education, policy statements, curriculum guidelines, and staff development criteria and opportunities. At the local level, the book can provide guidance for curriculum development, lesson planning, student assessment, and staff development. This user-friendly resource provides cognitive stimuli for individuals who care about quality educational learning experiences for children and youth—with dance education as a teaching and learning tool.

Content Overview

Chapter 1 provides a description and an interpretation of each of the revised seven standards for dance education. The text explains each benchmark and the relationship between the benchmark and standard. The text also provides a justification for reconfiguring the grade classifications for the revised standards and grade-level designation of the benchmarks. Chapter 2 defines the behavioral characteristics for each developmental domain (psychomotor, cognitive, and affective) on which the new dance benchmarks are based. The chapter explains the relationship between student learner characteristics and benchmarks and provides suggested teaching actions and instructional methodologies for each of the four grade categories (prekindergarten to grade 2, grades 3 to 5, grades 6 to 8, and grades 9 to 12). Chapter 3 explains the advantages and cautions of various teaching and curriculum environments common for dance instruction. Other factors that facilitate learning about and through dance are described, such as instructional time factors, types of performances, class organization and management, and teaching materials. Chapter 4 offers a detailed explanation of how to design, plan, and implement a standards-based dance curriculum. Chapter 5 focuses on options and processes for assessing student learning in a standards-based curriculum. Chapter 6 describes the role of technology in dance and suggests various options educators might use to strengthen the curriculum and challenge students' learning processes. Chapter 7 presents an in-depth description of a planning template. A novice or experienced educator might use the template to organize a one-day lesson or a multiple-day learning experience based on a particular theme or skills. The template can be valuable in different ways at various stages along the teaching continuum.

Based on the template described in chapter 7, the next four chapters (chapters 8 through 11) offer 32 sample learning experiences (LEs) for developing and implementing a dance curriculum from prekindergarten through grade 12. These learning experiences are included in PDF format on the accompanying CD-ROM. Chapter 8 presents 6 LEs for prekindergarten to grade 2. Chapter 9 introduces 8 learning experiences for use in grades 3 to 5. Chapters 10 and 11 each offer 9 LEs for grades 6 to 8 and 9 to 12, respectively. These four chapters emphasize the application of dance standards, benchmarks, and content knowledge in teaching dance to students with varying experiences and ability levels.

In the appendix, an extensive table presents the scope and sequence of exit-grade benchmarks for each of the seven dance standards. This section is also provided in PDF format on the CD-ROM.

The glossary includes necessary dance and educational terms. Finally, this book provides an extensive reference and suggested reading list designed to heighten knowledge of concepts and processes addressed in the book. This list of resources was developed by members of the CSC and contributing authors to this book.

Dance is a dynamic art. Dance is a means for communication. Dance is a process for linking cultures. Dance is an educational discipline. Dance is a facilitator for learning. Dance is a tool for healthy living. Students at various ages can learn about dance and how it relates to each of these areas in a variety of school and community settings. This book will help professionals learn strategies for addressing dance from these vantage points.

acknowledgments

The creation of any book involves a collaboration. This publication has been the ultimate collaborative effort over several years. We want to thank numerous people who invested many hours in the project. Words are inadequate to express our gratitude to individuals who participated in various developmental phases and sections of the book, even as the project evolved from one version to another. Discussions during planning, writing, reviewing, reconstruction, writing, reviewing, and refinement were extremely stimulating.

The expertise of each contributor to the chapter topics, benchmarks, and learning experiences is respected and appreciated. Their creative thoughts encouraged the thinking processes. Contributors to this book represent dance professionals from 21 states and Canada and from a variety of settings: prekindergarten to grade 12, higher education, studios, and parks and recreation programs. These professionals have served on writing and review teams and revision committees for dance standards and benchmarks at the local, state, and national levels. Throughout this project, it was a great pleasure to work with such dedicated, talented, and busy professionals who supported this project.

Most segments of this project were team endeavors, including developing concepts, constructing benchmarks, designing grade- and age-level-appropriate learning experiences, writing chapters, reviewing segments of works, reviewing the entire document, and producing the book. There were several individuals who participated on three or more teams that worked on this publication.

The American Alliance for Health, Physical Education, Recreation and Dance provided funding to support a few meetings of the central steering committee, the benchmark writers, and the learning experience designers. Other dedicated professionals used personal funds to attend meetings focused on writing the chapters and learning experiences, and reviewing the work at various stages of development.

Staff members in the Human Kinetics editorial and prepress departments deserve special acknowledgment. We are fortunate to have had such capable people on the team for this project. A special acknowledgment goes to Judy Patterson Wright, acquisitions editor at Human Kinetics. This project could not have happened without her guidance, leadership, and desire for developing quality, professional documents for practical use in dance education.

Central Steering Committee

Joan Burroughs

Liz Gallego

Cindy Hoban

Gayle Kassing

Kathleen Kinderfather

Mary Ann Laverty

Jody Lunt

Fran Anthony Meyer

Marcey Siegel

Marian Simpson

Becky S. Slettum

Peter Werner

Judy Patterson Wright

Expert Authors Providing Chapter Text

Joan Burroughs

Theresa Cone

Kacy Crabtree

Liz Gallego

Cindy Hoban

Gayle Kassing

Mary Ann Laverty

Jody Lunt

Fran Anthony Meyer

Lynnette Overby

Nancy Brooks Schmitz

Marcey Siegel

Marian Simpson

Becky S. Slettum

Peter Werner

Judy Patterson Wright

Contributing Authors for Sample Learning Experiences

Kathryn J. Acciari

John Bennett

Kelly H. Berick

Melinda Blomquist

Donna Cole

Theresa Cone

Janina Dobkowski

Kristin Eberhardt

Lynne Edmondson

Stephen Edmondson

Corine Esposito

Liz Gallego

Lori Head

Colleen Porter Hearn

Steve Hilton

Cindy Hoban

Barbara Kennedy

Debra Knapp

Mary Ann Laverty

Jody Lunt

Josie Metal-Corbin

Suzan Moss

Sherri L. Parker

LuTisha Roberts

Marcey Siegel

Marian Simpson

Becky S. Slettum

Al'Lisa Stallsworth

Peter Werner

Judy Patterson Wright

Laura Zavatto

Content Reviewers

Sandra Bowie

Judith Clark

Kristin Eberhardt

Colleen Porter Hearn

Cindy Hoban

Valerie Komkov Hill

Mary Ann Laverty

Kate Mattingly

Nancy Brooks Schmitz

Marcey Siegel

Debra Sparrow

how to use this book and CD-ROM

This book is designed to be a resource and a planning tool for future and current professionals at many educational levels. Each chapter opens with an overview of the essential points to be covered and closes with a summary that highlights and condenses key concepts discussed within the chapter. Sometimes the summaries provide thoughts for future consideration. This book may be used in its entirety to create a program or enhance an existing one. Alternatively, each chapter may be used as a stand-alone resource for specific information.

This book offers many special features to help professionals at varying levels better use its content in real-world applications.

- Revised action-oriented, outcomes-based National Standards for Dance Education
- New benchmarks for students at exit grades 2, 5, 8, and 12
- Descriptions of the progression of learner benchmarks across grade levels
- Detailed descriptions of learner characteristics by educational domain
- Concrete explanations for writing assessable learning objectives
- Definitions and explanations of key terms related to standards-based curricula, lesson planning, and assessment
- Suggested teacher strategies for addressing learner characteristics: physical, cognitive, and social and emotional
- Generic teaching tips for working with students within various grade and age categories

- Recommendations for working with students with disabilities and with those from other cultures
- Thirty-two in-depth learning experiences that cover grades prekindergarten to 2, 3 to 5, 6 to 8, and 9 to 12
- Description of a process for writing learning experiences in addition to those provided in the text
- Glossary of terms
- Extensive list of references and suggested readings

The CD-ROM contains the revised standards and new benchmarks, explanations of learner characteristics and implications for the curriculum planner, a template for planning learning experiences, and all 32 learning experiences. Curriculum planners and teachers can pull relevant standards, benchmarks, and learner characteristics from the CD-ROM as references for planning specific age- and grade-level-appropriate lessons. Teachers can make multiple copies of the planning template to use while organizing lesson content and sequence, deciding on teaching cues for specific points in a lesson, and coordinating the use of teaching materials and equipment. Having this information close by can help teachers function more efficiently and effectively while keeping learner objectives and desired outcomes at the forefront. Novice teachers may take the sample learning experiences from the office to the classroom and feel confident about using ideas that other professionals have found successful with their students. Experienced teachers may want new and innovative ideas to try with their classes.

part I

Teaching Dance Effectively

Dance is an art form through which movement communicates meaning and understanding. It is a movement form that facilitates mastery of physical skills. There is evidence that dance may enhance the learning processes and healthy development. Teachers who are engaged in the teaching of dance can be found in a variety of educational settings inside and outside the traditional school environment.

Part I of this book is designed to help dance educators in any environment develop or expand meaningful dance curricula and programs while operating within parameters available to them. Experienced educators can use the material in chapters 1 through 7 to become more efficient and effective in working through student-oriented learning approaches. New dance teachers or curriculum designers can use the material to become proficient in describing the program components, explaining the program rationale, understanding learners in their classes, developing model curriculums, using effective teaching methods, identifying appropriate resources for specific developmental levels of students, and creating meaningful assessment tools.

Chapter 1 sets the stage for the rest of the book. It describes the seven dance education standards and provides examples of how they might be addressed in class situations. The chapter also explains the connection between the exit-grade-level benchmarks and the standards. Chapter 2 offers descriptions of general student characteristics at targeted age and grade levels and implications for dance teachers at each level. The chapter recommends instructional methods that can help students reach dance education benchmarks at specific age and grade levels. There also is a description of the relationships among the learner domains, student characteristics, and benchmarks to help the curriculum designer and lesson writer.

Chapters 3 and 4 are critical chapters for curriculum designers. Information in these chapters helps in the decision-making processes regarding the type of program(s) to offer and at what age or grade levels, teaching spaces that can be used efficiently, and time factors available for effective teaching and learning. This information also provides a step-by-step process and progression for connecting the standards, the benchmarks, and the writing of objectives. The chapters provide sample models for teaching creative and structured dances. In Chapter 5, curriculum designers and dance teachers will learn about process- and outcomes-based assessment strategies that measure how well students progress toward or meet designated learning benchmarks. This information can help teachers develop blueprints for quality dance assessment to use with students of varying abilities.

Chapters 6 and 7 help dance teachers focus on effective planning and teaching. Chapter 6 provides information about technology, media tools, and resources available to dance teachers. This information can help add new dimensions to classroom instruction and program development as teachers learn how to apply technology standards and software within dance classes. Chapter 7 systematically takes teachers through a model process for planning dance learning experiences. It sets the tone for better using the information found in part II, chapters 8 through 11. The chapters in part I encourage all educators to reflect on ways the material might be most helpful in current and future teaching environments.

Setting the Stage to Use the Standards Framework

Implementing the National Dance Education Standards contains vital information that clarifies curriculum content selection and related performance outcomes. This chapter explains each of the standards and their interpretations and content implications. The chapter also highlights the relationship between content and performance outcomes inherent in each standard. The grade levels grouped together for the standards parallel the age and grade divisions predominantly found in schools.

Standards are statements that identify the essential knowledge and skills that should be taught and learned in schools and other educational settings. Essential knowledge is what the student should know; skills are what the student should be able to do. Knowledge includes principles, concepts, enduring ideas, issues, and dilemmas from the discipline. Skills are not only the specific motor skills usually associated with dance, but also skills related to the thinking, communicating, and investigative processes. Standards incorporate behaviors and attitudes related to success. The cognitive, affective, and psychomotor domains are integrated within the focus of each standard. At times, there may be more emphasis on a single domain but never to the exclusion of the other domains.

The general purpose of a standard, or a group of standards related to a discipline, is to provide direction for curriculum goals. We associate the term *standards-based curriculum* with a curriculum that is designed with a specific focus on standards. This means that learners have access to and can demonstrate attainment of the knowledge and skills identified within the standards. This text will provide samples of standards-based curriculum planning for all grade groupings (prekindergarten to grade 2, grades 3 to 5, grades 6 to 8, and grades 9 to 12) with the identified benchmarks, or reachable targets, for students to attain.

Interpreting the Seven Standards for Dance Education

Standard 1. Identifies and demonstrates movement elements and skills in performing dance

This standard addresses the acquisition of locomotor and nonlocomotor skills. It focuses on identifying and demonstrating these skills as they relate to the elements of dance. Although the normal progression for acquiring these skills usually capitalizes on the desire for movement by children in prekindergarten (pre-K) through grade 4, the progression becomes incrementally more complex and requires technical dance skills for students in grades 5 through 12. To attain success at higher levels, students need to build the foundation locomotor and nonlocomotor skills at the point in a school curriculum where formal

dance instruction begins. This may mean that middle school students with little background in dance will be learning and refining locomotor skills and combinations of such skills as walking, running, hopping, jumping, skipping, sliding, and galloping. The students also will be learning about nonlocomotor movements such as turning, twisting, bending, stretching, and swinging.

Movement forms the basis for dance. Planned changes in the position, placement, or location of the body use the elements of time, space, force, and relationships to create dance. The element of *time* refers to the rate of speed (tempo) and duration (length) of movement. *Space* relates to movements that take place in personal or general spaces where students may move on varied levels or in specific directions or pathways. The term *force* refers to the quality or energy associated with a movement. The movement may be light or heavy, percussive or sustained, free flowing or bound. When time, space, and force are combined, students may demonstrate movements such as floating, melting, shaking, punching, or exploding. The term *relationships* involves a variety of associations. The student may move over, under,

Students recognize musical time by walking or marching to steady drum beats, percussive sounds, or beats of music.

around, and between objects or individuals. Movements may be face-to-face, back-to-back, or side-by-side. Through applications of relationships, students may study how body parts relate to each other, how partners and groups relate to others in time and space, or how individuals relate to the environment or objects in the environment.

When a student can identify and demonstrate locomotor and nonlocomotor skills separately or in combination with the movement elements, the student heightens kinesthetic awareness of his or her body. The student can control his or her body while in the midst of others who are moving and has the foundation for creativity and self expression through movement.

Standard 2. Understands choreographic principles, processes, and structures

Discovering and inventing ways to solve specific movement problems is essential in dance education. The process of learning to comprehend and apply the principles of choreography is a progression from solving a simple problem involving perhaps a dance sentence—a movement with a beginning, middle, and end—to addressing a complex assignment that has a defined structure, such as ABA or rondo.

Among the commonly held principles of choreography are those of Margaret H'Doubler, dance education pioneer, and Doris Humphrey, professional modern dancer, choreographer, and teacher. H'Doubler often compared choreography to spinning a spider's web with attention to contrast, repetition, climax, variety, balance, transition, harmony, and sequence. She stated that the elements of choreography are form, rhythm, and space. Humphrey identified the four elements of dance movement as design, dynamics, rhythm, and motivation.

Choreographic principles are applied in most dance forms: cultural and traditional dances, ballet, jazz, modern, creative dance, hip-hop, and ballroom. The thoughtful application of the principles of choreography can create a phrase, study, or choreographic work that reveals the intent of the maker of the dance with great clarity.

Standard 3. Understands dance as a way to create and communicate meaning

When a teacher plans lessons that require identification and performance of movement elements within a short study, it is critical that students recognize ways in which body designs, pathways, levels, rhythmic patterns, and energy or movement quality convey meaning to the viewer. A simple observation might be that a dance seems happy. By asking questions such as "What movement makes this a happy dance?" or "What could we change in this dance to make it a sad dance?" you can direct attention to the quickness and speed of the footwork, the clarity of the steps, the body shapes used (open or closed), or the smooth or jagged flow of movement. With more advanced students, the teacher guides discussion by including questions about how the movement elements contribute to the whole work. The questions also encourage students to think about the choices of music, use of performance space (e.g., downstage or upstage), and the application of other art and movement forms (e.g., a Picasso painting, DVD excerpts, sports, or literature). Guided observation of the student's own dances and those of other students can foster thoughtful selection of movements and their combinations when communicating through dance.

This standard addresses the need for dance students to grow in the ability to observe and discuss their own intentions, their dance choreography, and the work of others.

Standard 4. Applies and demonstrates critical and creative thinking skills in dance

Even the smallest dance problem for a kindergarten child requires that choices be made before or while dancing in response to a posed problem: "Do I go in a straight pathway?" "How do I end the dance?" For those more experienced in dance, similar questions apply with more complexity: "Can I repeat this exactly the same way more than once?" "Why am I using this curved shape to both start and end the piece?" "Have I answered all aspects of this choreographic problem with clarity?" As students become more experienced in solving choreographic problems, while working alone or in small groups, they should be able to ask themselves more critical and thoughtful questions.

Critical and creative thinking skills relate to making choices that will clarify the intention of the dance for the performer(s) and the audience. You might ask such questions as "Now that we understand what Group 1 wanted to show, what might be changed (such as, design or rhythm) to make this clearer?" and "Why do you think that would make it clearer?" Asking students to reason, compare, analyze, and evaluate are all important in critical and creative thinking.

Standard 5. Demonstrates and understands dance in various cultures and historical periods

Dance permeates all cultures. There is ritual dance, popular dance, heritage dance, and theater dance. The culture of the United States is a rich mix of people and perspectives, drawn from many cultures, traditions, and backgrounds. The cultural diversity of America is a vast resource for arts education. This diversity can be used to help students understand themselves and others better. Students can learn that each art form has its own characteristics and makes distinctive contributions to its own history and heroes. Students need to learn that there are connections between the arts and connections between particular artistic styles and the historical development of the world's cultures. Subject matter from diverse historical periods, styles, forms, and cultures can be used to develop basic knowledge and skills in dance.

Using cultural traditions as a resource for learning requires more than memorizing the steps and formations of specific dances of a selected country. The historical context and the setting of a dance need to be taught. Students should be able to answer questions such as "Is the dance celebrating a form of work, rooted religiously, or does it express some other aspect of the culture?" Students also may be able to investigate these issues in social studies, history, and other arts classes. They may examine a country's form of government, traditions, games, and lifestyles. Students can bring this knowledge into discussions about how to create a dance using a particular style of movement that might be associated with a specific geographical region. Students benefit not only from practicing these forms and creating dances in the style of specific cultures, but also from observing performances of authentic cultural dance. Through dance, people learn to solve problems, express feelings, cooperate, accept and value individual differences, and gain awareness of their own and others' cultures.

Standard 6. Makes connections between dance and healthful living

Dance relies on the human body as its instrument of expression. As such, it is important that dance education include instruction about health, safety, and injury prevention. To meet this standard, dancers must learn basic anatomy (i.e., skeletal and muscular systems and body alignment).

Plan to incorporate this education early in dance experiences and continue throughout the dance curriculum. Dancers are athletes as well as artists. They need to know the importance of warming up and cooling down, correct stretching practices, injury prevention and care, and the need to rehabilitate. Using best movement practices goes hand in hand with information about nutrition, fitness, appropriate exercise, rest, and body image.

The growing field of dance science and medicine reinforces scientific principles for training and explains how injuries can be prevented when proper guidelines for training, rest, and nutrition are followed regularly. Students need to understand that differences in body types should not limit their ability to move creatively and in aesthetically pleasing ways. How the teacher shares this important information is crucial to the well-being of dance education students and future dancers.

Standard 7. Makes connections between dance and other disciplines

Interdisciplinary work and curriculum integration provide opportunities for students to make meaningful connections within the arts and across disciplines. These pathways to knowledge can take many forms: parallel instruction, cross-disciplinary instruction, and curriculum infusion. Parallel or correlation instruction involves two teachers working together to plan student projects in separate subject areas. Each class is taught independently, but the focus is on common topics, concepts, or standards between the disciplines. Cross-disciplinary instruction occurs when teachers in two or more subject areas address a common theme or concept and collaborate on planning and instruction. This collaboration synchronizes the approach and reinforces transfer of learning. Students can shift between content areas while making cross-disciplinary links. Infusion is a collaborative effort or single-teacher approach in which learning focuses on developing strong relationships between or among subject areas. This is the most sophisticated approach to dance education.

As noted in earlier discussions for each of the National Dance Education Standards, there is ample opportunity to help students make connections between dance and other subject areas. Some of the connections that are made easily in the early grades are between sport movements and music, math, science, literature, and visual

Dance classes offer students opportunities at many age and grade levels to work in small groups.

© Thinkstock Images/age fotostock

arts. Teachers can work cooperatively in these areas through the use of common themes such as rhythm and quality or force factors. Projects in middle and high schools may include additional subject areas, such as history, political science, and psychology. Teachers develop projects combining one or more subject areas to match the complexity appropriate for students' abilities. Working cooperatively with a teacher from a different discipline requires efficient planning by all. This collaborative effort provides an enriching opportunity that is meaningful for the students and teachers as it challenges professionals to bring new perspectives to their teaching.

Understanding What Students Should Know and Be Able to Do

The National Dance Education Standards outline the cumulative skills and knowledge expected of students engaging in dance activities. The dance standards consist of two components: content standards and benchmarks. The *content standards* specify what students should know and be able to do in the dance curriculum. In dance, this covers three modalities of learning: dancing, dance making, and dance appreciation. Students enrich these modalities by involving critical

thinking, understanding, aesthetics, and historical and cultural studies to enhance communication and creative activities in dance as an art form or dance as healthy physical activity.

The standards categorize knowledge by age and by what is developmentally appropriate. Chapter 2 addresses the general physical, social, and behavioral characteristics by specific age and grade levels and explains how these student characteristics are reflected in selected benchmarks. Students are expected to attain the benchmarks identified at the end of grades 2, 5, 8, 12, and at the advanced level. Grade classifications have been reconfigured from the earlier version of the dance standards to more closely match the current grade organization found in most schools.

A *benchmark* is a point of reference that identifies the level of performance for achieving excellence. There are several benchmarks for each dance standard. The benchmarks are the outcomes expected following instruction that is directed toward specific knowledge acquisition, creative work, cultural or historical appreciation, and performance of individuals or groups. A benchmark indicates what students should know and be able to do by the end of the planned dance education curriculum for a designated set of grade levels (e.g., grade 2 for student instruction in prekindergarten to grade 2). The sample benchmarks that follow have been selected as examples of the performance outcomes for two aspects of knowledge and skills encompassed within Standard 1. Sample benchmarks for grades 2, 5, 8, 12, and advanced show the learning progression and increase in complexity that is the developmental expectation in the comprehensive curriculum.

The first set of benchmarks is knowledge-based content that becomes more integrated with purposeful dance movement in grades 8, 12, and advanced. There is a natural progression in complexity of knowledge from identification of anatomical structures to application of that knowledge to strength, flexibility, and optimum dance performance.

Set one benchmarks for Standard 1: Identifies and demonstrates movement elements and skills in performing dance

Grade 2 Benchmark: Identifies body parts correctly (e.g., shoulder, elbow, knees, skull, ribcage, forearm, ball of the foot, and spine)

Grade 5 Benchmark: Recalls anatomical names for major and minor bones and muscles

(e.g., phalanges, femur, biceps, quadriceps, and gluteus maximus)

Grade 8 Benchmark: Describes the role that muscles play in the development of strength, flexibility, endurance, and balance

Grade 12 Benchmark: Analyzes the relationship between a balanced musculoskeletal system and optimum performance (e.g., how muscles work in pairs, benefits of cross-training, and functions of body levers)

Advanced Benchmark: Demonstrates a high level of consistency and reliability in performing technical skills

The second set of benchmarks is more obviously movement-based and reflects students' ability at each benchmark level to perform more complex combinations of movements and apply cognitive skills to meeting the benchmark.

Set two benchmarks for Standard 1: Identifies and demonstrates movement elements and skills in performing dance

Grade 2 Benchmark: Demonstrates simple nonlocomotor (axial) movements (e.g., bend, twist, stretch, and swing)

Grade 5 Benchmark: Creates combinations of locomotor and axial movements in a repeatable sequence of five or more movements

Grade 8 Benchmark: Demonstrates basic movement skills and describes the underlying principles (e.g., alignment, balance, initiation of movement, articulation of isolated body parts, weight shift, elevation and landing, and fall and recovery)

Grade 12 Benchmark: Applies appropriate skeletal alignment (e.g., relationship of the skeleton to the line of gravity and the base of support), body-part articulation, strength, flexibility, agility, and coordination in locomotor and nonlocomotor (axial) movements

Advanced Benchmark: Demonstrates technical skills with artistic expression, demonstrating clarity, musicality, and stylistic nuance

Relationship Between Benchmarks and Standards

The seven National Dance Education Standards provide the overarching framework for the dance education curriculum. Dancing, dance making,

Students at various age levels can learn and successfully participate in many traditional dances.

and dance appreciation are the three key areas of attention in building a well-rounded curriculum. The established benchmarks guide the selection of instructional content. The teacher uses the benchmarks to determine content progression so students can meet these goals successfully.

By using the example of the second set of sample benchmarks provided previously, the teacher knows to build movement vocabulary and kinesthetic awareness from prekindergarten to grade 2, including learning about and practicing a variety of movements that are done in place (nonlocomotor and axial). The emphasis from grades 3 to 5 for this benchmark is developing kinesthetic awareness of performing a nonlocomotor (axial) movement (bend, twist, stretch, or swing) combined with locomotor movements in a sequence that can be repeated. The aspect of repetition demands more physical refinement and control as well as mental concentration and focus. The benchmark for grade 8 calls for developing specific dance skills related to body alignment, movement of body parts in isolation, weight shift, and fall and recovery. The student must attend to where and how movement is initiated, and how to maintain balance by applying movement principles. The benchmark for grade 12 appears similar in focus to that of grade 8 and is directed toward development of sound body control, strength, and flexibility. At this level, more emphasis is placed on the subtle use of movement initiation, finishing movement phrases, and the use of more complex and simultaneous combinations of body movements (whole body or with body isolations). The advanced benchmark addresses the ability to meet all expectations for the grade 12 benchmark but with a mastery of technical skills.

The progression described in this one set of sample benchmarks is intended to help students dance with clarity while applying knowledge of the body and how it can move effectively and safely. The benchmark provides impetus for dance instruction with progression. However, linking a dance curriculum to only one of the standards, or using only one or two sample benchmarks from each standard, will not provide students with a full, comprehensive dance curriculum. By building a curriculum that incorporates all of the standards, students and teachers can integrate benchmarks to help determine appropriate goals.

Summary

Implementing the National Dance Education Standards offers a framework for building curriculum and teaching excellence in dance education. These components adhere to developmental learning characteristics and provide clear guidelines for creating appropriate assessment strategies and tools.

2

Knowing
Your Learners

Student characteristics and cultural backgrounds are critical to a teacher's decisions about lesson planning. This chapter provides information highlighting the general physical, cognitive, and socioemotional characteristics of students. (Additional information is provided at the beginning of chapters 8 through 11 in table format as an easy reference for the teacher.) Although teachers are mindful of the importance of the physical and cognitive characteristics in planning, other equally important factors in students' lives are the socioeconomic, religious, and cultural and heritage issues. All these elements, in addition to skill development, are blended in lesson planning materials that enable students to meet educational benchmarks for success.

Understanding Students' Physical, Cognitive, and Sociobehavioral Characteristics

The primary focus of contemporary education is to help children and youth develop to their full potential. As teachers of dance education, it is critical to understand the many aspects of students' growth and development to provide quality learning experiences and choose movement activities wisely. To make wise choices, you need more than a perfunctory knowledge of the stages of students' growth and development. You need to understand specific characteristics of each developmental stage and the implications that follow for designing a quality dance curriculum and meaningful daily lessons.

Those who study growth and development often use three primary categories, or domains, to make distinctions about changes that occur at general age levels: psychomotor, cognitive, and affective. The psychomotor (physical) domain includes characteristics dealing with patterns of physical growth and maturation, acquisition of motor skills, neurological development, and genetic abilities. The cognitive (intellectual) domain refers to changes that occur in memory development, conceptual understanding, reasoning, problem solving, and other intellectual skills. The affective (socioemotional) domain relates to changes that occur in understanding feelings and coping techniques, building relationships, developing morality, enhancing self-esteem, and actualizing self-efficacy.

Educators need to recognize that all the domains are interrelated and do not function independently. For example, a child cannot go through a physical life change without experiencing new feelings and seeing relationships in different contexts. In fact, all areas of development depend on broader experiences children have within their families, schools, community, and other social contexts, such as the effects of socioeconomic status, community dynamics, ethnicity, culture, religious beliefs, and historical events. Recognizing this will help you design successful curriculum and daily lessons.

This chapter will help educators teaching dance in prekindergarten to grade 12 settings explore child developmental stages in relevant ways. The general characteristics for the psychomotor, cognitive, and affective domains for grade levels and age groups are described in subjective terms because specific timetables for the development of basic characteristics can vary for children of the same age. Even so, there is a need to organize planning in a logical progression to address students' development along a learning continuum. This discussion (and the tables in chapters 8 through 11), describes students' developmental stages in four broad grade and age classifications: prekindergarten to grade 2 (young childhood, 2-7 years old), grades 3 to 5 (childhood, 8-10 years old), grades 6 to 8 (young adolescents, 11-13 years old), and grades 9 to 12 (adolescents, 14-18 years old).

General Characteristics of Students Grades Prekindergarten to 2

Children in the prekindergarten to grade 2 level (ages 2-7 years) are lively, curious, active learners who tend to tire easily and benefit from lessons that balance short, vigorous activity with quiet play or rest periods. They also benefit from relaxation exercises. The younger children tend to have longer torsos and shorter arms and legs, which influence body balance. Between ages two and seven, children's body shapes change as they experience a period of slow, steady growth and development in balance, large muscle skills, and later small muscle control. At these ages, there are wide ranges of cognitive development between children in the two- to four-year age range and the five- to seven-year range. Children in prekindergarten to grade 2 are naturally imitative and tactile; they readily learn by modeling behaviors observed in others. These children have small vocabularies and rely on nonverbal methods for communication (positive, animated facial expressions and body language, and gentle tones). Young children can benefit from more verbalization about thinking and learning processes (e.g., "How can we do . . . ?" "I wonder about . . ." "Where can we find . . . ?"). The children inherently display touching behaviors that help them in their learning processes as well as in their personal interactions with peers, other children, and adults.

In general, children ages two to seven are concrete learners that base their understanding of the world on what is familiar or tangible. They tend to have very active imaginations and are eager learners with short attention spans. At both preschool and primary education levels, children need to experience lessons that are well organized, structured in a logical progression, and incorporate variety and repetition into the activities. This age group is usually more interested in learning by experiencing and doing the activity. Although children in this age group tend to be egocentric, by grade 2 they are learning to make friends and work with partners and small groups. Adult attention and approval are important to them.

Professional Tips for Teachers

For children ages two to seven, dance provides a wonderful opportunity to develop the ability to express themselves nonverbally and to communicate ideas and feelings. Program emphasis at the preschool level that focuses on body awareness, sensory and perceptual-motor experiences, and fundamental spatial concepts taught in an inviting, supportive environment will create a firm foundation in dance as the children progress through the developmental levels. From ages five to seven, the primary program focus builds on body and spatial awareness by combining nonlocomotor and locomotor movements. Adding force, flow, and rhythmical elements to the curriculum increases dance options for students. A dance program that emphasizes creativity provides children with experiences that expand their critical thinking and problem-solving skills, helping them gain multiple ways of processing information. It is important to recognize students' responses of creative problem solving positively. The curriculum can foster positive self-esteem and is a meaningful way for young children to develop fundamental movement skills, dynamic balance, and motor control. Dance provides an opportunity for children to expand the world around them—to create, to learn, and to observe.

Highlights for Instructional Methodology

- Develop lessons that provide structure, variety, and repetition.
- Plan activities that revisit and practice skills previously introduced.
- Use short, simple verbal and nonverbal instructions.
- Design developmentally appropriate lessons that integrate the psychomotor, cognitive, and affective domains.
- Offer a wide variety of dance experiences that improve body balance, control, and coordination.
- Plan activities that consider the dance space size and number of students.

- Provide activities that center on process rather than product.
- Increase dance literacy by verbally identifying dance movements, elements, and concepts in the lessons.
- Balance lessons with short, vigorous activity and quiet play (and rest periods).
- Provide opportunities for older students to work individually, with partners, and in small groups.
- Use developmentally appropriate music and accompaniment.
- Use stories, fantasy and pretending, and familiar objects (animals, plants, appliances, or mechanical items) to develop lesson activities and concepts.
- Encourage students to create dances with a beginning, middle, and end.
- Plan lessons that explore movement elements, develop fundamental locomotor and nonlocomotor movement, incorporate sensory experiences, and involve movements that cross the mid line.
- Introduce prop manipulation (e.g., scarves, hoops) and later add rhythmic experiences.
- Introduce concepts first to a whole group or class. Later, allow students to work with partners or small groups of three.
- Use imitation, following, and leading as effective methods of introducing material and concepts (e.g., follow the leader, shadow imagery, mirror imagery, and call and respond).
- Offer praise and positive reinforcement generously.
- Embrace students' eagerness to be active and enthusiastic about learning.

General Characteristics of Students Grades 3 to 5

Children in the upper elementary grades (ages 8 to 11 years) are in a period of continued slow, steady body growth. Their body strength, balance, and coordination are improving, along with a sense of their own capabilities. Although some may be quite skilled and coordinated, others may appear uncoordinated, awkward, clumsy, inhibited, and insecure. No matter the skill level, students at these ages love to move, and they begin to have more endurance than students in the earlier grades. Students in the upper elementary grades enjoy additional challenges of more complex movements and use of props. They can move continuously for longer periods of time, but they still need short rest breaks to recover. Although they remain in the concrete-learning stage, they are beginning to think more logically and can understand cause-and-effect relationships. Their attention spans lengthen. The students want to perform activities in the proper way and will often have discussions with peers about rules and process. Students at these ages are becoming more social and often rely on the group for approval. Even with group approval, the children seek adult support.

Professional Tips for Teachers

Dance programs in the elementary school provide the foundation for a sequential dance curriculum. The programs should include lessons on progressive locomotor and nonlocomotor (axial) movements that address tempo, level, direction, range of movement, spatial pathways, and dynamics. Programs should offer students opportunities to create, perform, observe, and respond to dance. The elementary dance program is imperative because it serves as a way to learn

Elementary students can learn basic folk dance skills and steps that can be used in many dances throughout school and life.

and express, and it contributes to the acquisition of knowledge. The program should embrace a wide variety of educational dance experiences that use the core processes of doing, perceiving, knowing, understanding, creating, and evaluating. In doing so, dance can facilitate critical thinking in conjunction with the development of motor skills. Because dance education is one way children can learn about themselves and their environment, it can play a significant role in making concepts meaningful. It also can help elementary school children discover basic ideas that are applicable to science, social studies, mathematics, and language arts, as well as to music, theater, and visual arts.

Dance education in the elementary curriculum can increase children's sensitivity and stimulate new areas of awareness that can be carried into adulthood. Children learn that there are many appropriate ways to express himself or herself through dance. Such expression can help the child develop creativity and divergent thinking skills.

Highlights for Instructional Methodology

- Provide active learning experiences that improve combinations of locomotor and nonlocomotor skills.
- Plan activities that encourage large-muscle development and build strength, coordination, and balance while maintaining flexibility.
- Offer activities that provide for a wide range of abilities so that all children will succeed.
- Plan learning experiences that build short sequences while providing for student choice.
- Help students understand dance terminology and make movement-language connections.
- Integrate movement experiences with interdisciplinary concepts from language arts, mathematics, science, and social studies.
- Develop among students a sense of respect, fairness, and responsibility while working with others.
- Provide experiences that allow students to explore movement concepts and elements of space, time, and effort.
- Engage students in critical-thinking and problem-solving experiences.
- Emphasize partner and small-group learning experiences to encourage student input

and decision making when creating short movement sequences.

- Plan a variety of learning activities that include practicing skills and steps while using music and props.
- Ask students to choreograph dances while working by themselves, with a partner, or in small groups.
- Allow students to create, execute, and perform their own dance sequences or phrases and observe the work of others.
- Plan experiences that offer a variety of dance forms, including creative, folk, social, square, ballet, tap, and jazz.
- Plan sufficient practice time so that students may refine steps, dance patterns, and combinations.
- Help students develop knowledge of physical training and health and fitness concepts. Dance includes all fitness concepts for quality health.
- Help students learn that dance is for fun, enjoyment, and personal development and enrichment.

General Characteristics of Students Grades 6 to 8

During the middle school years (ages 12 to 14), young adolescents experience periods of dramatic change in body development, emotions, and social interactions. They experience fluctuations in hormones and metabolism that may cause extremes in body reactions. For example, students may feel anxious one minute and lethargic a short time later. At this age, students are concerned about their physical appearance and acceptance by peers. They are sensitive to criticism and are easily offended. As a result, young adolescents' behavior may seem abnormal (emotional, immature) to most adults. Young adolescents may demonstrate aggressive, daring behavior that sometimes seems argumentative and challenging toward authority. Youth want to show their growth in independence by testing the limits of rules and protocols in the family, at school, and in the community. Popular culture drives young adolescents' interests and decision making. As a result, they frequently use peers and media role models as sources for standards of behavior.

Young adolescents demonstrate increased attention spans and capabilities for understanding more complex issues. They understand time management better than younger children. They want more control and responsibility for planning their lives and evaluating their own work. As adolescents learn more about themselves and their world, they want to learn skills that can be applied to real-life problems and situations. At times, they will reject adult solutions in favor of their own resolutions.

Professional Tips for Teachers

Dance offers young adolescents a physical means to express their self-identity, emotions, and perceptions of the world around them. Students can use personal experiences as topics for creating movement studies and dances. Through creating dances and larger productions, students feel empowered to make decisions, formulate plans for dances, and revise ideas in cooperation with others. Learning about dance offers students the opportunity to gain an understanding of body anatomy, functions, capabilities, and potential for varied movement. Completing a dance can provide a sense of accomplishment. The dance also may be a statement about how the dancers perceive themselves in the world.

Highlights for Instructional Methodology

- Provide time for small groups to discuss a topic or theme for a dance from members' personal perspectives. For example, what do students think about the topic? What do they already know about the topic? And, what ideas for movement can be used to interpret the topic through dance?
- Organize students into small groups of three to five. Doing so can provide each person a voice, while allowing him or her to feel comfortable as part of a group.
- Teach dances that students are ready to accurately reproduce. Begin with dances that have short sequences so students easily feel a sense of accomplishment and are not frustrated.
- Plan dance experiences early on that relate to students' interests (e.g., music trends, popular television or film, or sports) to capture their attention and develop a comfort level for more traditional dance forms later in the program.
- Use props early in the curriculum to help students develop comfort zones about dance.
- Recognize individuals' needs to express ideas in a supportive and constructive atmosphere.

- Offer opportunities to create dances that begin with a structure or choreographic process while allowing for student decision making.

- Keep instructions and lecture to a minimum and provide more time for active engagement in learning and creating dances.

- Use specific and positive reinforcing statements that focus on what students have created or how they have performed, while offering a challenge to push further in the creative or performing process.

- Provide opportunities for boys and girls to mix without feeling uncomfortable.

- Allow students to set criteria for assessing a dance performance or choreography.

- Offer a range of possible types of clothing for participation in dance that are appropriate for the educational setting.

- Be approachable and willing to talk about physical changes, while maintaining respect and consideration for privacy, because teens are often uncomfortable with and embarrassed by their changing bodies. Acceptance of diversity is paramount.

- Ask questions that encourage students to problem solve and explore possible outcomes.

- Help students find solutions on their own by facilitating (providing supervision without interference) the process.

General Characteristics of Students Grades 9 to 12

During the high school years (ages 15 to 18), adolescents present a mosaic of distinct physical, cognitive, and socioemotional characteristics and behaviors. Their desire for independence, leadership, and physical maturity is counterbalanced by their need for guidance and support, group identity, recognition of value, and peer relationships. Adolescents are emotionally vulnerable and insecure. Feelings of inferiority and inadequacy are common. Praise and positive recognition from trusted adults are paramount to teens' healthy development.

On a positive note, adolescents have overcome the physical awkwardness of puberty, possess good small-muscle coordination, and have the ability to perfect movement skills. Their balance, coordination, and muscle strength are signifi-

cantly improved. Cognitively, adolescents have the ability to develop and monitor their own exercise and diet programs. They show maturity in the abilities to study topics in-depth, think systematically about relations and connections, understand abstract problems, and evaluate their own work. Socially, adolescents are concerned about body image and personal appearance. Teens frequently question rules in school, at home, and in the community. However, adolescents are developing a sense of fairness and community consciousness. They also demonstrate concern for the well-being of others, and many teens participate in community service projects.

Professional Tips for Teachers

Educators create positive learning environments when they demonstrate respect for adolescents, understand aspects of their development, provide assistance to low-achieving students, and engage teens in group-oriented activities. By communicating in ways that actively involve adolescents, teachers can spark students' interests in dance-related activities and career paths. Allowing students opportunities to make choices helps them to connect with learning projects and set

Teachers' understanding of adolescent characteristics is critical for ensuring that both male and female students find dance classes meaningful and rewarding.

standards for task performance. Holding teens to these standards creates an experience that can be challenging and rewarding.

Education in dance has been an integral part of human history. It is important for adolescents to gain a broad cultural and historical perspective of dance in society. It also is helpful for students to use current social issues as themes for their choreographic projects (e.g., climate and environmental change, relationships within families and peers, collaborations among political parties, feelings of trust and support, interactions and conflicts, genocide, famine, and health issues like drugs, young pregnancies, or violence). Decisions about the boundaries for a choreographic work and the refinement of a project engage the student in many critical-thinking skills: understanding, applying, analyzing, evaluation, and creating. Through repetition, reflective practice, and evaluation, students understand that dance is a product of intentional and intelligent physical actions. Continually learning about dance forms and working toward mastering dance techniques help adolescents respect the quality of their efforts and those of others.

Highlights for Instructional Methodology

- Avoid comments that may seem critical of a student's physical stature. Teens are sensitive about body image, especially when with peers.

- Allow students to fully explore ideas, make decisions, and evaluate outcomes. They need opportunities for independent brainstorming, making selections, and reflecting about choices that worked well and choices that need changing.

- Create opportunities for students to take responsibility for selected projects and expect them to follow through. This age group desires leadership and wants to feel ownership. Help them understand that with leadership and ownership comes the responsibility to complete all phases of the action plan or project.

- Provide opportunities that help teens explore their identity, values, and beliefs. Working on group projects allows adolescents time to learn about personal strengths and weaknesses and how they relate to other peer values and skills.

- Provide opportunities for students to plan some coeducational and some same-sex group projects. Students mature socially and cognitively when engaged in a variety of group environments.

- Provide optimal time for refinement of steps, dance patterns, combinations, technique, and choreography.

Meeting the Needs of All Students

To successfully provide dance education that is reflective of the three educational domains, educators should be aware of the students' varied backgrounds and abilities. Teachers must be dedicated and willing to work with the abilities students bring to class. Specific information about strategies for working with students with disabilities is available in chapter 7, and the learning experiences in chapters 8 through 11 include strategies for accommodation. Information in this section provides support for a focus on other areas that need attention.

At every grade level, most students enter schools eager to learn. They come as individuals with certain knowledge, beliefs, experiences, and abilities. They have expectations about their school experience. They also come as members of families and socioeconomic groups with a variety of customs, values, religious beliefs, and sometimes different languages and cultural backgrounds. Dance educators need to be knowledgeable about the diversity of individuals and cultural traditions represented by students in the classroom. Every teacher needs to know ways to incorporate the richness of unique student characteristics into the curriculum so that all will learn and benefit.

To gain the expertise and confidence needed to teach and relate to students in classrooms with diverse populations, work to understand the variety of ethnicities and cultures in your community and classes. Continually assess and reflect upon your personal values, attitudes, and biases toward the diverse groups that may be represented at your school. As dance teachers learn to value and honor aspects of different cultures and appreciate the individual learning styles of children, students will value and honor the content their teachers bring to the classroom.

There are a variety of sources to help you gain the knowledge and confidence to relate to students and families in a diverse community. The Chamber of Commerce in many cities and

The attire for specific dances helps express the origin, meaning, and spirit of a dance.

counties provides listings of community events and festivals celebrating different ethnicities. University dance departments can provide in-service workshops, seminars, and graduate courses on traditional and cultural dances, as well as information on common norms and values of specific groups. Professional associations, such as the National Dance Association and its district and state affiliates, can provide workshops at annual conferences and as specialty events in addition to publications related to dance and cultures. Local school systems can support teachers' attendance at targeted staff development events. The school systems also can provide a mentoring program where a successful educator working in classes with diverse students assists those with less experience. Further, dance educators may choose to participate in organized online or self-designed study programs. Such programs may include, but

not be limited to, reading journal and magazine articles, books, or governmental publications and reports. Such a program may involve conversations with individual representatives or families from diverse groups. Using these sources for guidance and skill building can have a significant impact on the success of the diverse learners.

After attaining certain proficiency, you can easily design a quality curriculum that represents the cultural values of the community and its resources. Dance educators have a unique opportunity to fully engage students in learning dance content while addressing each educational domain: psychomotor, cognitive, and affective. Table 2.1 shows how particular benchmarks might help guide a teacher in addressing learner characteristics within the psychomotor, cognitive, and affective domains.

TABLE 2.1   Student Characteristics as They Relate to Educational Domains and Specific Benchmarks

Educational domains		Sample Characteristics and Benchmarks by Grade Groups			
		Grades pre-K to 2	Grades 3 to 5	Grades 6 to 8	Grades 9 to 12
Psychomotor	Characteristic	Begins developing large muscle skills for more efficient patterns that use walks, runs, jumps, hops, gallops, skips, slides, and leaps	Imitates and creates complex physical movements and patterns; reaction time improves	Experiences accelerated physical development in gross motor and fine motor skills in varying degrees	Becomes capable of developing a regular exercise program
	Benchmark	Demonstrates simple locomotor movements (e.g., walk, run, jump, hop, leap, slide, gallop, and skip)	Performs more complex culturally-based folk and social dances with patterns (e.g., steps, formations, tempos, rhythms, and relationships)	Creates and performs combinations and variations with a broad range of dynamics (e.g., sustained, percussive, vibratory, swinging, pausing, or no action on beats)	Develop and implement a personal plan addressing health needs and issues to include regular healthy eating, flexibility, muscular strength, and endurance
Cognitive	Characteristic	Is creative in play and enjoys fantasy with peers; can communicate through stories and events	Can combine, separate, order, and categorize information with ease	Enjoys learning information and skills to apply to real-life problems and situations	Can think systematically and understand abstract processes; wants to experience real-life problem solving and critical thinking
	Benchmark	Improvises, creates, and performs dances based on personal ideas or concepts from other sources (e.g., stories, pictures, poetry, emotions, verbs, found objects, artifacts, or technology	Creates a dance phrase accurately, repeats it, then varies it (e.g., making changes in the time, space, or effort)	Describes the role that muscles play in the development of strength, flexibility, endurance, and balance	Creates a dance and revises it over time, articulating the reasons for artistic decisions and what was lost and gained by those decisions

~ continued

Table 2.1 ~ *continued*

Educational domains		Sample Characteristics and Benchmarks by Grade Groups			
		Grades pre-K to 2	Grades 3 to 5	Grades 6 to 8	Grades 9 to 12
Affective	Characteristic	Is learning to control self and identify what he or she can and cannot do	Enjoys group, cooperative activities and with same-age youth (especially same-sex groups); feels loyal to a group or club	Uses peers and media role models as sources for standards of behavior	Looks at the world more objectively, is developing community consciousness, and is concerned for others' well-being
	Benchmark	Demonstrates starting and stopping with control	Cooperates with a partner or in a small group to create a dance sequence with a beginning, middle, and end	Researches and explains how technology and social change have influenced the structure of dance in entertainment, movies, or the recording industry	Presents a dance that communicates a social theme (e.g., contemporary, historical, or cultural)

Summary

The discussion in this chapter (and information provided in the developmental characteristics tables in chapters 8 through 11) relate to the student characteristics within the three educational domains. Understanding the implications for these characteristics is important in planning meaningful lessons. Also, understanding the cultural and social backgrounds students bring to class is essential to accomplishing the dance benchmarks within a curriculum. The skillful teacher uses this material as building blocks to plan dance education curriculum and daily lessons.

3

Facilitating Effective Learning Environments

While planning and teaching a single dance lesson or unit, planning a yearly curriculum, or developing a district-wide dance program, you will need to consider multiple factors simultaneously. This chapter focuses on items that are essential to success in teaching dance, as well as items that make for a more ideal situation. Knowing the environment, maintaining class rules and expectations, organizing students in ways that facilitate learning, and budgeting wisely are essential to sustaining program excellence.

Identifying Classroom and Curriculum Environments

Preferably, dance is taught in a space designed to meet professionally acceptable standards for dance instruction. Unfortunately, most public schools, community buildings, and daycare facilities are not designed to house dance programs. Gymnasiums, cafeterias, classrooms, outdoor spaces, community common rooms, and even hallways are places where dance is taught every day. Although many of these spaces are not ideal, educators who have taught in these situations suggest that dance education can be taught anywhere, anytime, and in any available space, even though each of these spaces presents unique challenges for both the teacher and the student. Following are factors to consider when your classes or programs are assigned to the most common teaching areas for dance education.

Facilities for Instruction

Many dance classes at various levels of education are assigned to gymnasiums. To many administrators and those in the general public, this may seem like a good option. After all, the curriculum plan-ner specified time in the large space to be used only for dance instruction. Some features common to gymnasiums may support dance instruction: dividing walls (or nets) to designate additional teaching stations within the large area, bleachers that are folded back against the wall, and sprung flooring. However, dance educators assigned to such teaching spaces need to be creative if they expect to maximize this useable space. Teachers will need to brainstorm ways to store unnecessary equipment and address the impact on instruction when multiple sound sources and lessons (whether quiet or active) are offered simultaneously in adjoining classes. Dance programs also may be assigned to classrooms, hallways, outdoor areas, or other so-called empty areas.

Discuss facilities assignments with administrators or curriculum supervisors prior to program planning to share potential curriculum needs and priorities. Some administrators may be excited about including dance in the school curriculum but may not be familiar with needs of the discipline or teacher. In schools where dance is not frequently offered, facilities needs may be a foreign subject to those doing the planning. Some school leaders may believe their job is to supply an empty space, and the rest is up to the educator. Administrators want to be supportive of staff members

Teachers can teach meaningful dance experiences in a variety of settings, including the outdoors.

Darren Robb/The Image Bank/Getty Images

and may need additional information to make good planning decisions. It is important for the dance teacher and administrator to work as a team to ensure appropriate educational environments.

When teaching stations are in a gymnasium, classroom, hallway, or an outdoor space, there are several issues to consider:

- Safety—How many unnecessary items are in the teaching space, either stored or used by others during the day? Can the items be moved to minimize risk of injury? Are there doors or windows that open into the instructional space? How often is the space cleaned to keep floors sanitary for instruction?

- Floor surfaces—How will the space affect students' movement and learning? What footwear is recommended for the floor surface? What dance techniques are safe to teach on the given floor surface? What cleaning and floor care procedures should be followed depending on the specific dance genre or style?

- Sound—Will the teacher and students be able to hear each other during instructional times? What music or sound system is available? Is the sound equipment portable or attached to a fixed station? How accessible is the system to the teacher when he or she is instructing? Does the system work for students who are hearing impaired? Are others teaching in the same (or near) space simultaneously? How are the acoustics? If there are problems, how are they addressed?

- Environmental issues—How are issues related to indoor or outdoor temperature, noise level, sufficient teaching space, or sun glare addressed? Is this a dedicated instructional space, or is it a shared space? If the space is shared, how often does that happen? What options will be available if the class needs to move to a different location on short notice?

- Instructional tools—Is there an ongoing list of needed instructional equipment and supplies? Is there an area available when needs such as these arise: writing, watching video projections, playing CDs or DVDs, using the Internet, or observing a performance?

- Student needs—Do students have supervised areas to change clothes for class? Are the areas near the teaching station? Is there an area to store coats, books, or backpacks?

As people increasingly learn to value dance education within the school system's overall curriculum, decision makers seek to improve conditions for the dance teacher and students. Facilities planners and curriculum designers generally consult publications by the National Association of Schools of Dance (NASD) for recommendations and guidelines regarding facilities, instructional resources, staffing, and curriculum. Dance studios that meet the NASD standards will have

- a sprung floor (to support students as they jump, leap, land, roll, turn, control falls, and perform a variety of airborne and floor-bound movement);

- a smooth, unvarnished floor surface to prevent injuries that is adaptable for many dance genres;

- mirrors installed with equipment permitting their use uncovered or covered;

- ballet barres securely installed at appropriate heights and distances from the walls, especially for grades 6 to 12 and older students (though not ideal, portable, adjustable ballet barres may be purchased if fixed barres will not work in the teaching space);

- ceiling height that is usually 15 to 20 feet (4.6 to 6.1 m) to accommodate lifts, elevations, or prop extensions;

- acoustics that permit good sound resonance within the space while tempering the volume emitted into adjacent halls and rooms;

- sound equipment that permits an accompanist to work with percussion instruments or keyboard, or permits the dance instructor to play prerecorded music;

- storage for sound equipment and instructional resources (CDs, DVDs, VHS recordings);

- equipment for video playback and projection;

- security for expensive equipment and instructional resources;

- chalkboard or white erase board, bulletin board(s) for notices, rehearsals, and classroom rules;

- lighting that is conducive to learning and performing;

- temperature control capability to augment both movement and seat instruction (cooler room temperatures may work for the activity portions of classes); and

- windows strategically placed to avoid glare.

Appropriate facilities are critical to fundamental dance instruction and learning at all levels. Failure to provide adequate teaching spaces limits students' developmental potential and success.

Curriculum Environments for Dance Education

Dance can be an important part of the total educational program in schools. When included as part of the curriculum, dance helps students achieve specific knowledge, skills, and attitudes that increase their abilities to synthesize information, think critically, solve problems, make informed decisions, appreciate others' abilities, and work as team members. Dance can be offered many ways within curricula: as an isolated content area, within other disciplines, or both. Specifically, dance education may be taught as part of the physical education curriculum, incorporated within a dedicated fine arts program, infused or integrated into other subject areas, or combined with programs outside of school. The more opportunities offered students, the greater the success they will experience.

Physical Education

Although many prekindergarten to grade 12 schools offer dance as part of the physical education curriculum, it is most effective for *all* school systems to include this instruction throughout the grade spans. Usually, grade spans are divided into prekindergarten to grade 2, grades 3 to 5, grades 6 to 8, and grades 9 to 12. Dance and movement instruction within the physical education classes at the younger grades are often so integrated that it may be difficult for a casual observer to differentiate between dance and physical education objectives or lessons. In the early and upper elementary grades, much of the dance instruction is identified as creative dance or developmental dance. As students' skills and cognition advance, dance lessons evolve into more structured folk, square, recreational, and social dancing that also teach some basic choreographic elements. Students in elementary grades may experience one dance unit or several short instructional units during the academic year. Regardless of the number of dance units planned for each grade level, there should be progression from unit to unit and grade level to grade level.

In middle and high school grades that offer physical education, the curriculum generally includes one unit of dance per year of physical education instruction. The unit length may vary by school and available staff. Dance classes often focus on structured dances with social components: for example, line dances, traditional dances, various styles of ballroom dances, or call dances. The curriculum may challenge students to create their own partner or group dances. Dance lessons in the general physical education curriculum at the secondary level offer a stronger focus on dance for lifetime activity. In some schools at the middle and secondary levels, exploratory or elective dance classes may be offered as a choice within the physical education program. In these classes, there is more opportunity to strengthen dance technique, learn a new dance genre, and choreograph dances for class or other performance settings. Within any dance instructional unit, lessons should have recognizable scope and progression.

Longitudinally, dance instruction within the prekindergarten to grade 12 physical education curriculum might include one dance unit or more per grade level. Within the district-wide curriculum, it is important to identify the skills that can be developed and the varied dance experiences that can be offered in successive units. Using a curriculum based on the National Dance Education Standards will assure a balanced dance curriculum for all students. However, time constraints of the physical education dance units mean that fewer and less varied experiences can be offered than in a more dedicated dance curriculum.

Fine Arts

There are public and private schools dedicated to a fine arts curriculum or focus. These are often labeled as arts magnet schools and are found across the country at elementary, middle, and high school levels. There also are kindergarten to grade 12 schools that have coordinated fine arts curricula within the general education program. At both types of schools, there is an emphasis on the arts, and students have several concentrated units of dance instruction annually. These classes are in addition to the physical education dance units. Many students who graduate from schools with excellent fine arts curricula have credentials that allow them to successfully audition for major dance companies or prestigious undergraduate degree programs in the performing arts. To ensure sustained program quality, dance specialists are hired to design the curriculum and teach the lessons in these schools.

Infused or Integrated Arts

Another configuration used in curriculum design is infused or integrated arts programming. This design is focused on the learning processes more than on the specific arts content. The arts infused program encourages higher-order thinking skills that include the academic disciplines of dance, music, theater, visual arts, language and reading, math, science, and social studies. The instruction includes hands-on teaching and learning with the arts serving as a process for learning all disciplines. This is an exciting approach that encourages students to experience connections among disciplines and, simultaneously, establish a broader understanding of various content areas.

Integrated arts can mean melding the core principles of each art discipline simultaneously in the learning process. It can mean finding ways that the core principles of dance are used with other subjects to form a new idea or a new way of looking at content. For example, teachers plan dance activities for students to learn about negative and positive numbers, explore geometric shapes and lines, understand poetry, develop a story line, explore physics and other science principles, or learn about positive health practices. Studies regarding outcomes for students involved in the infused or integrated arts program approach show they have successful learning experiences and a deeper understanding in a variety of content areas (Fiske, 1999; Arts Education Partnership, 2002, 2003, and 2005; Burnaford, Brown, Dougherty, and McLaughlin, 2007).

Outside-of-School Programs

Outside-of-school programs are dance opportunities that occur before and after the traditional school class schedule. Before-school activity times are generally shorter in length than after-school time frames. Using the after-school block of time follows the traditional athletics or sports model for practice where students attend daily dance classes throughout the year or for a season. After-school dance instruction also may be organized as a voluntary dance club, meeting one or more times weekly. With either model, students have opportunities for involvement in a variety of choreographic projects as well as opportunities to practice techniques or learn new skills or dance genres. These experiences also offer opportunities for collaboration with other clubs (art, drama, and music) on musical theater productions or other unique cross-disciplinary projects. Additional benefits experienced through dance clubs or an outside-of-school program include opportunities to refine physical skills, develop leadership skills, establish group and team-building skills, and work through long-term creative projects. To establish outside-of-school opportunities for students, school staff members commit time and planning to ensure adequate facilities use and student transportation home after regular school bus runs have ended.

Considering Factors That Affect Instruction and Learning

The age and grade level of students; the length of the dance unit; the physical, cognitive, social, and affective characteristics of students; and the demands for informal and formal performances impact dance instructional blocks. Other chapters in this book address some of these specific topics. For example, chapter 2 identifies learner characteristics and their influence on instructional offerings. Chapter 4 explains ways curriculum planning is impacted by age- and grade-level traits, and how well-organized instructional strategies can maximize learning for students. Following are general suggestions to help educators working with students at various age or grade levels organize time frames for daily lessons and instructional units while considering student developmental patterns.

Instructing Grades Prekindergarten to 2

Dance instruction at the prekindergarten to grade 2 level is planned in relatively short units (two to three weeks) and may range from 15 to 20 minutes per lesson for prekindergarten students to 20 to 30 minutes per lesson for second graders. The lessons focus on structure, variety, and repetition as students explore the basic movement elements and develop fundamental locomotor and nonlocomotor skills. Creative tasks are planned for students to practice the same skills in many different ways. It is more important to gain body control and learn basic movement skills than to cover a large amount of content at this age and developmental level. This approach fosters self-esteem as children create, learn, observe, and explore the world around them. See chapter 8 for sample learning experiences for grades prekindergarten to 2.

Instructing Grades 3 to 5

Class periods for students in grades 3 to 5 typically last 30 minutes or more, and dance units may last three or four weeks. Students' longer attention spans and increased skills justify longer instructional time and educational units. Added length allows students to experience interdisciplinary concepts from other fields within the curriculum. Students are motivated to learn and practice more complex skills and content. Group work in creating dances can last more than one day for the upper-grade students, who are very concerned about getting the steps and dance right. See chapter 9 for sample learning experiences for grades 3 to 5.

Instructing Grades 6 to 8

Students in the middle school grades are more ready to learn skills that can be applied to real-life situations and, perhaps, within thematic concepts. Dance units are longer than in elementary school and commonly parallel grading periods throughout the curriculum. Class length is generally 40 to 45 minutes. The extended class and unit lengths offer opportunities for students to learn new dance genres, review and refine previous skills, and work in groups to complete creative projects over several class periods. As the teacher, select less, rather than more, content and use additional class time to extend learning around only a few thematic ideas. See chapter 10 for sample learning experiences for grades 6 to 8.

Instructing Grades 9 to 12

At the secondary level, dance units may extend for a complete grading period and may use a combination of 90-minute and 45-minute class periods for instruction. The number of days per week and the class length influence planning for learning experiences. Longer class periods provide more opportunities for in-depth planning and completion of student projects. Shorter class periods are useful for increasing skill development in different dance genres or polishing choreography projects. Longer class periods and units allow opportunities for self- and group-assessment activities. See chapter 11 for sample learning experiences for grades 9 to 12.

Planning Informal and Formal Performances

Performance opportunities vary within a grade level and according to the school curriculum. Potential options for informal performances (sometimes called *sharing*) are explained throughout this book for all grade levels. Well-planned informal performances hold high educational value for students. They learn focus, self-discipline, and self-confidence when they recall movements and dance their studies alone or with others. They learn to follow rules, make judgments about the worth of a dance work, and strengthen observation skills while creating and assessing studies using set choreographic criteria. This process also helps students gain appreciation of the dance aesthetic when the teacher guides the class in making evaluative comments about a work, always stressing positive points. Following are some basic questions a teacher might ask that will not focus on whether a specific student did well or performed poorly: "What movement did you see that was soft or very fast?" "Where did you see three of the straight line designs?" "Explain the group spacing at the beginning of the study and at the end. What changed, if anything?" "Where did part A end and part B begin in the two-part form you just observed?" These types of questions or challenges hold the focus of student observation and evaluation on actual dance criteria. When you ask more complex questions, you help students think intensely and view things with a critical eye. Informal performances are part of the planned learning experiences with expected outcomes for every student, and they help to meet the National Dance Education Standards.

Formal performances may be planned as a culmination of learning from classes or may be requested by administrators eager to share a visible part of the curriculum with superintendents, school board members, community advocates, or other special interest groups. These performances are common for any dance program and occur particularly in arts magnet schools, where there may be several formal performances annually. Sometimes student choreography is presented, and other times a professional choreographer may be invited to set a piece for the students. Sometimes the dance, music, drama,

Peter Cade/Iconica/Getty Images

Teachers can provide many opportunities for students to perform and view others' dances during classes throughout the year.

and visual arts classes collaborate on productions to showcase their programs. For any performance, dance teachers focus on the educational value for students. If student works and works by professionals are on the same program, ensure a positive experience for the emerging student choreographer. It is important that sharing of students' works create a further desire to perform and choreograph.

When preparing for formal performances, plan well to ensure educational value throughout casting, rehearsing, costume fitting, spacing, and technical rehearsals. Every student, from the solo artist to the company dancer, should feel valued and know they have experienced learning.

Managing Classes Effectively

Classroom management for the dance teacher is much the same as for any other teacher. You always need eyes in the back of your head. This means being aware of everything going on in all instructional spaces simultaneously. The following is a list of things to help maintain a safe and active learning environment:

- Post rules of conduct for the classroom in a visible area.
- Identify and reinforce expectations for good learning.
- Show respect for teachers and students.
- Respect the property and equipment of others.
- Have clear consequences for poor behavior.
- Use clear directions for class formations, shifts in groups, and the moving of equipment and props.
- Organize classes to deal with space problems and potential behavioral problems.

Following are procedures to think about prior to starting class to encourage positive classroom behavior.

- Plan how students will enter the classroom and where they will place shoes, personal articles, or book bags.
- Decide where to assemble students for the start of class (e.g., assign young children to a floor spot while older students gather or sit near a sign board that outlines work for the day).
- Designating spaces early in the school year will help with learning names.
- Decide on a process for students' respectful speaking, listening, discussing, and questioning.
- Plan ways to efficiently transition from large-group work to independent or small-group work.
- Organize efficient ways to set up and put away equipment and props.
- Decide how to end class and dismiss students to promote an orderly exit from the classroom.

Thoughtful use of the class space (from the beginning of class until the end) is a critical factor in promoting a safe learning environment for dance students. It can be overwhelming when 20 to 25 (or more) students move about simultaneously in a space to solve a movement problem. For a successful experience, establish outer boundaries for instruction that avoid walls, ballet barres, sound or other equipment, and windows. If young students need visual aids to help them learn about boundaries, place lines on the floor around the room perimeter.

Although you may want to use the entire space for movement, there may be times when it is appropriate to designate smaller instructional spaces. For example, designating spaces to complete paper and pencil assignments; create dance maps; view visual recordings; observe, discuss, and assess individual and group works; and participate in station work are most effective.

Planning learning experiences requires time commitment well before you greet students as they enter the dance space. Design movement problems with clear expectations for body control within the spaces. Organize ways to move students quickly from one group activity to another. For example, teaching authentic folk and square dances, with predetermined formations, requires advanced teacher preparation to allow students to move without bumping and shift from forma-

tion to formation seamlessly. Also, some dances may require students to move in rows or columns across the floor. There must be a preestablished transition plan for students to move across the floor in safe directions. The previous examples illustrate the need to plan carefully how instructional space will be used and how the students will shift from one formation to the next during class. Attention to these details will promote success for both you and your students.

Basics of Class Organization

The previous descriptions about creating class rules, establishing behavior expectations, and anticipating problems when planning lessons are grounded in learner characteristics. Very young children need to work independently, cannot follow complex directions, and have short attention spans. They require teacher guidance to learn how to move safely without touching or bumping others. For young students, working cooperatively in groups is a challenge. Therefore, formations must be simple and based on units of two. As children mature, so do their abilities to work in groups of three, four, or five. Likewise, upper elementary students can follow more complex directions about creating one formation and changing it to a new formation. The challenge for the teacher is planning dance work that will engage, rather than frustrate, students. When frustration occurs, behavior problems soon follow.

At the middle school and high school levels, it is easy to think there is no need for detailed organization because students comprehend directions easily, can build on previous dance experience, and have the ability to organize themselves. However, all aspects of the lesson require detailed planning. At the middle school level, it is important to establish the rules and expectations early in the school year. With guidance, students will acquiesce to the class organization and code of behavior. Without strict guidance, this age group will challenge authority, and it will be difficult to gain class control later. Peer group work is central to planning for middle school learners. High school students are less likely to challenge boundaries if there is student input on setting class rules. At this age level, students want to work in groups while seeking to fine-tune individual skills. These traits must be considered in planning the instructional units to achieve student success.

Coordinating Facilities, Equipment, and Props

Earlier, this chapter provided descriptions of common teaching spaces for dance education: gymnasium, classrooms, outdoors, and studios. These facilities offer areas for students to learn and practice their movement skills. In addition to these teaching spaces, especially at the middle school and secondary levels, students need access to dressing rooms with lockers to store school clothes, backpacks, and books during class, and dance apparel at other times. Dressing rooms also should have shower and toilet facilities to promote good hygiene.

Conducting safe dance classes requires large, unobstructed floor spaces (100 square feet [30.5 sq m] per student), high ceilings (recommended at 15 to 20 feet [4.6 to 6.1 m]), and uniform lighting. It is important to have access to the room's temperature controls. During periods of high activity, the room temperature can be lower than in another academic classroom. During inactive portions of a dance class (observing peer work or watching videos), the temperature should be higher.

Commercially developed sprung flooring promotes fewer injuries than other types of flooring. Sprung flooring can withstand many types of dance footwear and is resilient enough to be used for all dance genres. Dance floor longevity is affected by the care given it. That is, daily cleaning with specific cleaning products and procedures is critical. These procedures can reduce unsafe, unsanitary conditions created by bare feet and moist exposed backs, arms, and legs touching the floor.

Good audio and video equipment is a basic budget item for any dance teaching space. Although some dance facilities may use record players and records, many are equipped with a nonportable CD/DVD player and the necessary sound system to project the music throughout the space. Boom boxes (for both CDs and DVDs) are sophisticated in their capabilities and sound output, and they are less expensive than a fully installed sound system. When using a portable system, enhance the sound by placing speakers in strategic locations around the dance space.

Dance is a movement art and a visual art. Therefore, instruction must be supported by video equipment that can record and project dance work. DVDs need to be played through a projection system, such as with a laptop computer, LCD projector, and screen or whiteboard combination. Many dance videos originally in VHS format have been conveniently converted to DVDs. A recording camera is necessary to document and assess students' dance works. Any purchase of equipment for technical support in the dance program should be looked at as a long-term investment.

A wide variety of props are valuable resources for any dance program: scarves, stretch fabric, balls of many sizes that can support body weight, and hoops, to name a few. These can be used by individuals, partners, or groups. There should be enough props to engage all students simultaneously and be safe to use: clean, rounded ends; splinter-free wood, low-decibel sounds; and easily stored and accessed. Obtaining all these resources requires two types of budgets. A capital outlay budget is needed to obtain adequate facilities and purchase large equipment. Another budget is needed for renewable equipment (audio and visual players), instructional supplies (CDs, DVDs, props), and costumes.

Safety issues are addressed throughout this chapter and also in chapter 4. During dance lessons, continually monitor a wide range of safety issues: the condition of the teaching space; class rules; equipment maintenance; detailed learning experiences with careful consideration for class organization and behavior control; and the body care to ensure appropriate warm-up, stretching, strengthening, and endurance to perform specific dance skills and choreography.

Summary

This chapter provides descriptions of four classroom settings commonly used for dance lessons: gymnasium, classroom, outdoor space, and the dance studio. The chapter includes an explanation of what dance education generally provides within various structures: physical education, fine arts, outside-of-school offerings, and dance-infused or integrated classes. There is a section dedicated to factors that impact instruction and learning, such as class length, length of curriculum units, content by age and grade levels, and performance desires. Class organization and management factors are discussed: class rules, student behavioral expectations, developmentally appropriate dance content, and teaching methods that simultaneously invite and challenge students. The final section of the chapter summarizes important information on teaching facilities, equipment, and safety considerations for strong programs. Although similar topics appear in chapters 3 and 4, the perspectives from which they are discussed are different. Chapter 3 focuses on the learning environment, and chapter 4 emphasizes the curriculum environment.

Using Benchmarks and Effective Teaching Strategies

Following a standards-based curriculum requires teachers to construct effective goals, use appropriate teaching and learning strategies, and address benchmarks consistently. This chapter describes the relationship among goals; benchmarks; and cognitive, affective, and psychomotor objectives within the context of sample benchmarks by grade-level groupings for each of the seven standards. Accompanying examples of effective teaching activities and learning practices are identified in sample learning experiences in part II (chapters 8 through 11).

4

Planning a Dance Curriculum

Planning a dance curriculum requires thoughtful decisions so the end result is an organized progression of focused units of learning experiences. The flow and sequencing of the units can be selected from the broad spectrum of the dance field and from specific content. Many factors affect planning for the dance curriculum and instruction in the school and outside-of-school settings. Among these factors are the age and experience of the students; staff availability and qualifications; space, equipment, and instructional time available; and the intent of the dance curriculum within the overall school curriculum. Will the dance curriculum be an isolated content area? Will dance be taught as an arts integrated, arts infusion, or arts magnet or performance approach? Will dance continue as part of the physical education curriculum? Community enrichment potential also is a factor in successful program planning.

Both long- and short-term planning are part of the decision-making process in constructing an effective dance curriculum. As implied, long-term planning focuses on the total span of the curriculum under development. A person knowledgeable about dance education and the school system ideally should lead the project. This will insure a sequential, developmentally appropriate program that is consistent across the school system. For purposes of discussion, this person will be called the dance coordinator. This dance coordinator should have a solid understanding of

- curriculum development theory that includes current approaches to goal setting;
- long- and short-term planning strategies;
- relevance of progression;
- use of cognitive, affective, and psychomotor taxonomies;
- assessment tools;
- effective instructional strategies;
- integration of technology; and
- strategies for integration and accommodation of students with special needs.

The dance coordinator and all teachers responsible for teaching dance should do this planning as a team so that the overall emphases of the dance curriculum are understood and supported. In a district curriculum, there will be overall planning about where the units will be introduced in the curriculum and the overarching goals and benchmarks for accomplishment within the units of instruction. Upon completion of this planning process, teachers can be confident their own instructional units are contributing significantly to the total dance experience for every student.

The phrase short-term planning is applied to several parts of the preparation for teaching. The most obvious short-term planning is done for the daily and weekly lessons within the overall annual school and district curriculum. Before starting class instruction, identify clear goals and objectives for the unit and individual learning experiences. It makes no difference if the learning experiences are one day or five days. Sound goals and objectives help teachers plan sequential and developmentally appropriate learning experiences.

Goals and objectives selected for every instructional unit are content and achievement related. The National Dance Education Standards and the benchmarks provide a balanced framework for creating goals and objectives for the dance curriculum. The seven standards address the cognitive, affective, and psychomotor elements of learning. More specifically, the standards and benchmarks for dance education identify movement skills and elements of dance, choreographic principles, ways to create and communicate meaning, a direction for improving critical and creative thinking in dance, options for understanding various cultures and historical periods, ways to connect dance and healthful living, and opportunities for connecting dance and other disciplines (see chapter 1 for a brief discussion of each of the seven standards). The goals and objectives of the dance education curriculum need to focus on more than building a repertoire of fundamental dance skills and performing dances.

Knowing the skill level of students in the classroom is essential to selecting realistic goals and objectives and to planning units of dance instruction. When appropriate goals and objectives for achievement are selected, and the content is well taught, students are more likely to be successful and retain their motivation for future dance units. This should be an overarching goal for every teacher.

Instructional Time

Most school systems with sequential prekindergarten to grade 12 dance curriculums vary in the number of dance units taught per year, the space and equipment available, and the number of dance teachers or specialists within the school or system.

The length of classes also may vary by grade level. In general, classes in prekindergarten to second grade may range from 20 to 30 minutes. Classes in grades 3 to 5 may be scheduled for 30 to 40 minutes. Middle and high school planning may use a different daily total minutes per teacher, with times ranging from 45 to 90 minutes for instruction. The variations to class lengths are dependent on district standards and the number of teachers available for instruction.

The common pattern for dance instruction in the elementary grades, except in arts magnet schools, is through the physical education and music curriculum. Dance instruction may be infused throughout the curriculum within skill units, or it may be allotted a separate number of days and weeks on par with other skills units. It is recommended that a physical education curriculum, at prekindergarten to grade five, contain 20 to 30 percent dance skills and content infused over the school year. In some elementary schools, students participate in dance lessons as part of the overall arts instruction in addition to the physical education curriculum. When the dual opportu-

nity is available, the dance instructional lessons are planned cooperatively by the arts teachers involved. This keeps the focus on sequential dance instruction for each grade.

Delivery of dance instruction in the middle school curriculum also may vary by school district and by state. Dance coordinators and teachers should be thoroughly familiar with the state (and national) curriculum standards in both dance and physical education to determine the optimal time for dance instruction. Overall, the upper grades' dance units may be longer than those in elementary schools and generally parallel with grading periods. Dance may be offered, as within elementary schools, in the physical education curriculum and within an arts program, with 15 to 20 percent of the physical education curriculum dedicated to dance skills and content. In some middle schools, dance enrichment programs are offered before, during, and after school. All students do not participate in enrichment programs. Therefore, dance curriculum planners must ensure the inclusion of dance units within the regularly scheduled classes.

In advanced classes, students learn that weight and stance assist in counter balancing.

For high schools, most states have educational policies requiring a fine arts unit for graduation. To meet the general requirement, a half-year or one-year unit, high schools allow students to elect classes in dance, visual arts, theater, or music. In schools where the arts have a strong presence, there are opportunities for students to continue with elective dance courses for more than the required time frame. In high school arts magnet schools, dance instructional units may be offered separately for dance "majors" and for those who must take complementary arts courses to balance their general class work. At any high school, dance should continue as part of the physical education curriculum to promote dance as a leisure interest and as an avenue for lifelong physical activity. Minimally, 10 to 15 percent of the high school physical education curriculum should contain dance concepts, content, and skills. It is common for dance instructional units to parallel the high school grading periods, which are generally six or nine weeks long. The length of the grading periods will determine the total instructional days for dance and will influence the setting of content goals and objectives. Additional classes, graded or nongraded, may be offered in before- and after-school programs.

Space and Equipment

Space is a defining factor in determining how many dance classes can be offered daily and the possible genres that can be included in the curriculum. The class size, floor construction, proximity to dressing and locker rooms, technology connections for sound and visual support, and location and visibility of the instructor's office are serious considerations. Ceiling height, unobstructed areas, acoustical qualities, temperature controls, floor surfaces, and equipment placement (such as locations for mirrors, barres, and sound equipment) also are strong considerations in curriculum and lesson planning. Whatever instructional space is used, student safety is paramount. (More information on instructional facilities is found in chapter 3.)

The Purpose of Standards and Benchmarks

The general purpose of a discipline standard, or a group of standards, is to provide direction for curriculum goals that encourage high achievement for all students. A standards statement identifies the essential knowledge and skills that should be taught and learned in schools and other educational settings. Essential knowledge is what the student should know, and skills are what the student should be able to do following instruction. Essential knowledge includes the principles, concepts, and content relevant to the discipline. Essential skills include simple to complex motor, cognitive, and affective functions. Essential skills also include ways of processing: thinking, investigating, and communicating. The seven national dance standards statements identify the skills and knowledge that integrate thinking, feelings, and communications with movement.

Benchmarks are performance outcomes for each standard. Benchmarks set what a student should know and be able to do by the end of a planned dance education curriculum. (See the appendix for tables that describe benchmarks that address each of the National Dance Education Standards.)

Relationship of Standard, Benchmark, and Objective

Here is an example of the use of a benchmark to create an objective based on one of the standards. Standard 1 states that the student "identifies and demonstrates movement elements and skills in performing dance." There are many benchmarks for that standard; they are divided into appropriate performance goals for specific grade levels (prekindergarten to grade 2, 3 to 5, 6 to 8, 9 to 12, and advanced). One prekindergarten to grade 2 benchmark or performance goal states that the student "demonstrates a variety of shapes (e.g., wide, narrow, rounded, twisted, and linear)." The relationship between the standard statement and the benchmark is clear. The "demonstrate(s) a variety of shapes" identified in the benchmark description has a direct connection to "demonstrates movement elements and skills." Body shapes are considered elements of dance, specifically defined for very young children as nonlocomotor (axial) movements. An objective for a daily lesson plan derived from Standard 1 and the benchmark previously cited will clearly identify nonlocomotor movement and a selected set of paired shapes (wide and narrow) that need to be demonstrated. The objective might say, "The student will demonstrate with clarity two different wide-body shapes and two different narrow-body shapes while in personal space." To assess this action, the teacher would look for clear student understanding of wide and narrow

> **Standard 1:** Identifies and demonstrates movement elements and skills in performing dance
>
> **Benchmark Prekindergarten to Grade 2 Body d:** demonstrates a variety of shapes (e.g., wide, narrow, rounded, twisted, and linear)
>
> **Objective:** The student will demonstrate with clarity two different wide-body shapes and two different narrow-body shapes while in personal space.

by observing each student creating recognizable wide shapes and narrow shapes.

In the example shown in the sidebar, the benchmark included more shapes to be attained within the performance objective. However, the teacher who knows the ability of the class for whom the unit or individual lesson plan is designed will recognize that at prekindergarten to grade 2, it is not realistic to think students can demonstrate many different paired shapes during the first lesson within a series of lessons on body shapes. Therefore, the objective states that the student will successfully meet the objective if only wide and narrow shapes are demonstrated, and that each shape must be clearly wide or narrow. More body shape contrasts can be added progressively within the dance unit so that, by the end of grade 2, students will be able to demonstrate all the contrasting shapes identified by this particular benchmark.

Simple to Complex Progression

Benchmarks for each standard reflect significant progression from simple to complex motor, cognitive, and affective learning when studied sequentially from prekindergarten through grade 12 in the overall dance curriculum. The extensive set of benchmark descriptions for every standard is located in the appendix of this book and is also provided on the CD-ROM. The suggested outcomes have been sequenced within each item by grade levels. However, you will want to determine an appropriate sequence based on your knowledge of the students' experiences and capabilities. These benchmark descriptions are offered as a resource for all who are responsible for dance education. Each learning experience in part II clearly identifies the National Dance Education Standards addressed, as well as the benchmarks within each standard that provide the performance outcome for that learning experience.

Table 4.1 will help clarify how the benchmarks can be used to establish solid content progression within a dance unit, continuing with the previous example for prekindergarten to grade 2 body shapes related to Standard 1.

Integrating Knowing, Moving, and Gaining Satisfaction

Responding to stimuli in dance requires knowing and understanding what the task involves (cognitive), dealing with how both the task and the movement make the students feel as movers (affective), and actually doing the physical task (psychomotor). These three areas work simultaneously as students eagerly try to meet the expectation of the teacher. In the prekindergarten to grade 2 performance outcome described earlier, students intellectually grasp wide and narrow as concepts. They apply the concepts in shaping their bodies. Students gain satisfaction by successfully demonstrating wide and narrow shapes. The complexity level is increased by the grades 3 to 5 benchmarks Body b, c, and d (see table 4.2). As this table shows, both nonlocomotor (axial) and locomotor movements combine to create a pattern. This performance outcome is made intellectually complex by having students repeat a sequence of five or more movements.

Creating a pattern in a particular order and remembering that pattern is far more difficult intellectually than responding to a single stimulus (jump, or make a round shape). In the process, the student makes many decisions: "What locomotor movements will I use?" "What axial movement will I use?" "What will come first, second, and next?" "Will I use wide, narrow, or twisted shapes?" "How do I get from one part to the next in the sequence (e.g., fast, slow, varying speeds)?" "What feels more controlled?" "What feels good when I move through the sequence?" "How can I make this sequence clear for someone observing my work?" Physically, the student must demonstrate the decided-upon movements. The last action of the decision-making process is

TABLE 4.1 Example Content Progression

Content Standard 1. Identifies and demonstrates movement elements and skills in performing dance

Content and performance outcomes becoming more complex mentally, incorporating attitudes, emotions, and more challenging physical skills.

Grades pre-K to 2	Grades 3 to 5	Grades 6 to 8	Grades 9 to 12
BODY			
c. demonstrates simple locomotor movements (e.g., walk, run, jump, hop, leap, slide, gallop, and skip)	c. demonstrates more complex locomotor movements (e.g., schottische, polka, two-step, and grapevine)	c. identifies and demonstrates basic dance steps, positions, and patterns of dance from two different styles or traditions (e.g., ballet, modern, jazz, square, line, folk, tap, social, and indigenous dance forms)	c. identifies and demonstrates complex steps and patterns from various dance styles (e.g., dances of a particular performer, choreographer, or time period) and traditions (e.g., dances of bharatanatyam, noh, or folk dances of indigenous people)
d. demonstrates a variety of shapes (e.g., wide, narrow, rounded, twisted, and linear)	d. demonstrates complex shapes including asymmetrical and symmetrical	d. recalls and reproduces movement sequences either teacher or student designed	d. recalls and reproduces extended movement and rhythmic sequences (i.e., 2 to 3 minutes)

TABLE 4.2 Example Content Progression With Increased Complexity

Content Standard 1. Identifies and demonstrates movement elements and skills in performing dance

Content and performance outcomes become more complex mentally, incorporating attitudes, emotions, and more challenging physical skills.

Grades pre-K to 2	Grades 3 to 5	Grades 6 to 8	Grades 9 to 12
BODY			
b. demonstrates simple non-locomotor (axial) movements (e.g., bend, twist, stretch, and swing)	b. creates combinations of locomotor and axial movements in a repeatable sequence of five or more movements	b. demonstrates basic movement skills and describes the underlying principles (e.g., alignment, balance, initiation of movement, articulation of isolated body parts, weight shift, elevation and landing, and fall and recovery)	b. applies appropriate skeletal alignment (i.e., relationship of the skeleton to the line of gravity and the base of support), body-part articulation, strength, flexibility, agility, and coordination in locomotor and nonlocomotor (axial) movements
c. demonstrates simple locomotor (e.g., walk, run, jump, hop, leap, slide, gallop, and skip)	c. demonstrates more complex locomotor movements (e.g., schottische, polka, two-step, and grapevine)	c. identifies and demonstrates basic dance steps, positions, and patterns of dance from two different styles or traditions (e.g., ballet, modern, jazz, square, line, folk, tap, social, and indigenous dance forms)	c. identifies and demonstrates complex steps and patterns from various dance styles (e.g., dances of a particular performer, choreographer, or time period) and traditions (e.g., dances of bharatanatyam, noh, folk dances of indigenous people)
d. demonstrates a variety of shapes (e.g., wide, narrow, rounded, twisted, and linear)	d. demonstrates complex, shapes including asymmetrical and symmetrical	d. recalls and reproduces movement sequences either teacher or student designed	d. recalls and reproduces extended movement and rhythmic sequences (i.e., 2 to 3 minutes)

It shows when students are satisfied with their dance accomplishments—the creation of a beginning, a middle, and an end.

choosing what portions of the sequence to keep or change. This decision depends on the student's level of satisfaction with his or her work. If something does not feel right, the student can change or eliminate that portion until the whole physical sequence is satisfying personally and intellectually.

For students in grades 3 to 5, Standard 1 Body d, the focus is on knowing what symmetrical and asymmetrical mean, applying those concepts in creating or designing shapes alone or with others that meet the criteria for symmetrical and asymmetrical, and feeling successful in making clear shapes that meet the expectation of the performance outcome. Benchmark d circles back to work solely with shapes, as in the prekindergarten to grade 2 benchmark d. While this might seem less complex than the grade 3-5 benchmark b (that combined locomotor and axial movements in a sequence), the focus on new vocabulary (symmetrical and asymmetrical) adds a new dimension to shaping the body. Students learn that a wide-body shape (prekindergarten-grade 2) can be symmetrical (grades 3-5). These benchmarks add layers of cognition and understanding to the movement challenges.

Planning Progression: Step-by-Step and Spiral

An effective progression introduces knowledge and skills in small amounts. Then, new aspects of the skills and knowledge are added that require slightly more complex responses. Finally, the most recent skill and knowledge acquired serve as the foundation for even more demanding movements and concept application in later lessons. This process is a step-by-step evolution with a spiral progression. In a spiral process, the student revisits prior knowledge and skills while adding style, speed, directional change, or new movement vocabulary that eventually becomes a refined jazz technique, a flamenco performance, or a ballroom dance.

An example of the spiral progression concept and practice is found in the benchmarks, for Standard 1 Body, grades 6 to 8 and 9 to 12. The focus of benchmarks b, c, and d for grades 6 to 8 is dependent upon the student having achieved good body control; the ability to move safely using different speeds; the knowledge and skill to apply all axial movements as well as symmetrical and asymmetrical shapes; and the ability to move alone and with others in self-determined, repeatable sequences. The new focus for the body is the application of the basic principles of movement (e.g., alignment, balance, initiation of movement, articulation of isolated body parts, weight shift, elevation and landing, and fall and recovery) in doing basic dance steps, positions, and patterns from two different styles or traditions. For grades 9 to 12, there is added vocabulary that must be learned and applied with a focus on movement refinement (highest level possible), applying the basic principles of movement to complex dance step combinations and, ultimately, to additional dance styles and traditions.

Applying Bloom's Taxonomy

Understanding that knowledge is gained in progressively more complex thought processes is the foundation proposed by Benjamin Bloom and a group of educational psychologists in 1956. In the 1990s, a new group of educational psychologists, led by a former student of Dr. Bloom (Lorin Anderson), revised the taxonomy to reflect and support its broader use in the 21st century. In this revised taxonomy, the different levels of cognition are represented by verbs rather than the nouns used in the original version. Additional changes include renaming the lowest levels of cognition from knowledge to remembering and comprehension to understanding. Synthesis was renamed creating and inverted with evaluation. This new version of the taxonomy identifies creating as the highest level of cognition. To clarify information related to the taxonomy in this chapter and in chapter 5, the following lists compare the new language with the earlier Bloom's Taxonomy.

Bloom's Taxonomy

Original Version	New Version
Evaluation	Creating
Synthesis	Evaluating
Analysis	Analyzing
Application	Applying
Comprehension	Understanding
Knowledge	Remembering

Following is a description of how the revised Bloom's Taxonomy identifies the six levels of cognition and their relationships to dance education.

1. Remembering: recall or remember exactly; memorize facts, dance terminology, and dance elements, and identify simple details

2. Understanding: describe or demonstrate dance elements, facts, and simple details of a dance

3. Applying: solve a movement problem that has familiar dance terminology and dance elements; explore basic dance concepts

4. Analyzing: analyze parts of a dance created by self or others; break down parts of a technique sequence; examine historical period dance characteristics as seen in a dance performance or on a DVD

5. Evaluating: assess the artistic quality and value of a dance work; judge the worth of a dance lesson, unit, or program based on known criteria (standards)

6. Creating: arrange different pieces of information to create a new thought; organize several dance ideas into a new dance form or dance piece; compose an end-of-unit dance project that combines several aspects of unit content (Anderson and Krathwohl, 2001; Bloom, 1956)

The benchmarks for Standard 5 (Demonstrates and understands dance in various cultures and historical periods) illustrate how a link can be made between Bloom's cognition levels and the concept of spiral progression (see table 4.3).

Grades prekindergarten to 2 b: recalls the cultural significance of a folk dance (customs, special meaning, location; e.g., the Shoemaker's Dance is from Denmark and is about making shoes)

At this grade level, it is important that students understand that dance can be representative of and have meaning within the culture in which it was created. The Shoemaker's Dance imitates making shoes. This helps the students experience and visualize meaning. Within the dance, students work cognitively at the remembering and understanding levels of the new version of Bloom's Taxonomy.

Grades 3 to 5 b: describes the differences and similarities between folk dances of more than one culture

To discuss differences and similarities of folk dances, the students must know characteristics of the dances. To describe differences requires students to analyze information about the two

TABLE 4.3 Linking Cognition Levels Among a Sample of Benchmarks

Content Standard 5. Demonstrates and understands dance in various cultures and historical periods

Grades pre-K to 2	Grades 3 to 5	Grades 6 to 8	Grades 9 to 12
b. recalls the cultural significance of a folk dance (customs, special meaning, location; e.g., the Shoemaker Dance is from Denmark and is about making shoes)	b. describes the differences and similarities between folk dances of more than one culture (e.g., purpose, gesture, style, function)	b. describes the aesthetic qualities and traditions of more than one culture	b. describes the function of a particular dance within the society where the dance was or is performed (explains such things as religious or secular implications and cultural phenomena)

cultures. In all probability, the students will be guided through the applying process to answer specific questions about dances (e.g., How are the torso and arms held in English Country Dance and Middle Eastern traditional dances?).

Grades 6 to 8 b: describes the aesthetic qualities and traditions of more than one culture

This benchmark description offers a good example of a spiraling effect. The student reviews the traditions of one culture while adding a more difficult challenge by describing the aesthetic qualities. The student must think about performance cues the teacher provided when the student was learning the dance as well as the more subtle concepts of shifts in meter, use of accents, use of props, and whether the dance was designed for one sex or for both men and women. This performance outcome requires students to apply and analyze information.

Grades 9 to 12 b: describes the function of a particular dance within the society where the dance was or is performed (explains such things as religious or secular implications and cultural phenomena)

Although this performance outcome appears similar to that of the grades 6 to 8 benchmark b description, it is more complex because it requires a more in-depth background in the cultural or societal function of the dance. To reach this outcome, students will analyze information, evaluate possible primary or secondary functions of a dance, and create a response.

All learning experiences incorporate prior knowledge and skills, creating an ever-changing basis for spiral progression to occur. Dance content is complex and can be quite comprehensive. Many and varied dance experiences are necessary to help students progress through all levels of the new Bloom's Taxonomy.

Evolution of Benchmarks to Objectives

There is a clear relationship between benchmarks and objectives for a district and school curriculum, specific units within a curriculum by grade level, and daily lesson plans or learning experiences. Benchmarks identify the per-formance outcomes from which objectives are written. Dance teachers have the flexibility to modify the outcomes to ensure student success. Most likely, teachers will simplify concepts and skills for given benchmarks in the early grade levels. These adaptations are part of a planned, step-by-step and spiral progression that moves from simple to complex learning. Knowing dance content, learner characteristics, and the specific students in class are critical to building a strong curriculum. Using balanced objectives and sound progressions within a program will heighten students' enthusiasm for dance.

Strategies for Reaching Benchmarks

Teachers that organize their curriculums around standards and benchmarks want to ensure that their students have abundant opportunities for success. They want to know that achievement is progressing across classes and grade levels. A key to successful planning and teaching dance is to use a broad range of teaching styles or methods. The methods and approaches, however, will vary by teachers, classes, and schools. Even a teacher with multiple classes of the same age or grade level will find that some teaching styles or methods will serve better than others for covering the same content with a specific class or group of students. Teachers, therefore, should understand multiple styles and approaches to guide the individual learners' needs on a given day. This section offers ideas about learning practices and teaching activities that can be useful in planning standards-based dance curriculums and lessons.

Effective Learning Practices

Dance educators need to understand specific developmental characteristics of the students in their classes. Descriptions in chapter 2 and tables in chapters 8 through 11 highlight these characteristics by learning domains (physical, affective, and cognitive) for students ages 2 to 7 (prekindergarten-grade 2), 8 to 11 (grades 3-5), 12 to 14 (grades 6-8), and 15 to 18 (grades 9-12). Knowing these age and grade-level characteristics will help you write relevant objectives when planning curriculum and use effective learning practices when developing lessons.

For example, young children want to move and explore new ways of using their bodies. They want to please. They have short attention spans and tire easily. They do not have an extensive vocabulary with which to hold long discussions. Therefore, teachers of young children should identify performance outcomes that are simple, direct, and clear so that students know the day's expectations. Successful learning activities can be completed in a short time. The objectives will reflect progression within a lesson so that very simple movements are established before asking children to identify terminology, understand rudimentary dance content, or combine two simple tasks such as running in general space without bumping or going into another person's personal space. When students know the day's expectation, and feel it is achievable, they can focus intensely on the task.

Students in grades 3 to 5 display a wide range of development—cognitively, socially, and physically. In grades 4 and 5, some students will enter puberty, and differences in height, weight, strength, endurance, and body control will be noticeable. Students at these ages are more social. To help students succeed, performance goals and objectives need to acknowledge the range of abilities and allow for a wide variety of solutions to challenge and engage all students. Activities for developing both major and minor muscle groups must be included in lessons. At these grade levels, it is appropriate to emphasize group learning and decision making, possibly with choreographic problems. Groups can decide how to use all group members fairly, assess what is happening (in the process), and redirect actions as needed. Providing consistent and clear feedback is essential at this age to help students progress from working alone or with partners to being part of a small group learning team.

Students in middle school are physically more skilled in gross and fine motor control. However, they may lack endurance, strength, and flexibility due to rapid growth and hormonal changes. They are moody, restless, and often listless. Middle school students are interested in rules and regulations, but they tend to question rules and community norms. Cognitively, they recognize relationships between ideas and facts and can understand cause and effect. Middle school students prefer active over passive learning experiences. To address these factors, design a variety of active and fun learning activities. Plan for outcomes that encourage problem solving and help students find solutions on their own; provide guidance, not interference. When objectives require group planning, students need clear directions and expecta-

tions, strategies for addressing the task, and group self-evaluation techniques. Plan opportunities to help boys and girls feel comfortable working in mixed groups. Learning objectives need clear performance expectations and understandable boundaries to focus work for the class.

Adolescents in high school tend to have good muscle and bone development, advanced body coordination, and awareness of body image and appearance. These students can participate in prolonged activities that use critical-thinking and problem-solving skills. They enjoy testing home and school rules and often appear overconfident; however, they are often emotionally insecure and vulnerable. While seeking identity as a part of a social group, they also want independence to develop individuality. Learning objectives for the students in grades 9 to 12 dance classes should encourage refinement of technical skills, choreographic processes, and work ethics. Students can learn to organize projects, implement time lines, and evaluate their own and others' works. As with middle school youth, group learning activities are important for learning and developing both cooperative responsibilities and peer leadership skills. Focusing on these learning goals can heighten awareness of aesthetics and dance values.

In school systems where the dance curriculum is not offered until middle school or high school, dance teachers will need to plan activities to address learning associated with the content and benchmarks identified for students in the lower grades. This provides the older students with the necessary background and practice to be successful with the on-grade content and skills. Middle and high school students will progress faster through the learning of prior benchmarks than will younger students.

The teacher recommendations can help students achieve active learning in the psychomotor, affective, and cognitive domains while developing competence at the highest intellectual levels:

- Review the research findings about brain development to be effective in planning dance learning experiences.
- Help students feel safe as they move through learning experiences that increasingly challenge them to meet high expectations.
- Connect learning experiences to the real world so students will be engaged and motivated to learn.
- Recognize the importance of providing enriched environments.

Effective Teaching Activities

Following are samples of effective tools that a dance teacher may use to meet grade-level benchmarks. Selective use at appropriate grade levels is important. For instance, there should not be a large emphasis on journal or notebook work in the prekindergarten to grade 2 classes, although this kind of work can be very effective for students in grades 9 to 12.

Direct teaching is a teacher-centered approach to instruction. To use this approach, explain or show students what to do and then observe the learning process. The teacher makes all or most decisions about the lesson content and specific responses desired. The teacher sets practice or rehearsal times. The direct approach is most appropriate if students are learning specific choreography or dances, or if safety is a major issue. This is one option in a wide array of teaching possibilities.

Guided discovery is a student-centered approach to instruction. To use this approach, pose a series of questions or statements that will lead students to discover one solution to a task or learner concept. This approach promotes discussion among students and challenges their capacities to evaluate. It encourages exploration and experimentation. It leads to a greater understanding of how and why skills are performed the way they are. Although this approach is used primarily at lower grade levels, it can be effectively used to help all students gain a deeper understanding of many dance forms, including modern, jazz, ballet, tap, folk, square, and social dance.

Role-playing and mime are considered most effective with young children. However, when movement challenges are crafted sensitively, these forms of response can be used at all grade levels. The value of these forms of stimuli is that students become the role they play. They are more open about movement responses and lose some of their insecurity and inhibitions. This happens because there is a concrete reference from which to draw ideas, such as body design, strength or lightness of movement, and spatial boundaries.

Class discussion is a natural tool to engage students, bring focus to the day's work, and use selected criteria (student or teacher determined) for assessing peer dance studies. Class discussion can serve as a platform for review of previous class work as well as a means to make connec-

Role playing and cooperative group work enrich the process of creating a dance.

Peter Cade/Iconica/Getty Images

tions between different subjects and dance content. Effective use of class discussion requires thoughtful preparation of cues that will contribute directly to the day's lesson. The teacher guides the discussion to keep it focused.

Small-group discussion or cooperative learning is most effective when you have prepared a frame of reference to guide and focus the work. Small-group discussion and cooperative learning are important tools for upper elementary grades through high school. Breaking into small groups provides students with opportunities for some autonomy, self-direction, peer decision making, peer leadership development, and group identification.

Interviewing is a good way to get students involved immediately in a learning process outside of class. The objective is to systematically solicit information about specific dance topics (e.g., well-known choreographers, community dance companies, students' works, community programs of study, or cultural dance origins).

Students are asked to bring interview data back to class for sharing and discussion. In planning for data collection, one student may interview one person; one student may interview several people; several students may interview one person; or many students may interview several people. To ensure success, help students plan targeted questions for the interviewee, and explain the importance of gathering meaningful data to generate relevant class discussion. Before data collection, students may practice interview techniques alone or with others.

Brainstorming and improvisation are paired because they are good activities for trying new ideas or movements with no concern for editing or monitoring. Use phrases such as "explore" and "find as many ways as possible" as cues to encourage students to move freely and experience new ways of using their bodies. The term *improvisation* has different connotations for dance students, and its use is dependent upon their levels of dance experience. The goal is to increase movement range and options when provided with a single stimulus. Brainstorming is an excellent icebreaker for increasing students' repertoire of knowledge-based ideas that later may be used to focus a dance study or choreographic work. Brainstorming can be a paper-and-pencil activity or an oral response, either teacher guided or student-led discussion within small groups.

Problem solving offers students opportunities to construct knowledge for themselves. Although you most likely will pose the original task or question that needs a solution, students may create topics for investigation. This process can require individual attention or group interaction. Generally, the more students involved, the greater the learning can occur because of the number of variables that need experimentation and evaluation to determine a best solution. More learning also can occur when solutions are not easily apparent. Through problem solving, students gain a rich understanding of techniques that might be used in other learning situations outside the dance classes.

Debate, as a stimulus for dance learning, may seem odd. However, debate offers the obvious cognitive challenges and the need to acquire necessary factual information as well as the ability to draw relationships among ideas in order to present convincing arguments. Debate is a tool that can be very effective in a unit using social or political issues as a source for creating dance works. Debate is best used with high school students.

Journaling or keeping a notebook is often used to encourage students to think reflectively about their creative work and progress in class. Writing daily or weekly reports focuses on the work attempted and completed in classes. This reporting explains choices made, provides the rationale for revisions, includes descriptions of the final creative work(s), and serves as a guided opportunity for assessment of personal performance. Journals and notebooks provide a chance for students to share "aha" moments privately. These can be important breakthrough experiences that might never be freely shared orally with the class. Where school facilities permit, journals may be kept electronically. It is important to respond to journal entries but never in a judgmental way. If a teacher is not tactful and supportive with comments, the value of students writing about their works and themselves is lost. The students will no longer feel it is safe to expose their reflections about progress and difficulties.

Hands-on writing offers a way to describe short, in-class writing experiences. For the teacher, this means planning and organization prior to class. Writing materials must be available for each student. There must be an efficient means of distributing the supplies so that instructional time is not wasted. Children may draw shapes that connect with the lesson's content; more mature students can draw shapes and list words to describe ways of moving in the shape; older students can answer questions after viewing a video or DVD of a selected dance style. There are innumerable ways to use short written responses.

When using any teaching activity, stay focused on the idea that students are in class to move and dance most of the time. Writing should be used to reinforce content and help students analyze and combine materials in direct relation to an ongoing class dance project.

Peer tutoring is generally offered by individuals of similar ages or educational levels. In prekindergarten to grade 12 schools, the instruction is generally provided by another student in the same grade or a little higher. In higher education, the peer tutor is usually another student within the institution. This process is generally less intimidating or threatening to learners. Schools implementing peer tutoring programs generally establish guidelines for the tutors to ensure effective learning.

Computer simulation programs offer students and teachers opportunities to stretch their limits regarding movement and choreography. Dance is an art form that uses the body to communicate messages to audiences. Computer simulation programs may help dancers create different ways of delivering their messages. Certain programs allow students to explore new body shapes and dance movements through animated simulations. There are programs that allow for practicing movement sequences on screen, investigating dancers' positions while moving within a dance space, choreographing dances, or revising choreographed works. Dancers may use computer animation within dances to create interesting visual effects during performances. This teaching and learning approach would be most effective for use with experienced dance students at higher grade levels.

Part II contains sample learning experiences for grades prekindergarten to 12. Within the material are many examples of the teaching activities described in this chapter and stimuli for effective learning. The examples are embedded in the natural development of learning experiences. It may be helpful to note that some of the teaching activities may happen at different points within each lesson.

Additional Considerations

When dance teachers develop learning experiences, it is advantageous to consider other instructional components: optional activities, technology connections, accommodation and differentiation ideas, and connections to everyday living and lifetime wellness. This information must be planned at the same time dance content is determined. Following is a description of these additional instructional considerations.

Optional activities are those used to augment the lesson. They might be called emergency ideas. There are times when even the most perfect teaching plan does not work, so have a preplanned, content-related option ready to use as needed. Optional activities also may be viewed as enrichment opportunities.

Technology connections are increasingly found in teaching plans. Technology connections can be as basic as having a DVD player, screen, and access to a library of DVDs to augment visual understanding of spaces, patterns, dance genres, and great choreographic works. Computer-driven technology connections require a school-wide support system and budget to be useful on a daily basis. When all students have access to laptop computers for an entire school year, the possibilities for enrichment are endless. Individual student assignments and group projects can take on new dimensions.

Accommodation and differentiation in lesson preparation addresses the need to have a range of activities possible for a given task. This allows students of all abilities to succeed in class. Differentiated classrooms are successful when you focus on the most important content areas, are flexible, value student differences, work in partnership with the student to match the academic needs and the learning environment, develop plans to teach students at their levels of readiness, offer activities to complement students' interests and learning styles, and provide ongoing assessment with instruction. Teacher feedback early and often is important for everyone in the class.

Everyday living and lifetime wellness connections can be identified in many learning experiences to reinforce relationships to lifetime health and well-being and the need for regular activity, mental stimulation, and social interaction. Use your lessons to raise the level of consciousness about dance being a resource for lifetime health and wellness. Current television shows and movies that focus on dance can raise awareness of the long-term values of dance.

The learning experiences found in chapters 8 through 11 address most of the factors listed as additional considerations. These ideas are located at the end of every learning experience and are identified by a clear subject heading. When reviewing the learning experiences, look at lessons for the grade levels you teach, as well as lessons for grade levels at the next lowest and highest grades. There are many different, valuable suggestions that may be applicable at all grade levels.

Applying Effective Learning Practices and Teaching Activities

Models for teaching creative dance and folk dance are presented here independently from the learning experiences in part II. Using these models as examples illustrates a framework that can be used to prepare for and teach classes. These two models provide background for planning and an introduction to understanding the structure applied to the sample learning experiences in chapters 8 through 11.

Instructional Strategies for Teaching Creative Dance to Prekindergarten and Kindergarten Students

- Use basic concepts.
- Concentrate on dance content Standard 1.
- Keep lessons simple; do not include too many ideas in one class session.
- Use story dances with many movement words.
- Use music with clear contrasts and rhythms.
- Use verbal cueing for success.

The strategies that follow are useful when working with students prekindergarten to grade 2. With modifications, many of these strategies may be used successfully with upper elementary and middle school students.

Instructional Strategies for Teaching Beginning Creative Dance

- Start slowly. Do not rush.
- Begin with a comfortable concept and teach it as a short-term warm-up activity.
- Introduce one movement concept at a time. (Older beginners can be successful learning and exploring more than one concept in a lesson, such as level and body shape.)
- Allow students to work individually within a class to experience each movement concept.
- Encourage students to work in self-space with closed eyes to help increase creativity; make sure safety is considered.
- Use a drum or other percussion instruments to help with rhythm. (It is helpful for students to hear the pattern of rhythm or counting with a strong beat.) Listening and moving to an instrument can help students understand differences between even and uneven beats and rhythms. Practice at home to improve abilities to provide a strong, steady rhythm. Using a metronome can help at first.
- Use interesting music with strong beats. Instrumental music is best. Choose music of varying styles. Music should match the mood, feeling, or idea of the movement challenge.
- Eliminate possible student fears about the word *dance*. Use the word often with prekindergarten- and kindergarten-age students to lessen concerns.

- Encourage variety. There are many different ways to successfully meet a teacher challenge. Allow students the freedom to be creative. Gain new ideas from students and then incorporate the ideas into future classes.
- Remember that creating takes time. Finished products should not be the objective of school-based creative dance classes. However, as students create, it is important to offer opportunities for them to share their work with peers. Students learn how to improve their own dances by watching and then discussing those of their peers. Creative dance tasks may take two to four lessons.
- Emphasize process. Rather than creating a dance performance, the primary purpose of creative dance or movement is to facilitate learning by the students.
- Experiment. We all learn from less-successful lessons. Let students know that some lessons are an experiment to help all learn. It is important that they know teachers continue to learn, too. If needed, allow students more time to develop a dance concept.
- Model the movement for them. Students do not expect perfection, but they are willing to try activities if the teacher models in an enthusiastic manner. Students love to see their teacher doing unusual things. Be creative.
- Use descriptive language and imagery. Students of all ages respond well to this approach.
- Add props to a movement concept lesson. Students may lose inhibitions when they concentrate on a prop and ways to make it move. Balls, scarves, hoops, and elastic bands are successful ideas.
- Incorporate Standard 6: Makes connections between dance and healthful living in each dance experience. Help students understand the connections. Ask questions such as "What muscles worked really hard during this lesson?" or "Did you notice that you are breathing hard today? Tell me why that happened." Include statements such as "Dancing keeps the heart, lungs, bones, and brain healthy" or "Dancers are athletes. They need to warm up and stretch before a performance."

Imagery Examples and Ideas for Helping Students Improve Creative Movement

- To improve balance, have students imagine there are roots growing out of the foot (or the body part that is the support). Have students imagine the body as a marionette with a string coming out of the center of the head, and that the puppeteer is holding up the body.

- To understand pathways, ask students to think of a jet or skywriting plane; after it moves a pathway can be seen by smoke in the sky.

- To understand body direction, have students imagine that specific body parts are leading the movement (use the example of a puppet on a string for younger students). For example, for backward movement, imagine the calves or heels leading the way; for sideways movement, imagine the shoulder, hip, or side of the foot in the lead; for forward movement, imagine the toes, knees, or nose leading.

- To understand effort, ask students to imagine moving in a space filled with a substance such as water, peanut butter, or honey. To understand force, ask them to imagine pushing against a wall or something similar.

- To learn to use certain movement qualities, ask students to move the way an animal feels when it moves. Think about size, weight, tempo, and the relationship of body parts to each other and to the space around them. For example, ask students to move as heavily as an elephant, glide as gracefully as an eagle, and jump as far as a kangaroo.

- To improve posture, encourage students to stand straight and tall by asking that they pretend to be kings or queens who must keep beautiful crowns balanced on their heads.

Examples for Using Props

Using props can release inhibitions and self-consciousness of students. Props stimulate creativity and allow students to focus on things other than themselves.

- *Balls*—Incorporate the skills of tossing, rolling around the body, and bouncing and catching while in personal space. Transfer the ball from hand to hand or incorporate a body turn with tosses and catches. Move the body through different levels while manipulating the ball around and between body parts. Toss the ball in a curved pathway forward and run to catch it. Move the ball around the body or body parts (arm, leg, back) without losing contact with the ball. Move the ball slowly, quickly; then intersperse slow and quick movements.

- *Scarves*—Experiment with different ways of holding the scarves: one handed, by one corner, in the middle, or by two corners. Show the relationship of the scarf to the body: over, under, around, and through different body parts. Toss and catch the scarf, or drape the scarf and move in and through space. Explore movement with the scarf on various levels, at different tempos, and on varying pathways.

- *Cooperbands*—Explore movement with the medium or large band in groups of four to six or six to ten. After a mini lesson on safety, allow students to stay attached to the band and explore shapes and level changes. Experiment with unison movement: inward, outward, upward, downward, and turning. Allow music to stimulate movement.

Instructional Strategies for Teaching Folk Dance

Preparation

- ○ Select a developmentally appropriate folk dance.

- ○ Choose dances with themes that are relevant to the age group.

- ○ For prekindergarten to grade 2, use basic locomotor and nonlocomotor movements, and simple rhythmic patterns.

- ○ For grades 3 to 5, use more complex movement combinations: grapevine, polka, schottische, and other complex rhythmic patterns.

- ○ Review or learn the dance yourself.

- ○ Use available resources to learn about the dance: books, video, Internet, other teachers, or community members.

- ○ Acquire the appropriate music.

Implementation

- ○ Present students with the contextual information about the dance: country of origin, location, climate, and geography; time or era of the dance; style; meaning, purpose, or main idea of the dance; pictures, photos, or DVDs of the dance,

○ if available; and any historical information (who, when, why, where) related to the dance.

○ Introduce the music.

○ Ask students to listen for patterns, rhythm, and tempo of the music.

○ Demonstrate movement patterns in the dance.

○ Show students the entire dance through teacher demonstration or video.

○ Teach each part without music and allow students to practice.

○ Practice with a drum or voice cues to reinforce patterns, if necessary.

○ Practice patterns with music.

○ Perform segments of the pattern as described below.

  ○ Initially, teach dance movements out of formation to develop movement patterns correctly.

  ○ Have students follow you by mirroring or copying your movements.

  ○ Have students practice in partners or small groups.

  ○ Move the group in unison to practice with spatial awareness.

  ○ Explain and demonstrate how to keep space between the dancers consistent.

  ○ Have students practice maintaining spatial relationships between and among dancers at a slow tempo first.

  ○ Have students practice maintaining spatial relationships in the dance formation.

○ Have students perform dances using all the previously learned skills.

○ Remind students about the history and characteristics of each dance.

○ Encourage correct eye focus or body positions.

○ Expect rhythmic accuracy.

Assessment

  ○ For the creative dance model or the folk dance model, determine the knowledge, specific dance skills, and social behaviors that should be assessed for the lesson or dances.

  ○ Prepare the rubrics or other assessment tools.

  ○ Plan time into the lessons for quality evaluation of student learning and the teaching strategies used.

Summary

This chapter describes concepts for thinking about and planning a dance curriculum. The chapter includes discussion about the difference between standards and benchmarks, the relationship between benchmarks and objectives, the progression within units, and a process for daily planning from simple to complex learning activities. The chapter highlights examples relating to the benchmarks of the National Dance Education Standards. The text provides strategies for teaching and preparing successful learning experiences, including models for teaching generic creative dance and folk dance lessons. Using all these elements of good planning helps create meaningful learning experiences in dance.

5

Assessing for Success in Dance Education

Assessment is central to both teaching and learning as processes; it is also critical to meet student outcomes by demonstrating that students have acquired knowledge and skills in dance. An assessment strategy runs through a cycle. In the first part of the cycle, assessment is identified as the student outcomes that occur from designing learning experiences and selecting objectives for the experiences. During and after the learning experience, assessment shifts to determining if student outcomes have been attained. Keeping assessment strategies and goals in mind throughout teaching and learning experiences will enable dance instructors to guide students through the dance units and curriculum.

Assessing dance in relationship to standards has been an evolving process since it began decades ago. During much of the twentieth century, assessing dance was subjective and linked directly to the teacher's background, knowledge, preferences, creativity in developing learning experiences, and observational and analytical skills. Although it is difficult to disassociate personal perceptions about achievement from student production in any performing art, dance assessment has been proactive. As a field, dance education led the way in authentic assessment of classroom performance and began to use criterion-based evaluation more than three decades ago (Kassing and Mortensen, 1982).

In 1994, when dance joined other arts organizations in framing the *National Standards in Arts Education,* this was an important step forward. As a member of this coalition, dance, along with the other arts, was recognized as an important component in education. Many states moved beyond the national voluntary standards to mandating standards in dance and the other arts. These state standards impacted children at the school level and guided teachers in decisions about what to teach and assess.

Standards-based teaching makes connections among the national and state dance standards, use of learning experiences in the classroom, and student and curriculum assessment. This assessment sustains a process for connecting successful work in the dance classroom with student achievement as part of the nationwide effort to provide accountability in education.

The Arts and Authentic Assessment

Arts assessment and authentic assessment work together intrinsically. The arts provide content areas, skills, techniques, and concepts that are applied directly through performance processes, and products that strive to emulate real-world requirements. By using dance performances or products as the foundation, students naturally practice and hone

- critical-thinking and problem-solving skills,
- execution of real-world, meaningful tasks that strive to emulate quality performance or product,
- integration of research with the development of a performance or product, and
- analysis and evaluation of their work.

Dance education learning experiences provide a strong forum for students to perform and use high-level thinking skills in the production of dance works that meet and extend professional expectations and arts education standards.

Authentic assessment requires an evaluation of student learning through real-world experiences. This process encourages teachers and students to go beyond rote learning and traditional test taking that uses measures such as true-false, matching responses, fill-in-the-blank, or multiple-choice exams. Through the authentic assessment process, teachers guide students in using higher levels of thinking, problem solving, and analytical processes while performing tasks that create new meaning.

Authentic assessment is valid. It assesses necessary skills and knowledge in ways that are as close as possible to the real-world environment. Most performance tasks within authentic assessment involve well-crafted scoring guides or rubrics attached to specific curriculum assignments or learning experiences. A rubric sets criteria for different levels of performance, and unique scoring guides are developed for many types of curriculum products or performances.

In this chapter, performance refers to the creation or development of a dance work to be performed either in the classroom or in a public presentation. Product refers to oral or written responses, including reports, presentations, Web-Quests, lesson plans, reflective self-assessments, journals, and other similar documents. Both performances and products provide evidence that learning has occurred.

In both performance and product development, the teacher's role is to set the expectation for the performance or product, which can be a public presentation or a testing situation in the classroom. These performances or products include expectations of dance mastery and professional attitude. The teacher outlines the expectations for the written or oral product, which mirrors tasks and processes in real-world situation.

Standards-Based Assessment

Assessment is a cyclic activity interwoven throughout successful teaching and learning. The cycle starts with the students' learning goals and objectives in mind and ends with celebrating the

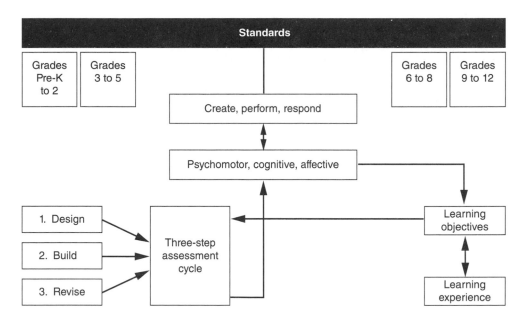

FIGURE 5.1   Standards outline expectations for different grade level ranges.

students' successes. Determining what students should know, what they need to learn, and what they need to do to meet identified benchmarks and standards is the teacher's starting place for developing learning experiences and assessing the outcomes effectively. This chapter covers writing objectives and identifying evidence that learning has occurred. These components connect the objectives to assessment strategies that complete the standards-based assessment cycle (see figure 5.1). Some of the pathways between the components are direct connections; other paths represent underlying relationships and strengths that also are part the assessment cycle. The dance assessment cycle draws on content from earlier chapters for the steps needed to implement assessment strategies in the dance class that will complete the assessment cycle.

Assessment Criteria

In dance education, teachers and students address three processes: dance making, dancing, and dance appreciation. Teachers assess these processes as students create, perform, and respond (known as CPR). Dance making involves creating; dancing involves performing; and dance appreciation involves responding to a dance performance, choreography, or writing.

The CPR teaching and learning modalities in dance relate to the types of objectives that guide student learning experiences in the classroom. CPR evolved as a key concept and common basis for national assessment in all the arts. CPR connects to dance making, dancing, and dance appreciation activities directly and supportively. Using CPR provides ways to make connections between and among dance learning experiences in class and across arts disciplines.

Creating

Creating includes making new movement; developing movement combinations; reproducing dance; improvising new, repeatable dance movements; or choreographing dances. Creating requires higher-level thinking skills, such as analysis and evaluation, to select dance movement that will match with the dance form and the style created. Creating a dance work is synergistically connected to how and where the work is performed. Likewise, creating connects to dance appreciation by the development of a written, oral, or media project requiring evaluation of dance processes or product. As students complete different types of projects and gain more experience, they are guided to use critical, higher-level thinking skills to develop these various projects.

Performing

Performing is central to dancing. It includes executing a wide range of age- and developmentally appropriate movements, steps, combinations, figures, and dances. Student performance can be as simple as an informal study presentation. The individual or group presentation may be shared informally in the classroom, gymnasium,

Students work cooperatively as partners to create mirror imagery.

or dance studio. The student performance may be formal, as in the case of a high-powered evening program with costumes, lights, and a paying audience in a large theater. Dance performance as an outcome of an assignment or project generally occurs at the end of a unit or series of units and as a testing situation where students present the work they have created or studied. Creating and performing are interrelated activities. Viewing a dance leads to creating a response to the work and making a critical evaluation of its structure and meaning.

Responding

Traditionally, responding to dance has been an important part of the dance education process associated with dance appreciation. Responses range from informal discussion to more formal activities, including group discussion during the creative process, student-to-teacher dialogue, self- or peer analysis of a work during its development, or the production of written documents through journaling, writing reports, making observations, or providing a critique of a dance performance or composition. Responding to and about dance also may extend beyond creating personal work to attending a live performance, viewing a video production, and even to restaging or reconstructing historical works.

The concept of CPR is the basis for assessing dance educational processes. It can help make clear connections to established learning domains so that teachers and administrators understand CPR and its relationship to dance as an educational discipline. Using CPR can help others view dance as one of many arts forms

that are part of the educational mission of the school.

Underlying the teaching, learning, and assessment processes are the educational learning taxonomies that focus on the cognitive, psychomotor, and affective domains. Correlating learning experiences and assessment within these domains provides a conduit by which dance education clearly demonstrates accountability as an art, as an educational medium, and as part of arts education within the school curriculum.

Educational Taxonomies

Taxonomies provide a convenient way to designate different learning levels that students should be able to demonstrate with competence as a result of teacher-designed learning experiences.

Traditionally, dance education has connected to three taxonomies: motor or psychomotor, intellectual or cognitive, and attitudinal learning or affective. Students demonstrate improvement in each taxonomy as their understanding and use of concepts is heightened, specific skills are enhanced, and attitudes and values are positively cultivated. The teacher determines the critical levels of student achievement expected for taxonomies connected to various lessons.

Psychomotor

Dance is a physical activity heavily based in the psychomotor learning domain. Scholars who created taxonomies for this domain come from diverse backgrounds: Elizabeth Simpson (1972), a home economics teacher, developed a skill acquisition taxonomy (see figure 5.2), and Ann Jewett

FIGURE 5.2 Psychomotor Domain: Skill Acquisition

1. Perception
   - Sensory stimulation
   - Cue selection
   - Translation (perception to action)
2. Set (readiness for action)
   - Mental set
   - Physical set
   - Emotional set
3. Guided response (instructor)
   - Initiation of other people
   - Trial and error
4. Mechanisms (learned response becomes habitual)
5. Complex overt response
   - Resolution of uncertainty
   - Automatic performance
6. Adaptation
7. Origination

Reprinted, by permission, from G. Kassing and D. Jay, 2003, *Dance teaching methods and curriculum design* (Champaign, IL: Human Kinetics), 134.

FIGURE 5.3 Psychomotor Domain: Creative Movement Taxonomy

1. Generic movement
   - Perceiving (identify, discover)
   - Imitating (replicate, pantomime)
   - Patterning (arrange into successive harmonious acts)
2. Ordinate movement
   - Adapting (adjust, apply)
   - Refining (control, regulate, improve)
3. Creative movement
   - Varying (alter, revise)
   - Improvising (interpret, extemporize)
   - Composing (design, symbolize)

Reprinted, by permission, from G. Kassing and D. Jay, 2003, *Dance teaching methods and curriculum design* (Champaign, IL: Human Kinetics), 135.

and Linda Bain (1985), both physical educators, developed a creative movement taxonomy (see figure 5.3).

Simpson's version of the psychomotor domain provides a clear path for student assimilation of dance skills and techniques. She named seven levels of development. The first category is perception, the use of sensory cues to guide motor activity. This is followed by five other categories: set (preparing to act), guided response (imitation and experiencing trial and error), mechanisms (habitual movements performed with confidence and mastery), complex overt response (quick, accurate, and automatic response requiring a combination of movements), and adaptation (modification of movements to fit unique or unpredictable environments). The final level is origination, where the individual creates new patterns to fit a particular problem or situation.

Jewett and Bain's psychomotor taxonomy, developed from physical education, provides an important basis to support the creative forms and aspects of dance. Each level of the taxonomy leads to self-actualization in the creative process, beginning with the use of generic (pedestrian) movement and gestures. Students then refine and adapt movements from the first category to improve their skills. The final level involves creating and varying movement patterns.

Throughout the physical activity of dance, many intellectual processes support and expand creating and performing as students' skills and techniques develop and they mature as dancers and dance artists.

Cognitive

Intellectual abilities underlie all dance processes. First, students have to achieve making the movement and connecting it with language so they can think and perform while using the language of the dance form. This process takes a conscious effort to simultaneously translate movement into action words or terms and then translate words or terms into movement. At specific ages, developmental stages, and experience levels, movements and verbal languages will vary. Benjamin Bloom (1956) and later educational psychologists, Lorin Anderson and David Krathwohl (2001), identified

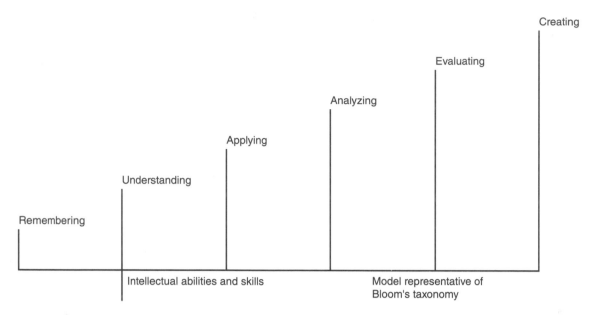

FIGURE 5.4 Cognitive domain of learning.

Reprinted, by permission, from G. Kassing and D. Jay, 2003, *Dance teaching methods and curriculum design* (Champaign, IL: Human Kinetics), 136.

a standard cognitive taxonomy that designates levels of knowledge and intellectual attainment (see figure 5.4). Chapter 4 provides information on a comparison of the original and the new versions of Bloom's cognitive taxonomies. Within the same section is a description of how the new version of Bloom's taxonomy relates to dance. The cognitive domain has strong relevance to students in dance education since intellectual abilities underlie all dance processes.

Cognitive abilities range from remembering (recall or recognition) of facts to higher-level thinking skills that combine in a variety of ways. The complex levels of analyzing, evaluating, and creating evolve as dance students hone their skills in observation, analytical interpretation, and problem solving so they can talk and write about dance works as competent dancers and artists.

Many dance activities require higher-level thinking skills. Dancing, dance making, and dance appreciation have deep cognitive roots. Purposely developed learning experiences can direct students to practice higher-level skills to refine their thinking processes and movement skills while creating, performing, or responding to dance.

Affective

In addition to engaging students physically and intellectually, dance education engages students in collaborative, group efforts. Creating and per-forming as a member of any size group requires wide-ranging social awareness, attitudinal adaptations and management, and reciprocal sharing. Working in groups to produce an ensemble performance or create a group dance study involves valuable individual and group skills that are an integral part of the affective domain (see figure 5.5).

The affective domain provides indicators regarding students' behavior, cooperation, and ability to function well in the classroom or as part of a group. Because dance is a nonverbal art, the teacher is required to observe and read students' dispositions: the nonverbal and verbal language in both the classroom environment and performance situation. Teachers can incorporate many strategies into learning experiences that facilitate students' development within the affective domain. For example, cooperative activities, peer and cross-age mentoring, group meetings to assess behavior, conflict resolution, and self-reflection journals are measures that help students take personal, social, and group responsibility.

The affective taxonomy is critical to assessing how well students communicate with peers and people in authority, express self-confidence in understanding and accepting others' viewpoints, negotiate through group dynamics, compromise, and serve in leadership roles within the class or dance group.

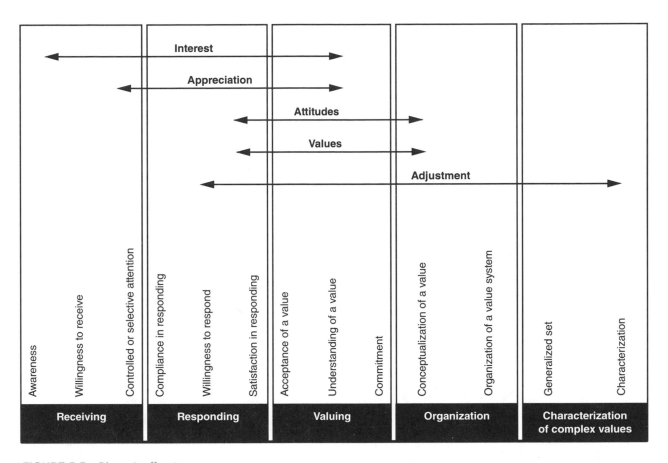

FIGURE 5.5 Bloom's affective taxonomy.

Reprinted, by permission, from G. Kassing and D. Jay, 2003, *Dance teaching methods and curriculum design* (Champaign, IL: Human Kinetics), 137.

Looking at the big picture of educational taxonomies illustrates the strong connections dance has to the three learning domains. These connections provide the educational basis for the teaching and learning processes in dance making, dancing, and dance appreciation.

Writing Student Learning Objectives

Knowing your students, their abilities, and the developmentally appropriate dance experiences for their age is crucial. This knowledge becomes the starting point in designing learning objectives, or student outcomes, for learning experiences that are observable, measurable, and attainable (see figure 5.6). There are several traditional ways to write student learning objectives. Following is a review of one commonly used system. Writing the objective begins with understanding the components that make up an objective and how each component relates to the others to make up

the whole. The objective states what you predict will happen during the assessment cycle for a particular learning experience.

The parts of an objective include the stem, the behavior, the conditions, and the criteria for performance.

- The *stem* describes what students will be able to do at the end of the learning experience, lesson, or unit. A traditional phrasing for the stem is "The student will . . . ."

- The *behavior,* or what the student has to demonstrate to prove that learning has occurred, describes the performance or product evidence that learning has occurred.

When you write objectives, use action verbs to indicate what the student will do. Choreograph, demonstrate, write, and perform are common action words used in writing dance learning objectives.

Correlate the verb to the level of difficulty indicated by the specific skill. The level of difficulty

FIGURE 5.6   Guiding Questions for Constructing Measurable Student Objectives

- What are the developmental and age levels of students?
- What are the students' learning styles?
- What are the students' previous learning experiences?
- What are the targeted standard or standards?
- What is the best teaching methodology to help students succeed (e.g., direct instruction, task setting, reciprocal learning, problem solving, collaborative learning, student-centered project, other)?
- Which learning domain is the focus?
- Where does this learning experience fit within the unit?
- What introductory set or review is needed for students' success?
- What is the intended outcome of the learning experience?
- What will motivate students?

Sample Student Learning Objective

Responding: Select a term from a level of the cognitive domain, such as "analyze." Then write an objective indicating the outcome: The student will write one paragraph analyzing a dance (study, learning experience, class performance) . . .

Performing: The student will demonstrate locomotor movements (hops, gallops, and runs) in a straight or curved pathway . . .

Creating: The student will create a one-minute dance study that includes three levels, two contrasting qualities, three different shapes, three different types of even-rhythmic locomotor movement, and two nonlocomotor movements demonstrating a beginning, middle, and end . . .

should relate to a level in the psychomotor, cognitive, and affective domains. Beyond connection to each the three taxonomies, the activity needs to link back to creating, performing, and responding. The sidebar above shows an example of how to write each part of the objective.

Writing the behavioral portion of a learning objective forms the basis for developing the next parts of the objective. The following components address when and where the objective will be met and what will constitute performance of that objective.

- The *conditions* explain where and when the performance of the objective occurs. For example, the performance may occur in the dance studio, classroom, or on stage. The performance may occur by the end of class, after a specific number of class meetings, or at the end of the learning experience or the unit.

- Following are examples of learning objectives that include conditions: The student will write one paragraph analyzing a dance learning experience by the end of two class meetings. . . . By the end of the class, the student will demonstrate locomotor movements (hop, gallops, and runs) in a straight pathway . . .

- The *criteria for performance* explain what is a successful performance and specify the evidence that learning occurred. The teacher determines the minimum acceptable performance level and expresses the criterion for performance as either a percentage or a ratio. For example, the student will correctly execute a hop, gallop, and plié 90 percent of the time (or 9 out of 10 times).

- When writing objectives, each one should contain the four components: stem, behavior, condition, and criteria for performance. Check each component by underlining it and writing above it the element to which it correlates. Then ask the following questions about the learning experience and the students in the class:

  ○ Observable? Can I see the learning product easily in a class of 30 students when they perform the combination or dance in small groups or as an entire class?

  ○ Measurable? Can I ascertain the level of the skill or technique, choreography, or response? How will I measure it as performed by that student in relation to others in the classroom?

  ○ Attainable? Are the planned learning experience and expectations something that will make students successful? Will the learning experience provide a challenge that will enable students to expand their skills and abilities? Do the objectives in all domains reflect the most important concepts, techniques, or dance elements in the learning experience? Will these learning experiences help students attain achievement of the goals? Will these learning experiences help students meet the standards?

Adapted, by permission, from G. Kassing and D. Jay, 1998, *Teaching beginning ballet technique* (Champaign, IL: Human Kinetics), 138-139.

In the objective, delineate the criteria for performance. Identify the tasks in the learning experience that will provide evidence of what has been taught. These tasks should be natural outcomes from the learning experience and should connect directly to the objectives. Students' ability to perform these tasks provides the evidence that learning has occurred during the learning experience.

When developing objectives, make sure they connect directly to the assessment strategies for the learning experience. Observing and evaluating the evidence of learning is the conduit for completing two parts of the assessment cycle (see figure 5.7, *a-b*). The first part of the cycle focuses on teaching and learning, with assessment as the background for each of these events. In the second part of the cycle, assessment comes to the foreground, gaining a more prominent role to determine if the evidence observed is linked to final learner outcomes that meet the standards.

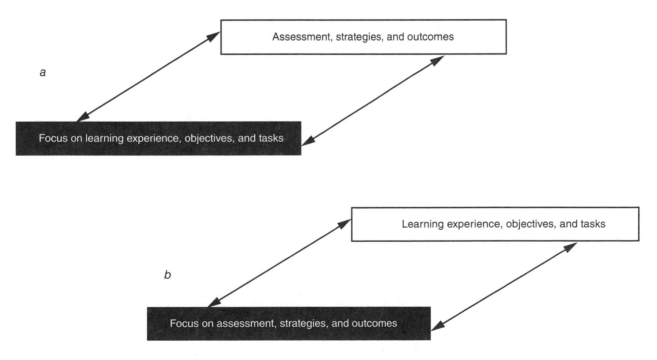

FIGURE 5.7 Evaluate the evidence of learning by focusing on *(a)* learning experiences, objectives, and tasks; and *(b)* assessment strategies and outcomes.

Implementing Assessment Strategies

An assessment strategy that includes a hierarchy of components ensures success. The assessment cycle begins with reviewing the standards and drafting objectives that delineate what students should be able to do at an appropriate level. The cycle then includes developing learning experiences that allow students to offer evidence they can meet these objectives. Selecting, implementing, and reflecting on assessments complete the assessment cycle. Effective assessment links learning experiences that involve creating, performing, and responding with the objectives or outcomes that stem from standards. Following this strategy makes implementing the dance standards much easier and more effective.

Strands, Standards, and Strategies for Student Outcomes

Both voluntary national and state-mandated standards provide the framework for dance education in the classroom for prekindergarten through grade 12. Overarching the standards are five strands modified from those described in the *National Standards for Arts Education* (pp. 18-19). The following strands provide short descriptions of the categories that guided development of the voluntary national dance standards and subsequent benchmarks:

- Knowledge, skills, and technique
- Creation and communication
- Critical analysis of works
- Cultural and historical connections
- Applications across curriculum and to life

The strands reflect key concepts and consistent themes for organizing dance subject content. Each strand supports one or more of the standards below. Many states and national organizations have adopted, adapted, or modified these strands to guide development of their dance standards and related documents.

Content Standard 1. Identifies and demonstrates movement elements and skills in performing dance

Content Standard 2. Understands choreographic principles, processes, and structures

Content Standard 3. Understands dance as a way to create and communicate meaning

Content Standard 4. Applies and demonstrates critical and creative thinking skills in dance

Content Standard 5. Demonstrates and understands dance in various cultures and historical periods

Content Standard 6. Makes connections between dance and healthful living

Content Standard 7. Makes connections between dance and other disciplines

The strands and standards provide a rich foundation from which to generate inventive dance learning experiences.

When some planners consider implementation of either state or national standards, they may start with the students, the standards, or a learning experience. The primary goal is to connect standards, objectives, and learning experiences with student growth in skills and knowledge.

Connect Objectives to Standards

After checking the objectives and learning experiences against the standards, the next steps are easy checkpoints in the process:

1. Use words that are meaningful to levels within the taxonomies.
2. Write the objective in the psychomotor, cognitive, or affective domain to make it a complete learning experience.
3. Implement CPR.

Collect Evidence of Performance and Products

The types of planned performances and products should provide students with a variety of experiences from which to learn and expand their dance making, dancing, and dance appreciation. The class size, the length of the unit of instruction, and the number of class meetings are factors that will influence how much evidence can be collected. When and how often you use learning experiences to provide assessment information and the types of evidence also are important components of the assessment cycle.

When and How Often to Evaluate

Gathering evidence is an ongoing process. However, there must be a balance between learning and evaluating the learning. The number of learning experiences provided and the number of experiences evaluated to assess student progress need serious analysis. Sometimes the balance is difficult to determine the first time a unit is taught, but an optimum approach should become clearer the more you analyze the successes of the students, the unit, and the learning experiences. Postteaching reflection time is important to assess what worked, what didn't work, how much time students needed to complete a project, how successful students were, and how the project could be done differently. This important self-analysis will help hone planning for the next group of students. It will also help you gain an inner sense about how long it takes for a student to accomplish certain tasks either individually or as part of a group.

Formative Assessment

Formative assessment is an ongoing process for teachers and students alike. Data are collected at various points along a continuum to determine if planning, teaching, and learning are on the desired path. The value of this process is to use feedback early on to make improvements before reaching the stage of conducting summative or outcome evaluations.

When planning the scope and sequence for a dance unit, place the learning experiences in progressive order. Teach the techniques and skills associated with the learning experience beforehand as a foundation so the learning experience will be successful, enjoyable, and beneficial for students. During the unit, students should develop a clear understanding of the expected vocabulary, techniques, and skills to be learned before the final assessments. While selecting or developing student learning experiences, plan specific time or "breathing spaces" between assessment times to help students assimilate learning before moving on to the next learning challenge. Throughout the instructional time or unit, periodically assess learning experiences of progressive difficulty. Record each student's progress at the end of the unit. Also, assess each student's progress toward meeting yearly goals and the benchmarks that are set by standards, either by grade or level.

Throughout the instructional units, use various types of evaluation tools to assess different types and styles of learning. There is no set formula for the number of learning experiences or assessments to use within a unit. The number of assessments often depends on the number of units taught during the term and the number of weeks in the term or semester. Sometimes outside deadlines

The teacher works collaboratively with the student at intervals to evaluate various aspects of her work.

require evaluation of students at certain times. Of course, midterm and final evaluation periods provide important indicators of student progress or accomplishment.

Summative Assessment

Final or summative assessment for a unit or term generally provides closure. It summarizes what students have learned and accomplished, and whether benchmarks were met. Summative evaluation can take different forms, such as a technique assessment, a choreographic project, a written paper, or an oral or media presentation for the class, another school audience, or a public presentation.

Make sure to allow adequate reflection and response time for a summative assessment. Often, summative assessments become part of product or process portfolios. These end-of-unit or term assessments verify learning at certain points within one or more year's learning. They present junctures to review how much has been accomplished and what needs to be addressed to satisfy outcomes and meet expected benchmarks. They are stop and pause moments that allow both teachers and students to gain a sense of where they are and where they will go next in their learning adventures.

The Three-Step Assessment Cycle

The three-step assessment cycle is easy to implement: design, build, and revise (see figure 5.1 on page 49). At the end of each step in the assessment cycle, either teachers or students can pose one or more questions to determine if each step has been completed.

To determine what will be the criterion for performance,

- identify and list the elements in the learning experience;
- make sure the elements relate to the standards; and
- verify that the list of criteria identified justifies an observable, measurable, and attainable performance or product.

Student portfolios can be a summative project for one or more years. Assignments or projects might include any of the following:

- Drafts, sketches, technique development, finished work, documentation of a work or performance
- Photos, audios, videos, multimedia projects, reflective writings
- Choreography notes, diagrams, videos of performances, analysis of the process and the work

Student portfolios can be in any of these forms:

- Process portfolio that exhibits mastery over time
- Portfolio of outcome-based products that demonstrate mastery of a standard
- Best-work portfolio that showcases the student's best work in a course as selected by students and teachers through informal or formal review processes
- Competition or high-stakes portfolio that includes applications for advanced studies, special programs, or competitions

Some dance portfolio examples found on the Web are:

Maryland Fine Arts Education, dance portfolio assessment: www.mfaa.msde .state.md.us/source/PDF/Portfolio_Dance.pdf

Texas, dance portfolio elements: http://finearts.esc20.net/dance/dance_ assessment/dance_as_example.html

New York, task and checklist for dance performance and portfolio items (pages 12 and 13): www.emsc.nysed.gov/ciai/arts/pub/artsampdance.pdf

FIGURE 5.8 Checklist for a Jump or Sauté

A jump or sauté is an extension of a plié.

Element	Yes	No
Stands in First position		
Executes First-position plié		
Extends legs to lift body into the air		
Lands in a small First-position plié (weight equally on both feet) using both feet on landing (touches first with the toes, then with balls of the feet, and last with heels)		
Centers and controls elevation and landing		
Keeps midsection (torso) upright and controlled on landing		
Ends standing in First position		

Decide if a performance or product is observable, measurable, and attainable by students, and whether the identified student outcomes are achievable. For example, create a checklist of criteria for executing a jump or sauté correctly (see figure 5.8). With this list in mind, you can easily observe and measure a student's performance.

Developing the criterion for each performance or product for student outcomes in relation to specific grade-level standards is critical to the three-step assessment cycle. Start with the end in mind: standards, benchmarks, and objectives. Identify the performance and product components of the learning experience.

- Generate criteria to evaluate the performance or product.
- Select observable, measurable characteristics and key principles or concepts that underlie the learning experience.

Ask: Has the objective been achieved and the standard been addressed?

Step 1: Design

The first step is to design the assessment tool. Performance evaluation has different levels of expectations that relate to how the teacher distinguishes evaluation of the dance and related performance components of the learning experience. This level of discrimination is more discrete as students move from the beginning to more advanced levels of performance.

Rating a dance performance takes developing a mind-set where the teacher has a clear sense of performance expectations for each component being assessed. This clear perception should not be swayed by variables such as student personality, attitude, or other attributes. Regardless of the performance evaluation tool selected, include the expectations for a competent performance of a demi-plié, for example, or find a description from a book that indicates the key points. Gayle Kassing and Danielle Jay's textbook, *Dance Teaching Methods and Curriculum Design* (2003), provides sample units.

Following is a brief description of common forms of assessment using rubrics. Rubrics help make evaluation of students' works objective and consistent. It allows for students to understand assessment criteria before starting any project. Deciding which tool is appropriate depends on the learner objectives, the students, the learning experience, and the expected outcomes. There are several examples of these assessment tools found in the learning experiences in chapters 8 through 11.

• Checklist: The tool provides structure for early formative assessment or for students at young ages. Checklists are useful to note accomplishments without assigning a rating scale. Students and teachers can easily identify the key elements of a performance or product that can be marked with a "yes" or "no" (see table 5.1).

• Rubric with a rating scale: A rating scale is an effective tool for assessing student-created, student-performed, or student-response products. It defines the performance objective, identifies the components to be assessed, and shows the levels or degrees of performance. Often a 3-, 4-, or 5-point scale is used, with the highest number indicating the best performance. A zero may indicate "not present" or "unable to perform." The point categories should be defined and communicated to the students early on so they know what each numerical value means and what is required to get a score of 5 rather than a score of 4 (see table 5.2).

• Rubric with holistic scoring: A rubric using holistic scoring includes a descriptive indicator for each level of performance. Qualitative words distinguish one level of performance from another. Measurements are less detailed than using a rating scale. Selecting a variety of terms for a rubric template provides terminology that can help explain

TABLE 5.1   Sample Checklist: A Qualitative Assessment of Student Work

Task components	No (Needs work)	Yes (Performed to expectation)
Part A has three distinct and different movements		
Part A movements are done to the rhythmic phrasing		
Part B travels in at least two different body directions		
Locomotor movement is performed with rhythmic accuracy		
Movements match the written description		

TABLE 5.2   Sample Rubric With Rating Scale for Research Paper: A Quantitative Assessment of Student Work

Elements	1 = Needs Work	2 = Improving	3 = Meets Expectations	Score
Organization	The beginning and end are unclear, focal points are not clear	Main points are not in a logical order	Clear beginning and end, focal points follow logical order	
Content	Both inaccurate and incomplete	Inaccurate or incomplete	Accurate and complete	
Writing mechanics	More than five errors (grammar, punctuation, spelling)	Three to five errors (grammar, punctuation, spelling)	Less than three errors (grammar, punctuation, spelling)	
References	Less than three sources	Three to four reputable sources	Five or more reputable sources	
			Total score	

TABLE 5.3   Sample Holistic Rubric for Creative Composition Evaluation: A Qualitative and Quantitative Assessment of Student Work

Criteria	1 point	2 points	3 points	Points awarded
Text interpretation	Literal (mimetic)	Predictable	Abstract	
Composition content	Flat with few choreographic elements	Demonstrates some choreographic elements, but is not fully developed	Well formed with varied use of directions, levels, rhythms, shape; developmentally complete with a clear beginning and conclusion	
Presentation	Unorganized with weak transitions, incomplete composition, and unclear or incomplete memorization of sequences	Complete with memorization in place but with movement is tenuously performed	Fully prepared with committed performance of movements, transitions, and content	
			Total points	

to students, parents, administrators, or even the school board why some students receive a score of 2 and others receive a score of 3. This type of assessment includes an accountability statement of the levels of learning that students have attained in a variety of areas (see table 5.3).

Rubrics are powerful instruments for teachers to make the case for dance education and its place in the school curriculum.

Step 2: Build

The criterion for the assessment is described in the written objective. Look at the objective to determine what will be evaluated, when it will be accomplished, where it will be produced, and what will constitute the criteria for different levels of performance needed to meet standard outcomes identified as the foundation for the assessment tool.

Next, select an assessment tool that relates to the students and the performance expectations of the event (e.g., in-class study, test, performance either in class or in public):

- Checklist: yes or no (observed performance)
- Performance rating scale (e.g., 1-3, 1-4, or 1-5)

○ Identify the items to be assessed as part of the learning experience.

○ Determine a scale.

- Holistic scoring

○ Select performance levels (e.g., 1-3 or 1-4).

○ Select descriptive indicators (criteria for each indicator) and check terminology.

○ Develop the criteria for each level of performance.

Then, decide if the criteria is analytical, holistic, or weighted.

- Analytical criteria include evaluation of the parts of an exercise, step, or technique. For example assessment of a demi-plié would include a performance evaluation of these steps:

○ Stand in First position.

○ Center body weight over the legs through the descent and ascent.

○ Turn out from hips through the legs; keep feet in the same position throughout the exercise.

○ Keep alignment stable throughout the exercise.

○ Bend knees directly over the second and third toes of each foot.

○ Maintain distribution of weight over the foot triangle throughout the exercise.

○ Keep movement continuous throughout the exercise.

Adapted, by permission, from G. Kassing and D. Jay, 1998, *Teaching beginning ballet technique* (Champaign, IL: Human Kinetics), 93.

• Holistic criteria looks at a movement sequence, combination, movement study, or even a dance as a whole. Within a movement sequence, the key elements or focus of the learning experience need to be identified. For example, in a creative movement study, did the student's movement have a beginning, middle, and end? In a modern dance movement study that explores levels, were all three levels—low, middle, and high—present within the study? In a technique study, were technique, sequencing, transitions, use of qualities or efforts, and coordination of

performance elements appropriate for the setting?

• Weighted criteria assign value to elements in a holistic and analytical manner so that one element may have more weight than another. For example, in a technique study, employing the correct technique may have more weight than the sequencing of the movement or another identified criterion. The weight assigned can change as the student gains technique competency; the focus might then be on the use of qualities of movements, seamless transitions, or coordination of performance elements to gain artistry.

• When weighting, effective assessment focuses on looking at the whole—the combination, the study, or the dance—and evaluating the entire product or discrete segments of the product. This requires establishing a criterion that can be used for a whole category of movement samples. In ballet, adagio, allegro, or grand allegro, what are common elements for any number of examples in each of these categories? Determining a generic

Knowing the performance benchmarks and objectives will help students determine the creative process to use to reach an end product.

criterion requires identifying the elements that constitute adagio, regardless of what the steps are, and determining which of the elements should be weighted for the performance assessment. Weightings might be given to some of these elements:

- Slow, continuous movement
- Technical execution of each step in the combination
- Transitions between steps
- Body directions
- Head coordination
- Appropriate qualities for each part of the adagio
- Deliberate beginning and ending to the combination

Last, determine how well the assessment tool connects to the learning outcomes—how well are each of these addressed in the assessment tool?

1. Overarching strands for dance education
2. The seven dance education standards
3. Benchmarks for grade levels or age groups
4. Student objectives to reach benchmarks

Step 3: Review and Revise

The final step of the assessment cycle involves reviewing and revising. This step makes the assessment tool more efficient, effective, and expressive of the evidence gathered through the learning experience. Repeating this important step will make the assessment cycle seamless.

After teaching the same level of dance for more than a year, you will be able to better identify the dance making, dancing, and dance appreciation elements that you believe meet the needs of students of a particular age and developmental level and the requirements of the established standards. Although teachers vary their learning experiences, the skills and techniques often remain the same—they are what students should know and be able to do at that point in their dance learning. This step of review and revise is important as you hone your evaluative techniques and assessment strategies for each new group of students.

Review

New teachers should consider pretesting an assessment tool prior to assessing a learning experience. One way to preview the assessment tool is to videotape a rehearsal of the performance planned for evaluation. Then, use the video as a way to check the assessment tool. After using the tool on several students' performances, review each item to determine how easy the tool was to use. For a class of 35 students, it is important to have tools that are quick, easy to use, and consistent in their results. Videotaping the student performance as a backup to the live performance allows any evaluator to confirm the appraisal of the performance. Ask yourself these questions following an assessment:

- How well did the assessment work? Determine this by doing an item analysis.
- What needs to be changed? Improved?
- Have all the connections been made among standards, benchmarks, and objectives?

Revise

Revision is the second part of this step. Revision can take place before the performance or technique test and again after the test. Revising the assessment tool after the test helps prepare for the next time the learning experience is assessed. Revision of the tool should take place immediately following your analysis of the testing session so that your impressions and knowledge of the situation are fresh. Additional notes about problematic areas will help you remember items to watch for during the assessment process so that the next time will go more smoothly. These notes provide a foundation from which to modify the assessment for the next group of students. Make an electronic version of the performance assessment tool so you can modify and print it for future projects. The content and standards are taught one or more times a year or semester. The learning experience may differ from class to class, but there will be similarities. Consider these questions to help build upon and continue to clarify the assessment cycle:

- Did the learning experience and its assessment meet expectations for student performance of the objectives?
- Did the learning experience and its assessment meet the identified standards?

Having Students Create Rubrics

Using the same three-step system, students can take the next step and write their own performance rubrics. Initially, this can be a joint project between you and your students. Later, student groups can develop the rubrics for their project. In this situation, the teacher facilitates and monitors the selection of items, weights, and tools. Developing the rubric could become part of the group assignment and include a one-page rationale documenting which tool, elements, and weights were selected to evaluate the project, and why. Having students create the performance rubric before embarking on the project will provide them with the criteria they need to attain.

Instead of starting with a blank sheet, provide students with templates so they can have examples to use to determine how to evaluate their own work. This prepares the dancers and dance educators of the future to take dance education to the next level of assessment.

Summary

The primary focus of this chapter is the role of standards-based planning and assessment in the process of improving instruction and learning at the classroom level. For this planning and assessment process to work, it is important to know the outcomes sought and the strategies available for helping students master the standards. This chapter provides descriptions of strategies and processes that can be used to assess student growth and development in creating, performing, and responding to identified benchmarks. Many types of assessment strategies are available to examine ways students learn physically, cognitively, socially, and emotionally. This chapter provides the teacher with options for assessing student growth in knowledge and skills.

Integrating Technology Into Dance Education

Dance technology seems like a contradiction in terms. Dance uses the human body for expression and communication. Technology describes media generators such as digital video recorders, computers, and some of the most advanced machines on the planet. These two fields come together to create dance technology. There is a synergy between the two that offers new avenues for studying and enriching dance, dance performance, and education.

Education technology has been around for decades, ever since the personal computer entered the classroom and the lives of students. Today, wireless Internet is widespread in schools and communities. Many high school and middle school students across the country are issued laptops for use during the school year. In addition to these school-based programs, students have access to computers in their homes, schools, and libraries.

Dance as a Multimedia Art

But how do dance and technology connect in the classroom? This connection happens easily because there is a great affinity between the two. Viewing and creating dance is a multimedia experience. Dance movement performed to music, in a specific dance space, often uses lighting effects and costumes. Music used in dance classrooms first came from records and later was recorded for playback on tape recorders and cassette tape players. This led to music on compact discs (CDs). Today, teachers and students download music directly from the Internet onto digital music players, sometimes called digital audio players (DAP), MP3 players, or personal laptops.

Technology has dramatically expanded the uses of lighting, both technically and artistically, as computerized lighting systems have evolved from manually sliding dimmers to computerized systems that can be preprogrammed. These systems allow for the design of complex lighting effects for dance spaces. Using gobos, slides, video, and other technologically enhanced backgrounds helps create interactive environments for dance.

Computer technology has fascinated dancers since the early 1960s when educators and performers launched experiments to connect dance and technology. During that period, dancers, dance notators, and educators sought ways to connect dance notation and computers. On stage, Alwin Nikolais, Merce Cunningham, and other postmodern pioneer choreographers created a wide variety of works that combined, integrated, or manipulated dance, various media, and computer technology. Throughout the next forty years, these unusual relationships blossomed in dance performance while educators experimented with ways to incorporate technology into dance education. Today, it is common to see technology used in dance classrooms.

With the dance boom of the 1970s, the *Dance in America* television series moved into America's living rooms, presenting dancers' classical and modern dance works. In that same decade, the videotape recorder revolutionized dance and dance education, enabling dance on demand in the studio or classroom. A teacher or artistic director could videotape rehearsals and performances to preserve them for restaging. Classroom studies, rehearsals, and performances were taped for student and teacher evaluation. Students began developing video projects and portfolios of their performances and choreography. The age of multimedia dance continues today.

In the late 1990s and early 2000s, the National Dance Association (NDA) hosted two conferences titled "Dancing with the Mouse: Dance and Technology." These conferences offered venues for educators and computer programmers to share their research, insights, pedagogy, and predictions for the future. Today, the use of technology within dance continues to grow as new resources emerge. Sessions at dance education conventions and pedagogy conferences often include sessions on the integration of media within the classroom and performance.

Incorporating the National Educational Technology Standards

Educational technology is an essential part of the American classroom. Multimedia connections have been made for and between academic subjects, including in the arts and dance through classroom work of creating, performing, and responding as part of academic curricula in public schools. It is important that students learn to use technological tools in preparation for the twenty-first century classroom and ultimately the workforce.

Supporting these new processes for skill and concept development are education technology standards and guidelines. In 2007, the International Society for Technology in Education (ISTE) revised the *National Educational Technology Standards for Students* (NETS), initially developed in 1998. These standards help teachers create appropriate lessons so that students can apply basic technological knowledge and skills to work on projects, solve problems, expand their abilities, and prepare for the digital work world.

Most states have developed mandated standards for classroom use of educational technology in public schools. Some states (e.g., Arizona, Louisiana, and Wisconsin) integrate educational technology standards within their arts and dance education standards. In addition to developing competent skills using the media and computers, students gain a variety of important skills across the learning domains that influence them as both millennium learners and future citizens.

Technological Literacy

Being technology literate means being able to use technology in a competent, skillful manner to attain information, conduct research, analyze and evaluate sources, and become effective producers of technology-rich products. Having the ability to use technology effectively is no longer an expectation for students, but a reality.

Media Literacy

Today, literacy extends beyond basic reading, writing, understanding, and analyzing subject matter. Media literacy is about gaining compe-

tency in evaluating messages presented through a variety of modes and forms. It necessitates analyzing messages, understanding varying viewpoints, identifying biases, and recognizing subliminal messages. It also is about helping students shape and produce meaningful media messages within multiple mediums.

Dancers have an advantage in becoming media literate. They constantly evaluate movement, sound, and visual sources—designs in space, shapes and poses, scenery, costumes, and lighting effects—so they can create, perform, and respond more effectively in dance. The values learned when observing, participating, and analyzing in the dance class can easily extend to media literacy.

Dance educators need to help students realize that the way a message is communicated is as important as the message itself. Teaching media literacy is an extension of dance interrelated with other arts, media, and computer-generated technology. Educators using the National Dance Education Standards and the National Educational Technology Standards for Students as well as their state standards can help students use appropriate technologies for dance to gain and strengthen cultural and media literacy.

AP Photo/Las Cruces Sun-News, Norm Dettlaff

There are many tools and resources students may use to choreograph dances. This dancer uses drawings of different shapes and patterns for inspiration.

Information Literacy

Information literacy and technology research capabilities work in tandem. Information literacy is the basis for students conducting technology research and becoming effective content producers. It is a critical part of prekindergarten through grade 12 education and higher education. Developing information literacy helps students prepare for postsecondary opportunities. Technology research capabilities are the extensions and products of information literacy. They include products that incorporate technology, media, and information literacy into a seamless multimedia product of high quality. For example, the use of PowerPoint software enables students to create presentations that include text, graphics, pictures, video segments, or music created or obtained from many sources.

The information literacy model includes seven steps for students to follow to become independent, lifelong learners:

1. Defining and focusing to recognize that an information need exists

2. Selecting tools and resources to locate and access relevant sources in libraries and media centers, from resource people, and from other sources

3. Extracting and recording resources for accuracy, unbiased positions; reading or scanning, identifying main ideas, synthesizing (chunking), and notating the materials

4. Processing information through categorizing, analyzing, and evaluating materials to make judgments about their information and findings

5. Organizing information by sorting, ordering, and determining how to use the information to communicate findings

6. Presenting findings by communicating through a variety of formats, including research report; illustration; portfolio; book report; oral, audio, or visual presentation; media presentation, dramatization; and more

7. Evaluating efforts throughout the process with the final product evaluated by the teacher and other qualified persons (Louisiana Department of Education 2003)

The first four steps are inherent in any project; steps 5, 6, and 7 produce finished products. Although this model is generic, it has implications for dance research and choreographic processes.

Gaining an understanding of concepts that underlie educational technology and following a constructivist approach to education, where students learn by doing, provide insight for how these concepts connect with technology in dance and other arts classes. In the introduction to the *National Standards for Arts Education* (Consortium of National Arts Education Associations 1994), the authors wrote, "The arts disciplines, their techniques, and their technologies have a strong historic relationship; each continues to shape and inspire the other. Existing and emerging technologies will always be a part of how changes in the arts disciplines are created, viewed, and taught" (p.14). The follow-up question is, "How do these ideas interface with dance concepts and standards?"

Dance Concepts and Technology Standards

Creating, performing, and responding are basic processes of dance and other arts. These processes connect well with technology and help students build the knowledge, skills, and dispositions needed to achieve national and state standards and benchmarks in dance and educational technology. These dance concepts are synergetic with using and integrating technology, as shown in figure 6.1.

Many state dance standards also present either general educational technology standards or arts technology standards; sometimes, states have designated dance technology and media standards. The dance technology standards, like others, indicate that students as individuals and in groups should be able to develop specified technology products within dance as well as in other subjects. Dance technology standards are unique to the states in which they are generated. Table 6.1 shows an example of one state's standard and benchmarks that provide infused dance education and technology standards at the elementary, middle school, and high school levels. This example may provide ideas and springboards for dance technology infusions in other states' standards.

Media Tools in the Dance Classroom

Just as in other classrooms, dance studios have needs for computers. The teacher can use the computer to check attendance, write lesson plans, make notes, and schedule reviews and test sessions. But, there is more to explore if dance educators are to

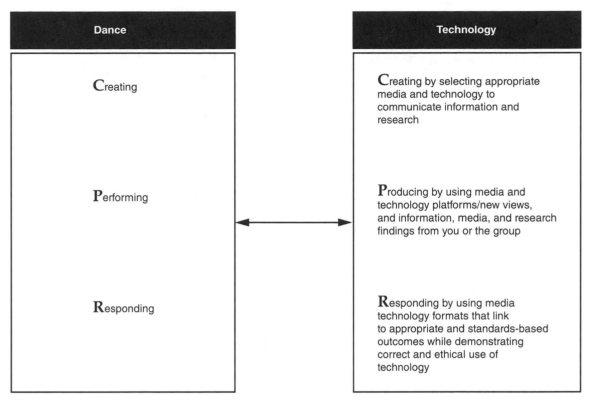

Dance	Technology
Creating	Creating by selecting appropriate media and technology to communicate information and research
Performing	Producing by using media and technology platforms/new views, and information, media, and research findings from you or the group
Responding	Responding by using media technology formats that link to appropriate and standards-based outcomes while demonstrating correct and ethical use of technology

FIGURE 6.1 Both dance education and technology education have a corresponding focus on creating, performing, and responding.

TABLE 6.1 Wisconsin Department of Public Instruction Dance Content Standard

Content Standard: Students in Wisconsin will expand dance horizons through the use of technology.

By the end of grade 4 students will:	By the end of grade 8 students will:	By the end of grade 12 students will:
Create a video portfolio of dance studies and performances	Add to a video portfolio of dance studies and performances	Continue to create an extensive video portfolio of dance studies and performances
Create and record audio tapes to accompany dance studies	Create and record audio to accompany dance studies	Create and record audio tapes to accompany dance studies
View videos of dances from other cultures and/or professional dance performances	View and discuss videos of dances from other cultures and/or professional dance performances	View and discuss with greater understanding videos of dances from other cultures and/or professional dance performances
Begin to use computer technology to facilitate dance-related research	Use computer technology to facilitate dance-related research	Use computer technology to facilitate dance-related research
Use the computer to note or describe a simple dance sequence or composition	Use a computer to note or describe a dance sequence or composition	Continue to use a computer to note or describe dance sequences or compositions
Create a short dance video	Create a dance video using technology to enhance the mood of the dance	Create an interdisciplinary project using media technologies (such as video or a computer) that present dance in a new or enhanced form (such as video dance, video- or computer-aided live performance, or animation)

create media- and information-literate dancers and dance educators for the next generation. Teachers may use a handheld computer or personal digital assistant (PDA) in ways similar to use of a laptop or desk-top computer. These devices can be used to discreetly record student behavior and make personal notes for individualizing classes.

Students are computer literate and have a built-in support system through the school's media literacy resource staff and centers. These centers and resource individuals can provide ideas, advice, applications, software, and in some cases the hardware needed to implement technology within the classroom. A variety of technology formats can be used for assessing student learning.

Media and Technology Extensions Into Dance Learning

Students need to learn to use technology effectively in relation to dance. When completing dance projects, students learn by making choices and then evaluating them, thereby using higher-order thinking skills. Using technology is no different. For decades, students have produced media products. Students can relate to creating, performing, and responding in dance and meeting technology education standards as parallel learning experiences.

Media and technology tools employed every day for professional and personal use have evolved so they are easier to use. The school library or media staff members have these items on hand and can share their expertise with students so they can learn by doing. The media resource person is invaluable as a supporter for implementing technology in the dance classroom.

Digital Video or Video Recorders

Video use in the dance classroom is a basic. The video recorder presents unlimited possibilities for the dance teacher and students, including reconstructing a work, recording a student performance or improvisations in class, assessing technical and performance skills, or creating opportunities for responding to a video performance by students or by a professional dance company. Video recordings can capture technical and creative products for later comparison.

There also are benefits to using a digital camcorder that can easily work with computer software programs such as PowerPoint, multimedia products, or Web-based products. Digital technology provides a perfect opportunity for students and teachers to enhance their abilities to create, perform, and respond immediately.

Computers

Computers offer students and teachers a means to record and manipulate images. Still photos

Students of all ages can successfully use computer resources in the classroom to enhance their learning about dance and the creative processes.

and video footage as well as sound can be used to create a new product. More sophisticated software such as iMovie and iDVD (for Mac platforms) assist in editing the digital footage. Storage on large capacity USB devices such as thumb drives or external hard drives provides a way to make recordings available for later use without overloading the computer. Each format has its benefits and its drawbacks. New technologies continue to evolve, and dancers and dance educators will find innovative ways to use them all.

Regardless of where the computers are located, they can easily be used for student dance learning experiences, assignments, research, and projects. Some software and media tools are professionally developed. Additional resources can be developed using generic tools such as word processing and spreadsheets, while others can be specifically created to meet unique needs of the dance project. The curriculum can be arranged so that students build technology literacy skills throughout the curriculum as they build skills in dance and need to use technology to implement their visions, record their work, or produce dance assignments.

Computers can be used to show commercial DVDs, capture digital photos, access the Internet's huge repositories of information, and hyperlink to specific Web sites. Students can prepare PowerPoint or other multimedia presentations on the computer. They can access WebQuests, which are Web-based reports or research projects that may use multimedia technology. School systems may subscribe to interactive course delivery, course management, and assessment systems. Teachers or students may wish to use blogs, Twitter, other online forums, and Web 2.0 communications for further contacts, sharing, and collaboration for after-class discussion.

Dance Software

There is little computer software that has been produced specifically for dance education. Of those that exist currently, some are presentation

Creative Ways to Use Dance Dance Revolution (DDR) in a Learning Experience

Dance Dance Revolution (DDR) is an interactive video and movement game produced by the Konami Corporation in Osaka, Japan. It is used in schools, gyms, and arcades as an aerobic exercise and dance tool. To perform DDR, players select specific songs based on varying speeds, foot patterns, and degrees of rhythmic complexity. Players stand on an electronic dance pad (labeled with directional patterns) and move to visual and musical cues. Teachers have used this game as a springboard to introduce dance to nondancers in middle and high schools. This product helps students increase endurance, balance, agility, and coordination. To make this experience a creative process where students perform, repeat, and reorder complex movement patterns, have students vary the movement with the following extensions:

1. Create DDR feet patterns away from the platform. Repeat the pattern two or three times.
2. Teach the foot patterns to two to four classmates. Repeat the patterns and change tempo of the steps.
3. Add arm movements to accompany the foot patterns.
4. Create a way to move through space (by stepping a bit farther than the original pattern) with at least one level and facing change during each repetition of the foot and arm patterns.
5. Clearly demonstrate tempo changes in each movement pattern.
6. Create a clear beginning and ending for the movement series.
7. Perform the movement study for other classmates periodically throughout the process.

The process can serve as a springboard to help students meet National Dance Education Standards 2, 4, and 6.

oriented, some are management oriented, and others are education orientated. Following are some examples of current software.

- *The Video Dictionary of Classical Ballet* and the *Video Dictionary of Ballet for Children* provide DVD presentations of various steps (www.allaboutdance.com).

- *Wild Child* and *Wild Child Mini,* by Jacqueline Smith-Autard, British choreographer and dance technology author. Working with Bedford Interactive Research, Smith-Autard and her colleagues produced CD-ROMs as multimedia tools to enhance the use of technology in education. Currently, Bedford Interactive Research offers four CD-ROM resource packs teachers can use to improve creating, performing, and responding to dance at elementary, middle school, secondary, and higher education levels. The Web site also provides publications for download and purchase (http://bedfordi.20m.com/index1.html).

- *DanceForms 1.0,* choreography software evolved from Lifeforms animation software. *DanceForms* uses a 3D environment for developing choreography that connects with dance technology applications. The animation allows for experimentation with movement phrases using an assortment of dance figures for modern dance, jazz, or ballet. Entire dances can be choreographed using this software (www.charactermotion.com/danceforms).

- *LabanWriter* is a software program, created on the Macintosh operating system, which permits dance to be copied and edited into the computer. It uses the symbols of Labanotation and can be downloaded for free from The Ohio State University (www.dance.ohio-state.edu/labanwriter).

- Other notation systems, such as EW Notator or Eshkol-Wachman Movement Notation, are available for Microsoft Windows (www.movement-notation.org/henner/EWNotator.htm).

General Software and Internet Functions for Dance Technology Projects

General software for word processing, spreadsheets, databanks, and PowerPoint or multimedia presentations provide formats for generating a wealth of dance assignments using technology.

- Word processing supports assignments, journals, and research projects that can be used for student-centered learning, performance evaluation, and rubrics.

- Graphics can be used for graphics-enhanced posters, flyers, programs, public service announcements, and other publicity items—even T-shirts for the dance company. Graphics are available on CD-ROM through different programs or can be downloaded free from the Internet.

- Drawing tools create pathways for dance compositions, floor and other designs, or graphic organizers (such as concept maps), flowcharts, and diagrams.

- Spreadsheets can be used to produce surveys and create data collection and analysis tools that can present information as bar or circle graphs and integrate data into word processing and other documents. Spreadsheets can be used for developing budgets for dance concerts, programs, and more.

- Databanks provide information that can be sorted and identified for further analysis.

- They can hold lists of people who attend concerts, lists of work in the repertory and by dancer, a history of works performed by the company, and costume and lighting instrument inventories.

- E-mail offers electronic communication with and between students, teachers, and other professionals. Specific etiquette applies, and students should use e-mail responsibly. This medium offers ways to send assignments, participate in discussion listservs, and communicate within the dance world and beyond.

Specialized Programs

Specialized arts technology can support dance performance or production, or it can stimulate development of new dance media.

AutoCAD and Vectorworks are 2D and 3D applications for lighting designs. These programs can create lighting plots and associated reports such as the instrument schedule, channel and dimmer schedule, and color schedule.

Computerized dimmer systems allow preprogramming of an entire dance concert's light cues. Moving lights or intelligent lights can enhance a dance performance by producing computer-controlled synchronized movement and color changes.

Computer Simulations

Digital video annotation is a tool to teach dance composition. Using video tracers that capture video so that it can be annotated and reflected upon is part of the choreographic process. At the University of Washington, dance researchers Gina Cherry, Janice Fournier, and Reed Stevens conducted a study to use this method for dance composition development (see http://faculty .washington.edu/reedstev/vt.html) (Stevens, Cherry, and Fournier, 2002).

Dance Videos or DVDs

As a staple of dance studies for viewing, analyzing, and reconstructing performances in the classroom, dance videos capture recordings of students, the dance company, a dance performance, or professional dancers and dance companies that are integral to dance education. Dance videos or DVDs provide a tremendous amount of variety for standalone media, work well with different kinds of technology, and enable students to produce their own products.

Digital Photos

Digital photos capture key shapes, choreographic moments, costumes, lighting, and stage effects. These photos capture the dance moment and even the essence of the dance; they can be integrated easily into a variety of technologies from word processing to multimedia to sharing locations on the Web.

Initially, students need to learn the technical skill basics, such as how to operate a digital camera, digital video recorder, and scanner, to create these integrated technology products. Later in the process, students should gain skills of downloading audio, photos and pictorial information, and video clips to their computers.

Internet Search and Research

The Internet offers huge repositories of information, and some are excellent for information collection and research for dance assignments and projects. Both teachers and students can search the Web sites of many national dance organizations, national or regional dance museums, libraries, dance company educational programs, university programs, or dance vendors, to name a few. The searches can help students learn about dance terminology, ways to perform specific skills, educational and health benefits of dance, origins of certain dance forms or styles, impact of dance on society during particular historical periods, or societal influences on dance. The possibilities are endless.

Internet Sites

General sites, such as those of dance libraries and others that link to a variety of information about dancers, dance companies, history, and other dance topics, provide good starting points. A list of some dance library and company repositories follows.

- Smithsonian Institution Libraries Web site provides information on the history of dance using authentic documents, video clips, and pictorial evidence—the American memory site (www.sil.si.edu). When looking at the homepage, key in "history of dance" or the specific dance genre of interest in the search box.
- New York Public Library at Lincoln Center, Jerome Robbins Dance Collection provides extensive sources for investigation and research (www.nypl.org/research/lpa/dan/ dan.html).
- American Ballet Theatre (ABT) history project provides a large repository of information about ABT choreographers and their works in a searchable way (www.abt .org/education/archive/index.html).
- PBS Great Performances dance site offers information about choreographers and their works (www.pbs.org/wnet/gperf/genre/ dance.html).
- Artslynx International Arts Resources is a portal especially designed to link to theater and dance resources worldwide (www .artslynx.org).
- Library of Congress offers a variety of dance resources, such as articles, books, audio sources, historical artifacts, and prints (www.loc.gov/index.html).

Create hyperlinks to these or any location by blocking, copying, and pasting Web addresses into documents for instant links to specific Web sites or specific pages in a Web site. These extended connections are easily integrated into word processing documents, PowerPoint presentations, multimedia hyperstacks and WebQuests, or Web pages. The links provide additional information and support of specific points a teacher chooses to make.

Internet Videos and Music

Some Web sites present video performance clips (e.g., the Smithsonian American Memory of historical dance, American Dance Companion, or Twyla Tharp Foundation). Students can link these Web sites to assignments or in some cases download them into projects.

Linking to general or specific audio sources provides connections to music or midi (synthesized music) resources. Many general music libraries are searchable by composer, composition, musical period, and style. Some midi sources provide downloading. If this is not a possibility, then incorporating an audio clip from a music CD-ROM into a new product or composition is another possibility. To ensure that copyright laws and technology ethics are respected, consult with the school's technology staff about updated copyright laws under educational fair usage.

Multimedia Presentations

PowerPoint presentations integrate words, pictures, video, and audio into a series of slides that can be designed to present a project. Multimedia presentations built on hyperstacks are similar to PowerPoints but often include several hyperstacks joined together into a larger project. The hyperstack series of screens can support written information, pictures, photographs, and audio, including music and voice. Animated and video elements can be integrated into the product.

Internet Projects and Products

Assigning a variety of Internet projects provides students with ways to demonstrate their creativity and mastery of integrating multimedia elements. In order to accomplish these goals, teachers need a basic knowledge of Web pages and Web site construction. This can be accomplished through a number of easy-to-use programs. Developing Internet projects such as multimedia presentations requires researching and selecting material, organizing the information, and presenting it through a multimedia format.

Web Pages

Web pages disseminate information or research presented either as part of the school's Web page on its intraweb or uploaded to an Internet site. It is easiest to start with dance projects that include information about class projects, an upcoming dance concert, or a community dance project.

WebQuest Research

WebQuests are Web-based projects that represent a culminating report or research project similar to a traditional written research project (see figure 6.2). A WebQuest presents a short- or long-term project using a multimedia environment that integrates pictures, photos, diagrams, audio, video, and hyperlinks in a series of Web pages. The WebQuest has a format similar to a traditional research project.

Evaluating Media and Technology Products

Prior to creating any projects, design the evaluation process so students will understand the criteria for assessment. Video performance analysis, multimedia, and WebQuest rubrics have long

---

FIGURE 6.2   Requirements for a WebQuest

- Clear introductory paragraph that sets the stage for the activity and provides some background information.
- Central task that is achievable and interesting.
- Set of information sources needed to complete the task. Provide all the knowledge sources, both from online and real-world sources, to students in the form of a WebQuest handout. These pointers to information are vital and ensure that students are centered on the task at hand.
- Description of the entire process students should go through to accomplish the task.
- Guidance on how to organize the information acquired. This can take the form of guiding questions or directions for completing organizational frameworks such as timelines or concept maps, ultimately resulting in the creation of new Web pages to demonstrate new learning.
- Conclusion that brings closure to the WebQuest, reminds students what they've learned, and encourages them to extend the experience into other domains.

From Classroom Connect, December 1996/January 1997.

been available. These were originally developed by educational technology experts or experts in other fields. Although many of the rubrics are generic, they can easily be used as is, adapted, or made specific for a project. Similar to guidelines for performance assessment, these rubrics are written as authentic assessments and connect well with educational assessment strategies. See, for example, *Rubrics for Web Lessons* (http://webquest.sdsu.edu/rubrics/weblessons.htm). The rubrics cover the technology, the individual or group process used, and the product.

Understanding Fair Use Guidelines

In 2009, the Dance Heritage Coalition released the "Statement of Best Practices in Fair Use of Dance-Related Materials." The document explains what individuals who work with dance-related materials need to know to apply the Copyright Act's fair use guidelines. The publication identifies contexts in which copyrighted materials may be used, ethical uses of noncopyrighted resources, and ways materials can be used for academic and scholarly work. A section of the document addresses use of copyrighted materials on the Web site. Initially developed for librarians and conservators, the publication also is useful for educators.

Copyright Laws and Technology Ethics

Technology does not exist without its laws and ethical standards. Students are expected to learn, work, and conduct research in an ethical manner. Since technology is an important part of developing the new workforce, it is important for students to learn and integrate technology ethics into assignments, research, and the development of all products. The standards provide the basis for reaching competency within the area of technology; the ethics ensure that everyone is acting as responsible individuals whose work mirrors the expectations of professionals. These technology standards include the basics of research, such as correct methods for citing sources. All sources—book, media, or Internet—deserve the same respect.

New Horizons in Dance Technology

The uses of technology within dance education and dance technology have two separate strands. One strand focuses on the use of technology to enhance dance education; the other strand, including technology such as telematic dance,

The Ten Commandments of Computer Ethics

1. Thou shalt not use a computer to harm other people.
2. Thou shalt not interfere with other people's computer work.
3. Thou shalt not snoop around in other people's computer files.
4. Thou shalt not use a computer to steal.
5. Thou shalt not use a computer to bear false witness.
6. Thou shalt not copy or use proprietary software for which you have not paid.
7. Thou shalt not use other people's computer resources without authorization or proper compensation.
8. Thou shalt not appropriate other people's intellectual output.
9. Thou shalt think about the social consequences of the program you are writing or the system you are designing.
10. Thou shalt always use a computer in ways that insure consideration and respect for your fellow humans.

Internet 2, and videoconferencing (http://dance .arts.uci.edu/lnaugle/files/telematic/index. html), focuses on the generation and composition of new dance. The process of integrating the second strand into dance education with the purpose of producing and analyzing student products is currently in development. As states integrate education technology standards into arts and dance education standards, the second strand will become more prominent. Additionally, as dance educators acquire the basic tools to integrate technology into dance and their students bring more technology literacy into the dance classroom, dance and technology will become stronger partners in dance education.

Summary

This chapter describes strategies a dance teacher may use to help students understand ways to enhance their learning about and through dance by using a variety of technological tools. The use of technology does not weaken the human value or quality of dance; rather, it can open new horizons for studying and connecting the body, movement, music and other sounds, interrelated arts, and other academic disciplines. Technology provides new ways of researching dance archives as well as ways to archive personal works. Technology offers varied sources to educators and students to self-assess and to critique others' works while in progress or as final productions.

7

Using a Template to Design Learning Experiences

This chapter focuses on how to use information from previous chapters regarding the learners, teaching environment, and effective classroom strategies to organize learning experiences that may be reflected in unit or daily lesson plans. The chapter includes a template you can use as a practical approach to plan dance content that meets specific dance standards and benchmarks. This model is designed to help maintain quality while building effective learning experiences.

What Is a Learning Experience?

A learning experience (LE) is a plan for student learning. It has a specific focus and an organized progression of tasks or activities that guide learning of movement, information, and peer interaction necessary to achieve the intended outcome. A learning experience may be considered in two different ways: (1) an overarching plan (e.g., mini-unit plan) that can be subdivided into smaller, time-appropriate lessons, such as the length of a class period; (2) a short-term learning experience (e.g., lesson plan) framed to meet a very specific goal for a single class period. Examples of mini-unit or overarching plans are found in chapters 8 through 11. One learning experience found in chapter 10 is the Sun Salutation. It is designed for middle school and contains far more content than is possible for a single 45- to 50-minute lesson. It is best to frame several lessons using sequential progression and content development from the materials within the Sun Salutation sample learning experience. Each learning experience has a stated goal, is designed for a specific group of learners (by age, grade, or developmental ability), addresses one or more of the National Dance Education Standards, and can help students reach specific benchmarks.

Designing Effective Learning Experiences

Designing effective learning experiences takes time and thoughtful practice. The teacher carefully chooses class goals, student objectives, dance content, assessment tools, realistic progressions, and instructional materials. This is done while considering students' developmental characteristics for each learning domain (psychomotor, cognitive, and affective). The teacher also seeks to address one or more of the National Dance Education Standards within each learning experience. Further, the teacher identifies ways to challenge students of all abilities throughout the learning experience. Chapters 3, 4, and 5 provide details of the background needed to design and assess sound learning experiences. This chapter provides information on how to use a specific learning experience template (figure 7.1) to design meaningful lessons. This template is also provided on the accompanying CD-ROM.

Using the Learning Experience Template

Figure 7.1 provides an outline with key components for planning learning experiences. Each item on the template has key points to remember. The brief text below describes the key points for each part of the template. After completing your study of the template, key points, and descriptions, you should be ready to write your own clear learning experiences.

Learning Experience Title: Identifies the primary content of the lesson or unit, for example, Flying Lindy Hop Swing Dance.

Description: The title for the lesson or series of lessons helps to focus attention immediately on the content and provides points of reference throughout the learning tasks and activities.

Overview: Includes one to three sentences that state the unit or lesson focus and expected outcomes.

Description: For example, the overview of the sample learning experience, the Flying Lindy Hop Swing Dance, states, "Expose students to swing dance in general and to the Lindy Hop in particular. Discuss how swing dance is an American art form that originated in the United States during the 1920s."

Grade Level: States the grade level for which a lesson falls within the overarching unit or school curriculum.

Description: This section might appear as follows: grade 11, beginning-level dance experience, lesson 3 in a 16-lesson unit.

Materials, Equipment, Space Needed: Includes specific information about each of these requirements.

Materials: List of titles of CDs, audio tapes, DVDs, and VHS tapes needed. May also list any hand props needed by the teacher or students.

Equipment: List of what is required to teach the lesson (e.g., percussion instruments, CD player, video playback equipment that matches the VHS tapes and DVDs listed in Materials section).

Space Needed: Identification, by name, of the specific space needed (e.g., Dance Studio #1; stage in a theater with audience seating capability).

Learning Experience Title

OVERVIEW _____

GRADE LEVEL _____

MATERIALS, EQUIPMENT, SPACE NEEDED _____

NATIONAL STANDARDS ADDRESSED   Content Standard(s)   (Benchmarks: _____)

GOAL _____

OBJECTIVES   As a result of participating in this learning experience, students will:
   [Psychomotor]
   [Cognitive]
   [Affective]

VOCABULARY

Management	Teaching Process	Teaching Points and Cues
Introduction		
(Time requirement)		
Review of previous material, warm-up		
(Time requirement)		
New material		

a. Exploratory activities
   (Time requirement)
b. Refinement activities
   (Time requirement)		

Recap of lesson, cool-down		
(Time requirement)		
Closure and assessment		
Rubric (criterion, evidence, scale— teacher, self, peer) (Time requirement)		

EXTENSIONS/MODIFICATIONS
   1. _____
   2. _____

OPTIONAL _____

TECHNOLOGY CONNECTION _____

ACCOMMODATION OR DIFFERENTIATION IDEAS _____

EVERYDAY LIVING (LIFETIME WELLNESS) CONNECTIONS _____

FIGURE 7.1   Learning experience template.

National Standards Addressed: Provides a location to list the standards addressed by the LE (see appendix).

National Standards: The content standard(s) by name and number.

Description: For example, the wording would be as follows: Content Standard 1: Identifies and demonstrates movement elements and skills in performing dance.

Benchmarks: Provides a place to list the preferred benchmarks addressed by the LE under each content standard.

Description: For example, the applicable benchmark(s), in this case for Content Standard 1, might be these: Body a, c; Relationships a, c; and Advanced b. If another national standard is addressed, it should be identified by number and title with the corresponding benchmarks listed under it.

The listing may be lengthy or very short. There needs to be a match between the lesson content and the selected standard(s); the identified benchmarks should correspond to the lesson goals and objectives. This part of the preparation is valuable to you in sharpening your focus on the content and assessment process. By choosing specific standards and their respective benchmarks, you know what to emphasize during the lesson or series of lessons.

Goal: States the broad purpose of the learning experience.

Description: Following is a sample goal statement: "To introduce students to swing dance, swing rhythms, and the history of swing dance in America." This statement is simple and offers a clear statement of the outcome of the lesson(s).

For this activity, the students will need to know and use swing dance terminology correctly and demonstrate these skills: musical phrasing, relationship between partners, dancing a planned sequence, and repeating the sequence multiple times.

Consistency should be evident between the learning experience title, overview statements, goal statement, and objectives. The selected standards statements and benchmarks should clearly match each of these components.

Objectives: Identify what the students will know and be able to do by the end of the learning experience. There may be one or more objectives in this section. For example, "As a result of participating in this learning experience, the student will apply correct swing dance terminology to specific swing steps and arm movements using a 144-count dance pattern."

Identify Domain: Text added in this section lists what will be addressed in each domain.

Psychomotor	(dance skills) locomotor, nonlocomotor, and movement combinations
Cognitive	knowledge, critical thinking
Affective	appreciation, feelings, values

Description: It is necessary, at this point in the planning, to break down the components of the lesson or learning experience into identifiable segments of learning. For example, the goal "to introduce students to swing dance, swing rhythms, and the history of swing dance in America" has subparts that must be introduced, practiced, and combined into a final dance pattern. Therefore, one objective needs to address the swing dance history and terminology. Another needs to focus on the arm positions for the male and female roles, while a third objective needs to focus on the basic steps and variations. Acquiring the historical knowledge and terminology and applying that knowledge to movement is a cognitive action. Working cooperatively with partners to make decisions that lead to the final dance is an affective concept. Successfully executing the swing steps with the appropriate rhythm, body positioning, and arm movement involves psychomotor actions. Objectives for lessons usually include psychomotor, cognitive, and affective statements.

Vocabulary: Lists the specific terms that students should know and use correctly by the end of this unit or lesson: open position, face-off position, swing out, pivot, and others.

Developing the Learning Experience Step by Step

The following format explains how to plan specific aspects of lesson management, teaching process, and teaching points and cues for a structured lesson.

Introduction: Provides a brief overview of the purpose of the lesson, how it relates to previous learning or to information from other disciplines (e.g., art, music, social studies), and what the learners are expected to know and be able to do by the end of the lesson. This overview may introduce the new unit or lesson or help students recall what they have been learning for the past several lessons.

Review of Previous Material, Warm-Up: Can function as a review of previously experienced knowledge and skills and can provide a stepping stone to learning new material in the planned lesson.

New Material: Includes exploratory and refinement activities.

Exploratory Activities: These planned activities may help students experience new skills, learn new information, and develop ways of working alone and with others. These activities can expand vocabulary, enhance skills, or combine learned skills in new ways.

Refinement Activities: Refinement requires critical thinking and observation. Refinement work can be alone or with others to determine the best response to a given problem or to present clear and clean movement to an assigned task.

Recap of Lesson, Cool-Down: Provides the summary of a lesson, reinforcing the focus of the session. It is usually teacher directed and can be done with everyone moving simultaneously. The cool-down can be incorporated in the recap activity, or it can be a well-balanced physical cool-down that includes some form of relaxation.

Closure and Assessment: Can be formal or informal and is a way of restating the purpose of the lesson and specific parts of the lesson. Closure usually includes some form of session assessment. Formal assessment may be done orally or in a paper-and-pencil format.

Informal assessment may be a simple show of hands in response to teacher questions or as complex as checking skills off using a rubric (see chapter 5: Assessing for Success in Dance Education).

Extensions or Modifications: Include pre-planned ways to increase or decrease challenges within tasks presented to the class as a whole and to specific students. A competent teacher has relevant learning activities planned to enrich learning or to allow for a change of direction if the originally planned activities are not successful.

Optional: It is helpful to plan a range of activities and tasks for classrooms with students of varying abilities. Students who master skills or tasks quickly may move on to new learning while those who need additional practice may continue to work at their own rates.

Technology Connection: The planned integration of DVDs, VHS recordings, WebQuests, and computer-generated research for dance projects are examples of ways to use technology within a learning experience. It is important to preselect class materials, cue them on the appropriate technology prior to class, and continuously reinforce the connection between the technology and the dance experiences (see chapter 6: Integrating Technology Into Dance Education.)

Accommodation or Differentiation Ideas: When implementing planned lesson strategies, consider the knowledge base, understanding, and capabilities of various students in the class. Develop reasonable approaches to carry out plans for each student effectively and efficiently. Think about processes for giving directions, building interest, transitioning from one lesson segment to another, providing individualized assistance, distributing materials, and checking for understanding. It is important to promote student success for all students.

Everyday Living (Lifetime Wellness) Connections: In classes at all levels, blend specific dance content with information that promotes students' personal health and safety. Knowledge of basic anatomy and body systems is crucial to heighten body awareness and alignment, avoid health risks, and prevent fatigue and injury. To develop healthy bodies and minds, students need accurate, age-appropriate information about healthy eating, body image, and weight management; dangers of tobacco, alcohol, and drugs; stress reduction and self-esteem; sleep; and safe workouts and training. Students need to understand the benefits of dance as a healthy, lifetime physical activity (increasing cardiovascular health, muscle strength, endurance, flexibility) and a way to prevent or control certain chronic diseases, including arthritis, diabetes, and osteoporosis.

Identifying Knowledge and Skills Needed to Develop a Learning Experience

Developing learning experiences places expectations on the teacher throughout the planning process. To facilitate the process, you need certain background knowledge, skills, and resources. It is important to be grounded in dance content and in the developmental characteristics (physical, cognitive, social, and emotional) of the students for whom the lessons are planned. Developing strategies to challenge learners of all abilities requires sound analysis of individual skills. You need to know how to execute specific dance technique, steps, or styles; apply cultural and historical aspects of selected dances and dance forms; make connections with other arts and educational themes; and develop critical-thinking skills. Planned informal and formal assessments permit feedback to the student and teacher.

Understanding Basic Dance Terminology

Following are definitions of four basic dance education terms that are important to understand and teach. Early on, teachers need to help students know their meanings to foster understanding of verbal instructions and written assignments.

Dance form or genre: Certain categories of dance are classified as a dance form or genre, such as ballet, modern, tap, ballroom, jazz, world dance, or hip-hop. Each form consists of specific cultural and historical background, dance movement vocabulary, and body positioning and movement skills.

Choreographic form: This "form" usually applies to the structure of a longer and more refined

Students studying any dance form, need to understand its specific terminology to execute skills appropriately.

dance, a work in progress, or a brief study for a short-term class assignment. The structure may be a two part (AB) form or have many parts (ABA). For example, the AB compositional form involves two definite sections of movement patterns that demonstrate a particular character or quality (e.g., tempo, spacing, relationship, or force). An ABA compositional form demonstrates two contrasting sections of a dance with a third section reminiscent of the movement and quality in the first section.

Dance style: This refers to distinctive characteristics or ways of moving that identify certain gestures, body alignment, or footwork with specific time periods, choreographers, or dancers within a variety of dance forms.

Dance techniques: Each dance form draws from a specific movement technique or fusion of techniques. A technique provides fundamental movements and recommended practices (including those to prevent injury), and require mastery of efficient, aesthetic movement. For example, exhibition clogging, Bournonville ballet technique, ballroom waltzes, and American square dance all require specific body carriage, subtle weight shifts, and specific turns. Knowledge that each dance form has characteristics that differentiate it from others is essential. Including a variety of dance forms and techniques in the curriculum helps students celebrate differences and similarities among cultures and individuals.

Teaching Dance Education

There are a number of basic skills required of a successful dance educator. These skills are broadly categorized into six components: knowledge of subject matter, organization, classroom management, instruction (teaching), assessment, and adaptability. A skilled dance educator weaves these categories into rich learning experiences for students. It is helpful if the teacher possesses a deep appreciation for dance as an art form and for its benefits for health promotion and sociological development. A teacher's personal traits and positive role modeling can inspire students to greater challenges and achievements. The inner passion can be a significant factor in energizing students and discovering new ways to engage them in learning about dance and other subjects.

Connecting Dance and Dance Forms With Other Subject Areas

There are obvious connections among dance, the arts, and other subject areas. The links between dance and other art forms are most evident. Noted choreographer Doris Humphrey (1959, p. 46), describes four elements that are also found in music, theater, and visual arts: design, rhythm, motivation, and dynamics. In her seminal dance education text, Margaret H'Doubler (1957, p. 144), identifies the principles of dance composition that are found in the other arts fields: transition, balance, sequence, repetition, harmony, variety, contrast, and climax. In chapters 8 through 11, sample learning experiences demonstrate ways that dance and other arts connect. (See sample learning experience, p. 213: grades 6 to 8 Visual Art, Dance, and Technology).

Over generations, dance developed significantly from its earliest religious origins. Many sociological patterns or events served as motivators for dance throughout history. Studying dance over time can help explain the many and reciprocal influences of dance, culture, and society. Teachers and choreographers find wonderful relationships between math, music,

and dance. The expanding science frontiers of earth science, chemistry, physics, and health, among others, provide rich resources for dance studies. Literature and poetry are fertile stimuli for dance making. Several learning experiences in part II are examples of connections between dance and other subject areas (grades 3 to 5, Working in the Coal Mine (p. 152); grades 6 to 8, Sun Salutation (p. 180); grades 9 to 12, Interdisciplinary Experience: Moving to Written Text (p. 247).

Teachers are encouraged to use the arts and other subjects as resources for enriching dance learning experiences. There is enormous educational material available for use, and the benefits of a well-planned lesson are notable. However, exercise careful thought in making these instructional choices. Combining even two academic topics (such as dance and poetry) takes careful planning to ensure optimal success for students and the teacher.

Benefits of the Learning Experience

Learning implies growth in physical well-being, intellectual abilities, social understanding, and psychological balance. The learning experience template is designed to help the teacher plan for growth in each domain while using dance as the essential learning tool. To address these areas for growth, recognize that each student comes to the classroom with life experiences that will affect that student's work. Those life experiences may be helpful, or they may be a distraction to learning.

It is important to have a large repertoire of tasks and activities to trigger students' attention. See chapter 2 and each chapter in part II for information regarding learner characteristics by grade levels and the implications for dance educators. See the appendix for benchmarks by grade level. Information in these sections of the book can help you establish realistic outcomes for specific students. Learning movement vocabulary, content, and skills at any age needs to occur in a planned progression. Although older students can intellectually process movement in refined movement phrases, younger students who are not ready for complex movement phrases can become frustrated by a lack of success. With a lack of success often comes a drop in motivation to learn. Good planning is necessary for students to have meaningful educational experiences that strengthen physical, cognitive, psychological, and social well-being.

Strategies for Integrating Dance With Other Curricula

There are several ways teachers can integrate dance with other subjects. This may be done individually, with a partner or team teacher, or as a small-group team project. Some schools emphasize subject matter integration and facilitate this work by creating dedicated time in the day for teachers to meet in planning teams. When meetings are not coordinated through the scheduling office, teachers work at the beginning or end of the school day, or after hours. Larger planning teams and the inclusion of more subject areas require extensive coordination for successful results. Following any group planning, individual teachers must prepare personal segments of the learning experience.

To be successful with any team approach, teachers need to understand the blended content so well that any in the group can serve as the lead teacher at any moment in the lesson. A teaching team does not compromise the subject matter expertise of any educator; rather, it enhances the learning of the subjects taught.

Often, student work developed as a result of pursuing integrated subject matter can become the subject of a formal assembly or informal presentation for peers. This venue is different from in-class sharing. A well-planned opportunity for peers to share work with others who have not participated in the learning experience allows for even more student exposure and learning. Students discover new connections with the subject areas and find ways to share that information using a variety of skills. Overall, the teacher planning teams, student planning groups, and the observers are enriched by the projects.

Strategies for Teaching Students With Special Needs

All children and youth have an innate desire to move and engage in arts experiences. They are drawn to activities that foster exploration, problem solving, and creative thinking. Educators can help this process by assuring ample opportunities for access to arts experiences, including dance. Dance is a unique kinesthetic art form that facilitates movement and learning. The experiential learning that dance promotes allows opportunities for critical thinking and creative ways to express thoughts, feelings, emotions, and ideas. Dance experiences can help youth develop the knowledge, skills, and abilities to understand and appreciate their communities and world in which they live.

Whether teaching in a public or private school, after-school activity, dance studio, or community-based program, you can provide strong programs for students, including those with special needs. There is often a vast range of abilities and special needs among students in classrooms. Some situations you may encounter involve students with diagnosed learning disabilities, developmental delays, hearing or visual impairments, emotional challenges, attention deficit disorder or attention deficit hyperactivity disorder, psychiatric disorders, or physical impairments. In these cases, you may want additional preparation to address the needs of students who speak English as a second language, are struggling with obesity, or are considered high risk due to socioeconomic or other environmental factors.

When planning a dance education curriculum, highlighting students' abilities rather than disabilities is critical to successful class experiences. This is true for all students. Several general points to consider when teaching classes of students with wide ranges of abilities are these:

- Get to know students well: physically, intellectually, socially, and emotionally.
- Integrate small-group teaching into the learning experiences.
- Hold students to high personal expectations.
- Use clear rubrics to teach for quality.
- Ensure obstacle-free teaching environments.
- Expand your repertoire of instructional strategies, including use of guided discovery and movement education techniques.
- Offer students a variety of ways to experience content and skills.
- Allow multiple responses to achieve a desired action.
- Provide a variety of teaching cues (e.g., auditory, kinesthetic, tactile, visual).
- Seek multiple ways for problem solving.
- Create or teach movement sequences in understandable chunks.
- Use informal assessments to monitor understanding.
- Allow students to work alone and with peers.
- Praise positive learning responses.

Realistic Reflections/Getty Images

Students with varying abilities can learn through dance education, experience success, and know the joy of movement.

Other, more specific instructional considerations for the dance instructor include

- focusing on the specific abilities and what can be enhanced through dance education;
- using clear, concise language for instructions, as well as for stopping and starting movement;
- refraining from talking or writing while your back is turned toward students;
- repeating class instructions in various ways, using auditory, visual, or print cues;
- developing unique lesson plans that consider the needs of all students in the class;
- breaking down dance steps and movements into manageable parts for learning, moving to slower musical or drum beats, and using repetitive movements;
- marking right and left hands or feet when needed;
- placing a speaker from the sound system on the floor so hearing impaired students can feel the music and sound vibrations;

- using instruments such as drums, cymbals, or wooden blocks to provide visual cues for rhythm and time;
- choreographing dances using different types of chairs so wheelchair-bound students can perform equally with others and to increase the awareness of non-wheelchair-bound students about life experiences of their classmates;
- encouraging students who can move from their wheelchairs to explore movement safely alone or with others;
- allowing more space between dancers when needed to accommodate individual needs;
- allowing partners to assist with body movements or assistive equipment when needed (while respecting the comfort level of the students about being touched);
- wearing brightly colored clothing (or soft bells on the wrist) to help students who are visually impaired;
- using additional verbal cues or bright floor markers as direction guides;

- walking the perimeter of the room to help a student develop a mental picture of the environment;

- using props such as scarves, ribbons, hoops, balls, fabrics, elastic bands, incline mats, poly spots, rope, balloons, chairs, hats, spandex body sacs, or canes;

- distributing handouts when relevant; and

- using teacher or student demonstrations as samples of activities or actions to experience.

Careful selection of instructional cues, materials, and class activities enables all students to achieve success. It is important to embrace and appreciate diversity in a classroom as a wonderful opportunity to broaden your skills as an educator, inspire creative lesson planning, and encourage collaboration and teamwork among colleagues.

Summary

This chapter describes necessary steps for thinking and planning a learning experience using the model template. A learning experience can occur on one day or class period or over multiple days or periods. Successful planning requires knowing the dance content and the physical, intellectual, social, and psychological characteristics of the age groups being taught. Planning is necessary to integrate other curriculum subjects with dance. Special consideration is needed to plan meaningful dance experiences for students with special needs. Careful planning of learning experiences creates positive, challenging, and motivating learning environments for all students.

part II

Sample Learning Experiences

Part II combines elements of the seven previous chapters of this book. A primary feature is the 32 learning experiences (LEs) set up by grade levels from prekindergarten through grade 12. The information in part II is designed to help educators best use these LEs and develop others. Part II builds on learner characteristics discussed in chapter 2, the learning environments described in chapter 3, the dance standards and benchmarks discussed in chapter 4, the assessment and technology tips identified in chapters 5 and 6, and the planning template described in chapter 7. The chapters in part II are included on the CD-ROM for easy copying and printing.

Chapters 8 through 11 are organized by grade levels. Each chapter begins by offering a set of tables that include developmental characteristics by educational domain. These tables support information found in chapter 2 regarding the general psychomotor (physical), cognitive, and affective (social and emotional) characteristics of students at specific grade and age levels. The left-hand column of each table identifies basic student characteristics by learning domains. The right-hand column describes implications for the dance teacher regarding specific characteristics for teachers working with students in these grade and age levels. The next table identifies grade-level benchmarks for each of the seven national dance standards. Keep this table close by while reviewing specific LEs.

Each chapter provides in-depth, developmentally appropriate LEs identified for use at specific grade levels. Some LEs are designed as sample, one-day lessons, and others are ideal for lessons that extend across multiple days. These lessons have proven successful for the experienced teachers who provided the samples included in this text. The names of professionals submitting LEs are found in the acknowledgments section of this book.

The grade-level LEs can help novice teachers learn ways to incorporate the National Dance Education Standards and their accompanying benchmarks into their curriculum. The LEs also can help experienced teachers enrich their programs. Specialists who currently use the LEs are dance educators, physical educators who teach dance, recreation specialists, and studio educators who base their curriculums on the national dance standards.

There are several LEs for grades prekindergarten to 2, 3 to 5, 6 to 8, and 9 to 12. The LEs offer samples of lessons addressing fundamental skills, creative dance, folk dance, creative square dance, choreography, dance technique, integrated curricula, yoga, recreational dance, and ballroom dance. These lessons can be easily adapted by teachers to fit unique situations at specific schools. These LEs provide roadmaps for creating relevant lessons or units for a variety of teaching situations. As with any instruction, it is important to be knowledgeable about students' developmental needs, their familiarity with the content, and their physical abilities before selecting any LE for your dance program. You also may want to review LEs a grade level below or a grade level above the grades you teach. With a little tweaking, some of the LEs might be appropriate for grade levels other than those identified here.

To fully understand how to use the LEs included in part II, review chapter 7. That chapter describes in detail each component and section of the template used for creating each LE. Knowing the definition of and the purpose for each component is valuable for understanding the depth and scope of the lessons provided.

8

Grades Prekindergarten to 2

Teachers of students in the prekindergarten to grade 2 classes will find information in this chapter helpful for lesson planning and class instruction. The chapter can help novice and experienced educators introduce the basic elements of movement, rhythm, and space to young students in early childhood programs, kindergarten, and the primary grades in school. The text offers encouragement to introduce some structured, yet simple, dances to eager learners. Having the grade-specific benchmarks for each standard separated from the other grade-level benchmarks can help focus the teacher's planning.

Table 8.1 provides a quick overview of learner characteristics of young children by educational domain (psychomotor, cognitive, and affective). It also offers instructional ideas that you might use to address specific characteristics of the young student. Using these two components can facilitate how program planning will help students achieve developmentally appropriate learning benchmarks.

TABLE 8.1   Developmental Characteristics by Domain

Psychomotor (physical) characteristics	Implications for dance education teachers
During young childhood, students (ages two to seven and in grades prekindergarten to 2) are . . .	
a. experiencing a period of slow, steady growth when compared with infancy	Provide plenty of opportunities to practice and reinforce skills previously introduced
b. adjusting to postural growth that changes the center of gravity over the base of support during the pre-K years	Provide many activities to practice body balance, control, and coordination
c. developing sensory systems (tactile, kinesthetic, vestibular, visual)	Introduce prop manipulation on various levels in personal space during pre-K years and through general space in the early grades; use props of varying shapes, sizes, textures, and weights
d. developing large muscle skills for more efficient patterns that use walks, runs, jumps, hops, gallops, skips, slides, and leaps	Incorporate many gross motor tasks that can be completed successfully by beginners; focus pre-K skills learning on the following progression: walk, run, jump, gallop, and hop
e. developing small-muscle control essential for eye–hand coordination	Incorporate body isolations and sensory experiences into class activities
f. learning to coordinate opposing hand and foot movements	Plan activities that allow for cross-lateral, oppositional, and across-midline movements
g. demonstrating boundless energy	Provide active, aerobic learning experiences
Cognitive (intellectual) characteristics	**Implications for dance education teachers**
a. thinking concretely (abstract and logical thinking and reasoning are limited)	Demonstrate activities (teachers or students); use visual, auditory, and kinesthetic cues with instructions
b. alert, keenly observant, and naturally imitative of others' actions	Plan lessons that include activities such as follow the leader, shadow imagery, mirror imagery, and call and response
c. significantly increasing vocabulary from pre-K to grade 2	Plan lessons that use action words, dramatic play, storytelling, and word cards
d. developing classification skills and reasoning ability (have difficulty generalizing or categorizing large numbers of items)	Chunk instructions and tasks in small increments; keep tasks and repetitions to short durations
e. basing their understanding of the world on particular examples, tangible sensations, and material objects	Ask students to create shapes and movements that reflect known items, events, or happenings, including letters, numbers, wind, rain, flying, or movements like that of a wind-blown leaf
f. thinking in images and symbols, and forming mental representations of objects and events	Ask students to create shapes and movements that reflect or illustrate letters, numbers, or colors
g. eager to learn and generally fearless	Offer a wide range of movement activities that may include new challenges
h. more interested in doing activities than in completing them	Provide activities that focus on process rather than on product production; plan a wide variety of activities that require a short time span to complete
i. ready to make and understand rules; can differentiate between procedural rules related to play and game making and conduct rules that regulate to sociomoral behavior	Set rules for classroom management
j. learning through movement experiences and doing for themselves	Allow for movement exploration and spontaneity in activities; be flexible in the instructions offered and the student responses expected
k. developing an understanding of the concepts of space, force, time, and flow	Allow ample opportunity to practice moving in varying spaces, at varying speeds, and with varying movement dynamics; use developmentally appropriate music and accompaniment

During young childhood, students (ages two to seven and in grades prekindergarten to 2) are . . .

Cognitive (intellectual) characteristics *(continued)*	Implications for dance education teachers *(continued)*
l. demonstrating short attention spans	Plan a wide variety of activities that take a short time to complete; use short directions; be able to change plans quickly to maintain interest
m. learning a balance between active and quiet play	Incorporate quiet movement into classes or deep relaxation at the end of class
n. curious and want to make sense of their worlds; ask lots of questions, including "how?" and "why?"	Provide teacher-guided questioning that allows for exploration and spontaneity in activities; be flexible
o. creative in play and able to enjoy fantasy with peers; able to communicate through stories and events	Plan activities where the students act out teacher-read (or self-created) stories, nursery rhymes, songs, or poems; use make-believe and role play

Affective (socioemotional) characteristics	Implications for dance education teachers
a. curious and spontaneous; need simple rules with clear boundaries of acceptable behavior; need to know the consequences of breaking rules; need repetition and stability to focus on learning and to increase competence and confidence	Establish and follow regular routines and rules with identified consequences for classroom management and movement activities; create short dance or movement sequences to help students experience appropriate, creative class behavior
b. learning to control themselves and identify what they can and cannot do by themselves	Introduce the concepts of spotting (weight supporting), modeling movement, mirror imagery
c. unable to understand causal relationships	Insist on adherence to classroom rules during activities
d. relating only to surface appearance of objects	Incorporate texture and pattern into movement
e. egocentric (believe everyone sees and experiences the world the way she or he does); yet, are beginning to sympathize with those in distress and beginning to experience empathy	Allow opportunities to observe student-created responses (interpretations) to a teacher-given task; provide creative role plays to help children think about emotions and the implications of actions
f. increasing abilities to take turns, share, and engage in group play	Plan partner and small group activities (possibly using props); use make-believe and role-play activities to help children understand how others think or feel; engage young children in mixed-gender activities
g. seeking approval for trying new skills or activities	Plan activities to practice skills and offer praise when milestones are reached; use gentle voice tones when giving directions
h. often demonstrating extreme and short-lived emotions	Use make-believe and role-play activities to help children understand how other people may think, feel, or express emotions
i. very imaginative; sometimes have imaginary friends	Use make-believe and role-play activities to help children distinguish between fantasy and reality
j. learning to postpone immediate gratification	Plan individual or group activities requiring students to learn outcomes after a given time period
k. impacted by cultural influences	Plan activities that respect culture and heritage; offer activities to broaden learning experiences to enhance understanding of other cultures
l. establishing social contacts with adults and imitating adult behavior	Model appropriate behavior for students to observe; demonstrate positive body language, facial expressions, and voice tones
m. establishing friendships with peers that last for short durations	Plan a variety of small group activities; facilitate situations that foster cooperation, not competition
n. cooperative with cleanup routines	Offer positive encouragement when responsible behavior is demonstrated; facilitate learning situations that foster cooperation, not competition

Table 8.2 provides teachers of young children with the benchmarks that students participating in a well-designed dance curriculum can accomplish by grade 2 (at approximately seven years of age). Students can reach the benchmarks through par-ticipation in specialized dance classes, a physical education curriculum, studio settings, recreation department programs, or other community-based instruction.

TABLE 8.2   Dance Content Standards and Benchmarks: Prekindergarten to Grade 2

Content Standard 1. Identifies and demonstrates movement elements and skills in performing dance
The student . . .

BODY

   a. identifies body parts correctly (e.g., shoulder, elbow, knees, skull, ribcage, forearm, ball of the foot, and spine)

   b. demonstrates simple nonlocomotor (axial) movements (e.g., bend, twist, stretch, and swing)

   c. demonstrates simple locomotor movements (e.g., walk, run, jump, hop, leap, slide, gallop, and skip)

   d. demonstrates a variety of shapes (e.g., wide, narrow, rounded, twisted, and linear)

SPACE

   a. demonstrates movement in both personal (self-) and general space

   b. demonstrates high, middle, and low levels

   c. demonstrates basic directions (e.g., forward, backward, sideways, upward, and downward)

   d. demonstrates movement pathways (e.g., straight, curved, and zigzag)

RELATIONSHIPS

   a. demonstrates the ability to dance alone, with a partner, or with a prop

   b. demonstrates basic movement relationships (e.g., around, apart, next to, between, over and under) with people, body parts, and objects

TIME

   a. demonstrates accuracy in moving to a steady musical beat

   b. demonstrates accuracy in changes in tempo

EFFORT

   a. demonstrates light and strong force

   b. demonstrates starting and stopping with control

Content Standard 2.Understands choreographic principles, processes, and structures
The student . . .

   a. uses improvisation to discover and invent solutions to simple movement assignments

   b. improvises, creates, and performs dances based on personal ideas or concepts from other sources (e.g., sto-ries, pictures, poetry, emotions, verbs, found objects, artifacts, or technology)

   c. creates a basic sequence with a beginning, middle, and end while alone or with a partner

   d. identifies the parts of a movement sequence or dance (e.g., beginning, middle, and end)

   e. creates and repeats a dance phrase with and without rhythmic accompaniment

Content Standard 3.Understands dance as a way to create and communicate meaning
The student . . .

   a. observes and discusses how dance is different from other forms of human movement (e.g., sports, everyday gestures)

   b. discusses in small or large groups interpretations and reactions to a dance (e.g., listening, speaking, or writing)

   c. presents dances to peers and discusses the meanings

   d. demonstrates appropriate audience behavior in formal and informal performance situations (e.g., respect for performers, applause at the end, and constructive feedback)

Content Standard 4. Applies and demonstrates critical and creative thinking skills in dance
The student . . .

a. chooses a favorite solution to a given movement problem and tells the reasons for that choice

b. observes two dances and discusses how they are similar and different in terms of one element of dance (e.g., space, shape, level, and pathway)

c. discusses opinions about dances with peers in supportive and positive ways

Content Standard 5. Demonstrates and understands dance in various cultures and historical periods
The student . . .

a. performs folk and social dances from various cultures

b. recalls the cultural significance of a folk dance (e.g., customs, special meaning, location; e.g., the Shoemaker Dance is from Denmark and is about making shoes)

c. names places, situations, and occasions where dance is seen or experienced (e.g., parades, festivals, theaters, weddings, movies, birthday parties, television)

Content Standard 6. Makes connections between dance and healthful living
The student . . .

a. states that dancing helps keep heart, bones, and brain healthy and strong

b. explains that dancing strengthens muscles

c. identifies two important things that a dancer can do to stay healthy (e.g., appropriate sleep, good nutrition practices, warm-ups, stretching)

d. demonstrates safe movement in personal and general space

e. recognizes the joy of dance as a lifetime activity to celebrate culture and community events

Content Standard 7. Makes connections between dance and other disciplines
The student . . .

a. discusses ways that dancers and athletes are alike and different

b. recognizes that emotions are expressed in dance and other art forms (e.g., dancing in response to music, literature, and the visual arts)

c. identifies common forms used in the various arts (e.g., pathway, rhythm, patterns)

d. creates a short dance sequence that reflects a concept from another discipline (e.g., action words, geometric shapes, workers in community, flowers growing)

e. draws a picture to explain a dance previously observed or performed

Ways of Walking

In this learning experience, students will explore different ways of walking. The tempo (speed) and quality of their walks will change based on verbal cues and speed of a drum beat. Students will explore this experience more than once and be encouraged to explore these walks in different directions (sideways or backward on the second and third repetition). Based on 30-minute sessions, this learning experience can be expected to take one session (see the following table for teacher instructions).

GRADE LEVEL   Prekindergarten to grade 1

MATERIALS, EQUIPMENT, SPACE NEEDED
- "Ways of Walking" poem (see page 97)
- Drum or similar rhythm instrument to keep a steady beat
- Poly spots or similar space markers for personal spaces
- Optional: music for each part of the poem

NATIONAL STANDARDS ADDRESSED   Content Standard 1. Identifies and demonstrates movement elements and skills in performing dance (Benchmarks: Body c, Space c, Time b, Effort a)

GOAL   To experience the various ways people can walk.

OBJECTIVES   As a result of participating in this learning experience, students will
1. move through general space with walking steps that are of varying tempos and effort. [Psychomotor]
2. demonstrate the difference between two types of walks (e.g., tiptoe and giant steps). [Cognitive]
3. state which type of walking they enjoy doing. [Affective]

VOCABULARY

Tiptoe	March
Stamping	Lazy walking
Giant steps	Directions: forward, backward, sideways

EXTENSIONS OR MODIFICATIONS
1. Repeat "Ways of Walking" poem in a new lesson without repeating the introduction to each section. Use the poem as a whole, with short drum beat sections between parts.
2. Repeat the poem, emphasizing body directions (forward, backward, sideways) during each type of walking step.

OPTIONAL   Use music for each section that reflects the quality and tempo of the different steps. Use only short (30 seconds at the most) segments. Music suggestions: Eric Chappelle, *Music for Creative Dance: Contrast and Continuum*, Vol. 2, Track 11 (stamping), Track 17 (tiptoe), Track 12 (giant steps), and Track 13 (marching).

ACCOMMODATION OR DIFFERENTIATION IDEAS   Students who might not be ambulatory can express the tempo and movement quality with their arms.

TEACHER INSTRUCTIONS FOR WAYS OF WALKING

Management	Teaching process	Teaching points and cues
Introduction		
(1-2 minutes) Have students stand on poly spots, looking at you.	Tell students they are going to begin walking to the beat of the drum, and that they will explore many different types of walking.	Remind students to stay away from everyone else as they move through the general space.
Warm-Up		
(1-2 minutes) Have students start from their spots and move through general space.	Play the drum in a steady beat and ask students to walk but stop when the drum stops.	Give students cues to walk backward or sideways as you play the drum.
	Stop and start the drum; alternate tempos (speeds) so you play the beats at a different tempo after each drum stop.	Ask the children if they can make their feet go slower or faster depending on the tempo of the drum beat. Say, "Match your feet to the beat."
New material		
Exploratory activities (5-15 minutes) Gather students near you to hear the first part of the poem (stamping). Then ask students to stand and move into general space.	Ask students to listen as you read a short poem. Ask students to • stand up and show you how they can make their feet "stamp." • move out to their poly spots to start exploring stamping steps as you read the poem for a second time.	Read the first part of the poem (p. 97) in a rhythmic way. You may want to reproduce an enlarged copy of the poem to post on the wall while teaching. Model stamping for them. Emphasize a downward push of the feet that is sudden and direct. Read the poem as the students walk around, stamping their feet. When the poem ends, keep a steady beat on the drum for the students to continue exploring stamping steps.
Gather students near you to listen to the second part of the poem (tiptoe).	Ask students to • stand up and show you how they can make their feet "tiptoe." • move out to their poly spots to start exploring tiptoe steps as you read the poem for a second time.	Encourage students to take their stamping steps backward or sideways. Read the second part of the poem in a rhythmic way. Model tiptoe for them. Emphasize light, small, quick steps on the balls of the feet, with stretched legs. Read the poem as the students walk around with tiptoe feet. When the poem ends, keep a steady beat on the drum for the students to continue exploring tiptoe steps. Make sure the drum beats are lighter and quicker than those used for the stamping steps.
Gather students near you to hear the third part of the poem (giant steps).	Repeat the above process using giant steps.	Ask students to reach their hands up to the sky while they tiptoe. Encourage them to take their giant steps backward or sideways.

~ continued

Teacher Instructions for Ways of Walking ~ *continued*

Management	Teaching process	Teaching points and cues
New material (continued)		
Gather students to hear the fourth part of the poem (marching steps).	Repeat the above process using marching steps.	Emphasize range of movement (reaching the legs out, far away from the body). These steps should be slower (more space needs more time for each step).These steps should explore a plodding quality. Be sure to play firm, slow beats on the drum. Cue students to travel in different directions. Emphasize lifting the knees up high with each step. The steps should be strong, with a steady, march-like tempo. Drum beats should be clear. Cue students to march in different directions. Students can pretend to be playing a marching band instrument during this section.
	Ask students to show you two different types of steps.	Objective 1: Conduct a visual assessment of the students during each part of the poem.
	Let several students demonstrate.	Objective 2: Observe for understanding.
Recap of lesson, cool-down		
(3-5 minutes) Gather students near you in a circle.	Lead students through seated stretches as you talk about the types of walks they did.	Model long-sitting stretch and butterfly stretch (soles of the feet together, hands holding ankles, and lean forward with a straight back). Be sure to use descriptive vocabulary about the steps: stamping is firm and downward; tiptoe is light and fast; giant steps reach far from the body and are done slowly; marching is performed with the knees lifted high.
Closure and assessment		
(1-2 minutes) Move students to the exit door or into their next activity.	Ask students to walk to the door using their favorite kind of stepping.	Remind students they can use stamping, tiptoe, giant steps, or marching. Tell them you want to know what their favorite is. Objective 3: Observe that students' personal feelings are expressed.

EVERYDAY LIVING (LIFETIME WELLNESS) CONNECTIONS   Students can feel their hearts beating fast or notice how their breathing changes during the dance. Ask them to observe how their pets walk or move through space and tell when there is a difference in the pet's heart beat and breathing.

Ways of Walking

Part 1–Stomping

Walking, walking down the street,
I like to watch my stomping feet.
I put them here, I put them there,
I put them down just anywhere.
So walking, walking down the street,
It's fun to watch my stomping feet.

Part 2–Tiptoe

I can stretch up high on tiptoes,
I can reach up to the sky.
Softly, softly reach and tiptoe,
Reach and reach and tiptoe high.

Part 3–Giant Steps

Giant steps, giant steps,
Who can take giant steps?
I can take giant steps
When I reach far out.
Giant steps, giant steps,
I can take giant steps.

Part 4–Marching Steps

Ta da rum tum tum,
I am marching to the drum,
Says the drummer boy
As he marches down the street.
Ta da rum tum tum,
I am stepping to the drum,
Says the drummer boy
Keeping time with marching feet.

Adapted from Ruth White 1960.

Dancing a Story

Students will explore locomotor and nonlocomotor movements suggested by the characters (cats and mice) in a story. They will create their own ending for the story and then perform these dances for classmates. Based on 30-minute lessons, this exercise may take two to three lessons to explore (see the following table for teacher instructions).

GRADE LEVEL Kindergarten to grade 2

MATERIALS, EQUIPMENT, SPACE NEEDED

- Copy of story (see page 101)
- Music (optional)
- Object to represent "cheese" (e.g., hoops, orange cones, carpet squares, balls)
- Large, open space

NATIONAL STANDARDS ADDRESSED

Content Standard 1. Identifies and demonstrates movement elements and skills in performing dance (Benchmarks: Body c; Space b, c, e; Relationship a; Effort a, b; Time b)

Content Standard 2. Understands choreographic principles, processes, and structures (Benchmarks: c, d)

Content Standard 3. Understands dance as a way to create and communicate meaning (Benchmarks: b, c, d)

Content Standard 4. Applies and demonstrates critical and creative thinking skills in dance (Benchmark: a)

Content Standard 7. Makes connections between dance and other disciplines (Benchmark: b)

GOAL To demonstrate how locomotor and nonlocomotor movements are used to express the characters and sequence of a story.

OBJECTIVES As a result of participating in this learning experience, students will

1. demonstrate simple locomotor (e.g., walk, run, jump, hop, leap, slide, gallop, skip) and nonlocomotor (axial) movements (e.g., bend, twist, stretch, curl). [Psychomotor]
2. demonstrate locomotor movements on pathways as both a leader and a follower. [Psychomotor]
3. demonstrate a sequence of movements that relate to the story. [Psychomotor]
4. observe and accurately describe the actions and movement elements in a dance. [Cognitive]
5. improvise and create a dance based on a story sequence and characters [Cognitive]
6. provide feedback to peers about their dances. [Affective]

VOCABULARY

Stillness	Light force or energy
Sequence	Strong force or energy

EXTENSIONS OR MODIFICATIONS

1. Create similar dances about other animals to elicit different movement qualities.
2. Prepare simple costumes and props, and perform for other students or parents.
3. Use children's stories and poems about animals to develop similar dances.
4. For prekindergarten students, simplify the lesson. Do not ask students to create a sequence. Concentrate on the movement qualities of cats and mice.

TEACHER INSTRUCTIONS FOR DANCING A STORY

Management	Teaching process	Teaching points and cues
Introduction		
(3-5 minutes) Have students sit near you.	Tell students they are going to create a story dance about a cat and mouse.	Ask this question: "Can you share ways in which you've seen cats and mice move?" Encourage a variety of responses.
Warm-up		
(2-3 minutes) Ask students to stand in personal space facing you.	Lead various locomotor and nonlocomotor movements.	Connect movements to characters in the story.
	Give students directions: • "Take quick, light running steps in place." • "Stop, stretch your arms up as high as they can go. Slowly bring them down and curve your back." • "Take more quick, light running steps." • "Stop, stretch your arms way out to the side, then curl them inward." • "Continue to alternate quick, light running steps in place with slow, whole body stretching and curling actions."	Emphasize contrasting qualities of movement: quick and light for the mice; slow and sustained for the cat.
New material		
1. Telling the story (2-3 minutes) Gather students close to you and tell the story.	Tell story on page 101.	Point out that the story has no ending, and that they will be creating their own endings for the story.
2. Cat exploration (15-20 minutes) Ask students to find personal space.	Instruct students: "Select and show three different locomotor movements that the cat might use as it searches for the mice."	Objective 1: Visually assess application of locomotor movement skills.
	"Create three cat shapes one high level, one middle level, and one low level."	Objective 1: Visually assess application of nonlocomotor movement skills. If students do not have experience with levels, take time to explore them now.
	"Develop a sequence that uses all three locomotor movements and all three shapes, but make sure to end with the low shape. For example: travel, high shape; travel, medium shape; travel, low shape."	Provide practice time.
	"Create a sequence of three stretching and curling actions that represent the cat going to sleep. End this with going to sleep in a still shape."	Talk about the different ways students have seen animals prepare to go to sleep.
	"Connect the locomotor shape sequence to the stretching and curling sequence; then practice the sequence."	Provide students with an opportunity to practice three or four times. Objectives 3 and 5: Observe and assess for • sequencing, • on-task behavior, and • movement quality actions.

~ continued

Dancing a Story

Management	Teaching process	Teaching points and cues
Ask students to gather in partners or trios (8-10 minutes).	Ask each pair or group to perform their sequence combination for partners while partners observe.	Review the cues for observing a classmate and good audience behavior. Objectives 4 and 6 (peer assessment): Ask partners to describe which three locomotor movements they see in the dance.
3. Mouse exploration (15-20 minutes) Have students work individually.	Tell students to • move through general space using light, tiptoe-like steps either quickly or slowly in response to directions; and • explore the light movement quality at different tempos using other locomotor movements.	Remind students to use different pathways as they travel.
Organize students into lines of three or four.	Tell students to follow the lead student doing the locomotor movement you indicate along a pathway chosen by the leader.	Give each student an opportunity to be the leader and encourage use of different pathways. Remind students to make their movements light like a mouse. Objective 2: Observe and assess; note students' use of pathways as leaders and followers.
4. Dancing the story (15-30 minutes) Divide student groups into cats and mice.	Instruct each group: • The mice group needs to wait quietly on the perimeter of the room, as if they are hiding. • The cat group begins on the perimeter in one of their shapes.	Play music during this section if desired. Remind students to begin in a still shape.
Gather students near you.	Have students listen to the story and dance their characters' parts.	Pause from time to time while reading the story to give dancers time to complete each movement sequence.
Divide students into groups of cats and mice.	Ask students to reverse roles and repeat the process. Engage the group in discussion about possible endings for the dance. Decide which ending to use. Repeat the story as the dancers perform their character movement sequences, including the chosen ending. Do this two times so that students have an opportunity to dance each role.	Write suggested endings on a board or paper.
Closure and assessment		
(3-5 minutes) Gather students near you.	Invite students to share their favorite movement of the dance.	Decide sharing pattern: can be with a partner, in a trio, or as a whole class if there is time.

TECHNOLOGY CONNECTION   The dance sequences may be captured on camera for playback later.

ACCOMMODATION OR DIFFERENTIATION IDEAS

- Increase or decrease the length of time for any part of the sequence.
- Write patterns and words on a board or chart paper.
- Show action pictures of cats and mice.

When dancing a story, children may successfully express themselves in different ways.

The Sleeping Cat and the Dancing Mice

Once there was a cat who lived in a house and loved searching for little mice to chase. One day the cat went searching for little mice. It looked everywhere in the house. [Pause for students to explore locomotor movements, levels, and shapes.]

Finding no little mice, the cat licked its paws, gave a big stretch, rolled up on its favorite rug, and quietly went to sleep.

Peeking out of the mouse hole, the mice looked from side to side and saw that this cat was asleep. The little mice started to tiptoe around the unsuspecting, sleeping cat.

They tiptoed in a circle around the cat, making sure they were at paw's length from each other. They did not want to bump each other or to step on the cat and wake it up! Sometimes, they would jump, and then hop, slide, and skip. Some mice played "follow the leader." And just for fun, everyone would turn around so that the last person in line became the leader and jumped, hopped, slid, and skipped with all the other mice following.

When they saw that the cat was still asleep, the mice tiptoed to a big piece of cheese on the other side of the room and began eating this cheese. Again, they moved back to the sleeping cat, sometimes pretending to tickle the soft, furry creature.

When all the cheese was eaten up, the mice decided to tickle the sleeping cat one more time and . . . (ask the children to suggest possible endings to the story. It is possible that more than one ending will be the "favorite" and will have to be performed by the students.)

Adapted from Ruth White 1960.

Dancing Balloons

In this learning experience students will explore the concept of directions using locomotor and nonlocomotor movements. They also will collaborate with others to compose a dance using the image of balloon movements. Based on 30-minute sessions, this learning experience will need two or three sessions (see the following table for teacher instructions).

GRADE LEVEL Kindergarten to grade 2

MATERIALS, EQUIPMENT, SPACE NEEDED

- Chalkboard or poster paper
- Music with fast and slow tempos (see the suggestions listed at the end of this learning experience).

NATIONAL STANDARDS ADDRESSED

Content Standard 1. Identifies and demonstrates movement elements and skills in performing dance (Benchmarks: Body a, c; Space a, c)

Content Standard 2. Understands choreographic principles, processes, and structures (Benchmarks: a, b, e)

Content Standard 3. Understands dance as a way to create and communicate meaning (Benchmarks: b, c)

GOAL To create and perform a dance inspired by the image of a balloon that emphasizes the space concept of directions.

OBJECTIVES As a result of participating in this learning experience, students will

1. create and perform a dance that expresses the different directions a balloon moves. [Psychomotor]
2. describe the movements and directions they used in their dance. [Cognitive]
3. work cooperatively in a group to create and perform a small group dance. [Affective]

VOCABULARY

Float	Forward
Rock	Backward
Sway	Sideways
Glide	Up
Inflate	Down
Deflate	

EXTENSIONS OR MODIFICATIONS

1. Add to the exploration and to the dance sequence the movements of a bursting or popping balloon using jumping or leaping in different directions instead of deflating.
2. Create an original story about the adventures of the balloon while it is floating in the space.
3. Create movements to express the story's events.
4. Emphasize a variety of movements and range of motion.
5. Before students create their dances, read the poem "Eight Balloons" in S. Silverstein, *A Light in the Attic*, 1981, New York: Harper & Row, or "Balloons" in D. Chandra, *Balloons and Other Poems*,1993, Canada: HarperCollins Canada. Or share the book *Elephants Aloft* by K. Apelt and K. Baker, 1993, San Diego, CA: Harcourt Brace.

TEACHER INSTRUCTIONS FOR DANCING BALLOONS

Management	Teaching process	Teaching points and cues
Introduction		
(2-3 minutes) Gather students to sit near you.	Tell students they will create a dance about the movements of a balloon.	Ask students to describe where they have seen balloons and ways they have seen balloons move. Provide cues: inflate, deflate, ascend, descend, float, pop, fizzle, spin.
Warm-up		
(3-5 minutes) Ask students to move into a scattered formation.	Lead a variety of nonlocomotor actions using music with both slow and fast tempos.	Emphasize directional terms while leading the warm-up.
	Tell students to • stretch and bend slowly reaching up high, down low, right and left;	Stretch and bend using directional terms up, down, and right and left.
	• twist slowly to the right and left; and	Twist using directional terms right and left.
	• swing arms quickly forward and backward and side to side.	Swing using directional terms forward, backward, and sideways.
New material		
Exploratory activities **1. Explore directional terms using loco-motor movements.** (15-20 minutes) Ask students to move in general space in a random formation.	Ask students to explore the following tasks: • Walk forward stretching arms out wide to the side.	Remind students to move into empty spaces while using locomotor movements.
	• Walk backward stretching arms out wide to the side. • Walk changing from a forward to a backward direction while stretching and bending arms in different directions.	Remind students to move slowly backward and look behind so they do not bump into others.
	Ask students what are other ways to travel moving forward and backward? Ask them to try different ways: • Try hopping, jumping, skipping, or galloping forward and backward.	Solicit responses from several students and ask students to try each suggested way. Running backward is not recommended for student safety.
	• Show different ways to travel sideways. Try different movements. • Slide to the right and then change to the left. What arm shapes can be used while sliding?	Solicit responses from several students and ask students to try each suggested way.
	• Find a way to move in general space by changing direction and using different locomotor movements.	After students have practiced, ask them to share with a partner or small group how they are moving in different directions.
		Objective 2 (self-assessment): As students share their movements, ask them to tell the partner or small group the type of locomotor movement and the direction they are moving.

~ continued

Dancing Balloons

Management	Teaching process	Teaching points and cues
2. Explore directional terms using nonlocomotor movements. (15-20 minutes) Ask students to be in personal space in a random formation.	Ask students to explore the following tasks: • Make a round shape low to the floor and stretch out sideways to a wide low shape. • Change from a low, wide stretched shape to a low, closed round shape.	Use the image of a balloon inflating and deflating.
	• Try stretching and bending in different directions while staying low to the floor. Can you stretch up, out to the right or left side, reach forward or backward in your stretch? • Find a way to move slowly from a low shape to a standing high shape. How wide outward to the right and left can you stretch in your high shape? • Can your shape twist to the right and left? • Make a wide-standing shape and find a way to make the shape sway or rock forward and backward and side to side.	Use the image of a balloon inflating.
	• Find different ways to move slowly from a high shape to a low shape. Can you bend forward, backward, or sideways as you move down?	Use the image of a balloon deflating. Remind students to move slowly to the floor so they do not fall and hurt themselves.
3. Create an individual dance sequence. (10-15 minutes) Divide the space into four zones and assign students to one of the four space zones to create and practice their dance.	Ask students to create a short dance about a balloon using the following sequence: • Begin in a low curled shape. • Stretch up to a standing wide shape. • Sway or rock forward, backward, and sideward. • Choose a locomotor movement and travel in general space maintaining the wide shape while changing directions. • Slowly move down to the floor and end in a low curled shape.	Use the image of a balloon that inflates, floats, or glides and then deflates to accompany the dance sequence. Write the dance sequence on the board or poster. Provide time for students to create and practice their dance sequences.
		If desired, introduce music that has a medium, steady beat. The students can move to the music: 8 counts to move to the beginning, low-level balloon shape; 8 counts to ascend to a standing shape; 16 counts to float in different directions; and 8 counts to deflate to a low-level ending shape. Objective 1 (teacher assessment): Divide the class space into four space zones. Assign students a zone to create and practice their dances. Ask all the students in each zone to perform their dances. Use a checklist to note if students can complete the dance sequence and demonstrate directional changes moving up and down while inflating and deflating and demonstrate using different directions while floating.

Management	Teaching process	Teaching points and cues
4. Create a group dance sequence. (15-20 minutes) Divide the space into four zones. Assign student groups of three or four to one of the four space zones to create and practice their dances. Several groups may share the same zone.	Ask students to collaborate with their group members to create a dance about a balloon that slowly inflates, floats, or glides in different directions in the space, and slowly deflates. All the students in the group move in unison as part of one balloon.	Provide time for students to create and practice their dance. Suggest to students that they can create different ways to inflate and deflate while standing and using different directions. They do not need to begin and end on the floor as they did in their individual dances.
	Ask each group to share their dance with another group in the zone.	Objective 3 (peer assessment): After each group shares their dance with others in their zone, ask each group to sit together and answer the following three questions either through discussion or in written form: • How did your group work together to create and perform the dance? • What part of your dance did you feel was the hardest to perform together? • What was the favorite part of your dance?
Closure and assessment		
(3-5 minutes) Gather students near you.	Ask students to identify the different directions they explored, practiced, and performed in their dance.	Encourage responses from many of the students. Students can tell or show their response.

EVERYDAY LIVING (LIFETIME WELLNESS) CONNECTIONS Discuss how breathing is part of blowing up a balloon as well as a part of dance.

MUSIC SUGGESTIONS Eric Chappelle, *Music for Creative Dance: Contrast and Continuum* Vol. 4, 2000, Seattle, WA: Ravenna Ventures, Tracks 1 and 17 slow-tempo music, Tracks 2 and 11 fast-tempo music.

Dancing Books

In this learning experience, students will explore different ways of performing locomotor and nonlocomotor (axial) movement through action words (verbs) in children's literature. Based on 30-minute sessions, this learning experience can be expected to take at least one session for each book used (see the following table for teacher instructions).

GRADE LEVEL   Prekindergarten to grade 2

MATERIALS, EQUIPMENT, SPACE NEEDED
- Children's book(s) that contain many movement words. Suggested titles:
  - J. Hindley. (2005). *Can You Move Like an Elephant?* St. Albens, UK: Corgi Childrens. ISBN: 978-0552548113.
  - S. Boynton. (2006). *Barnyard Dance.* New York: Workman Publishing. ISBN: 978-0761142942.
  - S. Andrews. (2001). *Dancing in My Bones.* New York: HarperFestival. ISBN: 978-0694013166.
  - R. Walton and A. Lopez-Escriva. (2001). *How Can You Dance?* New York: C. P. Putnam's Sons. ISBN: 978-0399232299.
  - J. Marzollo and J. Pinkney. (1990). *Pretend You're a Cat.* New York: The Trumpet Club. ISBN: 0-440-84514-9.
  - J. Schachner. (2007). *Spippyjon Jones Up & Down.* New York: Penguin Young Readers. ISBN: 978-0-525-47807-2.
- Optional: music such as hoedown music for *Barnyard Dance.*

NATIONAL STANDARDS ADDRESSED

Content Standard 1. Identifies and demonstrates movement elements and skills in performing dance (Benchmarks: Body b, c; Space a, b; Effort a, b)

Content Standard 2. Understands choreographic principles, processes, and structures (Benchmark: c)

Content Standard 6. Makes connections between dance and healthful living (Benchmark: a)

Content Standard 7. Makes connections between dance and other disciplines (Benchmark: c)

GOAL   To learn action word vocabulary by dancing the verbs.

OBJECTIVES   As a result of participating in this learning experience, students will
1. demonstrate various locomotor and nonlocomotor words. [Psychomotor]
2. demonstrate a connection between words they hear and actions they do. [Cognitive]
3. Show their favorite new action word. [Affective]

VOCABULARY   Words listed are a sampling from the suggested books; see your particular book for specifics.

Bounce	Sway	Slide
Run	Shake	Prance
Spin	Twirl	Skitter
Wiggle	Strut	Stalk
Glide	Promenade	Swing
Twist	Leap	Quiver
Tap		

TEACHER INSTRUCTIONS FOR DANCING BOOKS

Management	Teaching process	Teaching points and cues
Introduction		
(3-5 minutes) Ask students to sit in a group facing you.	Tell students they are going to hear a story that has lots of words that tell them how to move. Ask them to listen for the moving words.	Read the selected story, being sure to emphasize the action words (verbs) vocally and pause briefly to give students think time. Be sure to show students the illustrations.
New material		
a. Exploratory activities (10-15 minutes) Ask students to stand and move into general space ready to listen.	Ask students to • do the action words that they hear in the story. • stop and listen each time you begin to read a new part.	Begin to read the selected book again. Give plenty of time after each action word for students to explore that movement action. Be aware of words that are new for students and give them some connections or references (e.g., stalk: how a cat moves when it is moving slowly and getting ready to jump on something). Model movement for the students even if there is a book in one of your hands. Encourage students to use many different body parts as they experience each action. They can try the actions high and low, fast and slow. Objective 1: Complete the objective here.
b. Ask students to gather in a circle with you (3-5 minutes).	Ask students to tell (show) you their favorite moving words from the book.	Allow several students to share their favorites with the class. Objective 3: Assess the objective here.
	Ask students how their bodies felt while dancing.	Cue with questions about their breathing and heart rate. Tell them that dancing helps to keep their bodies healthy.
c. Have students move out into general space ready to dance the book's action words a second time (5-8 minutes).	Tell students to be ready to dance each action word of the story. They will have a shorter time to do each word.	Remind students to freeze and listen as you read each new phrase or idea. Read the selected book without giving students so much practice time with each word so that the story flows more smoothly. Objective 2: Visually assess for students' understanding of the various words.
Closure and assessment		
(1-2 minutes) Move students to the exit door or into their next activity.	Ask students to walk to the door using the action word they liked best.	When students are in line, ask each student to tell you his or her favorite word or action. Objective 2: Relate word to action. Objective 3: Observe that students' personal feelings were expressed.

EXTENSIONS OR MODIFICATIONS

1. For younger students, choose stories with fewer action words. Also, allow the students practice time to move to action words before hearing them in the story.

2. Repeat this learning experience with several different books.

3. Make a list of the favorite words and create a story that uses these words. Have students dance the new story at the next lesson.

OPTIONAL   If you will be using a book frequently or year after year, take the time to find music that compliments each movement word. Put together a music source of the selections; create silence in the music equal to the amount of time you need to read each section so that you will not have to stop and start the music during the reading and action parts of the lesson. Many selections will be found in Eric Chappelle's series of CDs: *Music for Creative Dance: Contrast and Continuum,* vols. 1, 2, 3, and 4.

EVERYDAY LIVING (LIFETIME WELLNESS) CONNECTIONS   Students can feel their hearts beating fast during specific movements. Suggest that students notice how their breathing changes during the dance.

Teaching Folk Dance for Understanding

Students will learn a traditional folk dance from Denmark about the actions of a shoemaker. They will learn that dances have patterns, require cooperation, and represent the work actions of a shoemaker. Based upon 30-minute sessions, this learning experience could be implemented in 3 or 4 sessions (see the following table for teacher instructions).

GRADE LEVEL   Prekindergarten to grade 2

MATERIALS, EQUIPMENT, SPACE NEEDED

- World map
- Music
- CD or tape player, or other music source
- Drum
- Poly spots or other personal space markers
- Paper for drawing and writing
- Crayons or markers

NATIONAL STANDARDS ADDRESSED

Content Standard 1. Identifies and demonstrates movement elements and skills in performing dance (Benchmarks: Relationships a, Time a, Effort b)

Content Standard 2: Understands choreographic principles, processes, and structures (Benchmark: b)

Content Standard 3: Understands dance as a way to create and communicate meaning (Benchmark: a)

Content Standard 5: Demonstrates and understands dance in various cultures and historical periods (Benchmarks: a, b)

Content Standard 7: Makes connections between dance and other disciplines (Benchmark: d)

GOAL   To learn the movements, patterns, and rhythms of a folk dance and how these concepts represent the folk culture from which they come.

OBJECTIVES   As a result of participating in this learning experience, students will

1. perform movement patterns accurately. [Psychomotor]
2. explain the cultural meaning of the actions in the dance. [Cognitive]
3. demonstrate the ability to dance with a partner and large group. [Affective]

VOCABULARY

AB Pattern

Shoemaker

Denmark

TEACHER INSTRUCTIONS FOR TEACHING FOLK DANCE FOR UNDERSTANDING

Management	Teaching process	Teaching points and cues
Introduction		
(10-15 minutes) Gather students in front of a world map.	Tell students • they are going on a trip across the ocean and back in time. • they are going to Denmark over 100 years ago.	Point to the United States and show students how they are going across the ocean to Denmark.
	• the dance they will learn is about a person who makes shoes, a shoemaker.	Explain to students that people create dances about things that are important to them, such as their jobs.
	• the story "The Elves and the Shoemaker" is a Danish story by the Grimm brothers. Show book or read story to students.	Make the connection between the dance and the story to show the importance of shoemakers to the Danish culture. • If shoemakers were important, shoes must have been important. • The connection can be made that the climate must have caused the need for shoes. • The clothing and dance style are connected, too. The people of Denmark used to wear tight, corset-like vests that required them to stand up very straight and tall. Therefore, they did not move the upper body much while dancing.
Warm-up		
(2-3 minutes) Ask students to stand up and move in general space.	Tell students to • begin walking in general space as if they were walking to a plane.	Encourage students to stretch their arms out as they are flying and be careful to use space safely.
	• jog in general space, pretending they are the plane flying over the ocean while counting out loud to 100. (This represents going back in time.)	Play 100 drum beats.
New material		
Exploratory activities (15-30 minutes) Gather students to sit near you.	Tell students to put their hands on their knees with their eyes closed and listen to the music. Ask them to put their hands on their heads when they hear the music change.	Focus on this activity as a discovery process for students to identify the two different phrases in the music.
	Ask students what they discovered. "How many parts did you hear in the music? What do you call something that has two parts and repeats over and over?" Demonstrate part A and tell students that part A of the dance is nonlocomotor and represents making shoes. (See p. 113 for the dance instructions.)	Connect the idea of two parts to the concept of AB pattern. A pattern is something that repeats over and over. This relates to their learning math.
	Instruct the students to reproduce the movements in part A with you.	Have students do part A while seated and repeat several times without music.
	Ask students to perform part A with the music; when part B begins, ask students to swing their arms and try to count the number of beats.	Play the music as pattern repeats several times. Ask students to count how many swings they do to part B. Ask students for responses.

Management	Teaching process	Teaching points and cues
	Ask students to repeat the part A movements and count out loud the 16 counts of part B as they swing their arms. Ask students to perform both parts to several repetitions of the music without you leading.	Tell students that the arm swings will be used while skipping to part B of the dance. Objective 1 (teacher assessment): Observe students to determine how many students can accurately reproduce parts A and B. Note students who demonstrate difficulty.
Ask students to stand in personal space. Use poly spots or space markers if needed.	Ask students to perform part A standing on their spots and during part B to skip and swing their arms around their spot.	
	Ask students, instead of skipping around the spot, to skip away from and back to the spot during part B. Tell students to figure out a strategy about how to use the 16 counts to make sure they are back to their spots by count 16.	Play music while students are dancing and encourage students to count the music out loud. The goal of this task is for students to gain an understanding of music phrasing using guided discovery. As a result, students will conclude that they need 8 counts to move away and 8 counts to return to the spot to complete part B. This process might take the students several attempts to discover a successful strategy.
	Ask several students to share their strategies with the class and discuss possible solutions.	Write students' responses on a board to demonstrate how their answers arrived at a total of 16 counts. For example, a student may respond by saying, "I used 10 counts to move away and 6 counts to return." Acknowledge this answer as a possibility but continue to ask students if anyone has discovered an equal number of counts needed to move away and to return.
	Ask students to perform part A and then part B using 8 counts to move away from their spots and 8 counts to return.	Tell students that when dancing as a group, it is important for everyone to move in one direction for 8 counts and then in another direction for 8 counts.
	Ask students to suggest what they think part B represents in the dance. "Why do you think the shoemakers are skipping?"	Encourage several students to offer ideas.
	Ask students to face their partners and perform part A; then perform part B while holding hands and skipping away from their spot for 8 counts and returning to their spot using 8 counts. Repeat the pattern several times with the music.	Act as someone's partner if there is an odd number of students. Model for students how to let go of hands at the end of 8 counts, turn, and rejoin the partner using the opposite hand as both return to their spots. Change partners several times, to reinforce the concept of sensitivity to a partner, which is an important aspect of folk dancing. Remind students to stand up tall and straight during the dance, like shoemakers working and wearing clothing of the time. Objective 3 (teacher assessment): Observe partners' behavior and look for • eye contact during part A. • skipping side by side while holding hands gently during part B. • willingness to dance with different partners.

~ continued

Teacher Instructions for Teaching Folk Dance for Understanding ~ *continued*

Management	Teaching process	Teaching points and cues
Organize students into a double circle. Partners face each other with one partner on the inside circle and one partner on the outside circle.	Tell students to practice part B first moving counterclockwise for 8 counts and then clockwise for 8 counts.	Use drum to beat counts while students practice as a whole group. Remind students to maintain equal space between partners. Use the image of horses on a merry-go-round.
	Tell students they will perform part A and then part B. Part A begins facing the partner, and part B is performed side by side.	Add music. Repeat dance several times using different partners.
Recap of lesson, cool-down		
(5-7 minutes)	Ask students to tell the main idea of the Shoemaker's Dance (making shoes), the pattern or the dance (AB), and the number of counts in part B (16).	Students may perform sitting or standing stretches mimicking the teacher's movement while questions are asked.
Closure and assessment		
(5-10 minutes) Ask students to find personal space.	Ask students to draw a picture that shows their understanding of what the dance is about. Students can add words or sentences to describe their drawing.	Objective 2 (teacher assessment): Present questions to students, hand out paper and markers or crayons, and provide time for the drawing response. Use the following rubric to determine level of response.

Drawing Rubric

+ = Picture, with or without words, that demonstrates an understanding of what the dance is about. Picture should include one or more of the following:

o   Shoe

o   Person making shoes

o   Spool of thread

o   Person or people doing an action from the dance (supported by a written or verbal explanation that refers to shoemaking for the older students)

o   Hammer and a shoe

? = Picture, with or without words, that does not clearly demonstrate what the dance is about.

– Picture does not include any items or words that relate to the meaning of the dance.

EXTENSIONS OR MODIFICATIONS   Students could do one of the following:

1. For younger students, use a walk rather than a skip. Practice each segment for longer time periods. Perform movements in scattered formation before getting into a circle.

2. For the advanced students, dance part B using 4 counts in each direction instead of 8 and repeat the phrase twice to complete the 16 counts. Compare the concept of four sets of 4 counts, which equals 16 counts, with two sets of 8 counts that equal 16 counts.

3. Perform the dance in smaller groups comprised of 6 to 10 students.

4. Teach the dance to parents or other students.

ACCOMMODATION OR DIFFERENTIATION IDEAS   Ask students to perform part B using the elbow swing, linking right elbows, instead of skipping and holding hands. When beginning partner work, keep the same partner throughout the dance.

Ask students to perform part B with the circles moving in opposite directions instead of holding hands and moving in the same directions. The inside circle moves clockwise, and the outside circle moves counterclockwise. Use 8 counts or 4 counts to move in each direction. At the end of part B, students should be facing their partner to begin the dance again.

EVERYDAY LIVING (LIFETIME WELLNESS) CONNECTIONS

- Connecting to others through folk dance promotes healthy relationships and contributes to personal overall health and fitness.
- Folk dance represents how a community comes together to celebrate, commemorate, support, and share common human experiences.

DANCE INSTRUCTIONS FOR THE SHOEMAKER'S DANCE

Part A (nonlocomotor)
This is done standing up straight and tall.
- Arms are held in front of the body, with elbows bent 90 degrees, hands in fists. Forearms are at chest level.
- Arms roll around each other 3 times forward, then 3 times backward (verbal cue: "Wind the thread, wind the thread").
- Elbows pull back sharply 2 times (verbal cue:" Pull it—tight").
- Hands in fists hammer each other 3 times (verbal cue: "And tap the shoe").
- Repeat all above 2 times.

Part B: (locomotor) 16 skips (gallops will work)
- Upper body should be held under control.
- Arms can be bent with hands resting on the small of the back when not working with a partner.

Music for the Shoemaker's Dance may be found online by typing the name of the dance into a search box. Many companies and dance organizations offer this music in various formats.

My Very Own Folk Dance

A Beginning Choreography Lesson

Working in pairs or groups of three, students will create a dance based on the form and rhythmic phrasing of the previously learned Shoemaker's Dance. They will use a theme of their own choice. The choreography will be performed for their peers and videotaped for assessment. Based on 30-minute sessions, this learning experience can be expected to take three to six sessions (see the table on page 116 for teacher instructions).

GRADE LEVEL   Grades 1 to 2 (recommended for grade 2)

MATERIALS, EQUIPMENT, SPACE NEEDED
- Music (see the resources on the following page)
- A music source with remote control
- Written assessment paper (see page 119)
- Pencils
- Video camera (tripod is helpful)
- VCR and television or DVD player and projection screen
- Chalkboard or large paper to write on

NATIONAL STANDARDS ADDRESSED

Content Standard 1. Identifies and demonstrates movement elements and skills in performing dance (Benchmarks: Relationships a, Time a, Effort b)

Content Standard 2. Understands choreographic principles, processes, and structures (Benchmark: b)

Content Standard 3. Understands dance as a way to create and communicate meaning (Benchmark: a)

Content Standard 4. Applies and demonstrates critical- and creative-thinking skills in dance (Benchmarks: a, b)

Content Standard 5. Demonstrates and understands dance in various cultures and historical periods (Benchmarks: a, b)

Content Standard 7. Makes connections between dance and other disciplines (Benchmark: d)

GOAL   To have students experience the satisfaction of choreographing their own dance while working with peers.

OBJECTIVES   As a result of participating in this learning experience, students will
1. create movement for a dance based on specific criteria. [Psychomotor]
2. perform their choreography the same way each time with rhythmic accuracy. [Psychomotor]
3. explain how their movement relates to the self-chosen theme. [Cognitive]
4. demonstrate the ability to cooperate with a partner or small group. [Affective]
5. show appreciation for the work of others as an audience. [Affective]

VOCABULARY

AB pattern	Relationships
Locomotor	Choreographer
Nonlocomotor	Choreography
Theme (main idea)	

Creating clapping dances, songs, or chants can help young children develop strong word-movement associations, bilateral movement, and cross-lateral coordination.

EXTENSIONS OR MODIFICATIONS   Students could do one of the following:

1. Teach their dance to the rest of the class.
2. Choreograph additional dances using other learned folk dances as the basis for structure or form.

TECHNOLOGY CONNECTION   Videotaping or recording. Students or a parent volunteer could be responsible for managing the camera and the recording.

ACCOMMODATION OR DIFFERENTIATION IDEAS

- Choose a theme for a group that is having trouble deciding. Help them process the three actions.
- With a nonambulatory student, others in the group can help an individual in a wheelchair or on crutches, or move around the student during part B. Students or class aides may assist students who have hearing or visually impairments.

EVERYDAY LIVING (LIFETIME WELLNESS) CONNECTIONS

- Performing folk dance promotes healthy relationships and contributes to personal overall health and fitness.
- Folk dances express feelings about subjects important to particular people.

RESOURCES   See Teaching Folk Dance for Understanding (p. 113) to teach the basic Shoemaker's Dance. This is the source for "Shoemaker's Dance": *Young People's Folk Dance, Folk Dances for Beginners*, Vol. 2 (MAV 1042). 1980. New York, NY: Merit Audiovisual. (An online search for "Shoemaker's Dance music" provides many options for locating music for this learning experience.)

My Very Own Folk Dance

TEACHER INSTRUCTIONS FOR MY VERY OWN FOLK DANCE

Management	Teaching process	Teaching points and cues
Introduction and warm-up		
(10-20 minutes) Have students in a single circle facing the center.	• Tell students they are going to do the Shoemaker's Dance in a circle. • During part A they will face the center. • During part B they will skip 8 counts counterclockwise and then 8 counts clockwise. • They need to think about the pattern of the dance.	Consider students' familiarity with the dance. Students should already know this dance well, but any new students may need to be placed between students who are accomplished at the dance. Play the music and do the dance three or four times through the AB pattern.
	• Tell students they are going to become choreographers. • Ask if they know what a choreographer is or does.	Explain that a choreographer is a person who creates dances, just like a photographer is a person who creates photos. Encourage students to make other connections to this word.
	• Ask students to tell you the theme of the Shoemaker's Dance (making shoes).	Remind students that people create dances about things that are important to them.
	• Tell students they are going to choreograph a dance about a theme that is important to them. It will be based on the form and use the same music as the Shoemaker's Dance.	Ask them to watch you perform your dance and see if they can tell what your theme is. Perform a simple dance about a theme, perhaps about "teaching," with three nonlocomotor movements and 16 counts of locomotor movements (part B). The nonlocomotor could be writing on the board, erasing the board, or correcting a child. Remember to make the movements exaggerated. Part B could be walking forward and then walking backward.
	• Ask the students to tell you what your theme was. • Ask students how many nonlocomotor movements were there. • Ask students how many nonlocomotor movements are in the Shoemaker's Dance.	Confirm the theme. Students should answer three for both questions about movements: shoemaker's are winding, pulling, tapping; teacher's are writing, erasing, correcting.

	• Tell students that there are several criteria for their dances:
	  - Theme must be something important to them.
	  - Group must agree on theme.
	  - There needs to be three distinct, nonlocomotor movements (not necessarily just with the arms) for part A.
	  - Part B must take 16 counts but can use any locomotor movement they can do to the rhythm and tempo of the Shoemaker's Dance music.
	  - Locomotor movements must travel in at least two directions (forward, backward, or sideways).
	  - They can use any kind of relationships with the partner or group as they do part A and part B.
		Write these criteria on the board as you explain them.
		Themes are really up to the students. Some choose simple things like cooking with movements like stirring, pouring, or flipping a pancake. Others become very creative and choose things as varied as being a paleontologist (digging, brushing, packing) or playing outside (putting on a coat, opening the door, throwing a ball).
		Remind them that they can be on different levels, in whatever formation they'd like for part A (e.g., circle, triangle, line).
		During part B they can choose to travel together, apart, or around. But each dancer must travel in two different body directions. They may use any kind of pathway they desire.

Management	Teaching process	Teaching points and cues
New material		
a. Exploratory activities (5-10 minutes) Organize students into groups of two or three.	Tell students to discuss and come up with a theme for their dance. It should be something that is important to them. Ask them to try to create three different nonlocomotor gestures.	Group students in any way that works for you. It is nice to let students choose their own groups for this choreography because they need to come up with a common favorite theme.
	Ask students to continue working on their choreography, making sure to include all the criteria. Tell them that the goal for the next period of time is to complete their choreography.	This task might be too much to do for the time left in a particular session. Use your own judgment as to how much to ask them to do. Make sure the criteria are listed on the board.
		Play music during the entire exploration but tell students they can ignore it as they are planning. The music is on to help them. Circulate among the groups to assess whether or not they are meeting the criteria. Help those groups that are having a difficult time deciding. Remind all students to make sure that their movements are exaggerated: bigger than life.
b. Refinement activities (5-15 minutes) Ask students to stay seated in their area with their group.	Ask two or three groups to demonstrate their dances for the others. Tell the audience to watch for when and how the criteria are met. Ask them to describe what they see when the dance is finished. Ask students to compare the dances they saw and then talk with their own group to decide how to improve their own choreography.	Objective 4: Visually assess cooperation with a partner or group. Choose groups that seem to have met the criteria and have interesting formations, pathways, or relationships. Objective 5: Visually assess audience appreciation.
c. (5-15 minutes) Ask students to work in their areas.	Ask students to return to refining and editing their dances and get them ready for performance.	Suggest that students need to think more about relationships (apart, around, in front of or in back of) and to make sure they use different body directions during part B. Students may need a reminder about the body directions. Circulate the room and give suggestions, praise, and critiques.
d. (15-20 minutes) Ask students to be seated in front of the board.	Tell students they are going to write about their dance to demonstrate their understanding.	Show a copy of the worksheet (p. 119) to the students. This may be done on a poster, using an LCD projector, or other projection system. Explain how to fill out the worksheet.
Ask students to move back into their group areas to complete the worksheets.	Tell students • they may work together, but each student needs a worksheet turned in. • if they travel in different body directions during part B, make sure they put down correct information for themselves.	Hand out the worksheets and pencils. Have students fill in their names and the classroom teacher's name. Circulate to give spelling help or to guide the writing process. Objective 3: Use written work to assess this objective when the dance is viewed on video. Depending on the time, this written work could be completed as homework and brought back to class for the videotaping or performance.

~ continued

My Very Own Folk Dance

Management	Teaching process	Teaching points and cues
Assessment		
(5-8 minutes) Ask students to be in their group spaces ready to practice their dances.	Tell students they have five minutes to make sure the dance is performance ready.	Play the music while the groups practice. Make sure the video camera is ready for videotaping.
(10-20 minutes) Ask students to move to an audience area while one group moves to a designated performance area.	Tell students that each group will perform their dance three times (AB, AB, AB). The others need to be a polite audience and watch for when and how the criteria are met.	Review audience behavior if necessary. Review dance criteria if necessary. Define the performance space so that the camera can see the area.
	Tell students the groups will perform quickly one after the other.	Let students know which group is next just before each new performance. Control the music with a remote or enlist a responsible student to turn it on and off at a signal from you.
	Ask students to hand in their written worksheets before they perform.	All groups should have a chance to perform. If time allows, ask students to discuss the dances they have just seen. Objective 5: Assess during this time. It is usually easier to note the students who do not meet the criteria for audience behavior.
	Let students know you will assess their dances as you watch the video at home. Each student will be assessed individually.	Take the video home and watch each performance, several times if needed, and assess the students on the criteria at the bottom of the worksheet. Objectives 1, 2, and 3 are assessed at this point.
Closure		
(10-15 minutes) Ask students to sit in front of the VCR and television or another projection source.	Ask students to look at their performance rubric.	Pass back each student's performance rubric (worksheet).
	Ask students to watch the dances, paying particular attention to their own dancing so that they will understand how you evaluated it.	Play the video and monitor the watching. Conduct a discussion afterward about the variety of themes and nonlocomotor actions the class created.

My Very Own Folk Dance
AB Choreographic Form Based on Shoemaker's Dance Music

Answer the following questions to help others understand your dance.

1. The theme of my dance is _____.

2. In part A (nonlocomotor) my three movements are _____,
   _____, and _____.

3. In part B (locomotor) I use this type of locomotor movement to travel around:
   _____.

4. The directions I travel during part B are _____ and _____.

5. I worked with these people to create this dance: _____
   _____.

6. Circle the words that tell me how well you think you cooperated with your partner while working on this dance.

   Very well   Mixed (sometimes good, sometimes not great)   I did not cooperate at all

   _____

Teacher fills out this bottom part after watching the video tape.
Evaluation of dance movements:

Name of student: _____

Student receives either a 1 (criterion is accomplished) or a 0 (criterion is not accomplished).

____   There are three distinct and different movements in part A.

____   Part A (nonlocomotor) movements are done to the rhythmic phrasing.

____   All part A (nonlocomotor) movements relate to the theme.

____   Part A movements are repeated the same way each time.

____   Actions have an exaggerated, dance-like quality, rather than being mundane or mimed.

____   Part B travels in at least two different body directions.

____   Locomotor movement performed matches the written description.

____   Locomotor movement is performed with rhythmic accuracy.

Possible total of 8 points:

8-7 = exceeds expectations

6-4 = meets expectations

3 or fewer = needs more time to improve

Summary

When young students experience lessons such as the ones described in this chapter, they can develop critical perceptual-motor skills, kinesthetic awareness, and a joy of movement. Students in the primary grades can develop body and space awareness, make connections between shapes and sizes, create and repeat basic movement sequences, discriminate between movement force and flow, and understand movement to even and uneven rhythms. When students succeed in tasks that allow them to progress with manageable complexity, their self-confidence for new learning is heightened, and they are ready for new learning in the higher grade levels.

9

Grades 3 to 5

Students in the elementary grades enjoy moving and learning. Dance is an art and educational form that helps students develop the necessary skills and knowledge to be successful in dance and other learning environments. By using material in this chapter, dance educators can help students strengthen their body awareness, movement skills through space, rhythmical abilities, and capacities for independent work and cooperative activities. The dance teacher can help students practice the creative processes used in composing and performing dances with varying dynamics. Also, by using the learning experiences included here, teachers can provide students with opportunities to learn about other cultures and multiple ways of viewing their school and community environments.

Table 9.1 offers a quick overview of elementary school–age learner characteristics by educational domain (psychomotor, cognitive, and affective). It also offers instructional ideas that can be used to address specific characteristics of the elementary school student. Using these two components can facilitate program planning to help students achieve developmentally appropriate learning benchmarks.

Table 9.2 provides teachers of elementary school–age students with the benchmarks that students participating in a well-designed dance curricula can accomplish by grade 5 (at approximately 11 years of age). Students can reach the benchmarks through participation in specialized dance classes, a physical education curriculum, studio settings, recreation department programs, or other community-based instruction.

TABLE 9.1   Developmental Characteristics by Domain

Psychomotor (physical) characteristics	Implications for dance education teachers
During childhood, students (ages 8 to 11 and in grades 3 to 5) are . . .	
a. increasing body length, large and some small muscle development; improving strength, balance, and coordination, as well as visual-perceptual abilities	Plan activities that allow movement around the dance classroom and target movement of isolated body parts (e.g., head, shoulder, torso, knee, ankle)
b. imitating and creating complex physical movements and patterns; improving reaction time	Plan opportunities to observe strong role models in various dance forms; some may be ready for dance technique classes
c. becoming capable of more organized physical activity	Provide opportunities for participation in teacher- or student-choreographed dances and culturally based folk and social dances
d. active movers with high energy levels	Provide experiences that encourage aerobic activity (e.g., running, skipping, galloping, sliding, leaping)
Cognitive (intellectual) characteristics	**Implications for dance education teachers**
a. combining, separating, ordering, and categorizing information with ease	Provide opportunities for creating and performing dances with varying rhythmic and movement patterns and changing dynamics
b. imaginative, creative, able to internalize logical systems, and able to understand abstract concepts	Provide opportunities for creating dances that conceptualize, problem solve, analyze, and sequence movement patterns
c. experiencing rapidly changing interests and do their best when work is presented in small chunks	Provide many brief learning experiences using simple, short directions
d. varying in academic abilities, interests, and reasoning skills	Offer activities appropriate for a wide range of abilities so all children succeed; provide opportunities for interdisciplinary learning
e. easily motivated and eager to try new things; able to focus attention for longer periods	Offer experiences in a variety of dance forms to help students identify areas of interest; create or perform movement patterns of longer durations
f. developing basic skills in reading, writing, mathematics, and other academic subjects	Provide opportunities for interdisciplinary learning
Affective (socioemotional) characteristics	**Implications for dance education teachers**
a. needing stability to focus on learning and cognition, and avoid serious attention distractions	Establish regular routines and rules for classroom management and movement activities
b. enjoying cooperative group activities, especially in same-age and same-sex groups; loyal to a group or club	Emphasize varying partner, team, and group planning and learning experiences
c. demonstrating self control and the ability to handle more freedom; able to handle tasks with more responsibility	Allow opportunities for creating and repeating movement patterns and dances

Affective (socioemotional) characteristics *(continued)*	Implications for dance education teachers *(continued)*
d. demonstrating realism about their abilities; comparing their abilities with others	Help students identify their own successes by comparing present and past performances, rather than comparing their abilities with those of others
e. more interested in working with group members of the same sex; both sexes enjoy self-testing activities	Plan lessons for students to work with members of the same sex and the opposite sex to broaden knowledge of and respect for others' abilities; offer activities that challenge physical and mental abilities; discuss historical and cultural roles of males and females in dance
f. admiring and imitating older boys and girls	Encourage mentoring experiences with older youth who are positive role models
g. needing adult guidance to stay on task and perform at their best; can be boastful, aggressive, self-critical, and excessively emotional	Provide clear directions and instructions; monitor learning progressions; praise positive efforts; offer targeted, positive corrections as needed
h. able to follow rules of classroom operations	Establish classroom etiquette and consequences for infractions
i. able to understand basic rules of morality; have a strong sense of justice and fairness	Establish rules of morality for the classroom; discuss appropriate movements, music, and costuming for dances; discuss appropriate audience behavior; analyze popular media dance

TABLE 9.2 Dance Content Standards and Benchmarks: Grades 3 to 5

Content Standard 1. Identifies and demonstrates movement elements and skills in performing dance
The student . . .

BODY

a. recalls anatomical names for major and minor bones and muscles (e.g., phalanges, femur, biceps, quadriceps, gluteus maximus)

b. creates combinations of locomotor and axial movements in a repeatable sequence of five or more movements

c. demonstrates more complex locomotor movements (e.g., schottische, polka, two-step, and grapevine)

d. demonstrates complex shapes, including asymmetrical and symmetrical

SPACE

a. demonstrates movement in both personal (self-) and general space (follow-up from earlier grade levels)

b. demonstrates high, middle, and low levels (follow-up from earlier grade levels)

c. demonstrates more complex directions (e.g., right and left, diagonal, and turning)

d. creates movement patterns that combine two or more pathways

e. demonstrates changes in range of movement (e.g., large, small, distal, and core actions)

f. performs spatial elements used with locomotor and nonlocomotor movements (e.g., skipping forward on a curved pathway)

RELATIONSHIPS

a. demonstrates the ability to dance alone, with a partner, and in a small group with or without props

b. demonstrates spatial and temporal relationships (e.g., leading and following, mirroring, or matching)

TIME

a. demonstrates accuracy in moving to a steady musical beat (follow-up from earlier grade levels)

b. recalls and accurately demonstrates both even and uneven rhythms and accents at varying tempos

EFFORT

a. demonstrates a variety of movement qualities appropriately (e.g., punch, press, flick, float, glide, dab, wring, slash, sustained, percussive, vibratory)

b. demonstrates bound and free-flow movements

~ continued

TABLE 9.2 ~ *continued*

Content Standard 2. Understands choreographic principles, processes, and structures
The student . . .

___

   a. uses improvisation to discover and compose solutions to small-group movement assignments

   b. improvises, creates, and performs dances based on personal ideas or concepts from other sources (e.g., stories, pictures, poetry, emotions, verbs, found objects, artifacts, or technology) (follow-up from earlier grade levels)

   c. cooperates with a partner or in a small group to create a dance sequence with a beginning, middle, and end

   d. identifies the structure of the dance (e.g., AB, ABA, or canon)

   e. creates a dance phrase, accurately repeats it, then varies it (e.g., making changes in the time, space, or effort)

___

Content Standard 3. Understands dance as a way to create and communicate meaning
The student . . .

___

   a. observes and discusses how dance is different from other forms of human movement (e.g., sports, everyday gestures) (follow-up from earlier grade levels)

   b. discusses in small or large groups interpretations and reactions to a dance (e.g., listening, speaking, or writing) (follow-up from earlier grade levels)

   c. creates a dance that communicates topics of personal significance

   d. demonstrates appropriate audience behavior in formal and informal performance situations (e.g., respect for performers, applause at the end, and constructive feedback) (follow-up from earlier grade levels)

   e. demonstrates and describes the difference between exaggerated movement and pedestrian movement (e.g., taking a movement that is familiar and changing it in range, dynamics, or quality)

   f. explains how accompaniment choice (e.g., sound, music, spoken text) can affect the meaning of a dance

   g. practices safe, legal, and responsible use of technology and digital information

___

Content Standard 4. Applies and demonstrates critical and creative thinking skills in dance
The student . . .

___

   a. creates and demonstrates multiple solutions to teacher-designed movement problems; chooses the most interesting solution and discusses the reason for that choice

   b. compares and contrasts movement elements (e.g., body, space, effort, relationships) in two dance compositions

   c. discusses opinions about dances with peers in supportive and positive ways (follow-up from earlier grade levels)

___

Content Standard 5. Demonstrates and understands dance in various cultures and historical periods
The student . . .

___

   a. performs more complex culturally based folk and social dances with patterns (e.g., steps, formations, tempos, rhythms, and relationships)

   b. describes the differences and similarities between folk dances of more than one culture (e.g., purpose, gesture, style, function)

   c. answers questions concerning dance in a particular culture and time period (e.g., who, what, where, when, why, and how)

___

Content Standard 6. Makes connections between dance and healthful living
The student . . .

a. identifies two or more ways that dance is beneficial to health (e.g., flexibility, muscular strength, aerobic endurance)

b. explains how and why warming up helps a dancer perform effectively and prevent injury

c. identifies two important things that a dancer can do to keep healthy (e.g., appropriate sleep, good nutrition practices, warm-ups, stretching) (follow-up from earlier grade levels)

d. describes the difference between safe and unsafe ways of moving (e.g., knees bent on landing, static and dynamic stretching, protecting head and neck when falling and rolling)

e. recognizes the joy of dance as a lifetime activity to celebrate culture and community events (follow-up from earlier grade levels)

Content Standard 7. Makes connections between dance and other disciplines
The student . . .

a. describes places, times, or events where dance occurs today (e.g., television, movies, family celebrations, religious ceremonies, community events, festivals)

b. recognizes that similar themes, ideas, and concepts are expressed in dance and other art forms (e.g., loyalty, courage, jealousy, affection, hope)

c. cites examples of how similar elements are used in dance and in another art form (e.g., balance, design, contrast, texture)

d. creates a dance that reflects a concept from another discipline (e.g., language arts, math, science, social studies, or health)

e. interprets through dance an idea taken from another medium (e.g., visual arts, music, video, poetry, history)

Bound and Free

Verbs Lead the Way

Students will be introduced to the effort concepts of bound and free flow through literature and movement tasks. There is a variety of children's literature that is rich in action verbs to stimulate creative movement. The book selected for this lesson is *Kites Sail High* by Ruth Heller. Based on a 30-minute session, this lesson would take one session (see the following table for teacher instructions).

GRADE LEVEL   Grades 3 to 5

MATERIALS, EQUIPMENT, SPACE NEEDED

- R. Heller, *Kites Sail High*, 1988, New York: Grosset & Dunlap, ISBN: 0-448-10480-6
- Large, open space
- Chalkboard and chalk, dry erase board and markers, or large paper and markers

NATIONAL STANDARDS ADDRESSED

Content Standard 1: Identifies and demonstrates movement elements and skills in performing dance (Benchmark: Effort b)

Content Standard 7: Makes connections between dance and other disciplines (Benchmarks: d, e)

GOAL   To introduce students to the concepts of bound and free flow through the use of related action words.

OBJECTIVES   As a result of participating in this learning experience, students will

1. perform movements that demonstrate bound and free flow. [Psychomotor]
2. correctly interpret the meaning of a word through their movements. [Cognitive]
3. work responsibly on tasks throughout the lesson. [Affective]

VOCABULARY

Bound flow

Free flow

EXTENSIONS OR MODIFICATIONS

- This lesson can be adapted or modified for use in a grade-level classroom if dedicated dance instructional space is unavailable.
- You can create a partnership with a classroom teacher and repeat the lesson using different literature.

EVERYDAY LIVING (LIFETIME WELLNESS) CONNECTIONS   Remind students that dance helps people stay physically fit.

TEACHER INSTRUCTIONS FOR BOUND AND FREE

Management	Teaching process	Teaching points and cues
Introduction		
(10 minutes) Have students gather near you.	Define free and bound flow; provide example words and actions.	Free flow: loose, unrestrained movement like skipping or tree branches blowing in the breeze. Bound flow: tight, restrained movement like moving in molasses or walking like a robot.
Read the story to the students.	Ask the students to think about and identify words that suggest bound and free flow.	Free flow: sail, bloom, fly. Bound flow: inching, shrinking, creeping.
Review of previous material, warm-up		
(3 minutes) Ask students to work in self-space.	Provide verbal cues for students to respond to.	Free flow: skip, leaf blowing in the wind, mist rolling in over the garden, fish swimming in water. Bound flow: moving in mud up to your knees, walking as if you have chewing gum on the bottom of your shoes, swimming in a sea of solid goo.
New material		
Exploratory activities (10 minutes) Ask students to work in self-space.	Reread the story and ask students to move in response to the actions each verb suggests.	Selectively read pages that include words strongly related to action words. Check if students are interpreting each word correctly with respect to bound or free. Cue students as needed. Remind students to use the dance elements they already know (level, pathway, direction, shape, time). Objectives 1 and 2: Use observations to assess.
Recap of lesson, cool-down		
(1-2 minutes) Have students gather near you.	Tell the students that today they were introduced to bound and free flow through literature for children.	
Closure and assessment		
(3-5 minutes) Ask students to find partners and gather near you.	Tell students they have 30 seconds to define the concepts of free and bound flow in their heads.	Think to yourself what the definitions for free and bound flow are.
	Ask students to discuss the definitions for free and bound flow with a partner.	Have students share their answers with their partners.
	Discuss free and bound flow as a class.	Lead the discussion and include responses from several students.
	Ask students to identify movements that use free and bound flow.	List action words on the chalkboard or on a large piece of paper under columns titled Bound Flow and Free Flow.

Dancing Words

Students will explore movement qualities and create group dances while moving safely. They will use verbs (action words) as stimuli for exploring movement qualities. Based on 30-minute sessions, this learning experience could be expected to take three sessions (see the following table for teacher instructions).

GRADE LEVEL   Grades 3 to 5

MATERIALS, EQUIPMENT, SPACE NEEDED

- Large, open space
- Paper
- Crayons or markers
- Teacher-made word cards (using words such as dab, flick, quick, light, heavy, slither, glide, float, pounce, jiggle, dart, explode, pop, wiggle, waddle, sink)
- Music or percussion instruments (optional)

NATIONAL STANDARDS ADDRESSED

Content Standard 1. Identifies and demonstrates movement elements and skills in performing dance (Benchmarks: Body b; Relationships a; Effort a, b)

Content Standard 2. Understands choreographic principles, processes, and structures (Benchmark: e)

Content Standard 4. Applies and demonstrates critical and creative thinking skills in dance (Benchmark: a)

Content Standard 7. Makes connections between dance and other disciplines (Benchmarks: d, e)

GOAL   To explore verbs (action words) and the movement qualities they elicit, and create a small-group dance using selected verbs.

OBJECTIVES   As a result of participating in this learning experience, students will

1. perform a sequence of five movements that express different movement qualities. [Psychomotor]
2. demonstrate safe movements to protect their bodies from injury. [Psychomotor]
3. describe the movement qualities associated with selected verbs. [Cognitive]
4. identify the reasons for their choice of verbs. [Cognitive]
5. work in a cooperative and productive manner with peers. [Affective]
6. discuss the rewards and challenges of this learning experience. [Affective]

VOCABULARY

Collapse	Pounce
Contrast	Punch
Movement quality	

EXTENSIONS OR MODIFICATIONS

- Have students add an adverb for each verb.
- Have students perform a final dance for a peer group for feedback and revision before performing for teacher observation and evaluation.

OPTIONAL   Give final student self-assessment as a homework assignment.

TEACHER INSTRUCTIONS FOR DANCING WORDS

Management	Teaching process	Teaching points and cues
Introduction		
(8-10 minutes) Organize students into groups of three or four.	Ask students to • look at the words Verb (Action Word) written on the board. • send one person to get a pencil and paper for their group. • brainstorm and write down a list of 10 or more verbs. • bring you the list and pencils.	Ask students to provide one or two verbal examples before the group begins brainstorming. Circulate and monitor, providing cues or encouragement as needed.
Review of previous material, warm-up		
(2-3 minutes) Ask students to stand in circles with their group and face each other with enough space for movement.	Tell students the verb for the warm-up is *bounce*.	
	Ask students to • begin by making small bounces using their knees. • add bouncing their hips from side to side. • add their arms and shoulders to the bouncing. • add their heads. • keep the body bouncing and gradually make the bounces bigger until they are jumping.	Model each movement as you give the verbal cues.
	Ask the students to do a previously learned stretch in their space.	Monitor for safe stretching. Praise or correct as needed.
New material		
a. Exploratory activities (20-30 minutes) Ask groups to stay near each other but gather near the board.	Ask students to look at the words *punch, kick, collapse, fall, drop,* and *pounce* on the board and listen to the guidelines for moving safely.	Write the words *punch, kick, collapse, fall, drop,* and *pounce* on the board and discuss the following guidelines for moving safely.
	Tell students • all movements will be done without body contact when expressing words like punch, pounce, and kick. • everyone needs to use control to lower to the ground when expressing words like fall, collapse, and drop so that no one gets hurt.	Give students an opportunity to suggest additional safety guidelines.
Ask groups to move to work spaces.	Tell students to look at their list of verbs (action words). Ask each student to select one word and create a movement to express its meaning. Ask students to choose words that use contrasting amounts of energy and tempo. Then ask students to teach their movements to the group.	Provide each group with a list of their words. Objective 2 (teacher assessment): Observe that students are implementing the safety concepts. Make affirming and corrective statements where needed. Observe dancers to determine the range of movements. If contrast is not evident, make suggestions to help students.

~ continued

Teacher Instructions for Dancing Words ~ *continued*

Management	Teaching process	Teaching points and cues
New material (*continued*)		
	Ask students to choreograph a short dance that includes each person's movement word. Instruct students to determine the word order and then practice the sequence.	Objective 5 (teacher assessment): Observe how students are working together and how well they are focused on the task.
Pair two groups together for peer assessment.	Instruct students to • watch for contrasting movement qualities in the dance. • tell the performers which movement qualities they saw.	Tell students that one group will be performers and one will be observers, and that they will switch roles. Objective 3: (peer assessment): Students verbally express the observed movement qualities to the performing group. Listen to a sampling from the groups as they assess each other to make sure that they can identify movement qualities.
b. Refinement activities (20-30 minutes) Organize students into their small groups.	Tell groups to • choose five words that express different movement qualities. • create movements that express each word. • organize the words into a unison dance. • practice the group dance. • perform their dance for your assessment when completed.	Distribute a new list of verbs (action words). Review the choreographic process and remind students to clearly demonstrate contrast in movement quality. Remind students to include changes of level, direction, and pathway.
Ask groups to come to you when they are ready to demonstrate their dances.	Tell students to notify you when they are ready to perform.	Objective 5 (teacher assessment): Observe how students are working together and how well they are focused on the task. Conduct the assessment. Objective 1 (teacher assessment): Use the suggestions on page 131 for this assessment.
Recap of lesson, cool-down		
(5-7 minutes) Ask students to gather near you.	Ask student to discuss the rewards and challenges of completing this learning experience.	Objective 7 (self-assessment): List student responses on the board.
Closure and assessment		
	Tell students they will list the verbs (action words) they selected for the second dance and write about why they chose each word.	Objective 4 (self-assessment): Distribute papers and pencils for the self-assessment. Use the student self-assessment suggestion on page 131.

TECHNOLOGY CONNECTION
Videotape or record the final student performances and use the recorded performance for either student or teacher assessment.

ACCOMMODATION OR DIFFERENTIATION IDEAS

- Increase or decrease the number of verbs with students' work, depending on the students' developmental abilities.
- Limit the size of the word list.

EVERYDAY LIVING (LIFETIME WELLNESS) CONNECTIONS Ask students to apply the movement safety concepts learned in the lesson to other physical activities in which they participate (e.g., sports, shopping at the mall, playing on the playground).

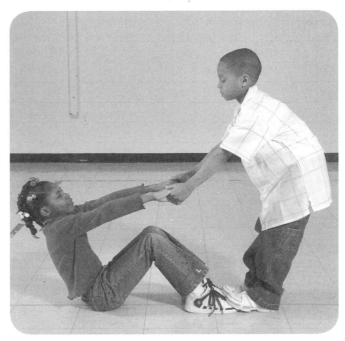

As these students respond to action words, they learn to think creatively while working cooperatively with a partner.

ASSESSMENT SUGGESTIONS

Teacher Assessment for Objective 1

Group includes five different words in their dance.	yes	no
Group clearly demonstrates contrasting movement qualities.	yes	no

Student Self-Assessment for Objective 4
Student writes about all five words and uses supportive statements.

Shapes-sepahS

Students will explore symmetrical and asymmetrical shapes individually, with partners, and in small groups. Activities that focus on the concepts of direction and relationships will be used to further develop movement tasks for this learning experience. Based on 30-minute sessions, this learning experience could be expected to take two sessions (see the following table for teacher instructions).

GRADE LEVEL   Grades 3 to 5

MATERIALS, EQUIPMENT, SPACE NEEDED

- Large, open space
- Artwork or pictures that provide examples of symmetry and asymmetry
- Geometric shapes that provide examples of symmetry and asymmetry
- Music (optional); suggested choices: Eric Chappelle, *Music for Creative Dance: Contrast and Continuum* Vol. 1, Track 1 and Vol. 3, Tracks 1 and 7

NATIONAL STANDARDS ADDRESSED

Content Standard 1. Identifies and demonstrates movement elements and skills in performing dance (Benchmarks: Body d, Space d, Relationships b)

Content Standard 7. Makes connections between dance and other disciplines (Benchmark: e)

GOAL   To develop a movement sequence of symmetrical and asymmetrical shapes with connecting actions that mirror or match the work of a partner.

OBJECTIVES   As a result of participating in this learning experience, students will

1. make symmetrical and asymmetrical shapes with their bodies. [Psychomotor]
2. make symmetrical and asymmetrical shapes that mirror or match those of the partner or small group. [Psychomotor]
3. manipulate (or reorganize) their movement sequence using changes in direction and relationship. [Psychomotor, Cognitive]
4. describe and compare the similarities and differences between their symmetrical and asymmetrical shapes. [Cognitive]
5. work cooperatively with a partner or in a small group when exploring the concepts of shape, direction, and relationship. [Affective]

Students explore the word *symmetry* with their body shapes.

132

VOCABULARY

Symmetry	Meet
Asymmetry	Lead
Mirror	Follow
Match	Relationship (e.g., side by side, front to front, back to back)
Part	

EXTENSIONS OR MODIFICATIONS

- Ask students to create movement sequences using symmetry and asymmetry with a focus on different levels.
- Ask students to look at visual artwork as a stimulus to explore a movement sequence with an emphasis on symmetry and asymmetry.

EVERYDAY LIVING (LIFETIME WELLNESS) CONNECTIONS Students can discuss the following statement: The human body is built symmetrically, yet most of the everyday actions the body performs are asymmetrical (e.g.,walk, run, leap, throw, bat, kick, crawl).

TEACHER INSTRUCTIONS FOR SHAPES

Management	Teaching process	Teaching points and cues
Introduction		
(1-2 minutes)	Tell students they are going to explore the concepts of symmetry and asymmetry.	Show students pictures or artwork that demonstrate symmetry and asymmetry. Compare geometric designs that show symmetry and asymmetry.
Warm-up		
(3-5 minutes) Have students spread out in self-space.	Encourage students to explore making a variety of symmetrical and asymmetrical shapes based on verbal cues you provide, changing shapes on the drum signal.	Ask students to explore symmetrical shapes such as wide, narrow, high, medium, low, long, and short.
Instruct students to maintain personal space while traveling through general space.	Have students travel through general space using symmetrical actions. Repeat using asymmetrical actions.	Ask students to explore actions such as walk, hop, skip, gallop, leap, run, jump, and slide.
New material		
a. Exploratory activities (15-20 minutes) Ask students to work in pairs or groups of three.	Have students mirror shapes using slow, sustained movement. On your cue, partners freeze in a symmetrical or asymmetrical shape. Students take turns being the leader and the follower.	Provide slow, sustained background music for slow movement, freeze, and leader change (optional). Encourage students to work in different • levels (high, medium, low); • extensions (wide, narrow); and • relationships (near, far, apart, together).

~ continued

Teacher Instructions for Shapes ~ *continued*

Management	Teaching process	Teaching points and cues
New material (*continued*)		
b. Refinement activities (15-20 minutes) Ask students to work in pairs or groups of three.	Ask students to create a movement sequence using actions that mirror or match the work of a partner while changing directions or moving apart, together, or side to side. • Option 1 *Slow:* symmetrical movement in place *Fast:* asymmetrical movement while traveling through space • Option 2 *Slow:* asymmetrical movement in place *Fast:* symmetrical movement while traveling through space	Use music for this activity. One option is Eric Chappelle, *Music for Creative Dance: Contrast and Continuum,* Vol. 1, Track 1 or 7. Look for students to move smoothly during the slow part. During the slow part, the leader should be moving slowly enough to allow the follower to mirror the actions. During the fast part of the music, students should be in time. During the fast part of the music, students should show variety in their direction and relationship choices.
Recap of lesson, cool-down		
(3-5 minutes) Ask students to spread out in self-space.	Review the learning experience: students explored making a variety of symmetrical and asymmetrical shapes based on verbal cues you provided.	Explain that the purpose of this learning experience was to explore symmetrical and asymmetrical movement while changing directions and relationships with partner(s).
Closure and assessment		
(2-3 minutes) Ask student pairs or trios to work with another pair or trio.	Ask students to discuss how symmetry and asymmetry affect line and design in art, math, and dance. Ask students to describe and compare the similarities and differences between symmetrical and asymmetrical shapes they created.	Circulate and monitor conversations to keep students focused on task.

Students will explore basic effort actions and create a group dance using art from the masters and artifacts from early industrial technology as stimuli. Based on 30-minute sessions, this learning experience could be expected to take three to five sessions (see the following table for teacher instructions).

GRADE LEVEL   Grades 3 to 5

MATERIALS, EQUIPMENT, SPACE NEEDED

- Large, open space
- Pictures of *Peasant Woman Tying Sheaves, The Reaper,* and *The Thresher* by Van Gogh
- Old tools and utensils (e.g., sickle, corn planter, two-person buck saw, hand mixer for baking, rolling pin)
- Chalkboard and chalk, dry erase board and markers, or poster paper
- Paper
- Crayons or markers
- Teacher-made word cards

NATIONAL STANDARDS ADDRESSED

Content Standard 1. Identifies and demonstrates movement elements and skills in performing dance (Benchmarks: Body b, Space e, Relationships a, Effort a)

Content Standard 2. Understands choreographic principles, processes, and structures (Benchmarks: a, c)

Content Standard 3. Understands dance as a way to create and communicate meaning (Benchmark: c)

Content Standard 4. Applies and demonstrates critical and creative thinking skills in dance (Benchmark: a)

Content Standard 7. Makes connections between dance and other disciplines (Benchmarks: d, e)

GOAL   To explore the eight basic effort actions of Laban and similar actions elicited from the interpretation of art and artifacts, and to create a small-group dance using selected verbs (see the assessment rubric and sample script on page 140).

OBJECTIVES   As a result of participating in this learning experience, students will

1. combine locomotor and axial movements in a repeatable sequence of four to six movements. [Psychomotor]
2. demonstrate the movement qualities associated with selected effort actions. [Cognitive]
3. identify a movement theme and the reasons for their choice of words within their theme. [Cognitive]
4. work in a cooperative and productive manner with peers. [Affective]
5. discuss the rewards and challenges of this learning experience. [Affective]

VOCABULARY

Laban effort elements provided for teacher information are: strong or firm, light, direct, flexible or indirect, sudden, sustained

Laban effort actions for students to explore: dab, glide, flick, float, punch, press, slash, wring

EXTENSIONS OR MODIFICATIONS

- Use fewer than eight words for younger students.
- With younger students, leave out the Laban effort actions and explore effort actions through selected occupations used as stimuli.
- Have fewer criteria for choreography created by younger students.
- Ask older students to research information on their chosen historical vocation.
- Share information about Rudolph Laban and the impact of his work with older students.

TEACHER INSTRUCTIONS FOR ART AND ARTIFACTS

Management	Teaching process	Teaching points and cues
Introduction		
(3-5 minutes) Ask students to sit near you.	Show students a variety of tools and implements you have brought to class. Discuss how the tools were used. Ask students the types of movement actions used with each tool. Tell students they will work in a small group to create a dance sequence based on their choice of movement theme or occupation.	Discuss differences in how work was done in pioneer times and now. The Laban effort elements are provided to assist the teacher in cueing the appropriate effort for each action. Be sure to choose phrasing the students will understand. Provide cues such as these: Saw back and forth: direct, sustained, firm Sew or weave: indirect, sustained, light Pound or hammer: direct, sudden, firm
Review of previous material, warm-up		
(3-5 minutes) Have students spread out in self-space.	Tell students to use a locomotor action that moves on a straight pathway to another space. Tell students that this is direct movement since they are moving directly to another place. Move to a different place while moving on a curved, wavy, or zigzag pathway. Explain that this is called indirect movement. It is like taking the long way to get somewhere. Move quickly to another space. Ask them to move in slow motion to another space. This is called sustained movement. It is continuous without jerks or bumps. Then have students choose another locomotor action and perform it very softly and lightly. Then have students perform the same movement, but this time with a lot of force and weight.	Direct or straight forward, backward, or sideways Indirect or flexible, wavy, curved, sharp angles, zigzag Fast: quick, rapid Slow Soft or light Heavy or firm Show changes in locomotion: walk, jog, hop, jump, skip, slide, or gallop in different ways. Focus on one element at a time.

Management	Teaching process	Teaching points and cues
New material		
a. Exploratory activities (20-25 minutes) Ask students to gather near each other in front of you and close to a chalkboard or poster paper.	After students warm up, tell them that they will be exploring the effort elements in self-space (axial or nonlocomotor movements and gestures in one place) and then in general space (traveling actions throughout the room). They will work on one element at a time, then combine elements.	Use the chalkboard or poster paper to explain or define each of the words. Space: direct, indirect Time: sudden, sustained Weight: firm or strong, light Ask students for suggestions of combinations of effort elements (e.g., direct, sudden; direct, sustained; direct, firm; direct, light).
Have students spread out in random formation to perform axial actions in self-space and then traveling actions in general space.	While students are in self-space, have them explore the concept of direct using axial actions. Ask students to pick a body part (hand, elbow, head, foot) and move it in a straight line from point A to point B. Instruct students to use air pathways and change directions (e.g., up, down; forward, backward, side to side; up, down). Have students do this several times and change the use of different body parts. Ask students to explore the concept of direct movement using traveling actions across the floor from point A to point B. Have students vary the traveling actions (e.g., move forward, backward, side to side, on a diagonal).	Check the children for a variety of responses. Encourage the use of different body parts.
	Have students perform the same sequence using indirect actions. Instruct students to perform indirect axial actions first, then indirect traveling actions.	Coach students on indirect actions: wavy, curved, circular, angular changes, and zigzag. Encourage a variety of responses.
	Ask students to explore the concept of time in the same fashion. Have students perform axial (nonlocomotor) movements first in self-space, then, do traveling actions.	Sudden: quick, over in a flash, fast, rapid Sustained: lasting, taking a long time, slow, smooth Encourage a variety of responses.
	Ask students to combine space and time actions together. Have students make direct (straight) movements in sudden and sustained (smooth) ways using axial (nonlocomotor) and traveling actions. Have students combine indirect movement with sudden and sustained time qualities.	Objective 2 (teacher assessment): Observe that children are interpreting the words correctly. Can they combine two elements simultaneously?
	Ask students to explore the concept of weight. Have students perform axial (nonlocomotor) movements first in self-space, then with traveling actions.	Firm: heavy pressure or energy, strong Light: soft pressure or energy
	Ask students to combine weight and space. Have students use a strong force in direct and indirect manners, then use a strong force in fast and slow ways. Ask students to vary the combinations.	Objective 2 (teacher assessment): Observe that children are interpreting the words correctly. Can they combine two selected elements simultaneously?

~ continued

Teacher Instructions for Art and Artifacts ~ *continued*

Management	Teaching process	Teaching points and cues
New material (*continued*)		
a. Exploratory activities (20-30 minutes) Ask students to gather near each other in front of you and close to a chalkboard or poster paper. Distribute effort action chart to students (see page 141).	Introduce eight (or fewer) new words to students: punch, press, slash, wring, dab, glide, flick, and float. These words represent combinations of the elements of space, time, and weight.	This explanation is for the teacher: Punch: direct, sudden, firm Press: direct, sustained, firm Slash: indirect, sudden, firm Wring: indirect, sustained, firm Dab: direct, sudden, light Glide: direct, sustained, light Flick: indirect, sudden, light Float: indirect, sustained, light
Ask students to spread out in random formation. Have students first perform axial actions in self-space, then perform traveling actions in general space.	Have the children explore the concept of each of the effort actions in sequence, first using axial actions, then traveling actions. Encourage the use of different body parts when performing axial actions and different methods of moving through space while performing traveling actions. • Punch with the hand, elbow, head, knee, foot • Punch while jumping, hopping, stepping • Float with the hand, head, foot • Float while stepping, sliding For additional guidance on developing effort action words see page 141.	Encourage a variety of responses. Objective 2 (teacher assessment): Observe that children are interpreting the words correctly. Are they aware of all three factors simultaneously? Objective 2 (teacher assessment): Observe that children are interpreting the words correctly. Can they combine three elements simultaneously into each of the effort actions?
b. Refinement activities (20-30 minutes) Organize students into groups of three to five. Have student groups gather near you for a discussion about vocations and the use of tools and machines in pioneer times.	Conduct a discussion about vocations and work in the period 1600 to 1800 in the United States. Talk about how labor intensive work was before modern technology. Connect actions used during work to the effort element students have practiced (see page 140). • Farmer: till, plough, plant, grow, cut, bundle, thresh • Baker or cook: break egg, sift flour, mix ingredients, knead dough, let dough rise, cook, cut, serve Analyze specific words as examples. • till or plough: direct space, sustained time, firm weight • break egg: direct space, sudden time, light weight	Show students examples of old tools and utensils (e.g., scythe, corn planter, bucksaw, hand mixer, rolling pin). Discuss how these tools were used. Optional: Work with the classroom, art, and music teachers to the extent possible on a theme of the historical period and vocations. What were the work and tools like for the farmer, miller, cooper, tailor, baker, candle maker, and so on? Have students research and write about their discoveries. Show paintings depicting different vocations. Listen to music from that time period.
b. Refinement activities (20-30 minutes) Ask students to work in small groups, choose a vocation, select four to six words that describe different actions related to that type of work, and relate the actions to space, time, and weight.	Tell groups to • identify two or three different vocations typical of the time period. • brainstorm and write down four to six words related to a chosen vocation during the identified time period.	Circulate and monitor, providing cues or encouragement as needed. Use fewer words for younger groups.
Have groups experiment with actions appropriate to each of the chosen words in their assigned space.	Have students experiment with a variety of actions for each of their words. Then, they should choose their most unique or best response for each action.	Circulate and make sure students are correctly associating effort elements with actions. Make sure that students give a creative, expressive interpretation to their selected actions. They are not trying to imitate the actions literally. The movement should be exaggerated.

Management	Teaching process	Teaching points and cues
New material (continued)		
Ask each group to develop a movement sequence with a beginning shape, action sequence, and ending shape to interpret their chosen vocation.	Have groups practice their sequences several times to memorize and refine the actions.	Review the choreographic process and remind students to clearly demonstrate contrast in their movement qualities and in their beginning and ending shapes. Objective 4 (teacher assessment): Observe how students are working together and how well they are focused on the task.
Performance		
(15-20 minutes) Have students gather as an audience. Ask each group to perform its dance as you and the other students assess the performance.	Ask each group to state the chosen vocation and the words depicting that vocation.	Objective 1 (peer and teacher assessment): Use the assessment rubric on page 140 to accomplish this objective.
Recap of lesson, cool-down		
(5-7 minutes) Gather students near you.	Ask the students to discuss the rewards and challenges of completing this learning experience.	Objective 5 (self-assessment): List student responses on the board.
Closure and assessment		
(15-20 minutes)	Tell students to write their action verbs from their vocation. Would they prefer to have lived then or now? Why?	Objective 3 (student self-assessment): Use the back side of the assessment rubric.

OPTIONAL   Collaborate with the classroom, art, or music teacher(s) to integrate the learning experience in an interdisciplinary fashion.

TECHNOLOGY CONNECTION   Record the final student performances.

EVERYDAY LIVING (LIFETIME WELLNESS) CONNECTIONS   Discuss ways that modern technology in many work places contributes to an active or inactive lifestyle.

EXAMPLE JOBS

Baking or cooking: break egg, sift flour, mix ingredients, knead dough, let dough rise, cook, cut, serve

Blacksmithing: use bellows, use heat or fire, pound, bend or shape

Farming: till or plough, plant, grow, cut, bundle, thresh

Lumberjacking: chop, saw, haul, split

Washing clothes: agitate, wring, hang on a line, dry in the breeze

Other jobs: basket maker, broom maker, candle maker, carpenter, cooper (barrel maker), tailor or quilter (sewer), weaver

Name _____ Teacher _____ Final score _____

Assessment Rubric: Objective 1
Art and Artifacts Creative Movement Sequence

Clear Beginning Shape of Individual
Pulling and pushing a heavy plough: _____ Yes   _____ No

SAMPLE THEME: FARMING

Word	Body, shape, effort, and relationship components						Movement interprets the selected components	
	Space		Weight		Time			
	Direct	Flexible	Firm	Light	Sudden	Sustained	Yes	No
Till	x		x			x		
Plant	x		x		x			
Grow		x		x		x		
Cut		x	x		x			
Bundle		x	x			x		

Clear Ending Shape of Group: Bundle or pile of straw or vegetables

Your theme _____

Persons in group _____

Clear Beginning Shape of Individual or Group: _____ Yes   _____ No

Word	Body, shape, effort, and relationship components						Movement interprets the selected components	
	Space		Weight		Time		Components	
	Direct	Flexible	Firm	Light	Sudden	Sustained	Yes	No

Clear Ending Shape of Individual or Group: _____ Yes   _____ No

Scoring for rubric. Place a 3, 2, or 1 at the top of the form after viewing the final project.

   3: Clear beginning and ending shape with all selected movements interpreted correctly and consistently using BSER components.

   2: Clear beginning and ending shape with most (3 or 4) selected movements interpreted correctly and consistently using BSER components.

   1: Beginning or ending shape is not clear. Two or fewer selected movements interpreted correctly or consistently using BSER components.

From National Dance Association, 2010, *Implementing the national dance education standards* (Champaign, IL: Human Kinetics).

References

Laban, R. (1963). *Modern educational dance.* London: MacDonald and Evans.

van Gogh, V. (1889). *Peasant woman binding sheaves.* Amsterdam: van Gogh Museum.

van Gogh, V. (1889). *The reaper.* Amsterdam: van Gogh Museum.

van Gogh, V. (1889). *The thresher.* Amsterdam: van Gogh Museum.

Possible Script for Exploration of Effort Action Words

Punch—direct, sudden, firm

- Punch with your arm – like boxing.
- Use your other arm to punch.
- Use both arms at the same time to punch.
- Punch up, down, to the side.
- Use your foot—like kickboxing.
- Punch with your elbow, head, or other body part.
- Use two different body parts at the same time to punch (e.g., foot and arm, knee and elbow).
- Take a step as if you are punching—stamp, jump. Use lots of energy; be vigorous.
- Use your punching steps to take you in different directions—forward, backward, sideways.
- Use your punching steps to help you move in different pathways—straight, curved, zigzag.

Float—indirect, sustained, light

- Let your arm or hand float away from you—like wandering clouds.
- Let your other arm or hand float away from you.
- Let your arm float side to side, up and down, front and back.
- Use other body parts (e.g., elbows, feet, head) to perform floating actions.
- Perform floating actions with two body parts at the same time.
- Move about in the general space, taking steps while floating.
- While traveling through general space taking steps, simultaneously use other body parts to perform floating actions.

Combine punching and floating actions

- In self-space, perform punching actions for 8 counts, then floating actions for 8 counts.
- Travel through space while performing punching actions for 8 counts, then floating actions for 8 counts.

Explore other action words and then combine contrasting words

- Press—flick
- Dab—slash
- Wring—glide

~ *continued*

~ *continued*

Written Assessment for Art and Artifacts Dance

Work with classroom teachers to support writing conventions emphasized in grade-level classrooms.

Criteria for the rubric can include:	Yes	No
Lists four to six action verbs from their dance.	___	___
Uses dance vocabulary to support verbs selected.	___	___
Students provide three or more statements about what life was like during the 1600-1800s.	___	___
Students identify three or more reasons about why they would like to live during that period or now.	___	___

Dancing With Scarves

In this learning experience students will explore level, direction and pathway while using scarves and moving to different music tempos. Based upon 30-minute sessions, this learning experience could be implemented in one session (see the following table for teacher instructions).

GRADE LEVEL   Grades 3 to 5

MATERIALS, EQUIPMENT, SPACE NEEDED

- Music with fast and slow tempos, such as Eric Chappelle, *Music for Creative Dance: Contrast and Continuum*, Vol. 3, Tracks 1 and 2
- Scarves (ideally one for each student) of light, soft fabric from stores cut into appropriate sizes; juggling scarves can be used as substitutes.
- CD or other music player

NATIONAL STANDARDS ADDRESSED

Content Standard 1: Identifies and demonstrates movement elements and skills in performing dance (Benchmarks: Space d, Relationships a, Time b)

Content Standard 4. Applies and demonstrates critical and creative thinking skills in dance (Benchmark: b)

Content Standard 6. Makes connections between dance and healthful living (Benchmark: d)

GOAL   Students will explore level, pathway, and direction using scarves as props while working independently and in pairs or trios. Fast and slow music will be used to guide the exploration of movement elements.

OBJECTIVES   As a result of participating in this learning experience, students will

1. move their scarves at high, medium, and low levels; along straight, curved and zigzag pathways; and in various directions around their bodies while traveling through space. [Psychomotor]
2. work independently and in pairs or trios while working with a prop and moving to fast and slow tempos. [Psychomotor]
3. discuss how the tempo of the music and working independently or in pairs or trios guided movement choices. [Cognitive]
4. discuss safe and unsafe ways of moving while using scarves. [Cognitive]
5. identify and discuss their favorite tempo and way of moving individually or with a pair or trio. [Affective]

VOCABULARY

Movement elements: level, pathway, direction

Tempo

Relationships

EXTENSIONS OR MODIFICATIONS

- Repeat the process using other props (wands, hoops, balls).
- Use music with different dynamics (loud and soft, high pitch and low pitch).
- Use a station format with different props in each area.
- Develop a repeatable sequence using props and music with varied tempo.

TEACHER INSTRUCTIONS FOR DANCING WITH SCARVES

Management	Teaching process	Teaching points and cues
Introduction		
(1-2 minutes) Have students gather in front of you.	Tell students they will be using scarves as props to explore the movement elements of level, pathway, and direction while moving to fast and slow music.	Remind students that the scarf becomes an extension of the body. It is more than a piece of equipment to play with. Students will need a larger self-space to work in.
	Introduce safety as a factor.	Demonstrate how you hold the scarf so it is a length that prevents you from stepping on it and then slipping and falling to the floor.
Review of previous material, warm-up		
(3-5 minutes) Ask students to get their scarves and find a self-space.	Check to make sure students are spread out away from neighbors and walls.	Give students an initial task to permit exploration while equipment is being distributed to others. Or, have students sit with the scarves in their laps until everyone has a scarf and is seated.
Ask students to stay in self-space and move scarves around their bodies in time with slow music.	Provide verbal cues to guide the students as they explore movement elements of level, direction, and pathway.	Ask students to move the scarves • high overhead, • at a medium level around the waist, and • low, close to the ground. Ask students to make the scarves go • up and down, • side to side, and • forward and backward. Ask students to move the scarves • in straight pathways, • in curved pathways, and • in zigzag pathways. Have students experiment with different ways of holding the scarves, including • with one hand, • in one corner, • in two corners, • in the middle, and • for toss and catch.
New material		
a. Exploratory activities (8- 10 minutes) Have students explore the movement elements while traveling through space in time with slow music.	Ask students to show variety in the use of level, direction, and pathway.	Remind students to be aware of others around them so they do not bump into someone.

Management	Teaching process	Teaching points and cues
New material *(continued)*		
	Remind students to be aware of others around them and to hold their scarves in a safe way.	Remind students to hold the scarves at a length that prevents students from stepping on it, then slipping and falling to the floor. Objective 4: Assess by using observation. Provide verbal cues as needed.
Have students explore the movement elements while traveling through space in time with fast music.	Repeat the process described previously.	As students are moving faster, caution them to be more aware of others. Objective 4: Assess by using observation.
Ask each student to find a partner that is close by and return one of the scarves because each pair will only need one scarf.		If there is an odd number of students, ask one set of students to work in a trio.
b. Refinement activities (8-10 minutes) Pairs and trios will explore the movement elements in self-space and while traveling through space in time with slow and fast music.		Provide verbal cues to guide student exploration (e.g., in place, traveling: "Let's see use of level." "I want to see more pathways."). Objectives 1 and 2: Assess through observation.
Recap of lesson, cool-down		
(2-3 minutes) Have students work in pairs or trios.	Ask students to select their favorite way to move to the slow and fast music while exploring the movement elements. Students will perform their favorite movements to the music.	
Closure and assessment		
(3-5 minutes) Have students sit in pairs or trios and discuss closure questions.	Ask students to discuss how the tempo of the music and working independently or in pairs or trios guided their movement choices.	Guide the discussion, reminding the students to make comments concerning their use of movement elements and how the tempo of the music influenced their movements.
	Have students discuss safe and unsafe ways of moving while using scarves.	Ask students to talk about what they needed to be aware of to use the scarves safely.

ACCOMMODATION OR DIFFERENTIATION IDEAS   Consider safety issues regarding the use of props for students with specific special needs (e.g., visually or hearing impaired).

EVERYDAY LIVING (LIFETIME WELLNESS) CONNECTIONS   Dance helps people to stay fit. Using props of many sizes and weights as an extension of the body allows students to vary the force needed to produce controlled movement.

Line Dance Fun

This dance experience is designed to introduce students to rhythmic patterns commonly found in line dances and to provide strategies for students to understand how they might create their own line dances. Based upon 30-minute sessions, this learning experience could be implemented in a couple of sessions (see the following table for teacher instructions).

GRADE LEVEL Grades 3 to 5

MATERIALS, EQUIPMENT, SPACE NEEDED

- Music in 4/4 time with a strong beat
- CD player
- Open area

NATIONAL STANDARDS ADDRESSED

Content Standard 1. Identifies and demonstrates movement elements and skills in performing dance (Benchmarks: Body b; Space c, d; Effort b)

Content Standard 2. Understands choreographic principles, processes, and structures (Benchmark: e)

Content Standard 4. Applies and demonstrates critical and creative thinking skills in dance (Benchmark: a)

Content Standard 6. Makes connections between dance and healthful living (Benchmark: d)

GOALS To guide students to use basic locomotor movements, combination movements, and dance-specific movements within rhythmic patterns of selected line dances and to create their own line dances.

OBJECTIVES As a result of participating in this learning experience, students will

1. demonstrate common movements used in line dancing and improve agility. [Psychomotor]
2. recognize the rhythmic pattern, including the number of weight changes within the selected movements used, either in their own execution or after viewing other classmates' performances. [Cognitive]
3. participate in the activities and display the character and style of the music as they execute the movements. [Affective]

VOCABULARY

Agility: ability to change directions quickly, such as shifting body weight from moving forward to backward, or from one side to the other side

Locomotor movements: walk (weight change from one foot to the other foot), hop (weight change from one foot to the same foot), and jump (weight change from either one or two feet onto two feet)

Nonlocomotor movements (e.g., tap, kick, heel): no weight change on these actions

Rhythmic patterns: recurring number of weight changes or footwork actions that corresponds in some way to the underlying beat of the music, for example, within one measure of music (using popular, 4/4 time music, a measure would have four beats)

Dance specific movements and rhythmic patterns: grapevine (step side, behind, side; three weight changes), three-step turn (step side, back, front—travel to one side on each step; three weight changes; can be done on both sides of the body)

Rhythmic elements: underlying beat (starting with four beats per measure; listen to the drum) and accent (an action that stands out differently than other movements by being louder or stronger or somehow different)

EXTENSIONS OR MODIFICATIONS

- To increase difficulty, have students repeat the rhythmic patterns or dances by starting with the opposite foot (reversing the entire pattern on the other side for ambidexterity).
- Challenge students to create their own line dances using simple criteria: limit themselves to 4 measures for 16 total counts, or for more challenge, use 8 measures for 32 counts total.
- If space is a problem, challenge students to create a line dance that fits the space available, perhaps using the rows in between students' desks in a classroom.

TEACHER INSTRUCTIONS FOR LINE DANCE FUN

Management	Teaching process	Teaching points and cues
Introduction		
(2 minutes) Explain to students that there are literally hundreds of line dances. The goal is to recognize the common movements that are used in line dances. For example, about 70 to 80 percent of all line dances use a grapevine step. Explain that in this learning exercise, they will explore some of these moves and learn how line dances are structured.	Organize students into a scatter formation, all facing the front wall (toward the music).	Ask students to stand in personal space, arms extended, without touching anyone, and facing the music (i.e., the designated wall). Explain that line dances may be choreographed to start with either foot first. Dancers need to be ambidextrous when preparing to recognize rhythmic patterns and moves used in line dances. Note: An easy way to challenge students is to repeat starting with the opposite foot.
Warm-up		
(10 minutes) Instruct students to 1. march in place to verbal counts in sets of 4 or 8 counts. 2. walk in each of the following rhythmic patterns to verbal counts: a. forward 8 counts, then backward 8 counts. Repeat. b. forward 4 counts, then backward 4 counts. Repeat. c. forward three steps and accent count 4 with a tap step, then backward three steps with a tap step. Repeat. d. Move to each side (i.e., side, together, side) with a tap (to accent count 4) to the right side (starting with the right foot), then to the left side (starting with the left foot). Add slow tempo music to repeat steps in the last two rhythmic patterns, then repeat to a moderate or fast tempo.	Have students in a scattered formation. • Start with rhythmic pattern "a" until students can change directions and keep the constant beat while walking. Then try rhythmic pattern "b," which requires more agility. • To increase difficulty, alternate rhythmic patterns "a" and "b" until students can change directions easily in time with the counts. • For a rhythmic challenge, adjust the number of walks to create a decelerated rhythmic pattern alternating forward and backward directions by using the following number of walks: 8/8, 4/4, 2/2, 1/1/1/1. Then start with the opposite foot and repeat. • Try separately, then alternate rhythmic patterns "c" and "d" together to counts, then for the length of a song.	Remind students to • step on each count, making a complete weight change from one foot to the other. They can start with either foot as long as there are an even number of steps in each direction. • bend their knees to lower the center of gravity and keep weight centered between both feet to quickly change directions. • start with the same foot to keep the group moving together to the same side in pattern "d" when adding side directions and a tap or other nonweighted accent. Remind students that moving in four directions creates a basic line dance facing one wall that requires agility and timing as well as sequencing movements.

~ continued

Line Dance Fun

Management	Teaching process	Teaching points and cues
New material		
a. Exploratory activities (5 minutes) 1. Introduce and practice a grapevine. Using pattern "d", vary the side movements by substituting a grapevine step for the side, together, side steps by executing a step side, cross behind, step side and then a tap. 2. Introduce turn option. Have students explore a three-step turn as a substitute for the grapevine. 3. Provide a combination challenge. Have students alternate forward and backward, side-to-side directions as they do three walks and a tap, or a grapevine and a tap to each side (i.e., the basic direction line dance with a grapevine). 4. Add accent options. Have students explore different ways to accent count 4: with a clap or a kick (to substitute for the tap), a hop, a heel dig, a slap of the heel of the non-weighted foot, and so on.	Ask class to face front wall (also called a one-wall line dance). Tell class each grapevine travels sideward and uses four counts: three weight changes and an accent or tap. The rhythmic pattern for four repetitions of the grapevine totals 16 counts (or four sets of four counts). Start and stop the entire class as needed until all are moving in unison to reflect the basic direction of travel within the dance. Add slow, then moderate or fast music.	Keep students moving by providing music and cuing the measures taken in each direction (e.g., **1**-2, 3, 4; **2**-2, 3, 4; **3**-2, 3, 4; **4**-2, 3, 4). Repeat. Initially, repeat each direction twice to give students time to react. Encourage students to step or perform an action on each underlying beat of the music. Add a clap on count 4 to make the accent stronger.
b. Refinement activities (15-20 minutes per dance) Cowboy Rodeo Line Dance (16 total counts) 1. Grapevine to right with a clap accent as tap left foot (4 counts). 2. Grapevine to left with a clap accent as tap right foot (4 counts). 3. Take three walks backward with a clap accent as tap left foot (4 counts). 4. Step left foot forward, drag or slide right foot behind left foot, repeat step left and drag right (4 counts).	Perhaps use "Elvira" as a slow song for this dance.	On the step and drag moves, tell students they can pretend that they are holding and circling ropes over their heads (like a cowboy's lariat). It is optional to say "Yaa-hoo" during these moves!
After students can repeat the four parts above while facing the front wall, add a quarter turn by having students slowly rotate to the left on the step and drag moves. This makes the dance a four-wall line dance.	Have students practice body awareness of laterality when facing a new wall by asking students to make a quarter turn to their left to face a new wall. Repeat four times to get back to the front wall. Remind students it can take a lot of practice time to repeat the entire dance facing each wall until all students can move in unison to the desired tempo—and execute a four-wall line dance. Use different music tempos, starting with a slow tempo and gradually increasing to a moderate or fast tempo. A faster tempo for this dance might be "Big Heart" by the Gibson-Miller Band or "Baby Likes to Rock It" by The Tractors.	Remind students this line dance has become a four-wall line dance because it begins again with students now facing a new wall. Remind students that with their sternums facing a new wall, they still have a "right" and a "left" side—in relationship to the wall they are facing.

Management	Teaching process	Teaching points and cues
New material (*continued*)		
Achy Breaky 1. Right toe fan (8 counts). Keep the right heel on the ground, lift the toes, rotate to tap floor once on the right side, then come back to parallel and tap the toes on the floor. Each tap takes one count. Repeat toe fan taps for a total of 8 counts: out and in, out and in, out and in, out and in. 2. Double heel forward, double toe backward, and around-the-world (8 counts). Use left foot to dig the left heel forward twice (2 counts), then dig the left toes backward twice (2 counts). Dig the left heel forward, tap toes to left side, slap heel of left foot behind the right leg with the right hand, step on left foot (each action gets 1 count). 3. Grapevine (or vine) to the right with a scuff (brush the heel of the left foot forward with no weight change) for 4 counts. Vine to the left with a scuff (brush the heel of the right foot forward with no weight change) for 4 counts (total of 8 counts). 4. Repeat vine to the right (4 counts) and then vine to the left (4 counts), ending with a right foot stomp (total of 8 counts).	Consider these ideas: • This is a four-wall line dance that rotates counterclockwise to face each new wall and repeat the dance. • A toe tap can be substituted for the heel slap. • Start the dance as a one-wall line dance. • Modify the dance to a four-wall line dance rotating counterclockwise on the second vine (while moving to the left), then face the next wall to complete two more vines, one to the right and one to the left. • The song "Achy Breaky" by Billy Rae Cyrus works well for a slow tempo for this line dance. • For a faster tempo, try the "Boot Scootin' Boogie" by Brooks and Dunn.	• Note that structure of this line dance is five sets of 8 counts, or 40 total counts, which is commonly used when choreographing line dances. • Encourage students not to worry about making mistakes; rather, encourage them to realize that it happens to everyone at some point, and the goal is to identify where in the routine they can join in again. Once they understand the subparts of the dance, it could be when the group moves to one side or the other, or when the entire dance is started again, and so forth. • Encourage students to personalize the accent on count 4 or add the optional three-step turn on the grapevines if they choose to do so. Or, they can do the "plain vanilla" version of the line dance; that is, how it was choreographed. • Observe that students are connecting to the music with either a weight change step or an action or accent with each beat of the music. • Create a demonstration challenge by having half the class demo the dance while the other half watches. The students must do the "vanilla" version for the first two walls; then they can personalize and add some other flavors to the dance by varying the accents, adding turns, and so on, as long as the basic structure and directions are followed.
Cool-down		
(2 minutes) Slow down the tempo.	Have students repeat any of the warm-up activities with basic direction changes, or slowly repeat a favorite line dance.	

~ *continued*

Teacher Instructions for Line Dance Fun ~ *continued*

Management	Teaching process	Teaching points and cues
Closure and assessment		

(2 minutes)
Bring students into a semi-circle around you.
	Select appropriate review questions for content covered in class.	Use the assessment rubric on page 151. The rubric can be used by the teacher or for peer or self–peer assessment.
		• Ask students to name the following:
		  a. the number of beats in a grapevine (4);
		  b. the number of weight changes in a grapevine (3; stepping on counts 1, 2, 3);
		  c. the number of accents in a grapevine (1; tapping on count 4); and
		  d. two different accents that could be used on count 4 of each measure of this basic line dance (e.g., clap, kick, heel, point, slap foot, hop, jump, or any other nonweight action).
		
		• Ask students to define *agility* and give an example from class movements or patterns (i.e., agility involves changing directions quickly when stepping forward to backward, backward to forward, or from either side to the other side; one example occurs at the end of a grapevine prior to moving to the other side).
		• Ask students how to keep the beat when changing directions quickly (bend your knees to lower your center of gravity and anticipate the direction change).
		• Ask students what the difference is between a one-wall and a four-wall line dance (four-wall dance repeats facing a new wall after making a quarter turn within the dance to face each of the four walls in the room, but a one-wall dance only faces the front wall).

OPTIONAL

- Culminate the learning experience with half the class performing while the other half watches to identify movements executed.
- Teach other line dances to give students more movements to select from.

TECHNOLOGY CONNECTION Record students performing.

ACCOMMODATION OR DIFFERENTIATION IDEAS

- Have different groups within the class at different levels working on a progression of activities leading to the basic line dance and variation challenges.
- Clarify definition of terms used in class for all students' understanding.

EVERYDAY LIVING (LIFETIME WELLNESS) CONNECTIONS

- Line dancing helps students understand how to be an individual within a group routine.
- Line dancing is an excellent low-impact, lifelong, aerobic activity that can be done to meet the general cardiovascular endurance criterion.
- Line dancing helps with counting, sequencing movements, and recognizing rhythmic patterns.

ASSESSMENT RUBRIC

4 points: Demonstrates the line dance rhythmic patterns using some flair and energy, variety of accents, very good execution and precise connection with the music (i.e., consistently keeps the beat and personalizes with at least two different accents either within the length of one song or for a minimum of 45 seconds).

3 points: Demonstrates the line dance rhythmic patterns as choreographed using good execution and connection with the music (i.e., keeping the beat most of the time either within the length of one song or for a minimum of 45 seconds).

2 points: Demonstrates the line dance rhythmic patterns using satisfactory execution but has inconsistent connection with the music (i.e., inconsistently keeping the beat either within the length of one song or for a minimum of 45 seconds).

1 point: Demonstrates the line dance with inconsistent execution and poor timing with the music (i.e., not consistently executing the rhythmic pattern correctly and not consistently keeping the beat either within the length of one song or for a minimum of 45 seconds).

0 points: Didn't try or was absent.

Working in the Coal Mine

An Integrated Approach to Folk Dance

After viewing a videotape of Tanko Bushi, students will learn this Japanese folk dance about coal mining. They will discuss facts about the history, culture, politics, and economy of Japan and facts about coal mining in America. Based on 30-minute sessions, this learning experience can be completed in two sessions (see the following table for teacher instructions).

GRADE LEVEL   Grades 3 to 5

MATERIALS, EQUIPMENT, SPACE NEEDED

- C. Lane and S. Langhout, *Multicultural Folk Dance Treasure Chest*, Vol. 2, 1998, Champaign, IL: Human Kinetics
- J. Hendershot, *In Coal Country*, 1987, New York: Alfred Knopf
- CD or other music player
- Videotape or DVD player
- Handouts on Japan and coal mining (see pages 156 and 157)

NATIONAL STANDARDS ADDRESSED

Content Standard 1. Identifies and demonstrates movement elements and skills in performing dance (Benchmarks: Body c; Space d, e; Relationships a; Time b, Effort c)

Content Standard 5. Demonstrates and understands dance and various cultures and historical periods (Benchmarks: a, c)

GOAL   To perform a folk dance from another country; learn facts about the history, culture, politics, and economy of that country; and discuss how the origin of a dance can be developed from themes such as vocations or occupations (see the suggested performance checklist on page 158).

OBJECTIVES   As a result of participating in this learning experience, students will

1. perform the complete folk dance (Tanko Bushi) from a circular formation using forward and backward stepping actions and the gestures of digging coal, throwing coal, wiping sweat, pushing a cart, and clapping. [Psychomotor]
2. state the cues for each step of the Tanko Bushi dance. [Cognitive]
3. discuss five facts they have learned about Japan. [Cognitive]
4. discuss five facts they have learned about coal mining in America. [Cognitive]
5. work cooperatively in a group while performing a folk dance. [Affective]

VOCABULARY

Brow

TEACHER INSTRUCTIONS FOR WORKING IN THE COAL MINE

Management	Teaching process	Teaching points and cues
Introduction		
(3-5 minutes) Have students sit near you and face a video monitor.	Tell students they will watch a video, listen to music, and learn a folk dance about coal mining.	Note that hearing the music and seeing a folk dance before learning the steps and formations helps students in the learning process.
Warm-up		
(3-5 minutes) Organize students in scatter formation facing you.	Lead a variety of locomotor and nonlocomotor actions to the rhythm of the music Tell students to • walk, hop, and jump through general space to the rhythm of the music; and • make various actions to the rhythm of the music (e.g., pushing, pulling, circling, digging, wiping sweat).	For beginners, teach foot movements and hand movements separately before combining them. For advanced students, introduce foot and hand movements together.
New material		
1. Introduce background of the dance (2-5 minutes) Have students sit in personal space facing you.	Discuss how coal mining was done before modern machinery was available.	Introduce facts about Japan (e.g., economics, government, industry, culture; see handout on p. 157). Provide facts about coal mining: digging with shovel, picking with ax, throwing coal into cart, pushing coal carts out of the mine, wiping sweat from brow (see handout on p. 156).
2. Teach part I: Digging the Coal (1-2 minutes) Have students stand in personal space facing you.	See dance description in the right-hand column.	Demonstrate part I. Pretend you have a big shovel in your hands. Part I lasts 8 counts. Cue: Dig, Dig (or RR) Dig, Dig (or LL) Remind students to tap foot on the same side of the body at the same time as they dig with the shovel.
3. Teach part II: Loading the Cart (1-2 minutes) Have students stand in personal space facing you.	See dance description in the right-hand column.	Demonstrate part II. Pretend you are putting coal in the cart with both hands up and palms facing back. Part II lasts 4 counts. Cue: Throw (R) Throw (L) Remind students to step forward with the right foot when throwing over right shoulder and step forward with left foot when throwing over left shoulder.

~ continued

Working in the Coal Mine

Teacher Instructions for Working in the Coal Mine ~ *continued*

Management	Teaching process	Teaching points and cues
New material (*continued*)		
4. Teach part III: Wiping Sweat (2-4 minutes) Have students stand in personal space facing you. Have students step backward with the left foot while wiping sweat from the brow with the right forearm.	See dance description in right-hand column.	This is the tricky part. Demonstrate stepping backward with the left foot while wiping sweat from brow with the right forearm. While wiping sweat from brow with the left forearm, step backward with the right foot. Part III lasts 4 counts. Cue: Wipe, Wipe (R, L)
5. Practice parts I, II, and III together (3-5 minutes) Have students stand in personal space facing you.	Perform the sequence with students while providing verbal cues. Tell students to practice the sequence without music and then practice the sequence with music.	Cues: Dig, Dig, Dig, Dig, Throw, Throw, Wipe, Wipe Objective 1: Use observation to complete assessment of this objective.
6. Teach part IV: Pushing the Cart (1-2 minutes) Have students stand in personal space facing you.	See dance description in right-hand column.	Demonstrate this part. Push the coal cart out of the mine while moving forward. Push forward with both hands while taking a step forward with the right foot, then the left foot. Part IV lasts 4 counts. Cues: Push, Push
7. Practice parts I, II, III, and IV together (3-5 minutes) Have students stand in personal space facing you.	Perform sequence with students while providing verbal cues. Tell students to practice sequence without music and then practice sequence with music.	Cues: Dig, Dig, Dig, Dig Throw, Throw, Wipe, Wipe Push, Push Objective 1: Use observation to complete assessment of this objective.
8. Teach parts V and VI: Clapping Sequence (3-5 minutes) Have students stand in personal space facing you.	See dance description in right-hand column.	Note that the clapping part of the dance is like the flag of Japan, a rising sun action (visual imagery). Demonstrate these parts. Palms are up in the cart-pushing position. Spread arms to side (like the breast stroke), then move them up and around in a circle and end with a clapping sequence. Remember to rock forward right, rock backward left as you spread the arms sideways. Close your feet together while doing the arm circling action. Clap rhythm: long, quick, quick, long
9. Practice the dance (3-5 minutes) Have students work with partners in scatter formation.	Tell students to • review entire sequence verbally, • practice dance sequence without music, and • practice dance sequence with music.	Cues: Dig, Dig, Dig, Dig Throw, Throw, Wipe, Wipe Push, Push Spread, Around Clap: (slow, quick, quick, slow) Objective 1: Use observation to complete assessment of this objective.
10. Perform the dance (3-5 minutes) Ask students to be in a circle formation moving counterclockwise.	Review entire sequence verbally. Tell students to practice dance sequence without music and then practice dance sequence with music.	Ask students to state the cues for parts I through VI. Objective 2: Observe performance and provide appropriate comments.

Management	Teaching process	Teaching points and cues
Integrated activities		
1. Review and perform sequence for Tanko Bushi (5-7 minutes) Ask students to work with partners in a scatter formation and then in a circle formation.	Tell students to review and practice sequence with partner and then perform whole dance with music.	See cues from page 154, number 9.
2. Review facts about Japan and coal mining and introduce coal mining in America (10-15 minutes) Organize students in small groups of four to six.	Assigns each member of the group a section of the Japan fact sheet to read (section 1, 2, 3, 4). Use jigsaw groups. Send each group to a different location in the gym to read and discuss their portion of the fact sheet. Tell students to go back to their original group and share information. Repeat the process with the coal mining fact sheet.	For younger students, share the information from one of the fact sheets and have students jigsaw the second sheet. When possible, encourage classroom teachers to team teach this part of the lesson (integrated learning). Ask students: "What facts do you remember about Japan?" (see fact sheet). "What facts do you remember about coal mining?" (see fact sheet).
3. Explore new movements related to coal mining (5-7 minutes) Have students stay in their jigsaw groups in their area of the gym.	Tell students to create new coal mining dance actions and to perform those actions in 4- or 8-count phrases.	Objective 1: Observe for the relationship of their actions to coal mining. Objective 5: Observe for cooperative behavior.
Closure and assessment		
(3-5 minutes) Have students work with a partner or in groups of three.	Ask students to each share three to five facts they learned about Japan or coal mining.	Encourage each student to talk about different information. Objectives 3 and 4: Use observation to assess.

EXTENSIONS OR MODIFICATIONS

- Repeat the process with dances from other countries or other occupations.
- Have students create an original Americanized version of a coal mining dance based on facts they have learned about coal mining in Japan and the United States.
- Ask students to perform this dance as part of a PTA program or at a local nursing home.
- Have students write about what it must have been like to live in the time period 1600 to 1800. Ask them to answer the question "Would you like to have lived in that time period? Why did you answer 'yes' or 'no'?"
- For classes with students at lower reading levels, you may choose to read the fact sheets on pages 156 and 157 to students or find other creative ways to share the content.

TECHNOLOGY CONNECTIONS

- Use PDAs to download checklists of each dance step to check for student competence.
- Students can wear pedometers while learning and performing the dance to check the number of steps they took.
- Record the performance for student or teacher assessment.

EVERYDAY LIVING (LIFETIME WELLNESS) CONNECTIONS

- Connecting to others through folk dance promotes healthy relationships and contributes to personal overall health and fitness.
- Folk dance represents ways a community comes together to celebrate, commemorate, support, and share common human experiences.

Coal Mining Fact Sheet

Coal has been mined for more than 1,000 years. Large-scale mining started in the 18th century. The first coal mine in the United States opened in Virginia during the 1780s.

In the early years, coal was found underground. It was cut from hard rock called a bed. Miners got to the coal through tunnels, also called shafts. They moved the coal by hand. Miners used picks and bars to carve the coal from its solid bed. It was shoveled into baskets, boxes, and wheelbarrows. Then it was dragged to the outside. Later, large wagons, called cars, were built to carry the coal. The earliest cars were pulled by humans, even children. By the mid-18th century, cars that rode on rails were pulled by mules, ponies, or horses.

The coal mines were far away from towns and cities. The workers lived in camps built near mine sites. The railroad was the best way to move people and coal out of the far-away communities. Houses were built on both sides of the tracks. Most coal camps had an elementary school, a church, and a company store. Usually, owners of the mines also owned the company store. The miners were paid in a special type of money called scripts. The money could be used only at the company store. This hooked the miner and family to the store owner by strong bonds. The coal miner had to purchase all his food, clothing, and tools from the company store. Store owners charged high prices for all the goods. If the miners could not pay the prices, they bought things with an agreement to pay in the future. This means the miners were in debt to the company store. The miners worked hard. But many could not earn enough to pay all debts to the store.

Life was very difficult for the miners and their families. They had complaints about their jobs. The underground work was dirty, dangerous, and often damp. Shafts would be carved into the mountain. The area was like a dark hallway with walls of coal leading into various underground rooms. The ceilings of the underground rooms were not high. Many miners could not stand up straight. They walked hunched over or crawled to their workstations. The roofs of the mines were often supported by wooden timbers. Lamps on top of the miners' caps were the only light in the mines. Miners picked and shoveled coal for 10 or more hours a day.

Miners lived with the dangers of explosions, fires, gases, and cave-ins. Miners breathed stale, dusty air. Many developed a breathing sickness called black lung. Other problems for the miners were numbness, pains in joints of the legs and arms, violent headaches, and drumming sounds in the ears. Canaries were often used in the mines for safety reasons. If the canary was ill or died, it was a warning signal to miners that the gas levels were deadly.

From National Dance Association, 2010, *Implementing the national dance education standards* (Champaign, IL: Human Kinetics).

Fun Facts About Japan

- Japan is a country in eastern Asia. It is made up of a chain of islands. There are four large islands and many smaller ones. It is between two bodies of water, the North Pacific Ocean and the Sea of Japan. The islands have many mountains with active volcanoes.

- Japan is a little smaller than the state of California. Japan's capital city is Tokyo. The largest city also is Tokyo. People in Japan speak Japanese.

- These are the numbers in Japanese: 1: ichi, 2: ni, 3: san, 4: shi, 5: go, 6: roku, 7: shichi, 8: hachi, 9: ku, 10: ju.

- Japan's flag looks like a red sun on a white background. The Japanese call their country Nippon or Nihon. This means "source of the sun."

- Japan has the 10th-largest population in the world. In 2009, there were more than 128 million people. There are more today. (Note to the teacher: Look on the Internet or other sources to update the numbers.)

- Japan has three parts (branches) of government: executive, legislative, and judicial. This is like in the United States. Japan has an emperor. This is unlike what the United States has. The emperor inherits his throne. He is a symbol for the nation. The emperor leads many Japanese ceremonies. He has no real power in the government. The prime minister is the main leader for the government in Japan. In 1947, the people of Japan earned many new freedoms. They gained the freedoms of religion, speech, and the press.

- Rice and fish are important foods in Japan. Fish also is an important business. Fish caught in Japan are shipped around the world.

- Coal is Japan's chief mineral resource. It is mined from two of Japan's biggest islands, Hokkaido and Kyushu. It is difficult to mine. But, many businesses depend on the coal for energy. Coal helps to run these companies: Nissan Motors, Sony, Toshiba, and Toyota.

- Sports are popular in Japan. Baseball is the most popular. It started in Japan in 1932. Sumo (Japanese wrestling) is also popular. It is the national sport. Many Japanese study the martial arts. Some of them are aikido, judo, and karate.

- There are several types of dance in Japan. Some types of dance describe history and religious beliefs. Others are performed only by men. Today, dancers combine dances around the world to the rich history of Japanese dances.

- Many Japanese things are valued around the world: futon (bed), sushi (raw fish), bonsai (small potted trees), origami (art of folding paper), haiku (short poem), and kimono (robe).

From National Dance Association, 2010, *Implementing the national dance education standards* (Champaign, IL: Human Kinetics).

157

Name _____ Teacher _____

Tanko Bushi Performance Checklist

National Dance Content Standard 1. Identifies and demonstrates movement elements and skills in performing.

Performs the following steps using

	Correct form		Proper tempo	
	Yes	No	Yes	No
Dig (R), dig (R), dig (L), dig (L)	___	___	___	___
Throw, throw, wipe, wipe	___	___	___	___
Push, push	___	___	___	___
Spread, around	___	___	___	___
Clap: slow, quick, quick, slow	___	___	___	___
Performs the dance sequence in the correct order	___	___		

From National Dance Association, 2010, *Implementing the national dance education standards* (Champaign, IL: Human Kinetics).

Linking to the Traditional

Having participated in the learning experience Working in the Coal Mine: An Integrated Approach to Folk Dance, students will create a new folk dance. This experience will extend knowledge and skills presented in the previous lesson and use contemporary coal mining songs as a music source. Based on 30-minute sessions, this learning experience may take two to three sessions (see the following table for teacher instructions).

GRADE LEVEL   Grades 3 to 5

MATERIALS, EQUIPMENT, SPACE NEEDED
- C. Lane and S. Langhout, *Multicultural Folk Dance Treasure Chest*, Vol. 2, 1998, Champaign, IL: Human Kinetics
- "Sixteen Tons," *Tennessee Ernie Ford Greatest Hits*, 1995, Hollywood, CA: Capital Records
- "Big John," *Jimmy Dean 20 Great Story Songs*, 1999, Nashville, TN: Curb Records
- "Working in the Coal Mine," Lee Dorsey, *Wheelin' and Dealin'*, 1997, New York: Arista Records
- J. Hendershot, *In Coal Country*, 1987, New York: Alfred Knopf
- CD or other music player
- Learning experience titled "Working in the Coal Mine: An Integrated Approach to Folk Dance" for teaching Tanko Bushi

NATIONAL STANDARDS ADDRESSED

Content Standard 2: Understands choreographic principles, processes, and structures (Benchmarks: d, e)

Content Standard 3. Understands dance as a way to create and communicate meaning (Benchmark: c)

Content Standard 7. Makes connections between dance and other disciplines (Benchmark: b)

GOAL   To create original coal mining dances based on facts learned about coal mining in Japan and the United States.

OBJECTIVES   As a result of participating in this learning experience, students will

1. create an Americanized version of a coal mining dance based on facts they learned about coal mining and Japan. Contemporary, folk, or country music may be used. [Psychomotor]

2. list a minimum of two facts about Japan, one similarity and

Students can take movements and steps learned in previous folk dances to create new dances.

difference between Japanese and American cultures, and three facts about coal mining. [Cognitive]

3. work cooperatively within the group and contribute ideas to the composition of the group coal mining dance. [Affective]

4. express in writing how they feel about coal mining and working in a group to choreograph a dance. [Affective, Cognitive]

VOCABULARY

Choreography

Choreograph

Choreographer

TEACHER INSTRUCTIONS FOR CREATING NEW FOLK DANCES

Management	Teaching process	Teaching points and cues
Introduction		
(2-4 minutes) Have students sit near you.	Tell students they are going to • warm up by performing the Tanko Bushi dance, and • choreograph a new dance about coal mining based on information they learned about mining in Japan and America.	Provide a review as needed: • How the actions of coal mining imitated the actions in the Tanko Bushi dance • Facts about coal mining in Japan and America
Warm-up		
(5 minutes) Have students review and perform the sequence for Tanko Bushi. Ask students to work with a partner in scatter formations first and then in a circle formation.	Tell students to review and practice the sequence with a partner and then perform the whole dance in a circle formation with music.	Cues: Dig, Dig, Dig, Dig Throw, Throw, Wipe, Wipe Push, Push Spread, Around Clap: slow, quick, quick, slow
New material		
1. Introduce aspects of coal mining by style (3-5 minutes) Have students sit near you.	Tell students they are going to choreograph a new dance about coal mining in America.	Discuss different aspects of coal mining and how they could be choreographed into a dance: • Feeling dizzy in the coal mine (gas fumes) • Miner's helmet with lamp • Large pin to attach to a coal cart when finished loading • Exhaustion from a long day of labor • Getting up early • Going into and out of the mine on an elevator • Disasters in the coal mine
2. Practice creating one phrase as a whole class using an action about coal mining (2-4 minutes) Organize students in a scatter formation.	Tell students to develop one action that takes a musical phrase of 4 or 8 counts.	Help students develop a coal mining action and put it to music.

Management	Teaching process	Teaching points and cues
New material *(continued)*		
3. Introduce coal mining music (5-10 minutes) Gather students near you.	Listen to song(s); see music references on page 159.	Select music options: • You choose the song for the entire class. • Students choose the song for their group. • Class votes on one song for entire class Ask: "Did the music or lyrics give you any ideas about coal mining actions or feelings that you could use in your dance?"
4. Provide instructions for creating the dance (3-5 minutes) Organize students in groups of four to six.	Tell students that their dance must • include four or more different coal mining actions or feelings of coal miners, • use each coal mining action for 4 to 8 counts in a phrase, and • be repeatable.	Students can choose members of their group, or you can assign members of each group.
5. Students create dances (10 minutes) Have students work in their own areas of the gym.	Have students select actions, refine sequence, and practice their chosen movements.	Instruct each group to decide on four or more movements with music playing in the background. Circulate among groups and assist where necessary. Keep students on task. Provide feedback.
Closure and assessment		
(minimum of one 30-minute session; the time for this section will depend on assessment method) 1. Students perform dances	Use the Tanko Bushi Performance Checklist on p. 158.	Perform dances in one of the following ways: • Students work in stations, with one serving as the teacher performance assessment station. • One-half of the class performs while the other half observes using the rubric. Repeat. • Groups are videotaped for you to evaluate later using the rubric.
2. Students do homework assignment	Tell students that they must finish and turn in assignment by next class period (see p. 162 for assignment).	

Creating a Folk Dance
Understanding and Feelings

National Dance Content Standard 3: Understanding dance as a way to create and communicate meaning.

National Dance Content Standard 7: Making connections between dance and other disciplines.

1. List at least three facts you have learned about coal mining.

2. List at least two facts you have learned about Japan.

3. Can you name one thing that is the same and one thing that is different about coal mining in the United States and coal mining in Japan?

   The same: _____

   Different: _____

4. Circle the words that tell how you felt as you worked on this folk dance choreography project with your group. Circle all the words that express **your** feelings.

happy	excited	included	left out	not interested
useful	awkward	helpful	annoyed	challenged

5. As a group member I was cooperative and used my best effort:

   always   most of the time   not very much

From National Dance Association, 2010, *Implementing the national dance education standards* (Champaign, IL: Human Kinetics).

Summary

After participating in activities triggered by the learning experiences offered in this chapter, students will discover that their bodies can be instruments for expressing thoughts, feelings, and life experiences. They will understand that dance education can help them learn how to learn, connect with other cultures, and respect others' abilities. Students will recognize that dance can be connected with other learning disciplines. They will also discover that dance can be a means for improving health. The information learned in this chapter can help students achieve success at the higher grade levels and in more challenging learning environments.

Grades 6 to 8

During early adolescence, students' bodies change rapidly. As a result, growth varies widely among adolescents. However, they still can master certain motor skills, analyze material, and respond well to movement-oriented challenges. Problem-solving abilities are heightened. Students are more interested in their personal health and well-being. Dance teachers will find that dance classes can be valuable in helping students make healthy and safe decisions about their bodies and movement options. The learning experiences found in this chapter can help young adolescents practice new ways of moving, working with peers, increasing dance knowledge, performing, and communicating with others.

Table 10.1 provides a quick overview of learner characteristics of young adolescents by educational domain (psychomotor, cognitive, and affective). It also offers instructional ideas that can be used to address specific characteristics of the young adolescent student. Using these two components can facilitate program planning to help students achieve developmentally appropriate learning benchmarks.

TABLE 10.1　Developmental Characteristics by Domain

Psychomotor (physical) characteristics	Implications for dance education teachers
During early adolescence, students (ages 12 to 14 and in grades 6 to 8) . . .	
a. experience accelerated physical development in gross motor and fine motor skills in varying degrees (boys are stronger, girls are more flexible)	Plan activities that isolate movement of body parts to develop control; and that enhance strength, endurance, balance, coordination, and flexibility
b. experience the onset of puberty (increases in weight and height) and mature at varying rates (girls generally develop physically earlier than boys)	Prepare opportunities for youth to discuss body development as a natural, normal process; listen to their fears without judging or trivializing
c. need more attention to improve physical fitness levels, including endurance, strength, and flexibility	Offer lessons on the components of physical fitness and ways that dance can influence the fitness levels for each component
d. experience fluctuations in metabolism causing extreme restlessness and listlessness; have appetites for particular tastes; may overtax their digestive systems with large amounts of improper foods	Discuss strategies for improving the sense of well-being, including good eating habits, the digestive system, and ways proper eating affects energy levels for active movement
e. have intense sexual feelings and a keen interest in their own bodies	Offer opportunities for youth to discuss body development as a natural, normal process; offer activities to help build confidence in their abilities
f. are interested in organized physical activity	Encourage a wide range of active and fun learning experiences in social, recreational, and performance dance
Cognitive (intellectual) characteristics	**Implications for dance education teachers**
a. are intensely curious	Offer many opportunities for problem solving
b. are beginning to think more abstractly and hypothetically; can think about "thinking" and how they learn; are becoming skilled in logic and cause-and-effect reasoning; can project thoughts to the future; establish goals; consider ideas contrary to fact; question attitudes, behaviors, and values	Provide activities for creative productions; ask questions that encourage predicting and problem solving; help students find solutions on their own by providing supervision without interference
c. can handle exposure to advanced academic content in specific subject areas (increased attention span)	Continue offering opportunities for interdisciplinary learning; plan more activities to improve technique and other skills
d. ask broad, unanswerable questions about the meaning of life	Challenge students to create movement studies and dances that reflect on the forces that have influenced or shaped their multifaceted lives
e. prefer active over passive learning experiences and cooperative learning activities	Offer clear, concise instructions with limited lectures; allow students to work with partners and teams
f. enjoy learning information and skills to apply to real-life problems and situations	Provide movement tasks reflective of a common activity (note passing in class, phone texting, or healthy food selections at school) to problem solve a potential outcome

Cognitive (intellectual) characteristics *(continued)*	Implications for dance education teachers *(continued)*
g. reject solutions from adults in favor of their own; feel entitled to challenge existing order	Considering class health and safety, allow students to set class ground rules and consequences for broken rules; ask questions that encourage predicting and problem solving
h. can take responsibility for planning and evaluation of their own work; have improved management skills	Allow young teens to plan dances and productions and expect follow-through; help them evaluate the outcome
i. broaden their worldview beyond peer groups and families; cannot understand why school, governmental, and ecosystems are difficult to fix	Allow for the study of the history and meaning of dance in many cultures; encourage participation in productions outside the classroom setting
Affective (socioemotional) characteristics	**Implications for dance education teachers**
a. are egocentric; believe that personal issues are unique to themselves; are easily offended and sensitive to criticism	Allow students opportunities to observe student-created responses (interpretations) to a teacher-given task; use clearly stated assessment tools for class observations; offer positive reinforcement for quality efforts
b. exhibit temperamental emotions and restless behavior	Accept feelings as results of hormonal changes; be careful not to embarrass or criticize; explore activities related to the wide range of human emotion and body language; offer movement tasks that allow students to create dances describing exaggerated gestures and extremes in emotion and behavior
c. periodically challenge rules and boundaries set by parents, teachers, and others in authority	Set clear and concise classroom rules with known consequences for infractions; hold students accountable for their actions and impose appropriate consequences when rules are broken; involve students in setting class rules
d. are concerned about their physical appearance, grooming, social rules, and being liked by peers	Organize classes so that students feel comfortable discovering and understanding selves and in building positive relationships; be patient with grooming behaviors that seem excessive; plan opportunities for achievement and recognition of accomplishments; concentrate on developing individual skills
e. are moving from dependency on parents to dependency on peers' opinions, yet strongly dependent on parental values	Find ways to involve parents in class activities, projects, or dance concerts
f. understand basic rules of morality and justice	Establish rules of morality for the classroom; discuss appropriate movements, music, and costuming for dances; discuss appropriate audience behavior; analyze popular media dance; plan activities that require trust in a partner or group
g. trust adults who show sensitivity to adolescent needs	Encourage educators, parents, and other community members to get involved in school dance activities
h. are interested in activities that involve the opposite sex or, simultaneously, the same sex	Offer after-school dance activities for students from a wide range of socioeconomic and cultural backgrounds; provide opportunities for boys and girls to mix without feeling uncomfortable
i. use peers and media role models as sources for standards of behavior	Discuss positive and negative behaviors of peer groups, media personalities, and icons
j. are optimistic, hopeful, and idealistic	
k. are reflective, introspective, and analytical about their thoughts and feelings; strive for a sense of individual uniqueness	Allow planning time and privacy to work on creative, individual projects and productions
l. have an emerging sense of humor	Offer tasks that allow for creating dances that describe exaggerated gestures and extremes in emotion and behavior

Table 10.2 provides teachers of young adolescents with the benchmarks that students participating in well-designed dance curricula can accomplish by grade 8 (at approximately 14 years of age). Students can reach the benchmarks through participation in specialized dance classes, a physical education curriculum, studio settings, recreation department programs, or other community-based instruction.

TABLE 10.2   Dance Content Standards and Benchmarks: Grades 6 to 8

Content Standard 1. Identifies and demonstrates movement elements and skills in performing dance
The student . . .

BODY

a. describes the role that muscles play in the development of strength, flexibility, endurance, and balance

b. demonstrates basic movement skills and describes the underlying principles (e.g., alignment, balance, initiation of movement, articulation of isolated body parts, weight shift, elevation and landing, and fall and recovery)

c. identifies and demonstrates basic dance steps, positions, and patterns of dance from two different styles or traditions (e.g., ballet, modern, jazz, square, line, folk, tap, social, and indigenous dance forms)

d. recalls and reproduces movement sequences either teacher or student designed

SPACE

a. improvises, choreographs, or performs in varied settings (e.g., studio, proscenium stage, theater-in-the-round, television, gymnasium, outdoors)

b. travels through space using a pattern drawn on paper or displayed on a computer screen

c. travels through space using self-generated patterns on paper or on a computer screen

d. creates movement patterns that combine two or more pathways (follow-up from earlier grade levels)

e. demonstrates changes in range of movement (e.g., large, small, distal, and core actions)

f. uses appropriate movement terminology and dance and anatomical vocabulary to describe the actions and movement elements observed in a dance

RELATIONSHIPS

a. demonstrates the ability to perform dances with groups of varying sizes

b. demonstrates partner skills: using complimentary shapes, using contrasting movements, taking and supporting weights, and counting phrases to maintain unison (e.g., counting in canon and understanding counts of the phrasing)

c. demonstrates kinesthetic awareness, concentration, and focus in performing dance movements

TIME

a. demonstrates accuracy in moving to a steady musical beat (follow-up from earlier grade levels)

b. translates a complex rhythmic pattern from the auditory sounds to the movement patterns (e.g., syncopation and polyrhythms)

EFFORT

a. demonstrates a broader range of dynamics (movement qualities) during improvised and choreographed works (e.g., sustained, swinging, percussive, collapsing, and vibratory)

b. creates and performs combinations and variations with a broad range of dynamics (e.g., sustained, percussive, vibratory, swinging, pausing, or no action on beats)

Content Standard 2. Understands choreographic principles, processes, and structures
The student . . .

a. uses improvisation to discover and compose solutions to small-group movement assignments (follow-up from earlier grade levels)

b. improvises, creates, and performs dances based on personal ideas or concepts from other sources (e.g., stories, pictures, poetry, emotions, verbs, found objects, artifacts, or technology) (follow-up from earlier grade levels)

c. cooperates within a small group to create dances demonstrating choreographic principles such as contrast and transition

d. identifies the choreographic structure (e.g., call and response, theme and variations, narrative) and choreographic principles used (contrasts, transitions, unity, and variety) in a movement study or dance

e. demonstrates the process of reordering (i.e., specific movements or movement phrases that are separated from their original order and restructured in a different sequence) and chance (i.e., movements that are specifically chosen and defined but randomly structured) to create a dance or movement phrase

f. cooperates with a partner to demonstrate the following skills in a visually interesting way: creating contrasting and complementary shapes, taking and supporting weight

g. cooperates with a partner or small group to produce an original work involving technology-based tools

Content Standard 3. Understands dance as a way to create and communicate meaning
The student . . .

a. compares and contrasts different styles of dance (e.g., high-kick routine, folk dance, ballroom, hip-hop)

b. explains how personal experiences influence the interpretation of a dance (e.g., journal writing, class discussion)

c. creates a dance that communicates topics of personal significance (follow-up from earlier grade levels)

d. demonstrates appropriate audience behavior and etiquette in formal and informal performance situations and explains how audiences and venues affect choreography

e. demonstrates and describes the different meanings evoked by specific body language, shapes, and movement choices (e.g., low, round shape: fear or repose; high, angular shape: defiance or power; symmetrical shape: harmony)

f. explains how accompaniment, lighting, technology, and costuming can contribute to the meaning of a dance

g. practices cultural and social etiquette related to technology (e.g., does not post harmful or inappropriate material, does not reveal personal information, follows school policy)

h. researches a theme using the Web site or media to create a short dance study

Content Standard 4. Applies and demonstrates critical and creative thinking skills in dance
The student . . .

a. creates and demonstrates multiple solutions to teacher-designed movement problems; chooses the most interesting solution and discusses the reason for that choice (follow-up from earlier grade levels)

b. compares and contrasts movement elements (e.g., body, space, effort, relationships) in two dance compositions (follow-up from earlier grade levels)

c. discusses opinions about dances with peers in supportive and positive ways (follow-up from earlier grade levels)

d. identifies aesthetic criteria for evaluating dance (e.g., originality, visual and emotional impact, variety, transition, contrast, skill of performers)

~ continued

TABLE 10.2 ~ *continued*
Content Standard 5. Demonstrates and understands dance in various cultures and historical periods
The student . . .

   a. performs folk, square, social, theatrical, and contemporary dances demonstrating awareness of various cultures and time periods

   b. describes the aesthetic qualities and traditions of more than one culture

   c. researches and explains how technology and social change have influenced the structure of dance in entertainment, movies, or the recording industry

Content Standard 6. Makes connections between dance and healthful living
The student . . .

   a. describes how dance is a lifelong, healthful physical activity (e.g., aids in weight management, helps prevent diabetes and osteoporosis, and promotes a strong cardiovascular system)

   b. describes and demonstrates three or four safe warm-up practices that relate to personal needs (e.g., hyperextended knees, swaybacks, rounded shoulders, or lack of abdominal tone)

   c. explains the importance of good nutrition in achieving peak performance

   d. applies safe movement practices in both technique and choreography (e.g., plié: knees over toes; relevé: alignment of ankle, knee, and hip; balance: vertical alignment of spine)

   e. recognizes the joy of dance as a lifetime activity to celebrate culture and community events (follow-up from earlier grade levels)

Content Standard 7. Makes connections between dance and other disciplines
The student . . .

   a. creates a project (e.g., aural, visual, oral, kinetic, or technological) that reveals similarities and differences between dance and another art form (e.g., tone, color, symmetry, dynamics)

   b. recognizes that similar themes, ideas, and concepts are expressed in dance and other art forms (e.g., loyalty, courage, jealousy, affection, hope) (follow-up from earlier grade levels)

   c. cites examples of how similar elements are used in dance and in another art form (e.g., balance, design, contrast, texture) (follow-up from earlier grade levels)

   d. creates a dance that reflects a concept from another discipline (e.g., language arts, math, science, social studies, or health) (follow-up from earlier grade levels)

   e. interprets through dance an idea taken from another medium (e.g., visual arts, music, video, poetry, history)

Students will create a movement phrase that demonstrates their understanding of the connection between inhalation and exhalation, and fall and recovery. This phrase will be incorporated into a short dance in ABA form. Based on 45-minute sessions, this learning experience may take two to three sessions (see the following table for teacher instructions).

GRADE LEVEL   Grades 6 to 8

MATERIALS, EQUIPMENT, SPACE NEEDED

- CD player
- Instrumental music in 3/4 or 6/8 time

NATIONAL STANDARDS ADDRESSED

Content Standard 1. Identifies and demonstrates movement elements and skills in performing dance (Benchmarks: Body b, c, d; Space c, f; Relationships a, b, c)

Content Standard 2. Understands choreographic principles, processes, and structures (Benchmarks: b, d)

Content Standard 4. Applies and demonstrates critical and creative thinking skills in dance (Benchmark: d)

Content Standard 6. Makes connections between dance and healthful living (Benchmark: d)

GOAL   Students will apply the principles of breath phrasing in their own 16-measure choreographic phrase that will be used in a short dance using ABA form.

OBJECTIVES   As a result of participating in this learning experience, students will

1. demonstrate basic movement skills and describe the underlying principles. [Psychomotor]
2. identify aesthetic criteria for evaluating the breath phrase. [Cognitive]
3. apply safe movement practices in both technique and composition. [Affective]

A well-executed fall and recovery can add new dimensions and dynamics to a dance.

Photo courtesy of Cindy Hoban.

VOCABULARY

Fall and recovery	Choreographic form: ABA
Inhalation and exhalation	Suspension
Phrase	Swing

EXTENSIONS OR MODIFICATIONS

- Include the forward fall as additional material.
- Explore the concept of collapse and successional movement.
- Show excerpts of Paul Taylor's *Esplanade*.

ACCOMMODATION OR DIFFERENTIATION IDEAS

- Extend the number of measures.
- Make a more complex choreographic assignment.
- Modify ranges of movement and motion for orthopedically challenged students.

EVERYDAY LIVING (LIFETIME WELLNESS) CONNECTIONS   Practice and stress the importance of proper use of the diaphragm in breath control.

RESOURCES   Options for musical accompaniment:

- Singer, composer Enya, *Paint the Sky with Stars*, Reprise Records
- B. Botsford, *Movin' Up-Percussion Grooves for Dance.* Hand to Hand Recording Company, Asgard Productions
- Compilation of numerous artists' recordings onto a series of CDs, *Moods I, II, III*, Virgin Records

TEACHER INSTRUCTIONS FOR LETTING GO

Management	Teaching process	Teaching points and cues
Introduction		
(1-3 minutes) Ask students to lie on their backs in assigned spaces.	Introduce the focus of the lesson.	Say, "Today we are going to focus on some principles that will make you a better dancer."
Review of previous material, warm-up		
(10 minutes) Review previous material students have had experience with: directions in space, 3/4 and 6/8 meter, dynamics, phrase. Have students follow your verbal guidance during the warm-up.	Direct a warm-up focusing on inhalation and exhalation as they initiate movements of the body. Students will move from a stationary prone position lying down on the floor to standing in personal space.	Say, "Close your eyes and focus on how you breathe in and out. Breathing in is called inhalation, and breathing out is called exhalation. Pay attention to the opening and closing of your ribcage as it expands and contracts. Feel your spine lengthen and open the space between each vertebrae when you breathe in, then sink into the floor as you exhale. As we explore the use of inhalation and exhalation, pay attention to the rising, floating feeling as you breathe in, and the melting, sinking feeling as you breathe out. Explore this with your right arm, left arm, shoulders, legs, and so on. Gradually, breathing in and out using your whole body will lead you to standing up."

Management	Teaching process	Teaching points and cues
New material		
a. Exploratory activities (20-30 minutes) Ask students to stand in personal space.	Model the teacher-guided movement experience using swing as the impetus.	Say, "I will now direct you through a series of movements that use inhalation and exhalation in different ways. Start by inhaling as your arm rises into a suspension that is vertical and directly over your shoulder. Now exhale and let your arm drop while I count to six (count is moderately fast). Right away, inhale and raise the arm again to reach vertical by count 6." Continue to repeat this exercise and gradually increase the tempo. Model the continuation of the movement into the free release of a swing. Say, "Now experiment using the other arm, both arms at once, your head, and your shoulders. Try swinging one leg and then the other. Next, try swinging your head at the same time that you swing your arms or shoulders, and so on."
	Affirm that students will travel from place to place, away from and back to their spots.	Say, "Now let the momentum lead you away to a new place in space. When you start another swing, let the swing take you back to your original space."
Ask students to stand in personal space.	Demonstrate how to execute a side fall and a back fall (Doris Humphrey and José Limón style). In order to prevent students' kneecaps from hitting the floor, continuously remind students with verbal cues to fall safely.	Say, "I will demonstrate a side fall and recovery up to tempo, and then I will break it down for you." Analysis: side fall to the right side • The right arm circles in across the body from high left to low right and leads you to the floor. • This movement on your exhalation takes the body out onto the floor, extended on your right side. • Engage your core abdominal muscles at all times, fold the right knee in toward the center of the body as you take the weight off of the right leg. • As you lower the body with the left leg folded, that leg is supporting your weight. • Do not let the right knee touch the floor at all. Slide the right arm and let your fingertips guide you out straight to the side in line with your right shoulder. • To recover on the inhalation, your body parts will be folded into your center simultaneously. Your left foot is directly under your body, and your foot is flat on the floor to take weight. Imagine a string attached to your left ribcage; as the ribcage pulls, it pulls you up to the left foot. • Complete the inhalation to return to your starting position.

~ continued

Teacher Instructions for Letting Go ~ *continued*

Management	Teaching process	Teaching points and cues
New material *(continued)*		
Ask students to stay in personal space to practice side falls to the right and to the left.	Monitor, count the movement, and add music. Introduce the back fall. Monitor and provide continuous feedback to prevent injury.	Say, "Swing both arms forward and upward and shift your weight onto your right foot. As your arms swing down, fold your body forward and down over the right leg as you simultaneously fold the left leg under you. (No weight on the left leg.) Slowly, in this tucked position, allow your left leg to take weight on the outside of the calf. Both hands will touch the floor to help guide the body down into a tightly rounded position. Begin to rock backward, keeping the body tightly tucked." "As you roll back onto the floor, the spine unfolds to a flat position on the floor. The left leg is folded and the right leg is extended on the floor. The right leg then swings upward." "As you begin to roll forward to recover, your arms scoop forward toward the front of the room. Engage the abdominal muscles and continue to shift the weight forward as your head curls forward over the right foot. Complete the upward swing of the arms and fully extend the body to standing."
Ask students to stay in personal spaces.	Teach students a teacher-designed phrase that includes two falls and two direction changes. The phrase takes 16 measures in 6/8 meter.	Demonstrate a teacher-designed phrase that includes two falls and two direction changes. The phrase takes 16 measures in 6/8 meter. Say, "Now we will learn a phrase that combines falls and traveling." "Follow me..."
	Have students practice the phrase with you and by themselves. First, count the phrase out loud for the students, then play music as the students practice.	Say, "Remember to use your inhalation and exhalation as an impulse to execute your movements."
	Have students perform the phrase as a class, then half of the class at a time with the other half watching.	Say, "As the other group performs, watch for the use of inhalation and exhalation as an impulse for the fall and recovery. Are the direction changes clear?"
(10-15 minutes) Have students find partners and choreograph their dances.	Ask students to create original phrases using two falls and two changes of direction while traveling in space.	Say, "Remember as you create your 16-count phrase to include a minimum of two falls and traveling in two directions. Use the inhalation and exhalation as the impulse for your movements."
	Have students use the same music used for the teacher's phrase.	Say, "We will be using the same 6/8-time music that you danced to earlier."

Management	Teaching process	Teaching points and cues
New material *(continued)*		
b. Refinement activities (15-20 minutes)	Divide the class into three groups. Allow pairs to perform their phrases to music one section at a time. Provide positive feedback about the dance phrases.	Say, "You will now perform your phrases for each other. As you watch, look for two falls, traveling in two different directions, and breath quality."
	Ask students to determine which phrase will be repeated twice to create a dance in ABA form. They will use their own 16-count phrase and your 16-count phrase as material.	Say, "Now we will use your phrase and my phrase to make a dance using ABA form. You have to decide which of those phrases you want to dance twice. Assign the letter A to the phrase you want to dance twice. Assign the letter B to the phrase you want to dance only once. The final form will be Phrase A, then Phrase B, and then end the dance with Phrase A again. We will use the same music again."
	Instruct students to practice ABA dances for 5 minutes and then perform for peers.	Say, "As you are watching, be prepared to share your observations about the use of breath quality in the falls, the clarity of the direction, and about extending the phrase to a longer dance using ABA form."
Recap of lesson, cool-down		
(5-7 minutes) Have students sit down in scattered formation.	Ask students to share their observations about the use of breath in the falls, direction changes in traveling, and ABA form.	Ask, "How does breath quality show in the movement? How were direction changes made clearly? What did you like best about performing a longer dance?"
Closure and assessment		
	Provide summary remarks.	Say, "Your comments reveal that there has been effective use of breath quality in side and back falls, clarity in the use of directions in traveling movement, and understanding of how to use ABA form as a way to extend phrases."
Assessment		
	Teacher Assessment of Pair Choreography _____ Used two falls _____ Used two directions _____ Breath quality evident	

Energy and Weight Sharing

Students will

- observe two examples of weight sharing,
- view selected highlights from a video clip,
- read a one-page handout and respond to a corresponding teacher-created worksheet,
- practice basic weight-sharing examples,
- explore variations of weight-sharing shapes,
- create their own sequence of weight-sharing shapes,
- perform a pattern of weight-sharing shapes, and
- assess the process.

Based on 45- minute sessions, this learning experience may take two sessions (see the following table for teacher instructions).

GRADE LEVEL   Grades 6 to 8

MATERIALS, EQUIPMENT, SPACE NEEDED

- Television monitor or projection screen
- VCR or LCD projector
- video clip of a performance that exemplifies weight sharing, such as from the Connecticut-based Pilobolus Dance Theatre, which can be found online
- copies of supporting text that describes the history and philosophy of the Pilobolus Dance Theatre
- worksheet with three to five questions directly related to the text

NATIONAL STANDARDS ADDRESSED

Content Standard 1. Identifies and demonstrates movement elements and skills in performing dance (Benchmarks: Body b, d; Relationships b, c; Effort c)

Content Standard 2. Understands choreographic principles, processes, and structures (Benchmarks: c, d, e)

Content Standard 6. Makes connections between dance and healthful living (Benchmarks: b, d)

GOAL   To create body shapes that demonstrate weight sharing using the concept of counterbalance.

OBJECTIVES   As a result of participating in this learning experience, students will

1. experience how to equalize shared weight, and establish safe alignment with partners. [Psychomotor]
2. demonstrate basic movement skills and describe the underlying principles (e.g., alignment, balance, initiation of movement, articulation of isolated body parts, weight shift, elevation and landing, fall and recovery). [Psychomotor]
3. demonstrate kinesthetic awareness, concentration, and focus in performing movement skills. [Psychomotor]
4. demonstrate partner skills in a visually interesting way, for example, contrasting and complementary shapes, taking and supporting weight. [Psychomotor]
5. apply safe movement practices in both technique and composition. [Cognitive]
6. establish mutual respect for safety and well being when moving with another person (trust). [Affective]

VOCABULARY

Counterbalance

Weight sharing

EXTENSIONS OR MODIFICATIONS

- Compose transitions between counterbalance shapes to create a movement sequence.
- Add accompaniment to the movement sequence.
- Introduce other types of weight sharing, for example lifts, drag, and carry.
- When introducing the concept of lifts, assign one student to act as a spotter.

TECHNOLOGY CONNECTIONS

- Students conduct Internet research on weight sharing in other dance companies or movement genres.
- Students record their work for self-critique and refinement.
- Students use software such as Lifeforms (from Credo Interactive, www.charactermotion .com) and Poser (from Smith Micro, http://my.smithmicro.com/win/poser/) to create graphic animation that illustrates shared weight designs.

TEACHER INSTRUCTIONS FOR KALEIDOSCOPE STUDY

Management	Teaching process	Teaching points and cues
Introduction		
(3-5 minutes) Ask students to sit in a semicircle in front of the monitor.	Ask for two volunteers to demonstrate. Class members observe and respond to questions.	Demonstration 1 Say, "The two students will sit back to back with knees bent and elbows hooked, feet flat on the floor. They will try standing up from this position simultaneously." "What happens if • the weight is not evenly distributed?" (Partners will be unable to stand). • the weight is shared equally?" (Both partners can stand which is an example of counterweight.) Demonstration 2 Say, "The two students will stand facing each other with feet underneath their hips. Partners grasp each other's hands. Make eye contact and slowly lean away from each other." "What happens if • one side is stronger or lower than the other?" • "the weight is shared equally?" (This is called a counterbalance.)

~ *continued*

Kaleidoscope Study

Teacher Instructions for Kaleidoscope Study: Energy and Weight Sharing ~ *continued*

Management	Teaching process	Teaching points and cues
Introduction *(continued)*		
(10-15 minutes) Ask students to remain seated in semi-circle.	Show video of Pilobolus Dance Theatre (PDT). Go to the PDT Web site (www.pilobolus.com) to gather information for preparing a one-page handout about the dance company and weight sharing. Prepare a worksheet with three to five questions that require student responses.	Say, "We are going to watch a brief video clip of a modern dance company called Pilobolus Dance Theatre. These dancers are well known for using weight sharing in their choreography. Look for examples of counterweight and counterbalance. Also pay attention to how the dancers move smoothly from one weight-sharing shape to the next. Much like with a kaleidoscope, the shapes change beautifully and seamlessly from one design to the next."
	Distribute handout. Students read the text and fill out the worksheet.	Say, "This handout will tell you more about the Pilobolus Dance Theatre. Read the text and answer the questions on the worksheet. All of the answers can be found in the text."
Review of previous material, warm-up		
(5-10 minutes) Move students to assigned personal spaces.	Direct students to warm up major muscle groups (e.g., spine, shoulders and arms, legs and feet) for the activities involved in weight sharing.	Say, "In personal space and in your own way, begin to stretch, bend, circle, and twist the different parts of your body . . . begin by stretching one arm, then the other; stretch your spine, then stretch your legs . . . " (In a class with less experienced students, you may choose to lead the warm-up.)
New material		
a. Exploratory activities (15 minutes) Group students in pairs.	Have students practice the two demonstration examples. Quickly pair up students by height and size to explore counterbalance shapes. Circulate and monitor student success. Provide specific feedback.	Say, "Get into position for the two-handed shared deep plié. Work together to create this counterbalance." "Now, explore making your own counterbalance designs that are successful." Teaching cues: Maintain • eye contact, • proper alignment, • location of shared center of gravity as partners pull away while sustaining contact, and • equal amount of effort.
	Have students practice alternating one-hand counterbalance.	Say, "Now try a counterbalance with only one hand holding onto your partner. Move smoothly and slowly into this design."
	Instruct students to balance with a partner with only one foot on the floor.	Ask, "What different ways can you create a balanced position with one foot on the floor?"
	Instruct students to use varying contact points while still maintaining shared balance positions.	Say, "Try a counterbalance shape with contact points being elbows, elbow and lower leg, and so on."
	Have students move through several different designs, making smooth changes between each design.	Say, "Continue to practice new counterbalance designs. As you change from one design to the next, make sure that the changes are smooth and seamless."

Management	Teaching process	Teaching points and cues
New material (*continued*)		
b. Refinement activities (10 minutes)	Have students make a kaleidoscope study. Students will create a sequence of three different counterbalance shapes. The changes (transitions) between each design must be smooth.	Say, "Set a pattern of three different counterbalance shapes so that you can repeat them in a performance. Think of the color chips in a kaleidoscope. The shapes change and move smoothly and beautifully from one design to the next. Do not rush through your designs. Think of your counterbalance shapes creating a brilliant kaleidoscope."
Recap of lesson, cool-down		
(10 minutes) Ask students to sit in their shared personal spaces.	Have students perform their prepared sequences on your cue.	Say, "As you watch the kaleidoscope studies, be respectful of each other's work and pay attention to the many ways the dancers create counterbalance shapes."
Closure and assessment		
(3-5 minutes)	Have students participate in an oral assessment responding to the question.	Ask, "What are three things to remember when creating a counterbalanced shape?" For example: • Shared distribution of weight • Proper alignment • Trust the partner(s) • Eye contact helps coordinate timing and cues • Maintain core body support • Develop safe grips through practice • Use positive partner communication • Create mental images of the bodies' shapes and movements in space

ACCOMMODATION OR DIFFERENTIATION IDEAS   Activities included in this learning experience are appropriate, with modifications, for students with special needs. Advanced students can

- create more shapes,
- create longer sequences with more elaborate transitions between shapes, and
- include different time components and different facings.

EVERYDAY LIVING (LIFETIME WELLNESS) CONNECTIONS
- Developing trust with partners
- Applying proper body alignment principles

RESOURCE
Artsource
Music Center Education Division
717 West Temple Street, Suite 400
Los Angeles, CA 90012

Gesture and Meaning

Students will learn introductory historical and cultural contexts as well as health benefits of the Sun Salutation, practice the Sun Salutation, discuss meaning and gesture, view a video clip of the authentic Indian dance, repeat the Sun Salutation with a focus on intentionality, experience partner observation of the Sun Salutation with peer feedback on intentionality, and identify and stylize a contemporary salutation gesture that becomes, for each student, a part of the traditional form. Based on 45-minute sessions, this learning experience may be done in one or two sessions (see the following table for teacher instructions).

GRADE LEVEL   Grades 6 to 8

MATERIALS, EQUIPMENT, SPACE NEEDED

- Sections of PBS *Dancing* video clips on classical Indian Dance
- VCR monitor and television, or LCD projector and screen
- Information on classical Indian dancing, a vocabulary handout, and worksheets for teacher, peer, and self-evaluation
- Large, open space
- Sun Salutation handout (see page 184)

NATIONAL STANDARDS ADDRESSED

Content Standard 1. Identifies and demonstrates movement elements and skills in performing dance (Benchmarks: Body b, c, d; Relationships b, c)

Content Standard 2. Understands choreographic principles, processes, and structures (Benchmark: e)

Content Standard 3. Understands dance as a way to create and communicate meaning (Benchmarks: d, e)

Content Standard 5. Demonstrates and understands dance in various cultures and historical periods (Benchmark: a)

Content Standard 6. Makes connections between dance and healthful living (Benchmarks: a, c)

GOAL   To create a personalized Sun Salutation that is an expansion of the traditional Indian movement form.

OBJECTIVES   As a result of participating in this learning experience, students will

1. create and perform traditional Sun Salutation with a personalized extension. [Psychomotor]
2. match movement of asanas (yoga postures) with correct terms. [Cognitive]
3. document in their journals the beneficial effects of personal practice of yoga other than in school. [Affective]

VOCABULARY

Yoga	Uttanasana
Asana	Downward dog
Sun Salutation (*Suryna-maskar*)	Intentionality
Mountain pose	Concentration
Plank	Zen Asana
Cobra	

TEACHER INSTRUCTIONS FOR SUN SALUTATION

Management	Teaching process	Teaching points and cues
Introduction		
(3-5 minutes) Ask students to sit in their assigned personal spaces.	Introduce the focus of the lesson.	Ask, "How many of you have ever practiced yoga?"
	Encourage student oral response to questions.	Say, "Tell me what you know about yoga. How can you describe it?"
Review of previous material, warm-up		
(5 minutes) Have students stand in assigned personal spaces.	Provide guided movement experience (mirroring) of the Sun Salutation.	Say, "Follow my movements exactly."
New material		
a. **Exploratory activities** (10 minutes)	Model each pose (in proper sequence) while explaining the specifics of the movements in the Sun Salutation. Talk about the meaning of the gestures and the terminology (Sanskrit and English versions). See Sun Salutation handout (page 184). Do several repetitions of the Sun Salutation.	Say, "Together we're going to repeat the Sun Salutation again and learn more about each pose."
In an 8-count transition, have students sit in a semicircle in front of the VCR monitor.	Introduce *Dancing* video clip.	Say, "You have 8 counts to move quietly to the VCR monitor." "Now we're going to view a short clip of traditional Indian dancing. Each movement has meaning. Each movement has a specific intent. Pay attention to the eye and the hand movements."
	Lead discussion about intentionality and meaning as it relates to the Sun Salutation.	Say, "In Hindu mythology, the sun god is worshipped as a symbol of health and immortal life. The Sun Salutation gives reverence to the internal sun (your inner spirit) as well as to the external sun (the sun that affects you from the outside in)."
	Ask students to look at the yoga handout. Lead discussion about the intention of the gestures and poses.	Say, "Look at the first pose in the series. It is called mountain pose. Hold your hands in the position while you are standing tall or seated on the floor. This is a symbol of reverence. It can mean that your are focusing inwardly. Any other ideas?"
	Ask students to respond to questions.	Say, "Look at pose 2. What's different about the intention of this movement?
	Ask students to study the handout independently and focus on the hand positions and their meaning, and the movement of the eyes.	Say, "Look at the other poses in the handout and think carefully about the intent of the positions of the hands and the eyes. When you do the Sun Salutation series again, you need to be very aware of what shape your hands are in, what that means, what and where your eyes are focused."

~ continued

Teacher Instructions for Sun Salutation ~ *continued*

Management	Teaching process	Teaching points and cues
New material (*continued*)		
Ask students to put handouts in their folders or away from the working space and go to assigned personal spaces.	Direct students to move into personal space in preparation for practicing the Sun Salutation again.	Say, "Put your handouts away and move quietly back to your personal space."
	Provide verbal cues as students move through the poses of the Sun Salutation.	Say, "I will give you verbal cues one more time [use the names of the poses] as you move from one pose to the next to complete the Sun Salutation. With every pose, be very aware of the positions of your hands and where your eyes are focused."
	Have students perform Sun Salutation series independently.	Say, "Pay attention to how you use your hands and your eyes and how you get from one position to another. This will show your concentration and your clear intent."
Ask students to sit down in their personal space.	Initiate discussion about contemporary salutation gestures.	Say, "Let's think about ways that we greet or say goodbye to people using gestures alone not words" (e.g., wave, high five, handshake).
	Model ways that a gesture can be stylized.	Ask, "How have I changed this handshake? You know it is a handshake, but it looks different."
	Explain ways to stylize a handshake.	Say, "The movement is bigger, smaller, slower, faster, or uses a smaller or larger amount of space than usual. Fewer or more body parts are used than normally." Ask, "What would it look like if you did a handshake with your foot or your knee? Show me a different way to handshake." Say, "Choose another greeting or goodbye gesture (not a handshake). Now stylize this gesture in at least two different ways."
Ask half the class to sit down while the other half performs.	Ask students to demonstrate their new gestures in two large groups.	Say, "Students on this side of the room sit down and watch how the other half has stylized their gestures."
	Make observations and reinforce different ways to stylize greeting or goodbye gestures.	Say, "I see the use of an elbow or head in your gesture. . . . I see how you made the gesture smaller . . . larger. . . ."
	Explain the next task.	Say, "The final task today is to select a greeting or goodbye gesture and stylize it the way we just practiced. Then you are going to add this gesture to your Sun Salutation. You may choose where in the series of poses you would like to add this gesture. As you move from a pose to your gesture and back to your pose, there should be clear intent and focus on how the hands, eyes, and your body move."
Ask students to practice their salutations.	Monitor student practice.	Provide encouragement or critique as needed.

Management	Teaching process	Teaching points and cues
New material *(continued)*		
b. Refinement activities (5 minutes) Ask students to pair off.	Ask students to pair off quickly in preparation for peer performance and evaluation.	Say, "Select a partner near you. One at a time, perform the Sun Salutation with your added stylized gesture. As your partner performs, watch carefully for clear intent and focus on how the hands, eyes, and body move. You are looking for concentration, quiet and steady flow of movement from one pose to the next. Concentration should not be broken. First partner, go!" Ask students to provide feedback to their partners.
Recap of lesson, cool-down		
(2 minutes) Ask students to stand in personal space.	Repeat the focus of the lesson.	Say, "Let's review one more time the origin and purpose of the Sun Salutation and this lesson." "In Hindu mythology, the sun god is worshipped as a symbol of health and immortal life. The Sun Salutation gives reverence to the internal sun (your inner spirit) as well as to the external sun (the sun that affects you from the outside in)."
Closure and assessment		
(3-5 minutes) Ask students to remain in personal space.	Direct students to end class with a final performance of their personalized Sun Salutations. Informal assessment is covered during partner feedback.	Say, "It is traditional to close a dance class with a form of reverence. Today the Sun Salutation will be our closure. Hold your concentration. You will perform at your own time. Remain still and quiet in your final pose until I tell you to look at me."
Ask students to sit in personal space.	Hand out journal folders or a piece of paper and pencil.	Say, "We're going to reflect about today's lesson. In one or two sentences, describe how practicing yoga today makes you feel. If you had the chance to practice the Sun Salutation outside of class what would be the best time of day for you?"

EXTENSIONS OR MODIFICATIONS

- Create a poem to complement the Sun Salutation.
- Add music to complement the movement.
- Add more than one stylized gesture.

ACCOMMODATION OR DIFFERENTIATION IDEAS   Students can develop their own Sun Salutations to accommodate their personal needs in terms of flexibility, strength, and balance.

EVERYDAY LIVING (LIFETIME WELLNESS) CONNECTIONS   Students keep a journal to record daily yoga practice.

Sun Salutation Handout

1 From Samasthiti (Mountain Pose), inhale and reach your hands up over your head, wide apart.

2 Stretch your arms and open the chest. Stretch your tailbone down toward the floor.

3 Exhale and press your palms together overhead, then down to your chest.

4 Inhale and press your fingertips toward the floor, then sweep them up over your head. Arch back gently, reaching out of the lower back.

5 Exhale and fold forward from your hips into Uttanasana (Forward Bend). Bend your knees if you need to, and relax from your neck to your tailbone.

6 Inhale and take a long step back with your right leg, coming into a lunge. Roll your shoulders back. Point your tailbone toward the floor and sink your hips lower than your front knee. Open your shoulders by pressing your hands toward the floor behind you.

7 Exhale and place your hands flat against the floor, shoulder-width apart. Step your left foot back, coming into a plank position.

8 On your next exhalation, bring your knees to the floor. Hug your elbows in to your sides and slowly lower your chest and chin to the floor, resting in Zen Asana.

9 Inhale and slide your chest forward and up, coming into Bhujangasana (Cobra Pose). Roll your shoulders open.

10 Curl your toes under and as you exhale, press firmly through your hands and lift your tailbone toward the sky into Adho Mukha Shvanasana (Downward-Facing Dog). Press your chest back toward your thighs. Roll your elbows down toward the floor. Breathe in Adho Mukha Shvanasana for five to eight breaths.

11 Inhale and step your right foot between your hands, coming back into a lunge with the left leg back. Open your shoulders by pressing your hands toward the floor behind you.

12 Exhale and step your left foot forward and fold into Uttanasana again.

13 Stretch your arms out to your sides and inhale as you lift your torso upright. Reach your hands above your head and press your palms together.

14 Exhale and bring your hands down in front of your chest.

From National Dance Association, 2010, *Implementing the national dance education standards* (Champaign, IL: Human Kinetics). Adapted, by permission, from K.L. Kappmeier and D.M. Ambrosini, 2006, *Instructing hatha yoga* (Champaign, IL: Human Kinetics), 69.

Students will select a theme based upon their perception of preselected photographs, and then choreograph and perform a "snapshot dance." Based on 45-minute sessions, this learning experience may be done in one or two sessions (see the following table for teacher instructions).

GRADE LEVEL   Grades 6 to 8

MATERIALS, EQUIPMENT, SPACE NEEDED

- An envelope for each group of four or five students (e.g., six envelopes for a class of 30 students).
- Six photographs per envelope that reflect themes like power, conflict, joy, sorrow, unity, fear, and so on. Each packet should contain two of the same photographs and four different photographs.
- Index card with assigned group theme included in each envelope.
- Handout for peer assessment with the following headings: Group number, Overall meaning of the dance, Describe one element of the dance that helped you decide the meaning. Teacher rubric for the student observation should be placed on the bottom of the handout page (see page 188 for the rubric).
- Pencils for each student.
- Accompaniment for improvisation.

NATIONAL STANDARDS ADDRESSED

Content Standard 1. Identifies and demonstrates movement elements and skills in performing dance (Benchmarks: Body d, Space f)

Content Standard 2. Understands choreographic principles, processes, and structures (Benchmarks: a, b, c)

Content Standard 3. Understands dance as a way to create and communicate meaning (Benchmarks: c, d)

Content Standard 4. Applies and demonstrates critical and creative thinking skills in dance (Benchmark: c)

Content Standard 7. Makes connections between dance and other disciplines (Benchmark: e)

GOAL   To create a dance that is based on interpretation of visual images.

OBJECTIVES   As a result of participating in this learning experience, students will

1. transfer spatial pattern from the visual to the kinesthetic. [Psychomotor]
2. demonstrate and describe the different meanings evoked by specific body designs and movement choices (e.g., low, round shape: fear or repose; high, angular shape: defiance or power; symmetrical shape: harmony). [Cognitive]
3. appreciate the body as a tool of expression and communication. [Affective]

Learning and applying proper dance technique allows dancers to feel the strength of their movements, while preventing injury.

VOCABULARY

Improvisation   Transition

Level   Phrase

Dynamics

EXTENSIONS OR MODIFICATIONS

- Extend the visual images to include works of art.
- Ask students to create their own visual images.
- Add musical accompaniment selected by the students or by you.

TECHNOLOGY CONNECTIONS

- Ask students to use the Internet to find visual images to incorporate into the learning experience.
- Record student performances for teacher or student assessment.

TEACHER INSTRUCTIONS FOR SNAPSHOTS IN MOTION

Management	Teaching process	Teaching points and cues
Introduction		
(3-5 minutes) Ask students to sit in their assigned personal spaces.	Introduce focus of the lesson.	Ask, "How do we use the human body to communicate an idea or feeling?"
	Encourage students' oral response to the question.	Ask, "How does your whole body react when you are feeling . . . ?" "What shape do you make with your body, when you are feeling . . . ?" "What level do you take? Do you move fast or slow, do you move light or strong . . . ?"
Review of previous material, warm-up		
(10 minutes) Review previous material students have had experience with: shape, space, time, and dynamics. During the warm-up improvisation, have students move freely around the room.	Direct a guided improvisation.	Say, "Walk your own pathway without touching anyone. Walk slowly; increase your speed and then freeze. Stretch high, wide, low, sideways, forward, and backward. Sink to the floor slowly and smoothly. Rise suddenly and freeze in a straight-line shape."
	Extend the improvisation by asking for different locomotor movements, dynamics, different body facings, pathways, and so on.	
New material		
a. **Exploratory activities** (15-20 minutes) Divide students into small groups of four or five.	Assign one of the following words to each group: power, conflict, joy, sorrow, unity, fear. Ask students to create shapes that represent the word. On your signal, students simultaneously create their own shapes and freeze in position. (If the responses are not clear, coach and provide more specific cues.)	Say, "Each group has been assigned a word. Using your whole body, create a shape that reflects the meaning of the word. Each member of your group does his or her own shape. You will perform your shape when I say, Ready, Go!"
	Identify one student from each group whose shape represents the clearest interpretation of the assigned word. Ask these students to perform simultaneously in front of the class as a group.	Say, "On my signal, repeat your shape and freeze."

Management	Teaching process	Teaching points and cues
New material *(continued)*		
	Ask students not presenting their shapes to sit quietly and become the audience.	Say, "As you watch, think about how the performers' bodies are communicating different meanings." Ask, "What shapes do you see?" (e.g., curved, twisted, low, high, angular, circular)
	Ask selected students to perform their shapes.	
	Ask students to move back to their original groups and individually prepare three shapes that reflect the assigned word. Students will have 4 counts to move between their shapes. Students will freeze in their new shape for 4 counts. Students must then determine how they move from one shape to the next. Students will complete a movement phrase that reflects the meaning of the assigned word.	Say, "Make three new shapes that reflect your word. You will have 4 counts as you change from one shape to another. You must decide how you want to move between the frozen shapes. For example, you may want to change the timing, level, or dynamics. Your phrase will be Shape-Move-Shape-Move-Shape."
	Ask students to stay with their groups and to be seated when they are the audience.	Say, "Remain seated with your group. You will now share your phrases one group at a time."
b. Refinement activities (15-20 minutes)	Distribute one envelope per group and introduce the contents (photographs and index card) to the class.	Ask, "How do you feel when you look at these photographs? Do they have meaning for you? Think about how you would communicate the meaning in each photograph with your whole body."
	Ask students to discuss the meaning of the word on their index card.	Say, "As you discuss the meaning of the word on your card, identify which dynamic qualities would best reflect the meaning—for example, vibration, float, slash, thrust, dab."
	Ask students to study the photographs and discuss the meaning of each photograph in relation to the assigned group theme (word on index card).	Say, "Once you have looked at the photographs and discussed how they connect to the word on the card, arrange the photographs in an order that has meaning for you."
	Have students arrange the photographs in an order that will communicate the meaning of the word on the card. The shapes and movements that they create and link will make a dance.	Say, "Create shapes and movements that are based on your group's interpretation and ordering of the photographs. All group members will perform the same movements and shapes in unison."
	Have groups practice the dance to prepare for performance.	Say, "Make sure you can go through your dance exactly the same way twice."
	Assign each group a performance order number; groups will perform their dances one at a time. Distribute a handout and pencil to each student.	Say, "As you are watching each group perform, record one sentence to answer each question on the handout."

~ continued

Teacher Instructions for Snapshots in Motion ~ *continued*

Management	Teaching process	Teaching points and cues
Recap of lesson, cool-down		
(3-5 minutes)	Gather students close to you. Ask students to share written comments and observations from their hand-outs.	Say, "Now it's time to reflect and share our observations."
Closure and assessment		
(2-3 minutes) Rubric (criterion, evidence, scale—teacher, self, peer)	Make closing remarks.	Say, "Your comments reveal that dance can communicate by using different shapes, dynamics, timing, and levels."
	Students turn in observation forms at the end of class.	
	Use assessment methods: • Teacher assessment of group performance • Teacher assessment of student observation sheets	
	Teacher Composition Evaluation Checklist: Group Performance (one point each) _____ shape _____ dynamics changes _____ level changes _____ unison _____ timing changes Total 5 points (one point each) Teacher Evaluation: Student Response Handouts _____ No Clear Response _____ Limited Clarity in Response _____ Clarity of meaning and dynamics Total 3 points	

ACCOMMODATION OR DIFFERENTIATION IDEAS   Advanced students go beyond the basic shape-move-shape formula to create more complex combinations in their dances.

EVERYDAY LIVING (LIFETIME WELLNESS) CONNECTIONS   Movement expression is a form of release and contributes to stress reduction and a sense of well-being.

RESOURCE

Artsource

Music Center Education Division

717 West Temple Street, Suite 400

Los Angeles, CA 90012

Introduction to Ballet Technique

Students will understand the origin of ballet and develop skills in fundamental ballet technique at the barre, center floor, and across the floor. Based on 45-minute sessions, this learning experience may be accomplished in two or more sessions (see the following table for teacher instructions).

GRADE LEVEL   Grades 6 to 8

MATERIALS, EQUIPMENT, SPACE NEEDED

- Music for ballet class
- *Nutcracker* video or DVD and equipment to project portions of the performance
- *Nutcracker* soundtrack
- Ballet barre, chairs, or wall space for support.
- Blank paper, pencils
- Copies of History of Ballet (see page 194)

NATIONAL STANDARDS ADDRESSED

Content Standard 1. Identifies and demonstrates movement elements and skills in performing dance (Benchmarks: Body a, b, c, d; Relationships: b)

Content Standard 6. Makes connections between dance and healthful living (Benchmarks: b, d)

GOAL   The students will learn basic vocabulary (verbal and motor) of fundamental ballet techniques at the barre, in center floor, and traveling across the floor.

OBJECTIVES   As a result of participating in this learning experience, students will

1. demonstrate on cue first, second, and third positions; plié, relevé, tendu, sauté, chassé, and reverence. [Psychomotor and Cognitive]
2. recognize and apply safe movement practices in ballet technique. [Psychomotor and Cognitive]
3. develop an appreciation of basic building blocks of ballet as they contribute to an art form. [Affective]

VOCABULARY

First, Second, Third positions	Sauté
Plié and relevé	Chassé
Tendu	

EXTENSIONS AND MODIFICATIONS

- Students can learn more ballet vocabulary and practice combinations.
- Students can use the ballet vocabulary to create movement phrases.
- Students can use music from ballets such as the *Nutcracker, Swan Lake,* and *Cinderella.*

TECHNOLOGY CONNECTIONS

- Students can use Internet connections to research ballet history, choreographers, companies, and dancers.
- Record portions of the classes for student feedback and assessment.

ACCOMMODATION OR DIFFERENTIATION IDEAS

- Arm positions can be introduced for more experienced dance students.
- Tempo can be slowed for less experienced students.
- Special physical challenges can be included to motivate male students.

EVERYDAY LIVING (LIFETIME WELLNESS) CONNECTIONS   Students might be inspired to become conscious of bodily alignment. Stress the importance of body alignment in movement to avoid injury.

RESOURCES   Music can be selected from a variety of record and equipment catalogs or online sources.

TEACHER INSTRUCTIONS FOR INTRODUCTION TO BALLET TECHNIQUE

Management	Teaching process	Teaching points and cues
Introduction		
(3-5 minutes) Ask students to sit in a semicircle in front of the monitor or projection screen to watch the video.	Introduce the focus of the lesson. Distribute History of Ballet text to each student (see p. 194 for text).	Ask, "What is ballet?"
	Refer students to the History of Ballet text. Ask students to take turns reading aloud.	Ask, "Where do you think ballet started?" "Who do you think first danced ballet?"
	Show video clip.	Say, "Notice how clearly each step is executed. You will be learning some of the same movements that you see here."
New material		
Barre work (20-25 minutes) Assign students to places at the barre.	Introduce a standard ballet warm-up. The first time through, move slowly. As students become familiar with the material, they can proceed with music (use the *Nutcracker* soundtrack) as a regular warm-up. Start with 4 counts down and 4 counts up on pliés and relevés.	Say, "Face the barre with both hands on the barre, stand tall, feet parallel and together."
	Demonstrate and have students practice the following:	
	• Four pliés (bend both knees with heels remaining in contact with the floor)	Say, "Bend your knees so that they are over the third toes; keep your torso lifted and hips in place. As you bend the knees, think of the torso as a rubber band that stretches toward the ceiling."
	• Four relevés (a rise to the balls of the feet)	Say, "Press the balls of the feet into the floor as the heels rise, keeping the body suspended and tall. Roll through all parts of the feet."
	• Four pliés and relevés in combination	Say each action as the students move: bend, straighten, rise and lower.
	Count aloud.	Say, "Plié 2-3, straighten 2-3 . . . relevé 2-3 . . . lower 2-3."

Management	Teaching process	Teaching points and cues
Refinement activities		
(3-5 minutes)	Lead and verbally cue complete warm-up with music using the following order: • Four pliés • Four relevés • Four demi-pliés • Four relevés • Hold balance	Say, "I will coach you through a warm-up using the ballet movements we just learned. Listen carefully to when I cue you to change from one step to the next. Ready, go . . ." "Hold the relevé and balance quietly on both feet."
New material		
(10 minutes) Ask students to remain facing the barre.	Demonstrate and ask students to practice ballet foot positions:	
	• First position (legs turned out, heels together)	Say, "Standing in parallel position, keep your toes on the floor as you rotate the legs and feet to a 45-degree, turned-out position. This is First position."
	• Second position (legs turned out, heels apart)	Say, "Feet are at least hip-width apart for Second position."
	• Third position (legs turned out, instep of the working foot placed at the instep of the supporting foot)	Say, "Keep your legs together and hips facing forward. Place the instep of the right foot at the instep of the left foot. This is called Third position."
	Call out positions in random order for student recall.	Say, "I will say different positions for you to take so you can practice these important positions several times."
	Demonstrate and ask students to practice battement tendu (to stretch the foot and leg from a closed position to an open position along the floor and return it to its original position).	Say, "Tendu forward. Starting in First position, lead the leg out with heel; on returning, lead with the little toe. Keep the heel in alignment with the center line of the body." "Tendu side. Starting in First position, lead the leg out in the direction of the big toe. Close by leading with the heel (First or Third positions)."
	Helpful strategy: Throughout lesson, ask informal questions about each specific technique.	Say, "Stay connected to the floor with your big toe as you slide your left foot forward. Remember to lift your torso."
Refinement activities		
(10-15 minutes)	Demonstrate and lead teacher-directed tendu combination. (First position): • Right foot: four tendus front, four tendus side • Left foot: four tendus front, four tendus side • Repeat using two repetitions • Repeat using one repetition	Say, "We will do a tendu combination now starting from First position. I will call out each movement; listen carefully for the number of repetitions of each movement so you will be ready to change to the next direction. Ready? With the right foot, four tendus to the front, four tendus to side; with the left foot, four tendus front, four tendus side. Listen carefully: right foot two tendus front, two tendus side; repeat with the left foot: two tendus front and two to the side." "Now, start with right foot and do just one tendu forward, one side; left foot, one tendu forward, one side."

~ continued

Introduction to Ballet Technique

Teacher Instructions for Introduction to Ballet Technique ~ *continued*

Management	Teaching process	Teaching points and cues
Refinement activities *(continued)*		
	Demonstrate and lead teacher-directed tendu combination. (Third position): • Right foot: four tendus, close back • Left foot: four tendus, close back • Repeat using two repetitions • Repeat using one repetition on each side four times	Say, "Starting in Third position, we will do another tendu combination. As with the last combination, follow my verbal instructions. Beginning right, four tendus (close back); left foot, four tendus (close front); right foot, two tendus (close back); left foot, two tendus (close front); alternate right foot, one tendu; left foot, one tendu. Repeat singles once more for each foot."
	Demonstrate and lead teacher-directed repetitions of both tendu combinations.	Say, "We are going to practice both tendu combinations again. Follow along as I call out which foot to use and in what direction to do the tendu. The pattern will always be 4-4, 2-2, 1-1-1-1. Ready? With the right foot, four tendus to the front . . . " (and so on).
New material		
Center Floor (10-15 minutes) Ask students to move to assigned personal spaces.	Direct students to assigned personal spaces. Lead a body roll and stretch downward and upward to end in a relevé as a tension-release series for students.	Say, "Move to your assigned personal spaces." "We will stretch the back out and loosen your muscles while you follow my directions. Inhale, exhale, tuck chin, and roll down for 8 slow counts. Roll up in 8 slow counts. Stretch in relevé." Do two to four repetitions.
	Introduce sauté (a jump: two feet to two feet)	Say, "Your starting position for the sauté is from First position. A sauté is a jump from two feet to two feet staying in place." "When you do a sauté you plié before you push against the floor with your feet to go into the air. Soften the landing so you roll through your feet as if returning from a relevé. Bend your knees as you land and then straighten them as you finish the final sauté."
	Demonstrate and lead this combination: • Sauté First position • Plié, relevé • Plié, relevé • Plié, hold, hold, hold • Jump 1 • Jump 2 • Jump 3 • Jump 4	Say, "The combination is plié-relevé; plié-relevé; plié and hold, hold, hold. Then jump1, jump 2, jump 3, jump 4, and hold your finished position."
	Demonstrate and lead the same combination in Second position. Have students perform a minimum of two repetitions of each combination. Don't worry about arms until the footwork is mastered. Coach students to place the hands on hips for balance.	Say, "Now follow my cues. Repeat this sequence in First position, and then we will repeat the whole thing from Second position." Speak the combination rhythmically to match the accompaniment.

Management	Teaching process	Teaching points and cues
New material *(continued)*		
Traveling Organize class into lines for traveling across the floor.	Progression down the floor: Direct the class with locomotor steps, moving quickly from one to the next in the series, without lengthy instructions about how to execute the steps. Repeat the basic traveling patterns so each group goes across the floor at least two times (number of repetitions can be increased depending on time available and the need for repetition for students to accomplish material with recognizable technique.)	Say, "We will travel across the floor going the length of the room. Each group will start 4 counts after the group ahead of them. This is not a race. Stay in your line as you work on your proper technique. First we will use a normal forward walk down the length of the room, starting on the right foot. Then we'll repeat from opposite side, starting with the left foot." "Next, we will stylize the walk. Ballet walks (tendu front, step forward alternate feet). Begin with the right foot and travel the length of the room. Repeat from the opposite side, starting on the left foot."
On the last chassé series across the floor, cue students to stop so that they are spaced out in center floor.	Chassé (the chasing step). Cue with voice and use of the uneven rhythm of "long, short, long, short" and "1 and, 2 and" to aid students in keeping the rhythm.	Say, "Chassé is executed in an uneven rhythm. Begin with right foot using a forward gallop and travel the length of the room. Repeat from the opposite side, starting with the left foot: 1 and, 2 and; long, short, long, short."
Closure and reverence		
(3 minutes) Organize students in center floor personal space.	Lead lesson review: teacher-directed call and respond. Observe student responses in order to evaluate student progress.	Say, "We will do a very quick review of some of the positions and steps we learned today. I will say the step and position cue and give you the rhythm you should use when you show me each step. This is what the cues will sound like: "On the count of 3, show me a plié in First position." Ready? On the count of 3, • plié in First position and 1, 2, 3, and so on. • relevé in First position. • tendus in Third position.
	Explain reverence: closing combination that honors both the teacher's and students' participation in ballet class.	Say, "Reverence is expected to be performed at the closing of each class."
	Ask students to follow you in performing reverence.	Say, "Follow me as I lead you in the reverence. Step to the right, left foot behind right, deep bow. Then repeat to the left."
	Provide final comments about the discipline of ballet.	Say, "Precise execution of technique is essential for accessing the artistic qualities that convey meaning in ballet."
Assessment		
(10-15 minutes) Ask students to sit near the television monitor.	Distribute paper and pencils. Show video again and ask students to identify movements that they have done in class. Use freeze-pause and ask the students to identify each movement based on what they have learned in class.	Ask, "What movements did you see that we did in class?" "How are they different?"

The History of Ballet

Dance as an entertainment was common in the late 15th century and throughout the 16th century; it generally included a mixture of acrobatics, mime, speech, and song. The performances were created on a large scale for royalty and on a smaller scale as traveling shows for common people. Court entertainments often had political agendas. Aside from being used to show off the magnificence of the court, court dances were written and conceived as subtle propaganda. For instance, a dance may have been designed to flatter a visiting dignitary who was about to start negotiations of state, thereby giving him an idea of the host's intentions. Or, on the other hand, a dance could be used to threaten the dignitary by a show of strength.

Catherine de Medici took the art of court dance with her to France when she married King Henry II. During this time, the ballet *Comique de la Reine* was created at Catherine's command. It was an epic piece that lasted over five hours and was meant to celebrate the wedding of the duc de Joyeuse to Margaret of Lorraine. It was from this point that the history of ballet is commonly said to have begun. It was around this time that court ladies began participating in the dances that were at one time limited to men. Much like in Shakespearean drama, the lead female roles could only be played by men. The ladies' involvement amounted to little more than elaborate walking while creating complicated floor patterns. Any intricate footwork, turns, or jumps would have been impossible because the ladies wore cumbersome hooped dresses—and continued to wear that style of clothing into the 18th century. It wouldn't be until a century later that women's dance repertoire would consist of a greater variety of movements. Men, on the other hand, wore tights as part of everyday dress and thus had greater freedom to show off a well-turned-out leg and finely pointed foot, both of which soon became necessities in ballet.

One important figure in the history of ballet was King Louis XIV, who had a great influence in the transition of dance from a court entertainment to a professional occupation. Louis performed in the next popular ballet of the day, *La Nuit,* where he played the Sun King. His own love of dancing gave dance respectability and encouraged others to work at perfecting the art. His courtiers, politicians, and one particularly talented field marshal devoted much of their energy to dance and to achieving greater proficiency. This was a period when the great Molière created the subjects, and Lully and Beauchamps wrote the music. Molière's plays usually included dance scenes, and it was from him that ballet acquired an occasional touch of comedy.

Louis XIV's first formal act to establish ballet as a professional theatrical art occurred in 1661 when he created the Royal Academy of the Dance and its associated Royal Academy of Music. Then, with the addition of a dance school in 1671, the Paris Opéra became what we know today. Louis's last significant influence on dance came when he retired from dance in 1669 because he was too fat. Naturally, his court had to follow suit, and the field was now left open for professional dancers.

By the late 17th and early 18th centuries, the foundations of ballet were established. Ballet masters began to codify teaching, and some attempts were made at dance notation. In addition, costumes began to change to adapt to more intricate footwork, and the female dancer, or ballerina, began to move to a position of prominence. Until this time, there were many restrictions on the art of ballet. Free-flowing movements, jumps, and lifts were not socially acceptable. Variations in effect could only occur through a change in floor patterns or tempo. Ballet continued to be a combination of dance, singing, and music, with singing usually taking precedence. Female dancers, who didn't appear on the stage until 1681, had strict standards of dress to adhere to. Marie de Camargo, one of the first ballerinas, was famous for her quick and intricate footwork. To show off her footwork, she shortened her skirt just a few inches, but similar actions wouldn't be considered completely acceptable for another 50 years.

From National Dance Association, 2010, *Implementing the national dance education standards* (Champaign, IL: Human Kinetics).

Reprinted from http://www.geocities.com/Heartland/Prairie/4302/history.html. Author unknown.

In 1760, ballet masters began to question the restrictions placed on their art, unwanted restrictions from the days when ballet was part of the court with its rigid protocol. The greatest of these ballet masters was Jean Georges Noverre (1727). In his *Letters,* Noverre was the first to propose ideas that were central to the development of ballet as a serious art form. According to Craig Dodd in his *Ballet and Modern Dance* (1980), Noverre believed that ballet should be a means of expressing a dramatic idea through the perfect combination of dancing, drama, and character. Speech, either declaimed or sung, was discarded, as were restrictive wigs, masks, and cumbersome costumes. Noverre shared his ideas with many students, dancers, and choreographers of the time, but the one person who really put Noverre's ideas into practice was the great choreographer Dauberval. In the romantic comedy *La fille mal gardée* (The Wayward Daughter), Dauberval created a grand ballet about a young maiden living in the French 18th-century countryside. The young lady must choose a husband. The meddlesome mother wants her to choose a young, uninteresting fellow from a wealthy family. But the daughter wants to consider a handsome, penniless farmer. The ballet, first performed in Bordeaux, France in 1789, is recognized as one of the oldest and most important works in ballet history. *La fille mal gardée* has survived more than two hundred years through many revivals of the classic story.

From National Dance Association, 2010, *Implementing the national dance education standards* (Champaign, IL: Human Kinetics).
Reprinted from http://www.geocities.com/Heartland/Prairie/4302/history.html. Author unknown.

Square Hip-Hop

Students will execute four to six square dance calls, create a mini square dance in groups of four, review four to six hip-hop movements, and call their own square dance using four to six hip-hop movements. Based on 45-minute sessions, this learning experience may be accomplished in two to three sessions (see the following table for teacher instructions).

GRADE LEVEL Grades 6 to 8

MATERIALS, EQUIPMENT, SPACE NEEDED

- CD player
- Square dance music without calls, such as "Turkey in the Straw"
- Instrumental hip-hop music
- Armbands or stick-on tags to identify males from females

NATIONAL STANDARDS ADDRESSED

Content Standard 1. Identifies and demonstrates movement elements and skills in performing dance (Benchmarks: Body c, d; Space c; Relationships a, c; Time a)

Content Standard 2. Understands choreographic principles, processes, and structures (Benchmarks: b, e)

Content Standard 3. Understands dance as a way to create and communicate meaning (Benchmark: a)

Content Standard 4. Applies and demonstrates critical and creative thinking skills in dance (Benchmark: a)

Content Standard 5. Demonstrates and understands dance in various cultures and historical periods (Benchmark: b)

GOAL To create a square hip-hop dance in groups of four.

OBJECTIVES As a result of participating in this learning experience, students will

1. transfer spatial patterns from the visual to the kinesthetic. [Psychomotor]
2. demonstrate the ability to work with groups of varied size. [Affective]
3. memorize and reproduce movement sequences either teacher or student designed. [Cognitive]
4. work cooperatively in small groups. [Affective]

VOCABULARY

Do-Si-Do	Charlie Brown
Grand Right and Left	Chicken Head
Ladies Chain	Heel Toe
Pass Through	Harlem Shake
Swing (Partner)	Crip Walk
Star (Right, Left)	Snake

TEACHER INSTRUCTIONS FOR SQUARE HIP-HOP

Management	Teaching process	Teaching points and cues
Introduction		
(3-5 minutes) Have students sit in designated positions in a circle (circle formation defined by poly spots).	Introduce the focus of the lesson. Encourage student oral responses to the questions.	Ask, "What do you think square hip-hop means?" "How would you describe square dance? What kinds of named formations are in square dance?" "What kinds of spatial formations would you use in hip-hop?"
Review of previous material, warm-up		
(6-8 minutes)	Call four to six basic square dance steps.	Say, "Practice the following calls to review: • Circle to the right and to the left • Do-si-do your partner • Elbow swing your partner • Right-hand and left-hand star • All circle to the left • All to the center and back
	Ask four to six students to volunteer to demonstrate and name different hip-hop steps.	One at a time, have students model hip-hop steps; have the rest of the class follow.
New materials		
a. Exploratory activities (45-60 minutes) 1. Designate groups of four within the circle formation.	Distribute armbands or tags to distinguish male or female roles in the dance.	Say, "We're going to form groups of four in mini square dance formation."
2. Set up the first four correctly in mini square dance formation (couples are facing each other).	Go to each group of four and quickly check to see that they are in the correct position. (To deal with someone left without a partner, ask the student to dance with an imaginary partner temporarily and later switch that student into a complete group.)	Put the first group into proper formation as other students watch. Say, "Two students will face counterclockwise standing side by side. The next two will turn to face them (clockwise) so that they are facing and directly opposite the other couple." "Circle right. Stop in your home positions."
	Direct mini square dances using square dance calls.	Say, "In groups of four (mini squares), all join hands and circle to the left, then to the right. Face your partner, do-si-do your partner, passing right shoulders, and do-si-do your partner, passing left shoulders. Now do-si-do your opposite right shoulders."

~ continued

Teacher Instructions for Square Hip-Hop ~ *continued*

Management	Teaching process	Teaching points and cues
New materials (continued)		
3. Have students practice to traditional square dance music.	Call a mini square dance using the steps just reviewed in a random order. (Whenever you finish calling, students must always end up in home positions with their original partners.)	Say, "Join hands; move to the center and out again and in once more and back out to your places." "Face your partner and right elbow swing once around to your home position. Face your opposite and left elbow swing and return to your home position." "Now turn your right sides in to the center with your right arm out to the center; place your right hands on top of the others to form a right hand star. Hold that position and walk around once until you return to your home position. Now go back with your left hand star." (Use same cues: e.g., circle left, do-si-do your opposite, right elbow swing your partner, star left, circle to right to home position.)
	Have students plan a mini square dance using three different calls that they select from those just practiced. (Students will need to practice this several times.)	Say, "In your groups of four, you will create your own square dances using three calls from what we just practiced. After you select the calls, you will say them as a group while you are moving. For example, everyone circle right, and you will all say that together. You will change your call every 8 beats, and I will clap the rhythm for you." "You have 30 seconds to decide which three calls your group will use and in what order you will call them. Now I'm going to turn on the music. On my cue of 'Ready, begin,' be ready to call your square dance for your own group." (Because all students know the order of their own dance, remind students they do not need to shout out the calls.)
	Then ask one student in each group to call the dance.	Say, "Select one person to become your caller. That person will use the same calls and add one new call. The last call must always end with everyone in home position. Ready, begin!"
	Then ask the remaining three members of the group to each take a turn calling.	Say, "Now we will take turns so that every member of your group gets to be the caller."

Management	Teaching process	Teaching points and cues
New materials (continued)		
	Extend vocabulary to include the grand right and left and the ladies or "people's" chain. Demonstrate with a pair how to revolve side by side 180 degrees counterclockwise.	Say, "In your mini square position (couples facing opposite each other), the person on the right of each pair raise your right hand. Look and turn to the person who has a hand raised in your set. Reach across with your right hands toward each other, walk forward, and join hands. Walk past each other, passing right shoulders until you've changed places. After you have exchanged places, make sure that you have turned so that you are facing into the center of the set."
	Provide direction. To complete this call and return home, the ladies must repeat the right-hand pull across pattern and pinwheel turn with their partners to return to the original home position. All sets practice the ladies chain.	Say, "Watch as we demonstrate how to do the next part of the ladies ("people's") chain." "Now that you know the formation and call, you don't have to raise your hand each time! Just reach your hand diagonally across and go!"
	Direct the grand right and left.	Say, "Now we will learn the grand right and left. Turn to face your partner. As we do this, you will continue in this direction until you return home and you're with your own partner again." "Reach your right hands toward each other and join hands. Walk past each other. Don't let go of your partner's hand yet. You should now be facing a new person." (Check to make sure students are facing correct directions.) "Reach your left hand out to the new person and let go of your partner's hand. Keeping left hands joined, walk past each other. You should end up facing your partner once again. Repeat right-hand and left-hand passing by, and you will end up in your home position."
	Instruct individual callers to add either ladies chain or grand right and left as they call the dance for their group.	Say, "Each group chooses one person to be your caller. This person will add either the ladies chain or the grand right and left to the sequence of calls used before. Each mini square dance will have four calls."

~ continued

Teacher Instructions for Square Hip-Hop ~ *continued*

Management	Teaching process	Teaching points and cues
New materials (continued)		
4. Ask students to remain in mini squares.	Quickly review the four to six hip-hop steps.	Say, "Let's review our hip-hop steps. Show me a chicken head, show me the Charlie Brown . . ." "Everyone freeze and sit down right where you are except this group in front of me. You'll stay standing. Tell me one of the square dance calls you learned . . . (students respond . . . do-si-do). Now tell me one of the hip-hop steps you just did . . . (students respond . . . Charlie Brown). This group will demonstrate how we can put together two very different dance forms to create a new dance style! Using the Charlie Brown to travel, the dancers will perform a do-si-do your partner."
	Play square dance music softly in the background as students develop their dances. At some point, change the music to an instrumental hip-hop song.	Say, "Now we've seen how to put together hip-hop and square dance. With your group, create your own square hip-hop. Use at least four different hip-hop steps and four different square dance calls."
	Have students quickly perform their square hip-hop dances one group at a time.	Say, "We will perform these dances for each other."
b. Refinement activities (10 minutes) Have groups stop practicing. Students remain seated with their group.	Direct students to practice refinements, present the final performance, and engage in group sharing.	Ask, "What steps in your dance need to be changed to make your dance more professional?" Say, "Make one or two changes or adjustments to make your dance clearer to an audience."
Recap of lesson, cool-down		
(3-5 minutes) Ask students to remain seated as an audience.	Ask students to reflect on their work.	Say, "Let's reflect on how we created a new dance style blending hip-hop steps and square dance."
Closure and assessment		
(3-5 minutes) Rubric (criterion, evidence, scale— teacher, self, peer)	Teacher Assessment: Students have incorporated four to six hip-hop steps with four to six square dance calls. Group 1 _____ 4 to 6 hip-hop steps _____ 4 to 6 square dance calls Group 2 _____ 4 to 6 hip-hop steps _____ 4 to 6 square dance calls	
	Student Assessment: Ask students to respond to questions.	Ask, "In your dance, what hip-hop steps worked best with the square dance calls? Why?"

EXTENSIONS OR MODIFICATIONS

- Individual callers can be exchanged between groups so students have to listen and react to a new caller and a new set of calls.
- Before the hip-hop activity, the teacher can be the caller for the class and use calls in a varied sequence.
- Two groups of four can dance together and combine their calls to create a longer sequence.
- One partner set can switch from each group to create a new mini square. Calls are exchanged to create a new pattern.

TECHNOLOGY CONNECTION   Students watch a video of an authentic square dance with costumes and music. Students discuss the possibilities of creating a recording of square hip-hop. Students discuss any special considerations for making their own video.

ACCOMMODATION OR DIFFERENTIATION IDEAS   For special needs populations, the music must be longer or slower, as needed. Space to do the figures must be larger. Differentiating instruction for more advanced dancers can include more complex square dance calls and the creation of longer sequences.

EVERYDAY LIVING (LIFETIME WELLNESS) CONNECTIONS

- The teacher provides information about square dance clubs within the community.
- Have students wear pedometers to count their steps during class.
- Ask students to periodically check their heart rates while dancing.

RESOURCES

- A. Pittman, M. Waller, and K. Dark. (2009). *Dance Awhile: A Handbook for Folk, Square, Contra, and Social Dance.* San Francisco, CA: Benjamin Cummings/Prentice Hall.
- S. Davis and C. West. (2001). *Recreational Folk Dance.* Dubuque, IA: Kendall Hunt Publishing.
- *Learn to Hip Hop,* Vol. 2, VHS. (2003 release). Joe's World Foundation (www.joesworld.org).

Rhythmic Patterns Into Aerobic Routines

This experience starts with everyday locomotor movements, combines two locomotor movements to create rhythmic patterns, and expands them into rhythmic aerobic dance routines. Based on 45-minute sessions, this lesson may be accomplished in one to two sessions (see the following table for teacher instructions).

GRADE LEVEL   Grades 6 to 8

MATERIALS, EQUIPMENT, SPACE NEEDED

- Two-page handout with step description for Skip Its (rhythmic aerobic routine; see pages 211-212)
- Variety of 4/4 time music with strong underlying beats, such as "We are Family" by Sister Sledge (for Skip Its) and "Ring My Bell" by Anita Ward (for creating own rhythmic aerobic routine). Both songs are from the album *Sounds of the Seventies: '70s Dance Party 1979* for Time-Life Music by Warner Special Products.
- CD player
- Open area

NATIONAL STANDARDS ADDRESSED

Content Standard 1. Identifies and demonstrates movement elements and skills in performing dance (Benchmarks: Body d, Space c, Relationships c)

Content Standard 2. Understands choreographic principles, processes, and structures (Benchmarks: c, d)

Content Standard 4. Applies and demonstrates critical and creative thinking skills in dance (Benchmark: a)

Content Standard 6. Makes connections between dance and healthful living (Benchmarks: a, d)

GOALS   To explore even and uneven rhythmic patterns; learn a prechoreographed, 32-count aerobic dance routine; and then create an original, small-group rhythmic aerobic routine.

OBJECTIVES   As a result of participating in this learning experience, students will

1. execute a 32-count routine to music. [Psychomotor]
2. know the difference between low-impact and high-impact aerobic movements, and how to make an activity aerobic. [Cognitive]
3. participate in the activities and cooperate within a small group to create an original group dance that satisfies the criteria. [Affective]

VOCABULARY

Even-rhythmic patterns: Either a weight change (whether from one foot to the other or from one foot to the same foot); a non–weight change action (e.g., kick, tap, heel dig, clap) getting equal value, such as walking that coincides with each whole count or beat of a measure (e.g., 1, 2, 3, 4); or running or stepping double-time with a weight change coinciding with each whole and half count or beat (e.g., 1 and 2 and 3 and 4 and).

Uneven-rhythmic patterns: Weight changes or actions that do not correspond with each beat of the music, either by holding select counts (for example, stepping on the first beat of each two beats of music) or by adding weight changes or steps in between selected whole beats or counts of the music (for example, 1-and, 2; also called a triple, or shuffle step).

Low-impact aerobic movements: Those movements where at least one foot is on the floor at all times, for example when walking.

High-impact aerobic movements: Those movements where both feet are off the floor momentarily, for example when executing a hop, leap, jump, run, skip, slide, or gallop.

Aerobic activity: Activities that produce cardiovascular endurance benefits. These benefits occur after a minimum of 10 to 12 minutes of continuous movements, for example, by keeping the feet moving. Start with a few minutes, then gradually add minutes to build cardiovascular endurance.

TEACHER INSTRUCTIONS FOR RHYTHMIC PATTERNS INTO AEROBIC ROUTINES

Management	Teaching process	Teaching points and cues
Introduction		
(5 minutes) Ask students to sit on the floor in a semicircle around you.	Ask, "How many like to listen to music? Do you like to move to music, too? Let's start by listening for the beat, which can be counted in whole numbers."	Explain: • Each measure of music (in 4/4 time) has four beats. • With a time signature of 4/4, the numerator represents the number of beats per measure, while the denominator indicates that each quarter note gets one count (students can count in sets of four to identify the measure).
Have students practice identifying 4 counts or beats. Gradually move to four sets of 8 counts to equal a 32-count phrase.	Say, "If we pat on the first beat of each measure, then we pat on the first count of each four counts. Try the following while seated: a. Listen to the music. With one hand, pat your fingers on your thigh on the first count of each set of four beats. b. Listen to the music and pat your fingers on your thigh on the first count of each set of 8 beats or counts."	Observe: • Observe students tap only on count 1, the downbeat, and hold for three more counts. • Observe students tap only on count 1, the downbeat, and hold for 7 more counts (grouping two measures together, which is a short phrase of music).
Have students stand in a semicircle and do something on each count or beat of the music.	Have students try the following while standing: a. Nonlocomotor sequence: • Snap fingers four times (4 counts) • Tap foot four times (4 counts) • Clap hands four times (4 counts) • Flap elbows four times (4 counts)	• Observe whether students can keep the actions to the tempos played. If students have difficulty, slow down tempo by using vocal counts and no music, slowly speeding up until the pattern can be executed at the desired tempo.
	b. March in place to beat or counts, then make a square: • March 8 counts forward • Make a quarter turn right and march 8 counts • Repeat until facing front wall again Keep counts (and feet) continuously matching the tempo.	• Observe students stepping or walking on each whole count to complete the square floor path.

~ continued

Rhythmic Patterns Into Aerobic Routines

Teacher Instructions for Rhythmic Patterns Into Aerobic Routines ~ *continued*

Management	Teaching process	Teaching points and cues
Warm-up		
(10 minutes) Have students start in a scattered formation using personal space, then travel in general space and stay within defined lines.	Say, "When walking to a beat or a count, the pace is external; that is, you need to move at the tempo of the music or counts called. Notice what part(s) of your foot hits the floor as you walk."	• Start slowly counting in eights and cue students to change direction prior to count 1. • Ask students which part of the foot hits the floor on the whole count as weight shifts from one foot to the other: heel, ball, or toe? (the ball of the foot) • Ask students where body weight should be on each whole count: back with heel forward, over heel, or over ball of foot? (over ball of foot)
	After students have heard the tempo with "5, 6, 7, 8," start them walking in general space without touching or bumping into anyone else while stepping on each whole count. After each 8 counts, change direction.	• Vary the task by counting in eights and selecting different locomotor movements (e.g., jump, hop, leap, skip, and so on). Repeat each move eight times.
	Now have students change direction after each four counts.	• Vary the task by counting in fours and selecting different locomotor movements.
	Still using four counts, ask students to try combining a walk for three counts, then adding a different locomotor movement on count 4. This is another way to accent count 4. Say, "Perhaps you can add your arms somehow (such as lifting them in the air or to the sides) or clap on count 4, too?"	• Select from the following to repeat multiple times before starting another combination: three walks and a hop, three walks and a jump, three walks and a leap, or other similar patterns. • Observe how students accent count 4. Share ideas with the class.
New material		
(15-25 minutes) a. Have students use scattered formation to explore the moves and decipher one way to annotate movement.	Skip Its (aerobic routine) Say, "Without consulting anyone else, read the step description and try to do this dance on your own." (See handout on pages 211-212)	Hand out the Skip Its example (two pages) for a 32-count rhythmic aerobic routine.
Have students use scattered formation, all facing the music and in personal space.	Say, "After walking through it, slowly try it all together. Notice the number of weight changes used in part A versus in part B of this routine." (Part A uses two weight changes per whole count [uneven-rhythmic patterns], while part B uses one weight change or action for each whole count [even-rhythmic patterns].)	Explain: • Part A uses a skip and a slide, which are both uneven rhythmic movements—they require two weight changes (i.e., ball of foot hits floor on count 1; hop to land or hit the floor on the "and"). • Part B uses a walk, jump, and a twist action. Observe students as they execute each move only on the whole counts (one weight change or hitting the floor with each count; jump needs to land on both feet). The twist action has weight on balls of both feet.
	Ask students to try the routine to a slow tempo, for example, "We Are Family" by Sister Sledge.	Gradually build cardiovascular endurance by having students repeat the routine at least four times, then for the length of a song.

Management	Teaching process	Teaching points and cues
New material *(continued)*		
	Say, "Now the challenge. Start the routine with the left foot in order to be ambidextrous; you never know which side of the body the choreography will use, so this is good practice! Now alternate your starting foot when executing the routine by executing it first with the right foot, then with the left foot."	After a few trials, confirm students understand how the directions change when starting with the opposite foot.
		Encourage students to add their arms somehow as they do the movements.
(30-60 minutes) b. Preassign students in small groups of four to six each, and place group numbers on the walls to create stations. Group students in a semicircle around you to discuss the assignment.	Create Your Own Rhythmic Aerobic Routine Say, "Notice your group number and read over the assignment. Then let's discuss it before you move to that station to get started."	Distribute the Practical Application handout (see page 207) and go over the assignment.
Rotate to each group to clarify that the criteria are being met, then to encourage use of arms and having fun with the moves. Finally, encourage students to transition from their ending formation back to their starting formation in time to repeat their entire 32-count rhythmic routine at least four consecutive times—which takes some practice!		Note that the assignment puts the even-rhythmic patterns in part A and the uneven-rhythmic patterns in part B (the opposite of what they did in Skip Its). Students often don't notice that they need to control their movements from part A to part B. The first part (A) is slow, then the second part is fast (B), then part A is slow again, and so on. The high-impact moves (uneven-rhythmic patterns) are more vigorous with two weight changes with one or both feet hitting the floor on each half count.
Cool-down		
(3 minutes) Remind students to use general space without bumping into anyone else and to use personal space without touching anyone else.	Ask students to walk slowly in general space at their own pace and slowly stretch muscles used.	Provide directions: • Slow down moves and slowly stretch arms as you walk slowly. • Hold stretches 20 to 30 seconds each.
Closure		
(2 minutes) Group students in semicircle around you and select questions to ask.	Ask, "What is the difference between an even-rhythmic pattern and an uneven-rhythmic pattern?" "Which is the best option if you want to do a low-impact routine?" "Who might need to use a low-impact option?" "Why are the uneven-rhythmic patterns in the Skip Its considered high impact?" "What makes a routine aerobic?" "How can you increase intensity?"	Note number of weight changes in relationship to the beat or count (should be either more or fewer weight changes than beats [for uneven; typically high impact]; one weight change or action for each beat [for even; typically low impact]). Explore definitions of cardiovascular endurance and benefits, especially the importance of keeping feet moving for longer periods of time (duration) and the option of adding arms at either middle or high levels (intensity).

EXTENSIONS OR MODIFICATIONS

- Decrease difficulty by selecting shorter routines; for example, use only part B of the Skip Its routine (which is also low impact) or only 16-count routines (versus 32-count routines).

- Increase difficulty by executing the Skip Its routine in a contra formation. Split class into two long lines; pair the lines up so that each student is facing across from a partner and is about eight giant steps away. Designate one line as Apples and the other line as Oranges. Have students move forward toward their partners for the first 4 counts of the routine. Randomly select one line to start on the right foot, while the other line starts on the left foot to execute Skip Its with one difference. During the last 8 counts (measures 7 and 8), the Apples become leaders so that anything they do for these 8 counts should be mirrored by the partners opposite. On the second repetition of Skip Its, the Oranges become the leaders (measures 7 and 8) so that the opposite partners have to mirror whatever the Oranges do for these 8 counts. Encourage unusual arm movements or any fun, free-choice movements during these 8 counts. Call out the leaders by their names—Apples or Oranges—to remind them. Try music with a faster tempo, such as "Ring My Bell" by Anita Ward.

TECHNOLOGY CONNECTION   Ask students to use a Word file, create a table, and describe their own rhythmic aerobic routines (similar to the Skip Its step description that they used in class). Or, ask them to design other ways of annotating their dances using computer software or drawings.

ACCOMMODATION OR DIFFERENTIATION IDEAS

- Gradually increase the tempo (speed) of the counts called until the class can match the tempo of the selected music.

- Vary the music for variety and to add practice with different musical songs (keep students' focus on listening for the underlying rhythm typically given by the drum beat versus the lyrics of the song, or the melody).

EVERYDAY LIVING (LIFETIME WELLNESS) CONNECTIONS   Aerobic routines are fun ways to improve the fitness of the heart and lungs. Putting together everyday locomotor movements is an enjoyable way to build cardiovascular endurance.

ASSESSMENT AND RUBRICS

- See the Practical Application handout describing criteria and rubrics for creating, presenting, and observing at least two other groups' use of different locomotor movements used in combination for parts A and B.

- See Master Observation Sheet on page 210, which can be used when guiding the small groups of four to six students to ensure that they know—and so others can recognize—the difference between even and uneven locomotor movements used to satisfy the criteria. Give students enough time to modify routines, as needed, in order to be successful at meeting the criteria prior to performing their routine.

Example: Skip Its

Part A: Uneven-Rhythmic Patterns

	Count #1	Count #2	Count #3	Count #4
Measure # a. List locomotor movement(s) corresponding to each count. b. List direction for each count. c. List weight changes (left or right) corresponding to each count.	Skip Forward (Fwd) Right (R) on both (Counts "1-and")	Skip Fwd Left (L) on both (Counts "2-and")	Skip Fwd R (Counts "3-and")	Skip Fwd L (Counts "4-and")
Measure #2 a. List locomotor movement(s) corresponding to each count. b. List direction for each count. c. List weight changes (left or right) corresponding to each count.	Slide Right side R (Count 1), L (Count "and")	Slide Right side R (Count 2), L (Count "and")	Slide Right side R (Count 3), L (Count "and")	Slide Right side R (Count 4)
Measure #3 a. List locomotor movement(s) corresponding to each count. b. List direction for each count. c. List weight changes (left or right) corresponding to each count.	Skip Backward (Bwd) L on "1-and"	Skip Bwd R on "2-and"	Skip Bwd L on "3-and"	Skip Bwd R on "4-and"
Measure #4 a. List locomotor movement(s) corresponding to each count. b. List direction for each count. c. List weight changes (left or right) corresponding to each count.	Slide Left side L (Count 1), R (Count "and")	Slide Left side L (Count 2), R (Count "and")	Slide Left side L (Count 3), R (Count "and")	Slide Left side L (Count 4)

~ continued

From National Dance Association, 2010, *Implementing the national dance education standards* (Champaign, IL: Human Kinetics).

~ continued

Part B: Even-Rhythmic Patterns

	Count #1	Count #2	Count #3	Count #4
Measure #5 a. List locomotor movement(s) and how they correspond to each count. b List direction for each count. c. List weight change (left or right) corresponding to each count.	Walk Fwd R	Walk Quarter turn in place L	Walk Fwd R	Walk Quarter turn in place L
Measure #6 a. List locomotor movement(s) and how they correspond to each count, b. List direction for each count. c. List each weight change (left or right) corresponding to each count.	Walk Fwd R	Walk Quarter turn in place L	Walk Fwd R	Walk Quarter turn in place L
Measure #7 a. List locomotor movement(s) and how they correspond to each count. b. List direction for each count. c. List each weight change (left or right) corresponding to each count.	Jump In place Both feet have weight (land together)	Jump In place Both feet have weight	Jump In place Both feet have weight	Jump In place Both feet have weight
Measure #8 a. List locomotor movement(s) and how they correspond to each count. b. List direction for each count. c. List each weight change (left or right) corresponding to each count.	Twist In place Both feet have weight	Twist In place Both feet have weight	Twist In place Both feet have weight	Twist In place Both feet have weight (end with weight more on L)

 From National Dance Association, 2010, *Implementing the national dance education standards* (Champaign, IL: Human Kinetics).

Name _____ Date _____ Group _____

Practical Application: Rhythmic Patterns Into Aerobic Routines

Group Problem to Solve

As a group exercise leader, you've been asked to create a group aerobic routine that is 32 counts long (using a typical structure of 4 sets of 8 counts, or 8 sets of 4 counts) with the following criteria:

Part A: Even-Rhythmic Patterns: two sets of 8 counts or four measures of 4 counts

For the first two measures (first set of 8 counts), combine two locomotor movements from the following list (walk, run, jump, hop, or leap) to create an even-rhythmic pattern that fits the music. Your combination needs to be easily repeated to the music by all group members. Select a starting formation for your group.

For measures 3 and 4 (second set of 8 counts), combine two locomotor movements from the list given previously to create a different even-rhythmic pattern that fits the music. Consider varying the direction, adding a turn, or changing the group's formation to make this second set of 8 counts unique.

Part B: Uneven-Rhythmic Patterns: two sets of 8 counts or four measures of 4 counts

For measures 5 and 6 (third set of 8 counts), combine two locomotor movements from the following list (skip, slide, or gallop) to create an uneven-rhythmic pattern that fits the music.

For measures 7 and 8 (fourth set of 8 counts), vary your combination of two locomotor movements from measures 5 and 6 in order to create a different uneven-rhythmic pattern that fits the music. Consider varying the direction or the order of the movements selected, adding a turn, or changing the group's formation to make this fourth set of 8 counts unique.

Your last measure needs to easily transition into the first measure in order to repeat the entire routine to the music, so plan how you will get back to your starting position and formation.

Complete the following tables.

Part A: Even-Rhythmic Patterns

	Count #1	Count #2	Count #3	Count #4
Measure #1 a. List locomotor movement(s) and how they correspond to each count. b. List direction for each count. c. List weight change (left or right) corresponding to each count.				

~ continued

~ continued

Part A: Even-Rhythmic Patterns *(continued)*

	Count #1	Count #2	Count #3	Count #4
Measure #2 a. List locomotor movement(s) and how they correspond to each count. b. List direction for each count. c. List each weight change (left or right) corresponding to each count.				
Measure #3 a. List locomotor movement(s) and how they correspond to each count. b. List direction for each count. c. List each weight change (left or right) corresponding to each count.				
Measure #4 a. List locomotor movement(s) and how they correspond to each count. b. List direction for each count. c. List each weight change (left or right) corresponding to each count.				
Part B: Uneven-Rhythmic Patterns				
Measure #5 a. List locomotor movement(s) corresponding to each count. b. List direction for each count. c. List weight changes (left or right) corresponding to each count.				

Part B: Uneven-Rhythmic Patterns *(continued)*

	Count #1	Count #2	Count #3	Count #4
Measure #6 a. List locomotor movement(s) corresponding to each count. b. List direction for each count. c. List weight changes (left to right) corresponding to each count.				
Measure #7 a. List locomotor movement(s) corresponding to each count. b. List direction for each count. c. List weight changes (left to right) corresponding to each count.				
Measure #8 a. List locomotor movement(s) corresponding to each count. b. List direction for each count. c. List weight changes (left or right) corresponding to each count.				

Group Presentation

Select one group member to cue the group when to start. Practice until your group can repeat the entire 32-count routine at least four times. Make sure you have a definite starting formation and relate in some way to the other group members during the dance.

Two groups at a time will demonstrate their aerobic routine while the others watch and complete the following observation sheet for at least two different groups.

GROUP OBSERVATION SHEET

Group number	Starting formation	Two locomotor movements used in part A	Two locomotor movements used in part B	Outstanding feature

~ continued

From National Dance Association, 2010, *Implementing the national dance education standards* (Champaign, IL: Human Kinetics).

~ continued

Assessment Items

Even-rhythmic patterns within part A

_____Meet criteria for measures 1 and 2 (4 points)

_____Meet criteria for measures 3 and 4 (4 points)

Uneven-rhythmic patterns within part B

_____Meet criteria for measures 5 and 6 (4 points)

_____Meet criteria for measures 7 and 8 (4 points)

Observation of two different groups

_____Accurately identifies four different locomotor movements used (4 points)

Total: _____ (20 possible points for Practical Application: Rhythmic Patterns Into Aerobic Routines)

MASTER OBSERVATION SHEET

Group number	Starting formation	Two locomotor movements used in part A	Two locomotor movements used in part B	Outstanding feature
1				
2				
3				
4				
5				
6				
7				
8				

From National Dance Association, 2010, *Implementing the national dance education standards* (Champaign, IL: Human Kinetics).

This learning experience is planned for work within class, independent work out of class, work in a computer lab that has been reserved by the teacher for use by dance class students for research and other preparation, and studio work in choreography and final presentation.

Students will

- view a piece of visual art and describe what they see;

- identify at least four elements of visual art;

- view excerpts from Bella Lewitzsky's "Impressions #2" (Vincent Van Gogh);

- identify elements of art and dance seen in the Lewitzsky dance;

- select a piece of visual art from four to six examples exhibited in the classroom gallery that will be the basis for Internet research about the painter and the painting genre;

- create a PowerPoint presentation with two or three peers that includes bullet points about the artist, the ideas behind the painting, and three to five elements of visual art that are dominant;

- compose a short dance (working in the same groups that created the PowerPoint presentation) based on their interpretation of the painting and using a minimum of three elements of visual art within the painting (e.g., line, dynamics, texture, intensity, patterns); and

- make a class (small-group) presentation with the PowerPoint material followed by the dance based upon the same painting.

Based on 45-minute sessions, this learning experience may be accomplished in two or more sessions (see the table on page 215 for teacher instructions).

GRADE LEVEL   Grades 6 to 8 (best for grades 7 to 8)

MATERIALS, EQUIPMENT, SPACE NEEDED

- Copy of Van Gogh's painting *Starry Night* (large enough for the class to see easily from a distance)

- Copy (video) of Bella Lewitzsky's work based on Van Gogh's *Starry Night* (this may be obtained by going to the Artsource Web site: www.musiccenter.org/education/artsource_dance.html#impressions)

- Studio (dance classroom) gallery with one well-known example of each of the following artists: Dali, Picasso, Degas, Da Vinci, Klee, Magritte, Monet

- Computer lab equipment (software and hardware, including an LCD unit) appropriate for research and for creating a PowerPoint presentation for small-group projects

- Accompaniment options (CDs) for student choreography project

- Chalk board or white board, chalk, appropriate pens

- Visual art, dance, and technology handouts for entire class (see page 218)

- Peer evaluation rubric copies for entire class, enough to match total number of groups (see page 219)

- Pencils for peer evaluation

NATIONAL STANDARDS ADDRESSED

Content Standard 1. Identifies and demonstrates movement elements and skills in performing dance (Benchmarks: Body d; Space c; Relationships a, c; Time a; Effort c)

Content Standard 2. Understands choreographic principles, process, and structures (Benchmarks: c, f)

Content Standard 3. Understands dance as a way to create and communicate meaning (Benchmarks: c, d, h)

Content Standard 4. Applies and demonstrates critical and creative thinking skills in dance (Benchmark: d)

Content Standard 7. Makes connections between dance and other disciplines (Benchmarks: a, d, e)

GOAL   Create a PowerPoint presentation (group work) about a selected artist and a selected painting to be presented to the class preceding the performance of a group-choreographed short dance (with a definite beginning, middle, and end) that uses the research-based materials as its impetus or stimulus.

OBJECTIVES   As a result of participating in this learning experience, students will

1. create a project that reveals the similarities and differences between dance and another art form. [Psychomotor, Cognitive]
2. appreciate the body as a tool for communication and expression. [Affective]

VOCABULARY

Visual Art	*Dance*
Line	Shape
Texture	Space
Color	Dynamics
Shape	Time
Patterns	Intensity
Contrast	

EXTENSIONS OR MODIFICATIONS

- Use a different art form.
- Extend the group dances by joining together other short dances that focus on the same art piece.
- Allow students to select any paintings they like and bring them to class.
- Ask students to write poems or short essays about one of the paintings.

TECHNOLOGY CONNECTION   PowerPoint presentations can be expanded to include a video of the student performance.

TEACHER INSTRUCTIONS FOR VISUAL ART, DANCE, AND TECHNOLOGY

Management	Teaching process	Teaching points and cues
Introduction		
(3 minutes) Ask students to sit in a semi-circle near television monitor and board.	Introduce the focus of the learning experience.	Say, "Today we are going to start on a project that relates visual art and dance as a means of communication and expression."
Review of previous material, warm-up		
(3 minutes)	Establish guidelines for behavior.	Say, "Be respectful as we begin to brainstorm."
New material		
a. **Exploratory activities** (35-45 minutes)	Ask students to look at a print of Van Gogh's *Starry Night* and describe what they see.	Say, "No talking, open your eyes and minds, look at this painting, and get ready to tell me what you see." By the end of the brainstorming session, the students should have talked about line, texture, color, shape, and patterns (see vocabulary list).
	Show students a video clip of Bella Lewitsky's "Impressions #2." After students view the video clip, their discussion should include the vocabulary: shape, space, dynamics, time, intensity.	Say, "Now we are going to look at a video clip of a choreographer's interpretation of this same painting. Open your eyes and minds and tell me what you see in the dance."
	Guide the discussion that points out the similarities between at least two elements that were used in the painting and the dance (e.g., visual art-color: dance-dynamics; visual art-contrast; dance-intensity).	Say, "Let see what connections we can make between the painting and the dance. For example, in the painting, you identified circles, and in the dance you identified circular pathways. Build more connections the same way, and I'll write them on the board."
Have students remain seated in a semi-circle.	Describe the project and distribute a handout. • Select one painting from our gallery. • Sign the sign-up sheet. • In teacher-assigned groups (from preference lists) conduct Internet research about the artist and the painting. • Create a PowerPoint presentation to be shared with the class. The PowerPoint will include bullet points about the artist, the ideas behind the painting, the historical context of the painting, and three or four elements of visual art that are dominant in the painting.	Say, "Let's go over the handout together." Tell the class that the next meeting will be held in the computer lab so that they can begin their research.
Organize students into small groups to view the gallery.	Direct students to circulate around the room so that they can view all of the paintings and sign up for their preferred painting for the project.	Say, "Our classroom is now an art gallery. I want you to circulate around the room, look at the various paintings, and select one that you are interested in for your project. Make your selection decision based upon the art elements that interest you and what you think will translate well into a dance."

~ *continued*

Teacher Instructions for Visual Art, Dance, and Technology ~ *continued*

Management	Teaching process	Teaching points and cues
New material (*continued*)		
Meet students in the computer lab. (45 minutes) Depending on the individual school situation, make arrangements to organize computer time.	Guide Internet search and maintain student time on task.	Say, "One way to start your search is to type in the name of the artist; you can also type in the name of the painting. Select the sites that will provide the information you need for your PowerPoint presentation. Once you review the sites and information, begin to create your PowerPoint slides using your handout as a guide."
Make sure discs or CDs are available for students to save their PowerPoint presentations.	Continue to circulate and monitor progress until computer time is finished.	Say, "Watch your time . . . make sure your group has created at least five slides before the end of the period. Save your work on the disc or CD."
(5-7 minutes) Have students return to the dance classroom and be seated with their project groups. The dance classroom must be preset with LCD, laptop, screen, or wall. Set up the equipment to the side of the performance space so that the audience has to adjust as little as possible to view the PowerPoint and watch the dances.	Describe the choreographic part of the project. Review the key points from the discussion about Bella Lewitsky's piece. Then go over the handout with the students.	Say, "Now you have gathered a lot of information about your painting and the artist. Remember the points we covered when we discussed Bella Lewitsky's dance based on a painting. You will now create your own dance about your painting. Let's go over the handout. Part B lists the requirements for this dance."
Organize students in groups to work on their dances.	Circulate around the room and monitor student progress, providing feedback if needed.	Say, "At the end of 15 minutes I will play three musical selections. At that time, your dance should be almost finished. You will sit down with your group and listen to all three selections. You will decide which piece of music your group will use."
Ask groups to sit down in their own work spaces to listen to the music.	Play each of the three selections once.	Say, "The music you choose should fit well with the style of the painting and your dance. You will hear three different musical selections. Your group will choose the music that best fits the style of your painting and your dance."
	Ask for a show of hands regarding the musical choices of the groups.	Say, "Raise your hand if your group chooses selection . . ."
	Explain how the groups will practice with the music.	Say, "Each musical selection will be played three times in a row. When your selection is played, your group will stand and practice. All other groups should remain seated without talking. This is the only time you will have to practice your dance with the music. We will start our performance with the PowerPoint and the dance presentations immediately following the practice."

Management	Teaching process	Teaching points and cues
New material (*continued*)		
b. Refinement activities (10 minutes) Ask students to sit with their groups as an audience.	Have groups practice with the music.	Say, "Be courteous and respectful as other groups are practicing."
	Orally assign each group a number for performance order.	Say, "We will perform our dances in the order to which they have been assigned."
Make sure the number of assessment packets corresponds to the number of the groups. Each member of the class will fill out a new assessment sheet for every dance.	Distribute student assessment forms (see page 219) and pencils. After each group performs, collect the sheets and clip them together to distribute to the group after all groups have finished. The form will be used for self-evaluation.	Say, "Now each group will present their completed project with the Power-Point presentation first, followed by the dance. As group 1 is preparing to show their PowerPoint, listen to the instructions for the assessment forms. Watch each group dance and fill out an assessment sheet at the end of the dance performance. I will collect the sheets at the end of each group's dance. I will return the sheets to each group after all groups have performed." "Group 1 . . . Go!"
Recap of lesson, assessment		
(5 minutes) Have students seated in their groups.	Return all peer evaluation sheets. Ask students to reflect on the feedback forms and discuss in their groups the question you pose.	Ask, "From the feedback forms, how closely does what the audience said line up with the elements that you intended to make clear in your dance?"
Closure		
(3 minutes)	Address one strength for part A and part B for each group and share these observations with the class. For example, the PowerPoint for Group A had clear information about the artist. The dance had a clear beginning, middle, and end and reflected some of the attitudes of the artist.	Say, "I'm very proud of the work you did on your PowerPoint presentations and dances. You demonstrated very clearly how the elements of visual art and dance are related. We know better how we can use ideas from one art form with another to communicate and express ideas."

ACCOMMODATION OR DIFFERENTIATION IDEAS

- Increase or decrease the number of paintings used in class.
- Increase or decrease the requirements of the PowerPoint presentation.
- Allow students to bring in their own music.

EVERYDAY LIVING (LIFETIME WELLNESS) CONNECTIONS   Students learn to appreciate a variety of art forms in relation to dance.

Name _____   Teacher _____

Visual Art, Dance, and Technology Handout

Vocabulary

Visual Art	Dance
Line	Shape
Texture	Space
Color	Dynamics
Shape	Time
Patterns	Intensity
Contrast	

Project Part A

1. Select one painting from our gallery.

2. Sign up to work with one painting.

3. In your teacher-assigned groups (from preference lists), do Internet research about the artist and the painting.

4. Create a PowerPoint presentation to be shared with the class. The PowerPoint will include
   - bullet points about the artist,
   - the ideas behind the painting,
   - historical context of the painting, and
   - three or four elements of visual art that are dominant in the painting.

Project Part B

1. Compose a short group dance based on your interpretation of the painting.

2. Make sure your dance has a clear beginning, middle, and end.

3. Base your dance on your interpretation of the painting and three to five visual art and dance elements.

4. Select from three pieces of teacher-provided music for your accompaniment.

5. Perform your dance in front of the class following your PowerPoint presentation.

From National Dance Association, 2010, *Implementing the national dance education standards* (Champaign, IL: Human Kinetics).

Name _____   Teacher _____

Peer Assessment: Visual Art, Dance, and Technology

Instructions: After seeing each dance, use this form to record your observations. The list of dance elements is in the left column. Beside each dance term, put a checkmark under the heading that is the best answer for how often you saw that element in the dance. Your choices are Not at all, Once, and More than once.

Group # _____

	Not at all	Once	More than once
Space			
Shape			
Dynamics			
Time			
Intensity			

Group # _____

	Not at all	Once	More than once
Space			
Shape			
Dynamics			
Time			
Intensity			

Group # _____

	Not at all	Once	More than once
Space			
Shape			
Dynamics			
Time			
Intensity			

Group # _____

	Not at all	Once	More than once
Space			
Shape			
Dynamics			
Time			
Intensity			

From National Dance Association, 2010, *Implementing the national dance education standards* (Champaign, IL: Human Kinetics).

219

Social Dance Etiquette

This dance experience will help students learn about several social dances and specific etiquette associated with each dance: merengue, four-count swing or hustle, and waltz. Based on 50-minute sessions, this learning experience is expected to take six to eight sessions to accomplish (see the table on page 222 for teacher instructions).

GRADE LEVEL   Grades 6 to 8; also appropriate for grades 9 to 12

MATERIALS, EQUIPMENT, SPACE NEEDED

- Music for each dance covered
- CD player or other audio sound source
- Microphone, as available
- Handouts of dance step variations
- Large area free of chairs and obstacles, such as a gymnasium, dance room, or other available recreation space

NATIONAL STANDARDS ADDRESSED

Grades 6 to 8

Content Standard 1. Identifies and demonstrates movement elements and skills in performing dance (Benchmarks: Body c, d; Space c; Relationships b; Time b; Effort b)

Content Standard 3. Understands dance as a way to create and communicate meaning (Benchmark: c)

Content Standard 5. Demonstrates and understands dance in various cultures and historical periods (Benchmarks: a, b)

Grades 9 to 12

Content Standard 1. Identifies and demonstrates movement elements and skills in performing dance (Benchmarks: Body b, c, d; Space d; Relationships c; Time a, b)

Content Standard 3. Understands dance as a way to create and communicate meaning (Benchmarks: c, e)

Content Standard 5. Demonstrates and understands dance in various cultures and historical periods (Benchmarks: a, b)

GOALS   To help students learn both partner and floor etiquette in social dance and to learn how to do even-rhythmic basic patterns with a partner.

OBJECTIVES   As a result of participating in this learning experience, students will

1. demonstrate the basic rhythmic pattern and at least two different variations with a partner to music for at least 45 seconds for at least two different even-rhythmic couples' dances. [Psychomotor]
2. dance at least four times demonstrating good posture, execution, and transition. [Psychomotor]
3. explain why the waltz (or 4-count swing or hustle, or merengue) is classified as an even-rhythmic pattern (versus an uneven-rhythmic pattern). [Cognitive]
4. explain the difference between the 4/4 time signature and the 3/4 time signature music for dancers. [Cognitive]
5. politely ask (and thank) a partner to dance when in a social dance setting. [Affective]
6. respect both the partner's and others' space on the dance floor by being polite and not bumping into other couples on the floor. [Affective]

VOCABULARY

Even-rhythmic pattern: Each beat of the measure gets one weight change to create a recurring rhythm.

Closed position: Partners are facing with the leader's right hand on the follower's left shoulder blade, and the leader's left hand holding the follower's right hand at approximately shoulder height. The follower's left hand is in front of the leader's right shoulder.

Social etiquette rules: This includes a variety of rules for conduct (e.g., absolutely no negative comments or criticism is appropriate on the dance floor, politely thank the partner after each dance or when changing partners).

Time signatures: A 4/4 time signature means there are four beats to a measure, and each beat gets one count. A 3/4 time signature means there are three beats to a measure, and each beat gets one count. Thus, students can step or walk on each beat for an even-rhythmic pattern whether it is 4 beats per measure or 3 beats per measure.

PRACTICAL APPLICATION ASSIGNMENT   After students have had time to practice the three selected dances, they are ready for a practical application of being at a social dance. Divide students into smaller groups (e.g., four to eight couples), let them complete the dance card by politely asking at least two (up to four) different partners to dance, and ask them to jointly decide on which two (of three) dances to dance and which two variations to use for each dance (see following Rubric Evidence and Scale). If there are uneven numbers (e.g., either few leaders or few followers), ask designated leaders to be on one side; then divide the designated leaders into smaller groups. Repeat for the designated followers.

Rubric Evidence and Scale

4: Dance four times for approximately 45 seconds with a minimum of two different partners and a minimum of two different even-rhythm couples' dances. Politely ask a partner to dance. Write your partner's name on your dance card and list the two variations to be executed each time you dance. Consistently thank your partner after each dance. Consistently demonstrate good posture, continuous footwork, and good transitions.

3: Dance three times for approximately 45 seconds with a minimum of two different partners and a minimum of two different even-rhythm couples' dances. Politely ask a partner to dance. Write your partner's name on your dance card and list the two variations to be executed each time you dance. Consistently thank your partner after each dance. Most of the time, demonstrate good posture, continuous footwork, and good transitions.

2: Dance two times for approximately 45 seconds with a minimum of two different partners and a minimum of two different even-rhythm couples' dances. Politely ask a partner to dance. Write your partner's name on your dance card and list the two variations to be executed each time you dance. Consistently thank your partner after each dance. Sometimes demonstrate good posture, continuous footwork, and good transitions.

1: Dance one time for approximately 45 seconds with a partner executing one of the even-rhythm couples' dances covered in class. Politely ask a partner to dance. Write your partner's name on your dance card and list the two variations to be executed each time you dance. Thank your partner after each dance. Rarely demonstrate good posture, continuous footwork, and good transitions.

0: No response, no effort, or unscoreable.

EXTENSIONS OR MODIFICATIONS   Create another unit using uneven-rhythmic couples' dances, such as the salsa, 6-count swing, polka, foxtrot, and so forth, as time permits.

TEACHER INSTRUCTIONS FOR SOCIAL DANCE ETIQUETTE

Management	Teaching process	Teaching points and cues
Introduction		
(5 minutes) Organize students in a semicircle around you.	Give examples of showing respect and demonstrating proper etiquette.	Say, "Have you ever seen dancers bow or curtsy to each other either at the beginning or at the end of a dance? Or, you might remember hearing 'Honor your partner' in square dancing calls, or 'Bow to your partner' in folk dancing. Why would dancers do this? We will learn social dances that involve a partner, which means that you'll be asked to be on your best behavior for demonstrating proper etiquette toward your own efforts, your partner, and the other dancers, including your hosts."
Option: Impose a penalty with some classes (e.g., if not demonstrating proper etiquette, students can be in a time-out, sit on the bleachers by themselves, or otherwise be exempted from disturbing the class).	Provide direction: • Review definitions of personal and shared space as needed with certain classes. • Show or post a diagram of where to dance on the dance floor for certain types of dances.	Say, "It is not appropriate to criticize or tell partners that they can't lead or follow or that they smell bad or that you don't want to dance with them. If they have a hygiene problem, it is better to let me know. Then I will announce to the class that everyone needs to practice good personal hygiene before coming to class. You will be with a partner for only a few seconds. You are not marrying the partner you dance with; rather, you will be asked to frequently rotate to a new partner. It is considered proper etiquette to introduce yourself to a new dance partner and to thank that dance partner after sharing any amount of dancing time."
		Other examples of etiquette are to avoid bumping into other couples and to follow the proper line of dance for the traveling dances (e.g., the flow of traffic for the waltz is to travel counterclockwise around the perimeter of the floor) or for spot dances such as the merengue and 4-count swing.
Warm-up		
(3-5 minutes)	Provide direction: • In couples' dances, leaders start with the left foot and followers start with the right foot. • Each person faces a partner; designate one person as the leader and one as the follower to repeat the marching to two different counts (grouping 4 counts, then grouping 3 counts). • Reverse roles and repeat to different tempos for each.	Ask students, "Who has been in or seen a marching band? What does a marching band do to stay in unison?" [All step on each beat or count at the same time with the same foot].

Management	Teaching process	Teaching points and cues
Warm-up *(continued)*		
Divide class in half to designate leaders on one side and followers on the other side.	• In couples' dances, leaders start with the left foot and followers start with the right foot. • Have students get in a ready position by lifting the heel of the starting foot.	Say, "Let's practice marching in place to a 4-count tempo. Half the class will be the leaders and the other half will be the followers. Each has a role, like the designated driver of a car and the passenger in the car (although the passenger is not entirely passive in this case)."
An alternative formation is to have the two facing groups of students walk forward until they stand in front of a partner (one leader facing one follower, ideally all leaders facing the same direction, and standing approximately an arm's length away from the partner).	Observe whether all students can consistently and individually step on each beat to the tempo provided. Leaders start with left foot while followers start with right foot. Repeat the tempo while mirroring the partner's steps and stepping on each beat.	Say, "Now, let's march in place to a 3-count tempo." [You can save this challenge until you teach the waltz.]
If you have more girls than boys, or vice versa, alternately ask students (or only the girls) to reverse roles and repeat to different tempos for each.	Once the basic step for a particular dance is learned, students can review the basic rhythmic pattern for a selected even-rhythm dance while in a group formation.	
New material		

Exploratory activities
(20-40 minutes per session)
Split the room in half to have leaders facing followers (can be two long rows facing each other as space permits, or set up rows of couples).
Once students can do the practice combo alone, then try it with a partner first facing (without touching), then in closed position.
	Either select from any one of the three even-rhythm dance styles presented, or follow the progressive order shown here:
	1. Merengue (basic):
	  • The merengue was created to honor a war hero from the Dominican Republic who was injured in one of the revolutions and could not bend one of his legs.
	  • Start by stepping in place, grouping 8 counts together before changing directions.
	  • Vary the direction of the steps to the side, rotating left or counterclockwise, then rotating right or clockwise.
	  • Can also travel forward or backward.
		Provide directions to students:
		• Modify march to be flat-footed. Barely lift feet off the floor to create the look of a Latin march to create styling.
		• Practice combo: Step for 8 counts in each direction: in place, to the side (left side for leaders, right side for followers); both rotate left; and both rotate right.
		• Demonstrate closed dance position: Leader's right hand on follower's left shoulder blade, follower's left arm gently touching above the leader's right arm. Grasp hands (leader's left and follower's right) and hold hands at approximately shoulder height for follower and halfway in between each partner.
		• For Latin dances, modify this hold by lifting the grasped hands higher (closer to ear level) and bringing the elbows closer together (leader's left and follower's right) with a more vertical forearm position.

~ continued

Teacher Instructions for Social Dance Etiquette ~ *continued*

Management	Teaching process	Teaching points and cues
New material *(continued)*		
Rotate the followers in a counterclockwise direction after approximately 30 to 45 seconds with a partner. You can call out the directions in a different order than in the practice combo.	• As time permits, add fun variations that are characteristic of the merengue (see handout on page 227). • Option: Challenge leaders to change the number of repetitions in each direction, keeping a minimum of 2 steps in each direction. Tell students to keep the feet moving to the beat at all times. • Observe that a minimum of 2 steps are executed in any one direction, that feet are constantly moving to the tempo, that both partners work together, and that each person thanks their partner when switching to a new partner.	
Match up partners in rows: All leaders face music, and followers have their backs to the music. Once students can do the basic rhythmic pattern alone, position them to face a partner and grasp both hands. Repeat the basic rhythmic pattern to verbal counts, then to music in 4/4 time.	2. The 4-count swing (basic): • Swing is an American dance style. There are many variations. The easiest to learn is the 4-count swing, sometimes called the 4-count hustle, which is a lead-up to the hustle (categorized as a club dance). The hustle is a mixture of salsa, swing, and disco that was popular after the movie *Saturday Night Fever* was released. The 4-count swing goes well with the music of the 1970s as well as many of the popular songs of today. • The basic rhythmic pattern involves 4 steps in 4 directions, each done on one beat of music in 4/4 time: forward, backward, backward, forward. • Add variations as time permits (see handout on page 227).	Say, "This is the only dance where both partners step toward each other when in a two-hands-joined position. Therefore, you will need to take small steps! Leaders start with their left foot and followers start with their right foot." Provide direction to students: • Face partner without touching: Rock weight forward as you step in a forward direction, then step backward (or replace weight onto other foot) for 2 counts. On both counts, feet should be in a forward-backward stride position (leader's left foot forward, or follower's right foot forward). • Step backward (only onto the ball of your foot) with leader's left foot (or the follower's right foot) on count 3. Shift weight in opposite direction, or forward onto the leader's right foot (and the follower's left foot) on count 4. • Gently push hands in to the center on counts 1, 2, then pull fingers back on counts 3, 4. • Keep elbows bent approximately 90 degrees with hands held at waist level and approximately halfway in between yourself and your partner.

Management	Teaching process	Teaching points and cues
New material *(continued)*		
Rotate partners frequently, with only 20 to 30 seconds for students to change to a new partner and to thank their previous partner. Either position students in two long rows facing each other (leaders on one side and followers on the other side, facing a partner, but not touching), or align rows of couples facing but not touching.	3. Waltz (two basics): • The waltz is the only social dance that uses three beats of music per measure. It is an elegant dance that originated from the beautiful music composed by Johann Strauss and Franz Lanner in the 1800s. • The waltz has an even-rhythm basic pattern in that you step on each beat of the music in sets of 3 counts. • The American waltz is covered in class because it is done to a slow tempo and is easy to learn. In contrast, the Viennese waltz is done to a faster tempo and involves more difficult footwork and coordination.	Provide direction: • Facing a partner, match palm-to-palm to experience how to lead or follow a direction change (like bumper cars) to alternately repeat the forward and backward balance. • Review the closed dance position.
Rotate partners every 30 to 60 seconds, keep students moving, and don't wait for them to get to the next partner before cueing to start again.	• To execute the forward and backward balance, take 3 steps (or weight changes) in each direction: forward, together, in place; and backward, together, in place. • Try the alternating forward and backward balance with a partner in closed position. • Add the sideward directions to create a side balance. Start with the leader's left foot to step to the left side, together, and in place, while the follower does the mirror reverse to step with her right foot to the right side, together, and in place. Then, reverse roles to execute the side balance to the opposite side. • Try a practice combo: Alternate the forward and backward balance 4 times with 4 side balances (8 measures or repetitions of the basic rhythmic pattern).	• Alternately repeat the side-to-side balance with a partner in closed position. The leader must keep his right hand firm and slightly press with the heel of his hand as well as keep the arms and shoulders in frame (in one unit). • Repeat practice combo in a closed position with a partner (8 measures) for the length of one song. • Keep the side step no wider than hip width. • Extend the length of the forward and backward steps to be longer than the side steps (to create a rectangular floor path).
• Vary tempos. • Slow down the pace near the end of class to cool down.	Add a box step (6 total beats). The box step is composed of 2 half-boxes, uses a rectangular box floor path, and alternates 2 directions as follows: forward half-box (i.e., forward, side, together) and backward half-box (i.e., backward, side, together). • Extended practice combo: 4 forward and backward balances; 4 side balances; 4 half-boxes. Do 12 measures in total, or 12 sets of 3 beats of music. • Add variations as time permits (see handout on page 227).	• Repeat practice combo in closed position with a partner to counts of 3, then to slow waltz music. • Ask leaders to choose the number of repetitions of each basic step or variation to create their own practice combo. The leader can lead a new variation when his left foot is free (i.e., after 6 beats of music), which groups 2 measures of music. The follower should be ready for a new variation when her right foot is free.

~ continued

Teacher Instructions for Social Dance Etiquette ~ *continued*

Management	Teaching process	Teaching points and cues
Closure and assessment		
(5-8 minutes) Group students in semicircle formation for easier discussion.	• Basics for even-rhythm couples' dances require a weight change on each beat of the measure. • Both the merengue and the 4-count swing are dances done to music in 4/4 time (that have measures of 4 counts each; each beat gets 1 count). • The waltz is done to music with 3 beats per measure (each beat gets 1 count). • Check that a circle of arms exists, such that the leader's left hand grasps the follower's right hand (held halfway in between each other) and the leader's right hand is on the follower's left shoulder blade (not lower on her back). The circle connecting upper bodies is a frame where each person has half of the space. Keep this distance when signaling a direction change or moving in another direction.	Ask a variety of questions depending on how much depth of response is desired: • Why are the dances called even-rhythm dances? [Each beat gets a step or weight change.] • Give an example of how proper etiquette is used on the social dance floor. [Thanking partner after dancing; being polite; not bumping into other couples; not jerking or pushing partner around; not criticizing or correcting partner.] • Which of the dances that you learned (either today or at the end of this learning experience) works best with music that has 4 beats per measure? • What is the only social dance covered that is done to music with 3 beats per measure? • Can you demonstrate a closed dance position or describe an important concept to help with leading or following?

TECHNOLOGY CONNECTIONS

- Video record students performing, then ask the class to observe the recording, discuss how the perspective changes, and record concrete visual examples to support their comments.

- Capture dancers on video, then use technology to modify selected scenes or moves, for example by adding split screens or creating a composite of various positions to form artwork (such as duplicating four times and overlapping or sharing the screen in an artistic manner.

ACCOMMODATION OR DIFFERENTIATION IDEAS

- For nonambulatory students, modify the dynamics of the moves to permit some body action on each beat of the music (e.g., substitute a head tilt, a finger tap, and so forth).

- For students with visual or hearing impairments, permit contact with another student (e.g., holding hands, hooking elbows, arms on shoulders, and so forth) so that these students can know where they are in space, including which direction they are facing, and can feel and replicate the rhythm alongside a partner.

EVERYDAY LIVING CONNECTIONS   Marching or walking to music is a low-impact activity that builds cardiovascular endurance if the feet keep moving consecutively for a minimum of 10 minutes. This can be a goal to work toward: Each day students can increase the number of consecutive minutes they march or dance to the music. Students also may wear pedometers or heart rate monitors to track steps or heart rate while dancing.

INTEGRATED ARTS IDEAS

- Students can prepare map drawings to show the footwork of selected direction changes. These drawings can be literal or abstract.

- Music students can provide drum accompaniment to create different tempos for other students to march to.

Practical Application: Even-Rhythm Couples Dances

Instructions: Demonstrate the appropriate rhythmic pattern while executing three or more variations, demonstrate proper dance floor etiquette, and thank at least five partners after dancing with them. After dancing, circle all variations executed, then tally your points.

Merengue Variations

1. In place: Alternate feet to step on each beat in place (one weight change on each beat)
2. Side steps: Alternate side, feet together to leader 's left
3. Couples' left turn (rotate counterclockwise) or right turn (rotate clockwise)
4. Slow underarm (right) turn for the follower
5. Slow underarm (right) turn for the follower with a hand change: Shake R to R (on top) and L to L; loop right hands over follower 's head, then loop left hands over leader's head

4-Count Swing (or 4-Count Hustle) Variations

1. Basic rhythmic pattern: Four weight changes, stepping forward, backward, backward, forward
2. Change positions: Both partners rotate clockwise to change positions
3. Inside (left) turn: Leader brings his left hand across his mid-line (under chin) towards his right shoulder and makes a counterclockwise loop over follower's head (as change positions)
4. Reverse (right) turn combined with a left turn: Lift leader's left arm to left side for follower's right turn under the arched arms; immediately lead an inside (left) turn for the follower in order to correct hands
5. Wrap and roll out: From two hands, bring right hand to leader's right side, left hand to right shoulder and counterclockwise over follower's head into the wrap; unwrap by releasing right hand and gently pulling with left hand
6. Wrap and arch out: From two hands, wrap to bring the follower to the leader's right side; unwrap by lifting the left hand and keep both hands

Waltz Variations

1. Balance forward and backward: Forward, forward with feet together, in place; backward, backward with feet together, in place
2. Balance side to side: Three weight changes to each side with side, feet together, in place
3. Box step: Forward, side, together; backward, side, together
4. Half-box progression forward: Alternate feet to travel forward, side, together
5. Slow underarm turn for follower: Leader does two full box steps (or four half-boxes); follower does one half-box as regular, second half-box step starts forward, then rotates clockwise, third half-box is taken forward and curves back to face partner, then forth half-box is forward to connect with partner in closed position again
6. Left turning box: One half-box forward, angle on backward half-box step (to rotate a quarter turn counterclockwise)

Self-Assessment

Merengue

____ Circle at least three variations executed (3 points)

____ Keep feet moving to step on each beat (2 points)

4-Count Swing

____ Circle at least three variations executed (3 points)

____ Keep feet moving to step on each beat (2 points)

Waltz

____ Circle at least three variations executed (3 points)

____ Keep feet moving to step on each beat (2 points)

Practice Etiquette

____ Thank at least five different partners (5 points)

Total: _____ (20 possible points)

Name _____   Date _____

From National Dance Association, 2010, *Implementing the national dance education standards* (Champaign, IL: Human Kinetics).

Summary

Dance teachers who provide a comprehensive standards-based curriculum that incorporates learner characteristics offer tremendous support to middle school students. The young adolescents can explore rich relationships between dance and other disciplines, connections between choreographic principles and movement possibilities, and links between the creative processes and assessment. Students learn to value their personal achievements and those of classmates. They can appreciate the unique qualities that each person brings to class. When these young adolescents reach identified benchmarks at the middle school level, they are better prepared to achieve success in the next grade levels.

11

Grades 9 to 12

At the high school level, dance education is designed to enhance students' competencies in dance as an art form, in self-expression, and in healthy living. As in lower grades, dance may be taught in specialized dance classes, as part of physical education, or in interdisciplinary classes across the curriculum. At the high school level, teachers will see great annual gains in students' psychomotor and cognitive skills. Social maturation also happens at a fast pace. Dance teachers can use materials in this chapter to advance students' development by offering challenging activities, both formative and summative, that promote critical thinking, problem solving, and self-assessment. Through these activities, teachers also can help adolescents to value systems and cultures of current and historical periods, appreciate achievements of peers, and recognize the qualities of the masters of dance.

Table 11.1 provides a quick overview of learner characteristics of adolescents by educational domain (psychomotor, cognitive, and affective). It also offers instructional ideas that can be used to address specific characteristics of the adoles-cent student. Using these two components can facilitate how program planning can help students achieve developmentally appropriate learning benchmarks.

TABLE 11.1 Developmental Characteristics by Domain

Psychomotor (physical) characteristics	Implications for dance education teachers
During adolescence, students (ages 15-18 and in grades 9 to 12) . . .	
a. have overcome most of the awkwardness and uneven appearance of early adolescence (although most have achieved sexual maturity and adult height, some boys are still growing)	Avoid comments that criticize or compare stature, size, or shape; plan class activities that foster achievement and success
b. experience better small muscle control and good large muscle coordination, even though bone growth is not yet complete; experience better fitness levels and can participate in pro-longed physical activity	Increase awareness of the maturation of bone structure and muscle development; plan safe activities for the students' developmental levels and refer any complaints regarding pain to the school nurse or other medical specialist as needed; plan more in-depth study of dance forms; work on perfecting steps, dance patterns, and movement combinations
c. form more mature eating habits	Incorporate information on good nutritional practices into the curriculum and provide special information for those choosing special eating practices or dietary patterns (e.g., vegetarians)
d. may demonstrate diet and sleep habits that lead to low energy levels	Plan discussion about time management, healthy eating and sleep practices, and strategies for making good deci-sions; discuss the impact of these behaviors on energy levels for active movement
e. are capable of developing a regular exercise program	Guide students in planning healthy and safe personal dance and exercise practices that may help those choosing professional or educational dance career paths and those who want to stay active in recreational dance as a healthy lifestyle
Cognitive (intellectual) characteristics	Implications for dance education teachers
a. are increasing self-knowledge and development of personal philosophies	Allow choices in planning activities or projects that express their personal viewpoints
b. have longer attention spans; participate in pro-longed tasks and activities; are capable of in-depth study of specific subject areas	Allow time for more in-depth projects; encourage learn-ing about dance technique while perfecting dance steps, patterns, and movement combinations; allow practice in training concepts related to upper-body strength, balance, agility, speed, flexibility, and aerobic capacity
c. can think systematically and understand abstract processes; want to experience real-life problem solving and critical thinking	Teach choreographic principles; provide opportunities for creating small-group dances that allows for conceptual-izing, problem solving, analyzing, sequencing movement patterns, and evaluating outcomes
d. can evaluate own work	Allow for using a variety of self-assessment processes such as video observation, rubric, peer critique, or journal docu-mentation

Cognitive (intellectual) characteristics *(continued)*	Implications for dance education teachers *(continued)*
e. tend to be perfectionists	Allow ample time to rehearse projects and dances; allow many opportunities to perform; plan opportunities to teach about dance appreciation of many forms
f. want more independence but need guidance and support	Provide ample guidance, support, and praise for student work
g. need life planning and school and career guidance	Offer information about dance and dance-related careers and places they may train; invite a variety of dance professionals to classes and events; plan activities addressing professional etiquette, standards, and behavior
h. recognize varied differences in achievement; begin to see lower-achieving students dropping out	Gather data to understand students' interests and motivational factors; plan activities to capture students' interests and those that will help them succeed (e.g., vary the use of music, props, and dance forms)
Affective (socioemotional) characteristics	**Implications for dance education teachers**
a. participate well in groups or on teams; have a strong desire for status within the peer group; are concerned about body image and appearance among peers	Establish a climate conducive to peer support; provide assignments that use choreographic devices such as canon or rondo format
b. want to be recognized as unique individuals	Place emphasis on personal development; focus on enhancing individual dance technique and achieving success
c. accept friends' general rules of behavior; are concerned about what others say and think of them; want to conform to a "contemporary dress code"	Analyze positive and negative implications of peer group behaviors; discuss rationale for appropriate attire in specific dance classes (e.g., safety, view alignment, expression of culture, and group uniformity)
d. use loud voices or extreme behavior to hide a lack of self-confidence	Find roles where students can express their positive voices and gain confidence (e.g., stage manager, group leader, class assistant)
e. want independence	Give teens responsibility and expect follow-through; provide opportunities that help teens explore their identity, values, and beliefs through dance-related projects
f. are interested in coeducational activities	Allow teens to plan coeducational and group-oriented projects or activities
g. look at the world more objectively, are developing community consciousness, and are concerned for others' well-being	Encourage students to give back to the community through service projects; connect dance projects to national and world issues
h. test limits and demonstrate a "know-it-all" attitude; frequently challenges existing rules and social norms; have a tendency to manipulate	Ensure that students know school and class rules, codes of conduct, and ethics; establish and discuss consequences of breaking rules or codes; help students set positive standards for behavior and achievement, hold them to the expectations, and provide guidance and support to meet the standards
i. identify with admired adults	Allow opportunities to meet, read about, and work with respected adults in dance-related areas
j. often want to serve in adult leadership roles	Provide opportunities for teens to hold positions of responsibility; allow time for planning of their own programs

Table 11.2 provides teachers of adolescents with the benchmarks that students participating in a well-designed dance curriculum can accomplish by grade 12 (at approximately 18 years of age). Students can reach the benchmarks through participation in specialized dance classes, a physical education curriculum, studio settings, recreation department programs, or other community-based instruction.

TABLE 11.2   Dance Content Standards and Benchmarks: Grades 9 to 12

Content Standard 1. Identifies and demonstrates movement elements and skills in performing dance
The student . . .

BODY

   a. analyzes the relationship between a balanced musculoskeletal system and optimum performance (e.g., how muscles work in pairs, benefits of cross training, and functions of body levers)

   b. applies appropriate skeletal alignment (e.g., relationship of the skeleton to the line of gravity and the base of support), body-part articulation, strength, flexibility, agility, and coordination in locomotor and nonlocomotor (axial) movements

   c. identifies and demonstrates complex steps and patterns from various dance styles (e.g., dances of a particular performer, choreographer, or time period) and traditions (e.g., dances of bharatanatyam, noh, or folk dances of indigenous people)

   d. recalls and reproduces extended movement and rhythmic sequences (i.e., 2 to 3 minutes)

SPACE

   a. improvises, choreographs, or performs in varied settings (e.g., studio, proscenium stage, theater-in-the-round, television, gymnasium, outdoors) (follow-up from earlier grade levels)

   b. creates choreographic phrases that incorporate movements at high, middle, and low levels

   c. travels through space using self-generated patterns on paper or on a computer screen (follow-up from earlier grade levels)

   d. creates movement patterns that combine two or more pathways (follow-up from earlier grade levels)

   e. demonstrates changes in range of movement (e.g., large, small, distal, and core actions) (follow-up from earlier grade levels)

   f. analyzes how the meaning of movement changes depending upon the dancers' location and facing position on the stage (e.g., upstage right, center, or downstage left)

RELATIONSHIPS

   a. demonstrates the ability to dance within classroom groups of varying sizes—with or without props

   b. demonstrates knowledge of group choreography using a variety of spatial and temporal relationships

   c. displays personal presence in formal and informal performance settings (e.g., confident presentation of body and energy to communicate movement and meaning to an audience, performance quality, positive sense of involvement)

TIME

   a. demonstrates accuracy in moving to a steady musical beat (follow-up from earlier grade levels)

   b. arranges various complex rhythmic elements in dance sequences and choreography (e.g., duple and triple meters, irregular time signatures such as 5/4 and 9/8)

EFFORT

   a. demonstrates a broader range of dynamics (movement qualities) during improvised and choreographed works (e.g., sustained, swinging, percussive, collapsing, and vibratory) (follow-up from earlier grade levels)

   b. creates and performs combinations and variations with a broad range of dynamics (e.g., sustained, percussive, vibratory, swinging, pausing, or no action on beats) (follow-up from earlier grade levels)

ADVANCED

   a. demonstrates a high level of consistency and reliability in performing technical skills

   b. demonstrates technical skills with artistic expression, demonstrating clarity, musicality, and stylistic nuance

   c. evaluates own technique and makes self-corrections

Content Standard 2. Understands choreographic principles, processes, and structures
The student:

   a. uses improvisation to discover and compose solutions to small-group movement assignments (follow-up from earlier grade levels)

   b. improvises, creates, and performs dances based on personal ideas or concepts from other sources (e.g., stories, pictures, poetry, emotions, verbs, found objects, artifacts, or technology) (follow-up from earlier grade levels)

   c. choreographs a duet or small-group dance using a variety of choreographic principles, processes, and structures (forms)

   d. demonstrates understanding of choreographic structures (e.g., retrograde or palindrome, theme and variation, rondo, canon, or contemporary forms selected by the student)

   e. demonstrates the process of reordering (i.e., specific movements or movement phrases that are separated from their original order and restructured in a different sequence) and chance (i.e., movements that are specifically chosen and defined but randomly structured) to create a dance or movement phrase (follow-up from earlier grade levels)

   f. cooperates with a partner to demonstrate the following skills in a visually interesting way: creating contrasting and complementary shapes, taking and supporting weight (follow-up from earlier grade levels)

   g. designs a multimedia presentation to accompany a dance (e.g., PowerPoint, camera, video, iPod)

ADVANCED

   a. demonstrates further development and refinement of the proficient skills to create a small-group dance with coherence and aesthetic unity

   b. explains accurately how a choreographer manipulated and developed the basic movement content within a dance production

   c. operates a complex technology system for a dance production (e.g., lighting or sound)

Content Standard 3. Understands dance as a way to create and communicate meaning
The student . . .

   a. formulates and answers questions about how movement choices are used to communicate abstract ideas and themes in dance (e.g., celebration, isolation, relationships, poverty, the environment)

   b. explains how personal experiences influence the interpretation of a dance (e.g., journal writing, class discussion) (follow-up from earlier grade levels)

   c. presents a dance that communicates a social theme (e.g., contemporary, historical, or cultural)

   d. demonstrates appropriate audience behavior and etiquette in formal and informal performance situations and explains how audiences and venues affect choreography (follow-up from earlier grade levels)

   e. demonstrates and describes the different meanings evoked by specific body language, shapes, and movement choices (e.g., low, round shape: fear or repose; high, angular shape: defiance or power; symmetrical shape: harmony) (follow-up from earlier grade levels)

   f. explains how accompaniment, lighting, technology, and costuming can contribute to the meaning of a dance (follow-up from earlier grade levels)

   g. describes and practices legal and ethical behavior with digital information (e.g., publishes photographs only with permission, follows copyright and fair use guidelines, and provides complete citations from electronic media)

   h. researches a theme using the Web site or media to create a short dance study (follow-up from earlier grade levels)

ADVANCED

   a. analyzes opinions concerning ways that a dance creates and conveys meaning from a variety of perspectives (e.g., audience, performer, creator, critic, historical context, use of technology)

   b. compares and contrasts how meaning is communicated in two personally choreographed works

   c. analyzes the impact of technology on the archival management of dance works (i.e., the preservation and access to artistic works)

~ continued

TABLE 11.2 ~ *continued*

Content Standard 4. Applies and demonstrates critical and creative thinking skills in dance
The student . . .

a. creates a dance and revises it over time, articulating the reasons for artistic decisions and what was lost and gained by those decisions

b. formulates and answers aesthetic questions about a particular dance (e.g., What is it that makes the dance unique? What changes to the dance will create a new concept?)

c. discusses opinions about dances with peers in supportive and positive ways (follow-up from earlier grade levels)

d. establishes a set of aesthetic criteria (e.g., transition, variety, contrast, repetition, sequence, structure, balance) and applies it in evaluating personal work and that of others

e. explains how skills developed in dance are applicable to a variety of careers

ADVANCED

a. analyzes the style of a choreographer or cultural form and creates a dance in that style

b. analyzes issues of ethnicity, gender, society, economic class, age, or physical condition in relation to dance or dance careers

Content Standard 5. Demonstrates and understands dance in various cultures and historical periods
The student . . .

a. creates a dance study demonstrating elements from a cultural dance (e.g., symbolic gestures, weightedness, posture, partnering, rhythms)

b. describes the function of a particular dance within the society where the dance was or is performed (explain such things as religious or secular implications and cultural phenomena)

c. uses technology to research cultural or historical perspectives surrounding the career of at least one professional in dance, choreography, or production

ADVANCED

a. performs in an informal or formal setting a dance from a selected resource (e.g., video, guest artist, family member, clubs, performance groups, dance society) and describes the cultural or historical context

b. choreographs a dance reflective of elements within a specific culture (such as history, spiritual beliefs, food, music, dress, family structure, artwork)

Content Standard 6. Makes connections between dance and healthful living
The student . . .

a. develops and implements a personal plan addressing health needs and issues to include regular healthy eating, flexibility, muscular strength, and endurance

b. designs a personal warm-up based on safe movement practices for a specific dance genre (e.g., ballet, modern, cultural dance, hip-hop)

c. explains findings from research on a personal health concern or a dance-related injury

d. explains how life choices affect the dancer's abilities and longevity (e.g., tobacco, drugs, alcohol, overtraining, overstretching, lack of sleep, eating disorders, emotional balance)

e. recognizes the joy of dance as a lifetime activity to celebrate culture and community events (follow-up from earlier grade levels)

ADVANCED

a. discusses challenges facing career-directed performers in maintaining healthy lifestyles

b. researches and explains potential dance genres that can be performed by older adults, individuals with disabilities, and others with unique abilities

Content Standard 7. Makes connections between dance and other disciplines
The student:

   a. creates a dance study demonstrating connections between dance and another discipline

   b. analyzes characteristics of works in various art forms that share similar subject matter, historical periods, or cultural context

   c. cites examples of how similar elements are used in dance and in another art form (e.g., balance, design, contrast, texture) (follow-up from earlier grade levels)

   d. identifies significant changes that occurred in dance as a result of technology, science, and history

   e. interprets through dance an idea taken from another medium (e.g., visual arts, music, video, poetry, history) (follow-up from earlier grade levels)

   f. uses a different art form to express an interpretation of a dance that students have observed or performed (e.g., drawing, poetry, musical composition, prose, technology)

   g. demonstrates how technology can be used to reinforce, enhance, or alter the dance idea in an interdisciplinary project

ADVANCED

   a. creates an interdisciplinary project based on a student-identified theme

   b. integrates technology into a group-generated interdisciplinary project

Social Dance Mixers

Mixers are designed to get students quickly moving to an external tempo and socially interacting with others in fun and novel ways. Based on 45- or 90-minute class sessions, this learning experience may be accomplished in four to six lessons (see the following table for teacher instructions).

GRADE LEVEL   Grades 6 to 8 and 9 to12

MATERIALS, EQUIPMENT, SPACE NEEDED
- Music in 4/4 time with a strong beat (can vary types of music for styling interpretation and interest)
- CD player or other music source
- Open area

NATIONAL STANDARDS ADDRESSED

Content Standard 1. Identifies and demonstrates movement elements and skills in performing dance (Benchmarks: Body c, d; Space d; Relationships a, b; Time a)

Content Standard 6. Makes connections between dance and healthful living (Benchmarks: b, d, e)

Content Standard 7. Makes connections between dance and other disciplines (Benchmark: b)

GOAL   To guide students to execute rhythmic patterns to music and to interact with others.

OBJECTIVES

As a result of participating in this learning experience, students will

1. match walking steps to the beat of the music and repeat the basic rhythmic pattern for the length of one song. [Psychomotor]
2. explain the relationship between beats, measures, and the rhythmic pattern, and understand diagonal left front direction. [Cognitive]
3. respect others' space and time while executing the mixers. [Affective]

When students learn a variety of social dances, they are confident in dancing at other family and community events.

VOCABULARY

Beat: The basic unit that reflects the duration of time; sometimes called the underlying beat, which is most often established by the drum in music

Accent: A stress on a particular beat to make it stronger, such as a clap; a stomp; or a different movement, action, or direction

Measure: One group of beats; for example, there are four beats per measure in 4/4 time music, which is used in most popular music

Rhythmic pattern: A recurring grouping of beats with footwork that corresponds in some way to the underlying beat

Diagonal left front direction: A movement in which the sternum rotates 45 degrees to face front left

RUBRIC CRITERION Executes the entire mixer for the length of one song in time with the music, demonstrates the proper rhythmic pattern for the dance, moves in unison with the other participants, and shows respect of others' space.

TEACHER INSTRUCTIONS FOR SOCIAL DANCE MIXERS

Management	Teaching process	Teaching points and cues
Introduction		
(2 minutes) • On either side of the room, line up leaders on one line and followers on another line opposite each other. Ask the leaders to follow you in single file to make a large circle. Then, ask the followers to follow you in single file and stop in front of a leader to create a second, outer circle. • Continue until there is a double-circle formation. Any extras can be paired up (because actual leading is not required in the set routines for the mixers).	Mixers are good icebreakers to help people get moving to music and dancing. They can be done at the beginning of an evening of dance or after a break and are great ways to meet a lot of new people as partners switch during each repetition of the basic rhythmic pattern of the dance.	
Warm-up		

(10-20 minutes)
• Face all paired partners in line of dance (LOD) or counterclockwise to start the dance.
• Repeat for the length of a slow song in 4/4 time.
• Increase the tempo for a second song.
• Music suggestions:
  a. Slow tempo: "Alley Cat"
  b. Moderate tempo: "Good Times" by Chic
  c. Fast tempo: "Hava Nagila"
  d. Optional ideas using holiday or show tunes or popular songs: "Jingle Bells," "Hey Look Me Over," "Hello, Dolly," merengue or Latin music
	• Students can start on either foot.
	• Use an add-on method to introduce the first 4 counts to a verbal count, then add on the next 4 counts, and so forth, until students can walk through the entire mixer to a spoken count. Gradually increase the spoken count to match the tempo of the music to be played.
	• The walking mixer is structured in 4 sets of 4 counts with a direction change to accent count 4 of each measure. For example, they can face the new direction or partner. Other accents are possible as well, perhaps a clap on the third set of 4 beats. An optional turn could be added when moving toward a new partner on the third set of 4 beats.
		An easy beginner mixer is a walking mixer (modified glowworm mixer). Direct students to do the following:
		• Walk 4 steps forward and face partner (4 counts).
		• Walk 4 steps back and face diagonal left (4 counts).
		• Walk 4 steps toward next partner's right shoulder and hook elbows (4 counts).
		• Walk 4 steps around partner and release elbows with followers quickly continuing to turn to face LOD again (4 counts).

~ *continued*

Teacher Instructions for Social Dance Mixers ~ *continued*

Management	Teaching process	Teaching points and cues
Warm-up (continued)		
• If students do not want to touch, other options for the elbow hook might be a do-si-do move around partner (back to back) or a high-five with hands as they walk around partner.	• Encourage students to acknowledge their partner. For example, they can introduce themselves as they hook arms and walk around their partner: "Hi, my name is . . ." • Depending on the music, it is fine to substitute skips for walks during the elbow hook turn.	Observe that students are walking at a constant pace or stepping on each beat of the measures for the length of the song played.
New material		

Use as many mixers as time permits.
• Double-circle formation: leaders on the inside with backs toward the center, and followers facing partners, or toward the center of the circle.
• Students love to revisit mixers, especially if different music is played.
• Music suggestions:
  a. Slow tempo: "Celebration" by Kool and the Gang
  b. Moderate tempo: "Some Kind of Trouble" by Tanya Tucker
  c. Fast tempo: "Wild, Wild West" by Escape Club
	a. Barn dance mixer
	(15-20 minutes)
	• The barn dance mixer is structured in 4 sets of 8 counts.
	• Encourage students to have fun with their body movements as they execute this mixer.
	• Observe students' footwork and actions; look for either a step or an action on each beat. You'll probably notice some smiles too—which is great!
	• Vary the types of cues given to the class.
		Direct students to do the following:
		• Grasp both hands. Leaders start with left foot. Followers start with right foot.
		• Step to side, bring feet together, step to side, touch. Repeat to other side (8 counts).
		• Leaders do same footwork while followers do a 3-step turn under the arch first clockwise, then counterclockwise (8 counts).
		• Both turn to face LOD, step on outside foot (farthest away from partner), kick across (away from partner). Step, kick inward (gently touching partner's heel). Repeat (8 counts).
		• Face partner, walk backward three steps, and tap foot on floor (or hitch, lift knee) while clapping. Walk 3 steps diagonally left to meet the next partner and tap foot on floor (8 counts).
		• Grasp both hands and repeat with a new partner. Introduce yourself to each new partner.

• Double-circle formation is same as used in the barn dance mixer.
• Music suggestions:
  a. Slow tempo: "Doudlebska Polka"
  b. Moderate tempo: Most any polka will work
	b. Pattycake polka mixer
	(10-20 minutes)
	Direct students to do the following:
	• Heel to side, toe to instep. Repeat (4 counts).
	• Slide to side in LOD 4 times (4 counts).
	• Repeat the actions on the other side (while moving in reverse LOD, 8 counts).
	• Clap right hands 3 times (2 counts). Clap left hands 3 times (2 counts). Clap both hands with partner (2 counts). Slap own knees 3 times (2 counts).
	• Hook right elbows and skip around partner (4 counts).
	• Leader skips forward in LOD to new partner. Follower skips in reverse LOD to new partner (4 counts).
		• Here are cues for first set of 8 counts: heel-toe, heel-toe, slide, slide, slide, slide.
		• Footwork cues for the slide to one side are "step, together, step, together, step-together, step." Counting cues are "1 and 2 and 3 and 4."
		• Cues for third set of 8 counts are "right, right, right; left, left, left; both, both, both; rotate quarter turn to your left (to avoid hitting heads when bending forward); then slap, slap, slap."
		• Use control to alternately slow down to do heel-toe actions with each beat, then speed up the timing to do the slides and the skips.

Management	Teaching process	Teaching points and cues

New material *(continued)*

Management	Teaching process	Teaching points and cues

• Double-circle formation with leaders on the inside and both partners facing LOD.
• Start in sweetheart position (sometimes called lariat or cape or varsouvienne position): follower holds hands in front of her shoulders while leader places his right arm behind the follower's shoulders and his fingertips in her hands.
• Both partners start with the left foot.
• Music suggestions:
  a. Slow tempo: "Indian Outlaw" by Tim McGraw
  b. Moderate tempo: "I Love a Rainy Night" by Eddie Rabbit
  c. Fast tempo: "Cotton-Eyed Joe"
	c. Cotton-Eyed Joe
	(10-20 minutes)
	• Try the dance without any partner changes until students have the pattern, then add the mixer option.
	• The Cotton-Eyed Joe mixer is structured in two parts, each with 16 counts, for a total of 32 counts.
	
	Mixer option:
	On the 6th shuffle, the leader brings his left hand over the follower's head and releases both hands; he is facing LOD, and she is facing reverse LOD. Both take two more shuffles to meet the next partner. The new leader extends his right hand to the follower's left hand and back to sweetheart position to start the entire dance over again.
		Direct students to do the following:
		Part A:
		• Cross or hook left foot in front of left shin (count 1), kick left forward (count 2), take three small steps while moving backward (left, right, left; counts 3 and 4).
		• Repeat, starting with right foot (4 counts).
		• Repeat for 8 counts.
		
		Cues for part A: Cross, kick, back 3 steps (4 times).
		Part B:
		• Shuffle (or triple step) to the left diagonal by stepping left, right, left (2 counts).
		• Shuffle (or triple step) to the right diagonal by stepping right, left, right (2 counts).
		• Repeat 2 shuffles 3 more times (12 counts).
		• Cues for part B: Left, together, left; right, together, right (repeat for left, right, left, right, left, right, or 8 total shuffles). Or, you might count each grouping of 2 counts needed for the shuffles: 1 and 2, 2 and 2, 3 and 2, 4 and 2, 5 and 2, 6 and 2, 7 and 2, 8 and 2.
		• Let the shoulders lean toward the side of the shuffles; alternate the left shoulder toward the left diagonal with the left foot, then the right shoulder toward the right diagonal with the right foot.

• Start in trios facing LOD, like spokes of a wheel radiating out from the center, and hold hands. Place the leader in the center with 2 followers (1 on each side). Or, place a follower in the center with 2 leaders on either side. Or place 3 leaders together, or 3 followers together.
• Give each person in the trio a role, that is, the center, the left side, or the right side. If there are extra students, place 2 together within the same role (e.g., 2 left-side persons).
• Keep distance in between trios approximately 4 walking steps.
• Music suggestions:
  a. Slow tempo: "Hot, Hot, Hot" by Buster Poindexter
  b. Fast tempo: "Proyecto Uno on Merenhits 2000"
	d. Caribbean connection mixer
	(10-20 minutes)
	• Ask students to raise a hand as you call out the role's name: center, left-side person, or right-side person.
	• The Latin music inspires more body movements and a flat-footed marching step on each beat of the music.
	• The structure of this mixer is 4 sets of 8 counts.
	• As an option, once students become comfortable with this mixer, you can call out who is to move forward during the last set of 8 counts (e.g., it could be any one of the 3 positions: right, center, or left), or any 2 positions can move forward (e.g., center and right).
		Direct students to do the following:
		• Walk 3 steps forward and touch, then three steps backward and touch (8 counts).
		• Left-side person goes under the arch on the right side. Leader follows under the arch while the right-side person walks or marches in place (8 counts).
		• Right-side person goes under the arch on the left side. Leader follows under the arch while the left-side person walks or marches in place (8 counts).
		• Center stays or marches in place as both sides move forward while doing 3 walks and a touch to the first center person, then continue until they meet the second center person (8 counts).
		• Repeat with a new center person.

~ continued

Teacher Instructions for Social Dance Mixers ~ *continued*

Management	Teaching process	Teaching points and cues
Cool-down		
(2 minutes)	Near the end of class, choose a slow tempo to slow down the pace.	
Closure and assessment		
(2 minutes) Bring class to semicircle around you.	Mixers are considered American social dances.	Ask students to give specific examples for each mixer to identify where the new partner change occurs. What makes a mixer different from other types of dances? [Somewhere in the dance, partners move to a new partner, which makes it a great way to meet new people.]

TECHNOLOGY CONNECTIONS

- Videotape the dances being performed.
- Create a video collage to motivate others to learn the mixers.

ACCOMMODATION OR DIFFERENTIATION IDEAS

- Pair students with visually impaired partners so that connections are made throughout the dance.
- Slow the tempo of the music.

EVERYDAY LIVING (LIFETIME WELLNESS) CONNECTIONS

- Work with others to share a common goal.
- Prepare the body and mind for expressive purposes.
- Participate in dance activities, which will help maintain or improve physical fitness if there are adequate frequency, intensity of movement, and performance time.

INTEGRATED ARTS IDEAS   Compare at least two different music styles for the same dance to see how the quality of the dance movements might be executed differently.

Celebrating Community Heritage Through Dance

Dance provides a vehicle for communities to celebrate their diversity. If a community has a vibrant expression of cultural heritage, there will be opportunities for gathering cultural information from direct observation at events such as weddings, holiday celebrations, and other social gatherings. Students and community leaders can provide a wealth of resources. If access to different cultures is unavailable, technology provides a means for studying cultures from afar. This learning experience takes students through four steps:

1. Gathering information about the culture
2. Studying the collected information
3. Creating variations and analyzing how much can be changed before losing the essence of the dance
4. Performing the dance to share the culture with others

Based on 45- to 90-minute sessions, this learning experience may be accomplished in five or six sessions (see the following table for teacher instructions).

GRADE LEVEL   Grades 9 to 12

MATERIALS, EQUIPMENT, SPACE NEEDED

- Video camera
- Television, VCR or DVD player
- Music

NATIONAL STANDARDS ADDRESSED

Content Standard 1. Identifies and demonstrates movement elements and skills in performing dance (Benchmarks: Body c, d; Space a, d; Relationships a, b; Effort a)

Content Standard 2. Understands choreographic principles, processes, and structures (Benchmark: a)

Content Standard 3. Understands dance as a way to create and communicate meaning (Benchmarks: b, c, d)

Content Standard 4. Applies and demonstrates critical and creative thinking skills in dance (Benchmarks: b; Advanced b)

Content Standard 5. Demonstrates and understands dance in various cultures and historical periods (Benchmarks: a; Advanced a, b)

Content Standard 6. Makes connections between dance and healthful living (Benchmark: e)

GOALS

- To collect and study cultural information on a dance in order to perform the traditional or popular form.
- To expand the traditional or popular dance form to stage it for presentation in a theatrical setting where it can be shared with others.

Students can learn about many cultures through dance education.

OBJECTIVES As a result of participating in this learning experience, students will

1. identify and execute appropriate steps within a traditional or popular cultural dance. [Psychomotor]
2. describe the significance of the cultural influences on the development of the dance (e.g., history, music, customs, geography, political events, economic situations, occupations, religion). [Cognitive]
3. recognize dance as an important means to celebrate important events in the community and in our lives. [Affective]

VOCABULARY

Culture

Community heritage

Diversity

TEACHER INSTRUCTIONS FOR MULTICULTURAL LEARNING

Management	Teaching process	Teaching points and cues
Introduction		
(20 minutes)	Take a survey of the students in your class to determine how many different cultural groups are represented. Are the students familiar with their cultural heritage, and if so, what is their favorite cultural dance? Do they know how to do it? Ask if any student's family members or friends can serve as a source for music, traditional movements, costuming, history, or videos of cultural events either in the United States or in the native country.	Say that everyone has a culture; some of us even have more than one. Studying the complexity of the development and origin of customs, traditions, and dance is a fascinating journey.
Research preparation		
Over a period of at least two weeks, collect videotapes of cultural events in your community (e.g., weddings, birthday parties, festivals, holidays). Scan the videos and copy only the sections that are rich with dance movement. If you have different cultural groups represented in your class, prepare one video for each group. When you have collected enough material, begin the analysis of the movement material.	Until you have gathered enough material to start this learning experience, continue the previous unit. Once the materials are ready, select group leaders. Allow time for the group leaders to become familiar with the dance material. While working independently or after school, student leaders can begin to identify and decipher representative steps of the dance. When the student leaders feel ready, have them introduce movements to their respective groups.	Consider these points in your planning: • Just because the majority of the students are from one country does not mean they share the same popular or traditional dances. Geography and economic status often play a role in what is acceptable. • Students from Mexico who live near the California and New Mexico border enjoy banda and quebraita; students who come from Monterrey, N.L., Mexico, may enjoy the dance Sonidero. Some students may not be familiar with either traditional or popular dances from their native countries. Children from upper economic classes may be unfamiliar with the folk dances of their native countries. • It takes time for students to learn to take movement from video.

Management	Teaching process	Teaching points and cues
New material		
a. Exploratory activities (90 minutes: exploring the movement; 2 weeks: choreographing a dance)	Have students • explore the choreographic potential. • view the steps from a variety of perspectives. • explore variations in tempo, direction, dimensions, and level. • develop a movement study or complete dance presentation.	Consider: The artistic maturity of your student leaders will help determine how the collected movement material is developed. If the group is brand new to dance, they may need to execute simple steps in a variety of floor patterns or with simple variations. If the group is proficient in the use of abstraction and choreographic elements, then many more options become possible.
b. Refinement activities (90 minutes: movement study; 1 week or possibly longer to polish for presentation: develop a theme, story, or poem)	Ask students proficient in choreography to develop a theme, tell a story, or interpret a poem using both traditional and interpretive movement.	
Recap of lesson, cool-down		
(10-15 minutes)	Discuss: How much can the traditional dance movements be changed and still remain true to the original intent? At what point does it become a different dance? Who determines if the dance is representative of the people it is meant to represent? Discuss the universality of human themes.	Note for class management: It is very easy for a couple of students to dominate group discussions. A group discussion should incorporate all members of the class. Discussions should stay on the topic. This is an excellent opportunity to practice cognitive coaching.
Closure and assessment		
(90 minutes) Rubric (criterion, evidence, scale—teacher, self, peer)	Create a rubric to evaluate each group's presentation based on the use of ethnic content and development. Peer assessment: provide each group with feedback. Self-assessment: write a journal entry on the learning experience focusing on what was learned about the culture studied, the dance studied, and process of choreographing a cultural project.	Take this opportunity to incorporate writing into the lesson.

EXTENSIONS OR MODIFICATIONS

- Advanced students can develop a theme; tell a story; or interpret a poem, lyrics, or a myth incorporating the cultural movement as well as the interpretive movement.

- Students can conduct historical research and write an introduction to the presentation or a short report on the history of the dance tradition studied. In what context is the dance performed? What is the historical origin of the tradition? This is an excellent opportunity for students to gather information from first-hand resources involving family, friends, and community members or artists. This is also an opportunity to use the Internet and other library resources.

- Students can explore a variety of ways to manipulate sounds or text by voicing themselves, adding a reader, incorporating music, or removing the words altogether.

OPTIONAL   The classroom learning experience can be extended and refined into a cumulative performance on a concert stage.

TECHNOLOGY CONNECTION   Videotape presentations of class projects. Performances of projects from this learning experience may lend themselves to the use of multimedia through the projection of words, symbols, artwork, textures, and more. If a foreign language poem or myth is used, students can provide and project a PowerPoint translation.

ACCOMMODATION OR DIFFERENTIATION IDEAS   English as a second language (ESL) students can select a poem in their native language.

EVERYDAY LIVING (LIFETIME WELLNESS) CONNECTIONS   This learning experience leads to appreciation of literature and the universality of human expression.

Assessment Check: Teacher Composition Evaluation

Criteria	1 to 3 points	4 to 6 points	7 to 10 points	Points awarded
Text interpretation	Literal (mimetic)	Predictable	Abstract	
Composition content	Flat with few choreographic elements	Touches on some choreographic elements but is not fully developed	Well formed with varied use of directions, levels, rhythms, shape; developmentally complete with a clear beginning and conclusion	
Presentation	Unorganized with weak transitions, incomplete composition, and unclear or incomplete memorization of sequences	Complete with memorization in place but with movement being performed tenuously and in an unfulfilled manner	Fully prepared with committed performance of movements, transitions, and content	
			Total points	

From National Dance Association, 2010, *Implementing the national dance education standards* (Champaign, IL: Human Kinetics).

245

Name _____   Teacher _____

Assessment Check: Cumulative Self-Evaluation Worksheet for Text-Based Composition

Respond to each question by providing rationale and detailed explanation: 10 points maximum per question.

Discuss the universality of human themes.

1. What tradition did you explore?

2. What were some of the ways you chose to develop the concept? What images, moods, qualities, or symbols did you use in developing the movement composition?

3. What problems did you encounter, and what solutions did you find in researching, developing the concept, and creating the dance?

4 Did the poetry, text, story, or cultural movement inspire you to move in different ways than you have previously moved? How?

5. How much of the traditional dance movements did you change, and does it remain true to the original intent of the dance form? At what point would or did it become a different dance?

6. What did you learn about yourself, the movements, and the concept you explored?

7. What aspect of this project did you enjoy? Why? What was hard about the project?

8. In repeating the project, how would you change the process used to develop the choreographic ideas?

9. If this project were to be extended into a dance concert piece, what multimedia images would you consider using to enhance the impact of the choreography?

10. What about your created dance demonstrates that it is representative of a people or culture you explored?

Moving to Written Text

Students will select from a variety of short written texts (e.g., poetry, short stories, song lyrics), conduct research on preselected authors or selected text, develop movement phrases in sections or entirety, and present the composition. Based on 45- to 90-minute sessions, this learning experience may be accomplished in two to four sessions (see the following table for teacher instructions).

GRADE LEVEL   Grades 9 to 12

MATERIALS, EQUIPMENT, SPACE NEEDED   Bring five different examples of written text for students to select: poems or short stories of various styles, cultures (Japanese, Harlem Renaissance, Aztec), and themes (nature, love, death); sonnets and lyrics; newspaper stories; and myths. Suggested authors include e.e. Cummings, Lewis Carroll, Langston Hughes, Edna St. Vincent Millay, Maya Angelou, Pablo Neruda, and Tupac Shakur.

NATIONAL STANDARDS ADDRESSED

Content Standard 2. Understands choreographic principles, processes, and structures (Benchmark: c)

Content Standard 3. Understands dance as a way to create and communicate meaning (Benchmarks: a, b, c; Advanced a, b)

Content Standard 4. Applies and demonstrates critical and creative thinking skills in dance (Benchmarks: a, b, d; Advanced a, b)

Content Standard 5. Demonstrates and understands dance in various cultures and historical periods (Benchmark: a)

Content Standard 7. Makes connections between dance and other disciplines (Benchmarks: a, b; Advanced a)

GOAL   To use text as a springboard for choreography.

OBJECTIVES   As a result of participating in this learning experience, students will

1. create and perform a completed work. [Psychomotor]
2. answer aesthetic questions about the completed work. [Cognitive]
3. create abstract movements and explain how personal experience influenced the interpretation of the written text and the resulting choreography. [Affective]

VOCABULARY

Cadence	Abstract gesture
Rhythm	Imagery

EXTENSIONS OR MODIFICATIONS

- Advanced students can create original poems, lyrics, stories, or myths.
- Students can conduct library research to select authors based on personal interest.
- Students can explore a variety of ways to manipulate sounds or text by voicing themselves, adding a reader, incorporating music, or removing the words altogether.

OPTIONAL   The classroom learning experience can be extended and refined into a cumulative performance on the concert stage.

TEACHER INSTRUCTIONS FOR INTERDISCIPLINARY EXPERIENCE

Management	Teaching process	Teaching points and cues
Introduction		
(10-15 minutes)	Divide class into groups of four or five students and distribute photocopies of selected poems to each group. Allow 10 to 15 minutes for students to review and select a poem.	Introduce the lesson: "People all over the world have universal feelings that are expressed through the arts: music, dance, visual arts, poetry, stories, and myths."
Review of previous material, warm-up		
(10 minutes)	Demonstrate a short movement composition based on written text. Following the demonstration, lead structured improvisation using words.	Model the use of movement inspired by sound, shape, texture, rhythm, cadence, and tone of words. Assessment Check and Teacher Observation: Guide students in improvisation by asking leading questions: Is the sound of the word light or heavy, flickering or sustained, staccato or smooth, grounded or ethereal, slow or fast? What images or moods are evoked by the sound of the word? Lead students to select movements based on their interpretations.
New material		
a. **Exploratory activities** (30 minutes)	Ask students to select three words from the poem and use breath, weight, imagery, and rhythm to create movement about the words. Have students execute quick improvisations to get a feel of moving to words.	Encourage students to avoid literal interpretation of the written text by concentrating on the sounds, shape, texture, rhythms, and cadence of repeating selected words.
b. **Refinement activities** (over a period of two days)	Have students revise their interpretations. Ask students to articulate the reasons for their artistic decisions on the worksheet, explaining what was gained and lost.	Encourage students to give shape and form to composition by using transitions, floor patterns, body parts, levels, directions, and so on.
Recap of lesson, cool-down		
(20 minutes)	Have students present the day's progress on their compositions.	During this recap, ask students to sit with their backs to the mirrors and provide an audience.
Closure and assessment		
Rubric (criterion, evidence, scale— teacher, self, peer) (15 minutes)	Provide students an opportunity to explain any problems encountered in the process.	Assessment Check: Ask peers to provide commentary and suggestions. Help students analyze the similarities and differences between choices made by different groups.

TECHNOLOGY CONNECTION Videotape presentation of class projects. Performance of projects from this learning experience may lend themselves to the use of multimedia with the projection of words, symbols, artwork, textures, and more.

ACCOMMODATION OR DIFFERENTIATION IDEAS English as a second language (ESL) students can select a poem from their native language.

EVERYDAY LIVING (LIFETIME WELLNESS) CONNECTIONS This learning experience leads to appreciation of literature and the universality of human expression.

Assessment Check: Teacher Composition Evaluation

Criteria	1 to 3 points	4 to 6 points	7 to 10 points	Points awarded
Text interpretation	Literal (mimetic)	Predictable	Abstract	
Composition content	Flat with few choreographic elements	Touches on some choreographic elements but is not fully developed	Well formed with varied use of directions, levels, rhythms, shape; developmentally complete with a clear beginning and conclusion	
Presentation	Unorganized with weak transitions, incomplete composition, and unclear or incomplete memorization of sequences	Complete with memorization in place but with movement being performed tenuously and in an unfulfilled manner	Fully prepared with committed performance of movements, transitions and content	
			Total points	

Name _____   Teacher _____

Assessment Check: Cumulative Self-Evaluation Worksheet for Text-Based Composition

Respond to each question providing rationale and detailed explanation: 10 points maximum per question.

1. What concept did you explore for your dance?

2. What were some of the ways you chose to explore the concept?

3. What images, moods, qualities, and symbols did you use in creating your dance?

4. What problems did you encounter, and what solutions did you find for each problem while creating your dance?

5. How did the poetry or text inspire you to move in different ways than you have previously experienced?

6. What did you learn about yourself, the concept you chose for the dance, and the movements you chose to represent the concept?

7. While viewing the video about your chosen concept, what were highlights for you?

8. What aspect of this project did you enjoy? What was not enjoyable about the project?

9. If you had a chance to start over, what part of the process would you change?

10. If this project were to be extended into a dance concert piece, what multimedia images would you consider using to enhance the impact of the choreography?

Comparative Study of Percussive Footwork Dances

Students will be introduced to various cultures that use footwork to make percussive sounds. Students will learn the basic use of the footwork involved in dances. Based on 45- to 90-minute sessions, this learning experience may be accomplished in approximately four to six sessions (see the following table for teacher instructions).

GRADE LEVEL   Grades 9 to 12

MATERIALS, EQUIPMENT, SPACE NEEDED

- Music
- CD player or other music source
- DVD player
- Tap shoes or hard-soled shoes
- PBS video series *The Power of Dance;* "Riverdance" or *Bojangles; Tap* or *White Nights* with Gregory Hines; *Stomp;* any Fred Astaire or Gene Kelly movie; *Cotton Club;* video of the Ballet Folklorico of Mexico

NATIONAL STANDARDS ADDRESSED

Content Standard 1. Identifies and demonstrates movement elements and skills in performing dance (Benchmarks: Body b, c, d; Relationships b; Time a, b; Effort b, c; Advanced a, b, c)

Content Standard 3. Understands dance as a way to create and communicate meaning (Benchmark: c)

Content Standard 4. Applies and demonstrates critical and creative thinking skills in dance (Benchmarks: a, d; Advanced a)

Content Standard 5. Demonstrates and understands dance in various cultures and historical periods (Benchmarks: a, c; Advanced a, b)

Content Standard 6. Makes connections between dance and healthful living (Benchmarks: e; Advanced a)

Content Standard 7. Makes connections between dance and other disciplines (Benchmark: b)

GOAL   To introduce students to various cultures that use the percussive nature of the foot to create dances. Students will also look at how cross-cultural fusion, such as that between the Irish and former slaves, has created new art forms (i.e., tap) in America.

OBJECTIVES   As a result of participating in this learning experience, students will

1. demonstrate one or two of the basic techniques of tap, Bharatanatyam, Mexican folkloric, and flamenco. [Psychomotor]
2. engage in discussion on how tap dance began in America. [Cognitive]
3. experience the etiquette and expectations of a dance class and how the dance traditions addressed in this lesson developed; work in collaborative groups to choreograph project. [Affective]

VOCABULARY

Toe	Irish
Heel	Pull backs
Ball	Riff
Shuffle	Stomp
Flap	Stamp
Ball change	Time step
Cramp roll	Wings

TEACHER INSTRUCTIONS FOR COMPARATIVE STUDY OF PERCUSSIVE FOOTWORK DANCES

Management	Teaching process	Teaching points and cues
Introduction to tap		
(Day one: 10-15 minutes)	The day before this learning experience begins, instruct students to bring either hard-sole shoes or tap shoes to class.	Explain that, "Today, we are starting a unit on tap. We will also talk about the history of tap and how it developed in America."
(25 minutes) Have students work in center floor or at the barre for balance.	Have students start at the barre or center floor depending upon the space available. The tap class may need to be taught in another room if the tap shoes dig into the floor. Alternatively, plywood can be laid down to prevent scratching. Students will learn the basic steps of tap: shuffle, flap, ball change, and a time step.	Explain the articulation of the foot (toe, ball, and heel; entire flat foot; inside edge of the foot; and outside edge of the foot) and how it is used to create sound. Demonstrate the distribution of body weight and the steps (e.g., flap) that take weight (step) and the movements that do not take weight (touch) (e.g., the shuffle). Provide posture explanation: the knees must be kept bent (loose and pliable); the dancer needs to stay balanced on the balls of the feet for quickness and agility.
(15 minutes) Have students move across the floor four or five at a time.	Have students progress across the floor, working on chainé turns, stepping ball, and heel.	Reinforce the idea of spotting while turning; the arms assist by moving from Second position to middle Fifth.
Recap of lesson, cool-down		
(5-10 minutes)		Recount how some of the tap movements developed historically in America because of occurrences such as slave masters banning drums and dancing, and the cross-cultural fusing of Irish clogging and former slave dances.
Review, introduction of new material		
(Day two: 60 minutes)	Review shuffles, flaps, ball change, and time step. Add cramp roll. Begin a combination to a Duke Ellington piece.	Review the basic steps, enforcing clearness of sound.
(20 minutes) Ask students to work in center floor.	Add riffs and pull backs. Have students sit in chairs to practice wings.	Explain the use of the outside and inside edge of the foot.
(10 minutes) Ask students to move across the floor four or five at a time.	Introduce cramp roll to turns. Turning combination will be ball-heel, ball-heel, ball-heel, cramp roll for every two chainé turns.	
(Day three: 40 minutes) Introduce theory and historical analysis.	View parts of the movie *Tap*. Discuss how tap dance was used in social settings for fun and entertainment, and how individuals would engage in friendly competition. Discuss the age of some of the men dancing. Tap dancing is a form of dance that does not require years of highly professional training and can be enjoyed by people of all ages.	Help students look for specific movements performed in class. Telephone local colleges to see if any of the fraternities have step teams that are willing to come in to demonstrate stepping.

~ continued

Comparative Study of Percussive Footwork Dances

Teacher Instructions for Comparative Study of Percussive Footwork Dances ~ *continued*

Management	Teaching process	Teaching points and cues
Review, introduction of new material (*continued*)		
(30 minutes) Have students work in small groups.	Divide the students into small groups and have them create various rhythms to explore using all body parts.	Ask students to review the rhythms used in the film. Have the students create some of those rhythms using various body parts, such as "ham-boning." Monitor groups to check progress on assignment.
Recap of lesson, cool-down		
(20 minutes)	Ask students to informally present their projects.	Have students give verbal feedback on informal presentations. Ask if any of the students are actively engaged in step teams.
Review, warm-up		
(Day four: 40 minutes)	Provide a quick warm-up. Review time step, riffs, pull backs; ask students to try wings in the center floor. Have students complete the Duke Ellington combination.	Reinforce vocabulary.
(20 minutes) Ask students to work in small groups.	Have students practice the dance combination to be performed for a skills test.	Spot-check to make sure all students know the combination and will be able to perform it for a grade. Observe the students as they work together in small groups to keep them focused on the task and provide feedback.
Closure and assessment		
Rubric (teacher assessment) (Day five: 30 minutes)	Ask students to refine their presentations and incorporate critiques; ask each student to perform so that you can evaluate the performance based on a rubric (see page 257).	Emphasize that all sounds and rhythms must be crisp and clear.
New material		
(45 minutes)	Help students learn basic hand-clapping contra rhythms. Have students begin the simple arm movements in "Sevillanas."	Introduce material: "We are going to look at some different cultures and how they primarily use the feet to perform percussive dance. Today, we will first look at flamenco. In flamenco music, the rhythm is predominately in 12 counts. Flamenco dancers also use contra rhythms, syncopating the rhythms of the feet with the clapping of hands." Discuss the use of castanets, although students will probably not be using them. You can bring in a pair to demonstrate. Discuss the similarities and differences between the tap and flamenco dance forms.
(10 minutes) Have students watch "Riverdance" video.		Cue the section in "Riverdance" to show the flamenco portion of the show.

Management	Teaching process	Teaching points and cues
New material		
(Day six: 30 minutes) Have students sit in a circle on the floor.	Have students go through all mudras seated in a circle.	Introduce the art form of Bharatanatyam. Discuss how the dance was performed only in the temples for religious purposes to tell the stories from the sacred Hindu texts. Show the mudras, or hand positions, and explain how each has a meaning, rather like sign language.
(10 minutes) Ask students to stand in lines and work in center floor.	Instruct students in the basic footwork to create rhythms of 2, 3, 4, 5, 6, 7, 8, and 9.	Begin footwork. Explain that the Hindu likened the earth to a gigantic drum that is played with the feet.
(40 minutes) Have students work on combination.	Instruct students in the beginning dance combination of the story of Shiva.	Reaffirm that dance in Indian society is of a religious nature with the goal of preserving Indian history and culture.
Closure and assessment		
(4-5 days) Students need the time to research a chosen culture, group rehearse, organize and obtain costumes. Students will also prepare a brief presentation so they can share information with the rest of the class about the process of the group's work.	Give students an opportunity to research a particular culture introduced in this learning exercise. Have students work in small groups to reconstruct a dance from that culture. Give added credit to students who include costumes or bring in a cultural food dish to accompany the presentation.	Check with local Indian or Mexican restaurants to see if they can recommend a dancer or a company to come to your school for a lecture, demonstration, or performance of Mexican folkloric or Indian dance.

OPTIONAL   Bring in a professional tap dancer or other international performer for a lecture, demonstration, or performance.

EXTENSIONS OR MODIFICATIONS   Have students write research papers on of the lives of professional tap performers. Discuss why so many tap performers are male.

TECHNOLOGY CONNECTION   Students can research historical presentations by professional tap artists on video or the Internet.

ACCOMMODATION OR DIFFERENTIATION IDEAS   Conduct research on a famous dancer in another culture. See how the training differs or compares to that of a ballet dancer.

TEXTS

- Any tap, flamenco, or Bharatanatyam manual.
- L. Fauly Emery, *Black Dance: From 1619 to Today*, 1989, 2nd ed., East Windsor, NJ: Princeton Book.
- R. Long, *The Black Tradition in American Dance*, 1995, New York: Smithmark Publishers.
- G. Jonas, *Dancing: The Pleasure, Power, and Art of Movement*, 1998, New York: Henry Adams.
- M. Fonteyn, *The Magic of Dance*, 1982, rev, ed., New York: Alfred A. Knopf.

EVERYDAY LIVING (LIFETIME WELLNESS) CONNECTIONS   Tap dancing is a form of social dance and can be performed late into life. Students can wear pedometers or heart rate monitors during class to track their steps or heart rate while dancing.

RESEARCH TOPICS   Students can select a professional tap dancer, or other international dancer, from the following list for the purpose of conducting research and presenting oral reports.

Fred Astaire

Charles "Honi" Coles

Gregory Hines

Maurice Hines

Gene Kelly

William Henry Lane "Master Juba"

Nicholas Brothers, Fayard and Harold

Bill "Bojangles" Robinson

Earl "Snakehips" Tucker

Bert Williams

Uday Shankar

Carmen Amaya

La Argentina

Lola Montez

Vicente Escudero

Balasaraswati

Rukmini Devi

Tap Combination Rubric

Criteria	1 to 3 points	4 to 6 points	7 to 10 points	Points awarded
Presentation	Performance is tentative and unsure	Performance is acceptable but without a sense of personal style	Performance is strong and well presented with style	
	Memorization of sequences is unclear or incomplete	Memorization in place but with movement being performed tenuously and in an unfulfilled manner	Fully prepared with committed performance of movements, transitions, and content	
	Sounds are muffled and unclear	Most of the sounds are clear	Sounds are clean and clear	
	Rhythm is off and missing sounds	On rhythm, but sounds are missing	On rhythm with clear, clean sounds	
			Total points	

From National Dance Association, 2010, *Implementing the national dance education standards* (Champaign, IL: Human Kinetics).

257

Ballet and the Early Ballerinas and Dancing Masters

Students will be introduced to ballet technique and the pre-Classic dance forms, choreograph their own pre-Classic dance, research one of the early ballerinas or dance masters, design costumes (on paper or in reality), and present findings in a group presentation. Based on 45- or 90-minute sessions, this learning experience may take several sessions of varying lengths over three or four days to accomplish (see the table on page 260 for teacher instructions).

GRADE LEVEL   Grades 9 to 12

MATERIALS, EQUIPMENT, SPACE NEEDED

- Music
- CD player or other music source
- DVD player
- Music of pre-Classic dance forms (pavane, galliard, courante, allemande, sarabande, and gigue)
- Dancetime DVD *500 Years of Social Dance Vol. I: 15th-19th Centuries; Orchesography* by Thoinot Arbeau, 1967, New York: Dover Publications.
- Ballet history books: *The Magic of Dance* by M. Fonteyn, 1982, rev, ed., New York: Alfred A. Knopf; *The History of the Dance in Art and Education* by R. Kraus, S. Hilsendager, and B. Dixon, 1990, 3rd. ed., Englewood Cliffs, NJ: Prentice-Hall, Inc.; *Pre-Classic Dance Forms* by L. Horst, 1987, Englewood Cliffs, NJ: Prentice-Hall.

NATIONAL STANDARDS ADDRESSED

Content Standard 1. Identifies and demonstrates movement elements and skills in performing dance (Benchmarks: Body a, b, c, d; Space c, f; Relationships a, b, c; Effort b)

Content Standard 2. Understands choreographic principles, processes, and structures (Benchmarks: c, d)

Content Standard 4. Applies and demonstrates critical and creative thinking skills in dance (Benchmarks: d; Advanced a)

Content Standard 5. Demonstrates and understands dance in various cultures and historical periods (Benchmarks: a, c; Advanced a)

Content Standard 6. Makes connections between dance and healthful living (Benchmarks: c, e; Advanced a)

Content Standard 7. Makes connections between dance and other disciplines (Benchmarks: b, d; Advanced b)

GOAL   To introduce students to ballet technique and the early history of ballet.

OBJECTIVES   As a result of participating in this learning experience, students will

1. physically demonstrate basic ballet techniques (see vocabulary list). [Psychomotor]
2. orally present research material as well as choreograph a historical piece of ballet. [Cognitive]
3. demonstrate the etiquette and expectation of a ballet class and how the traditions developed; work in collaborative groups to choreograph a project. [Affective]

Learning basic ballet skills can help students to master skills in other dance forms.

VOCABULARY

Adagio

Attitude

Arabesque

Balancé

Chainé

Changement

Chassé

Coupé

Croisé

Dégagé

Demi-plié

Derriere

Devant

Developpé

En dedans

En dehors

En face

Glisade

Grand battement

Grand plié

Pas de chat

Passé

Pique

Pirouette

Port de bras

Relevé

Rond de jamb

Sous-sus

Soutenu

Tendu

Tour jeté

OPTIONAL   Have students prepare a book report on *Orchesography* by Thoinot Arbeau, 1967, by Dover Publications in Mineola, NY.

TEACHER INSTRUCTIONS FOR BALLET AND THE EARLY BALLERINAS AND DANCING MASTERS

Management	Teaching process	Teaching points and cues
Introduction		
(Day one: 30 minutes) Have students start at the barre.	Introduce students to pliés, tondues, dégagés, rond de jambs, stretches on the barre, and grand battements.	Say, "Today, we are starting a unit on ballet. We will also talk about the history of ballet, beginning with Louix XIV, the first academy of dance, and the origin of the professional dancer."
(15 minutes) Have students work in center floor.	Have students come to center floor to work on en dehors pirouettes and adagio. Introduce the concept of spotting.	Guide students with verbal cues for slow, seamless movement in adagio and for the proper execution of pirouettes: 1. Use good, solid preparation in Fourth position. 2. Use arms to aid in the pirouette by preparing the arms in Third position and pulling into middle Fifth (Cecchetti method) during the turn. 3. Push evenly from both feet in Fourth position, pick up the back leg into passé devant, and turn toward the back leg. 4. Keep the torso solid, turning in one piece. 5. Focus in the mirror or on one spot; snap the head quickly to refocus on the spot to complete the turn.
(15 minutes) Have students move across the floor four or five at a time.	Ask students to move across the floor working on chaîné turns.	Reinforce the idea of spotting while turning and that the arms assist by moving from Third position to middle Fifth.
Recap of lesson, cool-down		
(5-10 minutes)	Lead students in a reverence, introducing croisé and en face.	Recount how some of the movements developed in the courts and how the turn-out movement is associated historically with the proscenium stage. Many of the moves were designed for athletic and quick moves. The positions were derived from fencing positions.
Review and introduction of new material		
(Day two: 40 minutes)	Review pliés, tondues, dégagés, rond de jambs, stretches, and grand battements. Add balances in coupé, passé, and sous-sus. Teach ways to turn to the opposite side of the barre with soutenu.	Review the five basic positions of the arms and feet. Reinforce how the arms and feet work together. Repeat the basic exercises at the barre.
(20 minutes) Have students work in center floor.	Add balancé, glissade, and pas de chat to the center floor work. Review adagio from previous class and set to a pavane.	Explain the difference between an en dehors (outside) and en dedans (inside) pirouette.
(10 minutes) Have students move across the floor four or five at a time.	Introduce piqué turns for students to practice as they travel across the floor.	

Management	Teaching process	Teaching points and cues
Cool-down		
(10 minutes)	Have students complete the reverence.	Reflect on the etiquette of the ballet class and the historical traditions still prevalent today, such as the reverence.
(Day three: 40 minutes) Have students explore theory and historical analysis.	Have students view "Dance Through the Times," showing the pre-Classic dance forms. Show pictures of the early ballerinas and describe their qualities as dancers. Listen to the music of the pre-Classic dance forms. Discuss the musical qualities and how they will transform into movement. Discuss the early role of dance in society.	Ask students to look for specific movement qualities that were explored in previous technique classes. Initiate discussion on the choreography viewed: Ask, "How does social dance fit into our society? Do you think any of our social dance forms today might eventually become a classic dance form?"
(40 minutes) Have students visit the library.	Ask students to review a list of early ballet dancers to select an artist of interest for an oral report (see list on page 262. Use the library resource material or Internet to research the early ballerinas, their dancing qualities, and their costumes. Have students work in small groups to develop a combination presentation.	Give students a list of the early ballet dancers and masters for their oral presentations. With students, look at the pictures of the early ballerinas. Note their stature as it differs from that of ballerinas today. Look at some of the classic female figures and discuss how the thin aesthetic developed. Talk about healthy choices for nutrition and the dancer.
Review of previous material, warm-up		
(Day four: 20 minutes)	Conduct quick barre warm-up.	Reinforce vocabulary.
(40 minutes) Have students work in small groups.	Give students some of the books and music resources available and allow them to choose one of the pre-Classic dance forms to choreograph. Ask students to review the qualities of the different dance forms and the costumes that were worn to accommodate the different footwork.	Spot-check to make sure all students have a topic and enough resources. Observe the students as they work together in small groups to keep them focused on the task and provide feedback.
Closure and assessment		
(20 minutes) Ask students to sit with their backs to the mirror to observe their peers performing.	Have students take turns presenting their combinations in the small groups of four to six.	Ask members from each group to perform while the other students observe. Have students provide general feedback to the members of their group.
Rubric (teacher assessment) (80 minutes)	Have students refine the performance, incorporate critiques, and then perform their combination for you to evaluate based on the rubric on page 265. Ask students to present their historical findings and costume designs orally.	
(10 minutes) Allow time for a recap.	Ask students to discuss what they learned. Address any questions they might have about their written assignment.	

EXTENSIONS OR MODIFICATIONS   Have students develop research papers on early ballerinas or dancing masters.

TECHNOLOGY CONNECTIONS
- Students can research historical presentations by early ballet artists on videotapes or the Internet.
- Students can prepare a multimedia presentation about their research.

ACCOMMODATION OR DIFFERENTIATION IDEAS   Encourage male students to research information about the history of men in ballet and early dance masters.

TEXTS
- T. Arbeau, *Orchesography*, 1967, New York: Dover Publications.
- M. Fonteyn, *The Magic of Dance*, 1982, rev, ed., New York: Alfred A. Knopf.
- R. Kraus, S. Hilsendager, and B. Dixon, *The History of the Dance in Art and Education*, 1990, 3rd. ed., San Francisco, CA: Benjamin Cummings.
- Other Texts: any ballet history books

EVERYDAY LIVING (LIFETIME WELLNESS) CONNECTIONS   Have students look at some photographs of early ballerinas and compare their body types to that of the classic female dancers' bodies.

ORAL PRESENTATION ON THE EARLY BALLERINAS   Have each student select an early ballerina or ballet master from the following list for the purpose of conducting research and presenting an oral report. Use the Rubric for Writing (page 263) to assist with project expectations.

Women	*Men*
Maria Anne de Cupis de Camargo	King Louis XIV
Maria Taglioni	Jules Perrot
Carlotta Grisi	Charles Diderot
Marie Salle	Jean-Georges Noverre
Fanny Elssler	Marius Petipa
Lucile Grahn	August Bournonville
Fanny Cerrito	Salvatore Vigan
Anne Heinel	Jean-Pierre Beauchamp
Augusta Maywood	Jean Douberval
	Raoul Feuillet

GROUP ORAL PROJECT   Provide these directions to students: You are to write a five-paragraph essay about your chosen ballerina or dancing master. You may write your information on cue cards so that you are not reading your essay verbatim. Try to use dance movements to demonstrate your findings. You are allowed to be creative in the interpretation of your historical findings.

   A five-paragraph essay consists of an introductory paragraph, the body, and a closing paragraph. Your three body paragraphs are to cite specific examples of your person's contribution to ballet and how ballet developed under his or her influence. Your opening and closing paragraphs should focus on what is known about the overall life and work of your chosen person.

1. Outline your thoughts before writing to ensure an original paper.
2. Submit a rough draft. Rough drafts will be accepted no later than one week in advance of the due date.

3. Papers must be typed on unlined paper, be double spaced, use a 12-point font, and have one-inch margins.

4. Include a title page with your name, grade, class, and date. Include a standard header or footer with the page number and your last name on each page.

5. Follow standard formal writing usage:
   - End your opening paragraph with a thesis statement.
   - Begin each paragraph with a topic sentence.
   - Use no contractions, abbreviations, or slang.

6. Use correct punctuation, spelling, grammar; if you are unsure, ask—or find another way to get your point across.

7. Do not use "I think" or "I feel." These are inappropriate in this type of paper.

8. For all other questions and issues, consult me, your English teacher, and texts.

Rubric for Writing

4: Superior Performance; Level: Distinguished

Addresses the topic directly.

Demonstrates an identifiable order and structure with a topic sentence, support, and a conclusion.

Focuses on the topic and demonstrates knowledge of content by providing excellent supporting details.

Displays effective use of language with a varied vocabulary.

Demonstrates proficiency of mechanics, including spelling, punctuation, and capitalization.

Produces error-free typing in the paper.

Offers complete and varied sentences.

3: Above Average Performance; Level: Proficient

Addresses topic directly.

Demonstrates an identifiable order and structure with a topic sentence, support, and a conclusion.

Focuses on the topic and demonstrates knowledge of content by providing adequate supporting details.

Displays appropriate use of language.

Demonstrates appropriate use of mechanics including spelling, punctuation, and capitalization.

Produces a paper that is nearly error-free typing.

Offers complete and varied sentences.

2: At or Below Average Performance; Level: Apprentice

Addresses the topic.

Demonstrates an identifiable limited order and structure with a topic sentence, support, and a conclusion.

Uses supporting details that demonstrate limited knowledge of content.

Displays limited use of language and vocabulary.

Demonstrates limited knowledge and use of mechanics, including spelling, punctuation, and capitalization.

Produces a paper with errors that may interfere with comprehension.

Generally uses complete sentences.

Occasionally uses sentence fragments or run-on sentences.

1: Low Performance; Level: Novice

Does not address the topic.

Has no evidence of order or structure.

Has few, if any, supporting details.

Displays incorrect or insufficient use of language and vocabulary.

Displays errors in mechanics, including spelling, punctuation, and capitalization.

Produces a paper with frequent errors in the typed material.

Often uses sentence fragments or run-on sentences.

Ballet Dance Culmination Project Rubric

Criteria	1 to 3 points	4 to 6 points	7 to 10 points	Points awarded
Presentation	Unorganized with weak transitions	Organized with smooth transitions	Fully prepared with sophisticated transitions	
	Combination is incomplete	Combination is complete	Combination is complete and complex	
	Memorization of sequences is unclear or incomplete	Memorization in place but with movement being performed tenuously and in an unfulfilled manner	Fully prepared with committed performance of movements, transitions, and content	
	Costume design incomplete or sloppily presented (e.g., no color, ragged paper)	Costume design complete on paper, in color	Costume worn by performers	
	No noticeable attempt to have created a living historical figure	Attempt made at creating a living historical figure, but student is confused on historical facts	Dancer(s) has taken on the persona of an early ballerina or dancing master, who is visibly and orally reflected	
			Total points	

From National Dance Association, 2010, *Implementing the national dance education standards* (Champaign, IL: Human Kinetics).

265

Graffiti and Hip-Hop

Exploring Modern Mosaics

Students will use graffiti and pop culture as a springboard to create a study in movement that is related to modern mosaics. This learning experience may be accomplished in several sessions of varying lengths over four or more days (see the following for teacher instructions).

GRADE LEVEL   Grades 9 to 12

MATERIALS, EQUIPMENT, SPACE NEEDED

- Music with a basic hip-hop beat (no lyrics)
- Access to a community with examples of artistic and destructive graffiti
- Digital camera or digital video camera
- Internet
- Artists within the community
- Paper and markers
- Copy of Alfonso Ossorio's "Breaking Chain" or other comparable mosaic

NATIONAL STANDARDS ADDRESSED

Content Standard 1. Identifies and demonstrates movement elements and skills in performing dance (Benchmarks: Space a; Relationships a, b; Effort a)

Content Standard 2. Understands choreographic principles, processes, and structures (Benchmarks: b; Advanced a)

Content Standard 3. Understands dance as a way to create and communicate meaning (Benchmarks: a, b, c)

Content Standard 4. Applies and demonstrates critical and creative thinking skills in dance (Benchmarks: b, d; Advanced b)

Content Standard 5. Demonstrates and understands dance in various cultures and historical periods (Benchmarks: a; Advanced a)

Content Standard 7. Makes connections between dance and other disciplines (Benchmarks: a, b; Advanced b)

GOAL   To manipulate graffiti and the hip-hop genre to explore and expand movement possibilities.

OBJECTIVES   As a result of participating in this learning experience, students will

1. expand their diversity of movements and their range of movement vocabulary to embrace elements of modern dance. [Psychomotor]
2. visualize the possibilities of expanding the staging of the hip-hop genre with the craftsmanship of modern dance. [Cognitive]
3. explain how personal experiences and group dynamics influence the development of the resulting choreography. [Affective]

VOCABULARY

Absence of focal point	Mosaic
Metamorphosis	Pattern
Predominance	Planes

TEACHER INSTRUCTIONS FOR GRAFFITI AND HIP-HOP

Management	Teaching process	Teaching points and cues
Introduction		
(Day one: 30 minutes) Have students work individually.	Tell students, "Create an abstract portrait of yourself in the graffiti style. Select one to three symbols, colors, shapes, and lines that represent your personality. Draw an 8.5 by 11 inch (21.6 x 27.9 cm) image using lines and colors that are representative of you."	Introduce the lesson: "Since the beginning of time, human beings have used symbols to express their feelings, thoughts, and accomplishments. Examples include pictographs on cave walls, hieroglyphics, totem poles, teepees, murals, and tagging. Society also places restrictions on the use of such symbols. Graffiti is a style of personal expression in the modern day pop culture."
Review of previous material, warm-up		
(30 minutes)	Ask students to create movement sequences that capture the line, color, and energy of the design—and imagine creating a three-dimensional canvas in space.	Guide students to shape, carve, mold, and explore the ceiling and floor of the imaginery canvas. Encourage each student to use full-body movements, various planes, and at least three levels to capture the essence of his or her name.
(30 minutes) Divide students into groups of four. Build on students' individual studies and create groups according to the designs that compliment or juxtapose one another.	Have students present individual movement studies that demonstrate understanding of the assignment. Ask students to take turns as performer and peer observer.	Check for comprehension of the assignment and assist individual students needing additional instruction. Students will provide verbal critiques to their peers for later refinement of each study. Encourage students to use appropriate language while critiquing other students.
New material		
a. Exploratory activities (Day Two: 30 minutes)	Ask students to work in their assigned groups of four to expand the movement studies into three-dimensional designs.	Ask students to, "Be spatially aware of dancers so that they can intertwine, overlap, and create new pathways allowing for complimentary and juxtaposing designs." Scan the class and assist students with the assignment as needed.
(20 minutes) Have students sit with their backs to the mirror and act as an audience.	Have student groups take turns presenting their three-dimensional adaptations of the original designs.	Provide feedback. At the end of the presentation, determine if the class as a whole is ready to move on to the last part of the assignment.
b. Refinement activities (40 minutes)	Encourage students to explore moving their three-dimensional designs through space by adding locomotor floor patterns. These will incorporate different rhythms into the previously conceived movements.	Make suggestions to stimulate students' choreography by suggesting moments such as hopping, sliding, skipping, running, leaping, swirling, gliding, and falling.
(Day three: 90 minutes) Based on the number of students in the class, decide how many groups will perform the assignment at once. If the class is very large, students may have to take turns.	Have each group draw a number. The numbers assign different sequences of the sections to be performed simultaneously: 1-2-3, 2-3-1, or 3-1-2. Because definite measures or counts were not assigned, the sections may overlap.	Remind students: Section 1 is the individual study, section 2 is the three-dimensional grouping, and section 3 is the locomotor section. Determine how many times each sequence will be performed so that all students will have equal time on stage.

~ continued

Teacher Instructions for Graffiti and Hip-Hop ~ *continued*

Management	Teaching process	Teaching points and cues
New material *(continued)*		
Pass out paper and markers for students to use to draw floor pattern designs.	Have students map out floor patterns. Students determine timing sequences by using mathematical equations.	Direct students to create a legend to color code each group member for easier navigation. Assist students with timing of the various sequences.
Recap of lesson, cool-down		
(Day four: 20 minutes) Begin class with a jazz or modern warm-up because all students will be dancing full out today in preparation for videotaping.	If space is available, have students recap previous day's practice in the auditorium prior to filming movement mosaics. Have students practice staging floor patterns and three-dimensional designs in the new location.	If an auditorium is not available, look for a large space such as a cafeteria, football field, or patio where the view angle of the camera will capture the entire group at once. For a mosaic effect, the camera should not pan.
(40 minutes)	Videotape the mosaic choreography. Have the class view the video recording of the moving mosaic.	
Closure and assessment		
(Day five: 90 minutes) Rubric (criterion, evidence, scale—teacher, self, peer)	Ask, "How does our movement study relate to Ossorio's mosaic 'Breaking Chain' in terms of metamorphosis, predominance, repetition, and absence of focal point?" Have class view the video to reflect on the question. Conduct class dialogue on the mosaic and respond to questions.	Say, "Dance and the visual arts share the same basic elements of design." Provide this information from the Whitney Museum of American Art in New York: "Despite the number and variety of the objects in Alfonso Ossorio's artwork, there is a sense of underlying organization in the work. Shapes and colors are repeated. The parts seem to flow, but within definite areas of the surface. They make up a loose mosaic that constantly rearranges itself before our eyes, like some strange living organisms moving in a drop of water under a microscope."

EXTENSIONS OR MODIFICATIONS Possible extensions or modifications for students include these:

- View a documentary film on the history of graffiti.
- Research the history of symbols and the universality of graffiti, famous graffiti and mosaic artists, origin of rap and hip-hop, or pop culture's influence on fashion.
- Perform a multimedia concert piece bringing together all aspects of the project, including
  - scanning and presenting the name graffiti drawing done at the beginning of the assignment,
  - displaying digital photos taken throughout the community that demonstrate both acceptable and destructive forms of graffiti, and
  - designing costumes that reflect pop culture's and graffiti's influence on fashion.

OPTIONAL

- Selected students investigate the positive and negative aspects of graffiti through the use of primary sources in the community (business and property owners as well as police officers).

- Students further investigate the positive and negative aspects of graffiti by taking digital photo images for a PowerPoint introduction or multimedia inclusion.

TECHNOLOGY CONNECTIONS

- Selected students can take digital photographs of acceptable and unacceptable graffiti in the community to share with classmates.

- Students scan and prepare a PowerPoint slide show using original student drawings as multimedia projections during a performance.

- Students find images on the Internet that exemplify the universality of graffiti.

EVERYDAY LIVING (LIFETIME WELLNESS) CONNECTIONS   This learning experience helps students develop respect for nonconformist artistic expression, appreciation of the universality of human expression, and respect for personal and public property.

Rubric for the Hip-Hop Mosaic

Criteria	1 to 14 points	15 to 19 points	20 to 25 points	Points awarded
Group participation	Absent or tardy, noncommittal, complains, whines, works poorly with others	On time; cooperative but offers few suggestions; has difficulty creating material and remembering sequences	Punctual; strong group leader and team player; offers suggestions and ideas; shares equipment; tutors peers	
Composition content	Flat with few choreographic elements; difficulty managing the overlapping time sequences; spatial patterns are not clear or evident	Touches on some choreographic elements but the composition lacks strong three-dimensional quality; adequate management of overlapping time sequences but with uninteresting results	Well formed with varied use of directions, levels, rhythms, shapes, and planes; strong development of planes that intertwine, overlap, show clear spatial pathways, and create a three-dimensional design(s)	
Presentation	Unorganized with weak transitions, incomplete composition, and unclear or incomplete memorization of sequences	Complete with memorization in place but with movement being performed tenuously and in an unfulfilled manner	Fully prepared with committed performance of movements, transitions, and content	
Audience and peer assessment behavior	**1 to 5 points**	**6 to 10 points**	**11 to 15 points**	
	Negative comments and inappropriate vocabulary or no comments given	Proper audience behavior; few comments, and difficulty using the applied vocabulary	Proper audience behavior, positive and well-thought-out critiques, and appropriate vocabulary	
Original graffiti drawing	**1 to 3 points**	**4 to 6 points**	**7 to 10 points**	
	Sloppy, ripped, smudged, dog-eared, no colors used, incomplete, no time taken	Complete; some use of color, adequate use of time; not in the graffiti style	Vibrant use of color, interesting shapes; full use of graffiti style; complete and on time	
			Total points	

From National Dance Association, 2010, *Implementing the national dance education standards* (Champaign, IL: Human Kinetics).

Assessment Check: Graffiti and Hip-Hop Worksheet

Respond to each question providing rationale and detailed explanation: 10 points maximum per question.

1. How does our movement study relate to Ossorio's mosaic "Breaking Chain" in terms of metamorphosis, predominance, repetition, and absence of focal point? What were some of the ways you chose to explore these concepts?

2. How did the mosaic imagery help you to appreciate another perspective of art and dance?

3. What problems did you encounter and what solutions did you use in creating a three-dimensional design?

4. How did the graffiti and hip-hop project inspire you to move in different ways than you have previously experienced?

5. What did you learn about working and performing with a group on the collaborative section of the project?

6. Based on viewing the video, how did we meet the objective of creating a movement mosaic and bringing to life the qualities associated with mosaics?

7. What aspect of this project did you enjoy? What did you not enjoy?

8. How did the hip-hop music support the choreographic project? What hip-hop movement qualities emerged from the use of the hip-hop beat?

9. How did the three sections of this project help you to expand or explore new movement possibilities? What problems did you encounter with the project?

10. If this project is extended into a dance concert piece, what multimedia images would you consider using to enhance the impact of the choreography?

The Influence of African-American Culture and History on Modern Dance

Students will be introduced to modern dance technique, view selected choreographic works, analyze the relationship to the elements of modern dance, and assess their knowledge through a short research paper. This learning experience may be accomplished in two or more sessions, depending on instructional time per day, students' knowledge-base, and their past experience in dance (see the following table for teacher instructions). Based on 45- to 90-minute sessions, this learning experience may take two to four sessions.

GRADE LEVEL   Grades 9 to 12

MATERIALS, EQUIPMENT, SPACE NEEDED

- Music and music playing source
- Improvisation evaluation form (page 278)
- Television and VCR and monitor or DVD player and projection screen
- Selected videos of modern choreographic works or those of the modern pioneers
- Choreographic Video Worksheet (page 279)
- Elements of Dance Handout (page 280)

NATIONAL STANDARDS ADDRESSED

Content Standard 1. Identifies and demonstrates movement elements and skills in performing dance (Benchmarks: Body c, Space a, Relationships b, Effort c)

Content Standard 2. Understands choreographic principles, processes, and structures (Benchmarks: a; Advanced b)

Content Standard 3. Understands dance as a way to create and communicate meaning (Benchmarks: a, b; Advanced a, b)

Content Standard 4. Applies and demonstrates critical and creative thinking skills in dance (Benchmarks: b; Advanced a)

Content Standard 5. Demonstrates and understands dance in various cultures and historical periods (Benchmark: c)

Content Standard 6. Makes connections between dance and healthful living (Benchmark: d)

GOAL   To introduce students to modern dance techniques and examine the contributions of African-American choreographers to modern dance forms.

OBJECTIVES   As a result of participating in this learning experience, students will

1. demonstrate 10 to 15 elements of modern dance. [Psychomotor]
2. recognize the influence of African-American culture and dance on modern dance. [Cognitive]
3. experience the etiquette and expectations of a modern dance class (e.g., dance barefooted, wear leotard and tights to assess body lines) to increase awareness of new ideas, movement, and music. [Affective]

VOCABULARY

Contract or release	Bound or free
Symmetrical or asymmetrical	Straight or curved
Heavy or light	Fall or recovery
Direct or indirect focus	Sharp or smooth
Tight or loose	

TEACHER INSTRUCTIONS FOR THE INFLUENCE OF AFRICAN-AMERICAN CULTURE AND HISTORY ON MODERN DANCE

Management	Teaching process	Teaching points and cues
Introduction		
(Day one: 30 minutes) Have students start at center floor.	Conduct a simple warm-up using the breath to facilitate movements (e.g., swinging, circling, twisting, collapsing and rising).	Introduce the lesson: "Today, we are starting a unit on modern dance and the contributions of the early modern dance pioneers."
Review of previous material, warm-up		
(30 minutes) Ask students to travel across the floor four or five at a time.	Have students travel across the floor using the same elements reviewed previously while incorporating locomotor steps. Ask students to perform progressions that increase in complexity: <ul><li>Collapsing, running, and rising</li><li>Swinging and skipping</li><li>Leaping and twisting</li></ul>	Guide students with verbal cues that expand on the qualities reviewed in the warm-up. Teaching cues: <ul><li>Weight transforms from heavy to light.</li><li>In fall and recovery, there are no placement of the arms. The arms are weighted. Let the gravity shape the arms.</li><li>Upper torso twists over the front leg.</li></ul>
New material		
(20 minutes) Ask students to return to center floor in a scattered formation.	Instruct students in a movement combination based on the warm-up and the progressions across the floor (32 to 48 counts).	
Divide students into small groups of four to six.		After you have demonstrated the combination and observe that the majority of students understand the material, assess the combinations performed in small groups.
Cool-down		
(10 minutes)	Have students follow you as you perform cool-down movements and stretches to bring closure to the class and prevent any muscular soreness.	The cool-down may replicate the warm-up process, only performed at a much slower pace and incorporating breath and stretching movements.
	If time allows, lead students through a quiet, meditative, deep relaxation.	Lead students gradually down to the floor into a supine position. Dim the lights if you want.
Recap of lesson		
(Day two: 20 minutes)	Have class view selected video.	Ask students to look for specific movement qualities that were explored in previous technique classes.
	Have students complete the Choreographic Video Worksheet.	Initiate discussion on the choreography viewed and guide students through the process of analyzing the video.
(10 minutes)	Ask students to review a list of modern dancers and choreographers. Ask each student to select an artist of interest for a book or magazine article report. See list on page 274.	Give students a list of modern dancers and choreographers. Ask each student to select an artist for further reading. Provide the criteria for successful reports.

~ continued

Teacher Instructions for the Influence of African-American Culture and History on Modern Dance ~ *continued*

Management	Teaching process	Teaching points and cues
Recap of lesson *(continued)*		
(20 minutes) Ask students to move to center floor.	Begin a warm-up using one or more of the modern movement elements, including • bending, • swaying, • shaking, and • stretching.	
(20 minutes) Recap the lesson.	Have students review and refine movement combinations from the previous lesson and add 8 additional counts of movement using the new elements presented during the warm-up.	Observes students as they perform the warm-up to determine if they are ready for independent work.
Closure and assessment		
(20 minutes) Ask students to sit with their backs to the mirror as an audience.	Ask students to take turns presenting their combinations four at a time.	Divide students into four groups. One member from each group will perform while the other members observe. No more than four dancers will perform at a time. Students will provide general feedback to the members of their groups.
Rubric (teacher assessment) (80 minutes)	Ask students to refine, incorporate critiques, and then perform as you evaluate the performances based on the rubric.	While students are working on their reports, evaluate their modern combination performances. Determine how many students you can evaluate at a time. Generally three or four at a time is recommended.
(10 minutes)	Ask students to discuss what they learned. Address any questions they might have on their written assignment.	Spot-check to make sure each student has a topic and enough resources.

WRITING ASSIGNMENT ON MODERN DANCE ARTISTS   Select a modern dance artist from the following list for the purpose of writing a report. Use the Rubric for Writing (page 276) to assist you with writing expectations.

Ruth St. Denis	Merce Cunningham
Ted Shawn	Twyla Tharp
Isadora Duncan	Katherine Dunham
Loie Fuller	Pearl Primus
Martha Graham	Talley Beatty
Doris Humphrey	Donald McKayle
Charles Weidman	Clay Taliaferro
Hanya Holm	Charles H. Williams
Mary Wigman	Bill T. Jones
Anna Sokolow	Joan Myers Brown
Alvin Nicolais	Chuck Davis
José Limón	Ulysses Dove
Paul Taylor	

EXTENSIONS OR MODIFICATIONS   Students can view videos or DVDs on a variety of modern dance artists and complete the Choreographic Video Worksheet on page 279. An online search can help students access materials to review.

ACCOMMODATION OR DIFFERENTIATION IDEAS   Advanced students can be challenged by conducting a study on Alvin Ailey using video(s) and his autobiography to write a research paper.

Texts

- A. Ailey, *Revelations: The Autobiography of Alvin Ailey*, 1995, New York: Carol Publishing.
- L. Fauly Emery, *Black Dance: From 1619 to Today*, 1989, 2nd ed., East Windsor, NJ: Princeton Book.
- R. Long, *The Black Tradition in American Dance*, 1995, New York: Smithmark Publishers.

Suggested videos on Alvin Ailey

"Dance Black America"

"Free to Dance" (PBS)

"Four by Ailey"

"An Evening with the Alvin Ailey" (American Dance Theatre)

"Ailey Dances"

"Hymn for Alvin Ailey" (PBS)

Dance Research Paper

Provide these directions to students: You are to write a five-paragraph essay about ways Alvin Ailey told his life experiences through his choreography.

A five-paragraph essay consists of an introductory paragraph, a body, and a closing paragraph. Your three body paragraphs are to cite an example of Ailey's choreography, which depicts some event in his life. You must specifically name the dance; describe the movements, mood, and structure of the dance; and interpret what you have described based on your knowledge of what Ailey is communicating in this dance from your reading of his autobiography. Your opening and closing paragraphs should focus on Ailey's overall life and work. Remember that the final sentence of the opening paragraph is the thesis statement, which lists the example (dance) you intend to discuss.

1. Outline your thoughts before writing to ensure an original paper.
2. Submit a rough draft. Rough drafts will be accepted no later than one week in advance of the due date.
3. Type your paper. Papers must be typed on unlined paper and double spaced; use a 12-point font and have one-inch margins.
4. Include a title page with your name, grade, class, and date. Include a standard header or footer with the page number and your last name on each page.
5. Follow standard formal writing usage:
   - End your opening paragraph with a thesis statement.
   - Begin each paragraph with a topic sentence.
   - Use no contractions, abbreviations, or slang.
   - Use correct punctuation, spelling, grammar; if you are unsure, ask—or find another way to get your point across.
   - Do not use "I think" or "I feel." These are inappropriate in this type of paper.

For all other questions and issues, consult me, your English teacher, and texts.

Rubric for Writing

4: Superior Performance; Level: Distinguished

Addresses the topic directly.

Demonstrates an identifiable order and structure with a topic sentence, support, and a conclusion.

Focuses on the topic and demonstrates knowledge of content by providing excellent supporting details.

Displays effective use of language with a varied vocabulary.

Demonstrates proficiency of mechanics, including spelling, punctuation, and capitalization.

Produces error-free typing in the paper.

Offers complete and varied sentences.

3: Above Average Performance; Level: Proficient

Addresses topic directly.

Demonstrates an identifiable order and structure with a topic sentence, support, and a conclusion.

Focuses on the topic and demonstrates knowledge of content by providing adequate supporting details.

Displays appropriate use of language.

Demonstrates appropriate use of mechanics, including spelling, punctuation, and capitalization.

Produces a paper that is nearly error-free typing.

Offers complete and varied sentences.

2: At or Below Average Performance; Level: Apprentice

Addresses the topic.

Demonstrates an identifiable limited order and structure with a topic sentence, support, and a conclusion.

Uses supporting details that demonstrate limited knowledge of content.

Displays limited use of language and vocabulary.

Demonstrates limited knowledge and use of mechanics, including spelling, punctuation, and capitalization.

Produces a paper with errors that may interfere with comprehension.

Generally uses complete sentences.

Occasionally uses sentence fragments or run-on sentences.

1: Low Performance; Level: Novice

Does not address the topic.

Has no evidence of order or structure.

Has few, if any, supporting details.

Displays incorrect or insufficient use of language and vocabulary.

Displays errors in mechanics, including spelling, punctuation, and capitalization.

Produces a paper with frequent errors in the typed material.

Often uses sentence fragments or run-on sentences.

TECHNOLOGY CONNECTION   Incorporate videotapes of various artists and conduct Internet research on modern dance artists:

"Dance Black America"

"Free to Dance" (PBS)

"Four by Ailey"

"An Evening with the Alvin Ailey" (American Dance Theatre)

"Ailey Dances"

"Hymn for Alvin Ailey" (PBS)

EVERYDAY LIVING (LIFETIME WELLNESS) CONNECTIONS

- Modern dance aesthetic tends to be accepting of different body types, is holistic in nature (breath and yogic principles), and can be enjoyed into adult life.

- From the onset, modern dance companies integrated artists of many cultures and body types into their companies, and this tradition continues today.

Modern Dance Culmination Project Rubric

Criteria	1 to 3 points	4 to 6 points	7 to 10 points	Points awarded
Presentation	Unorganized with weak transitions	Organized with smooth transitions	Fully prepared with sophisticated transitions	
	Incomplete combination	Complete combination	Complete and complex combination	
	Memorization of sequences is unclear or incomplete	Memorization in place but with movement being performed tenuously and in an unfulfilled manner	Fully prepared with committed performance of movements, transitions, and content	
			Total points	

Name _____ Teacher _____

Choreographic Video Worksheet

Title of video: _____

Title of dance: _____

Choreographer: _____

1. Describe the movement elements you saw in the video (e.g., use of body, space, energy, time).

2. Describe the nonlocomotor movements in the video that you also learned in dance class.

3. Describe the locomotor movements that you recognized in the video that you have performed in class.

4. Describe the variety of technical features in the video (e.g., costumes, props, scenery, lighting, staging).

5. What is your interpretation of this dance (e.g., the meaning, storyline, mood, and personal connection)?

6. What did you like? Why? What did you dislike? Why?

7. Why should this dance and the choreographer be appreciated? What would some individuals not appreciate about the choreographic work?

8. What were the main points in the video?

9. Describe or explain an aspect you found interesting.

10. Summarize the overall focus of the video and two or more things you learned from the experience.

Elements of Dance Handout

Note: Italicized words are subelements of each main element.

Body	Space	Energy	Time
Parts	*Shape* (symmetrical or asymmetrical)	*Weight* (heavy or light)	*Beat*
Nonlocomotor moves Stretch bend Twist shake Swing sway Circle rise Collapse	*Focus* (direct or indirect; gaze as well as concentration)	*Attack* (sharp or smooth)	*Rhythm*
Locomotor steps Walk run Leap slide Hop jump Skip gallop	*Size* (big or small)	*Strength* (tight or loose)	*Accent*
	Level (high or low)	*Flow* (bound or free)	*Pattern*
	Direction		*Duration* (long or short)
	Pathway (on the floor, in the air; straight or curved)		*Tempo* (fast or slow)

From National Dance Association, 2010, *Implementing the national dance education standards* (Champaign, IL: Human Kinetics). Adapted from M. Joyce, 1973, *First steps in teaching creative movement to children* (Mayfield Publishing).

African and African Diaspora Dance

Students will be introduced to African culture and dance. They also will examine the Atlantic slave route and how the African slaves adapted to their new environment and subsequently created new forms of dance as they integrated into a new culture and society. Some of these new forms to be explored are Haitian dances, plantation dances, the Lindy Hop, hip-hop, steppin', and jazz. This learning experience may be accomplished in sessions of varying lengths over four or more days, based on 45- to 90-minute sessions (see the following table for teacher instructions).

GRADE LEVEL   Grades 9 to12

MATERIALS, EQUIPMENT, SPACE NEEDED

- Music and music playing source
- VCR and television or DVD player and projection screen
- Various DVDs or videotapes: PBS video series *The Power of Dance*, "Pangols: The National Ballet of Senegal," "African Healing Dance," "Ipi Ntombi," "Les Merveilles D'Guinea: The Marvels of Guinea, West African Ballet Company," "Simply Funk," "Let's Hip Hop," and "Hip Hop Fusion."

NATIONAL STANDARDS ADDRESSED

Content Standard 1. Identifies and demonstrates movement elements and skills in performing dance (Benchmarks: Body a, b, c, d; Relationships a, c; Time a, b; Effort a; Advanced a, b, c)

Content Standard 3. Understands dance as a way to create and communicate meaning (Benchmarks: a, c)

Content Standard 5. Demonstrates and understands dance in various cultures and historical periods (Benchmarks: a, c; Advanced a)

Content Standard 6. Makes connections between dance and healthful living (Benchmarks: a, b, e)

Content Standard 7. Making connections between dance and other disciplines (Benchmark: b)

GOAL   To introduce students to African culture and the function of dance within that culture. To examine the Atlantic slave route and how the African slaves adapted their dance styles in the Americas and the Caribbean to create new dance forms. To explore how hip-hop is a direct link to African dance and uses the same qualities of polyrhythms, body isolations, and athleticism.

OBJECTIVES   As a result of participating in this learning experience, students will

1. physically demonstrate basic West African movements, Haitian movements, and hip-hop movement. [Psychomotor]
2. discuss how the African Diaspora created new dance forms. [Cognitive]
3. work in collaborative groups to choreograph project. [Affective]

VOCABULARY

Haitian	Kita
Yanvalou	Zepules
Congo	Body isolations
Obo	Polyrhythms

TEACHER INSTRUCTIONS FOR AFRICAN AND AFRICAN DIASPORA DANCE

Management	Teaching process	Teaching points and cues
Introduction to African movement and warm-up		
(Day one: 30 minutes) Have students stand in lines spread out in center floor.	See the script for the introduction and warm-up on page 284 of the learning experience.	See the teaching cues for the introduction and warm-up on page 284 of the learning experience.
(25 minutes) Have students travel across the floor four at a time.	Have students start by just walking on the beat. Add in body isolations starting with the head and progressing down the body.	Remind students to keep a clear, continuous beat with the walking feet to isolate the various body parts. The two separate beats are called polyrhythms.
(15 minutes) Have students come back to lines in the center to work on a combination. Once the combination is learned, they can perform the combination in groups of four.	Introduce the song: Fanga, a lafia, oshay, oshay (8 counts) Fanga, a lafia, oshay, oshay Greetings we bring to you, oshay, oshay Greetings we bring to you, oshay, oshay	Say, "First, we are going to learn the song 'Fanga,' the simple welcoming dance of West Africa."
	Teach the movement for the first line of the song: • Take four steps forward, right, left, right, left. Arms will pump forward from the shoulders in a spoke-like fashion on a forward, high diagonal. (4 counts) • Step two times on the right foot, lifting the knees to the chest as performed during the warm-up. • Reach the right arm to the side right, bent at the elbow, palm up. Put left hand on the back left hip, palm out. • Reverse left. (4 counts)	
	Teach the movement for the second line of the song: • Repeat movement from the first line but travel backward. • Repeat forward and back.	
Recap of lesson, cool-down		
	See the script for the recap and cool-down on page 285 of the learning experience.	Explain that, "We will use the breath to bring down the heart rate because much of African dance is aerobic."
Review and introduction of new material		
(Day two: 60 minutes)	See the script for the Review and Introduction of New Material on page 286 of the learning experience.	See the teaching cues on page 287 of the learning experience.
(Day three: 30–45 minutes) Have the students break into duets. Give each group a verse of the song to use to create a stepping pattern.	Introduce new material, "On the plantations in the United States, the slaves adapted their native rhythms, dances, and music to Western instrumentation. Some of the movement mimicked the work on the plantation and evolved into dances such as This Ole Hammer, Cotton Needs a Pickin', Cutting the Sugar Cane, and hambonin' or steppin'. Juba is a plantation dance performed in a circle."	Say, "We are moving historically through this unit. We're going to explore the use of African rhythms with Western language and instrumentation, starting with Juba." Monitor groups to check their progess on the assignment.
After each duet has completed their pattern, ask them to show the pattern to you for approval.		Have students give verbal feedback on informal presentations.

Management	Teaching process	Teaching points and cues
Review and introduction of new material *(continued)*		
		Ask if any of the students are actively engaged in step teams. Telephone local colleges to see if there are any step teams willing to come in to demonstrate stepping.
Closure and assessment		
(30 minutes)	Ask each duet to come into the circle on their own verse of Juba, engaging in a friendly competition. The opening verse goes like this: "Juba this, Juba that, Juba skinned a yellow cat. Juba. Juba."	Discuss the role of men dancing in other cultures.
Theory and historical analysis		
(Day four: 40 minutes)	Ask students to watch one of the hip-hop videos.	Explain that hip-hop is a direct link to African dance and uses the same qualities of polyrhythms, body isolations, and athleticism. Discuss how hip-hop is a reflection of today's youth in society, just as the Lindy hop was a reflection of the 1940s.
(30 minutes) Ask students to work in small groups.		Divide the class into small groups to work on their own hip-hop combinations. Discuss appropriate movement for school performances as opposed to what is seen in some music videos.
(20 minutes)	Have students informally present their projects.	
Warm-up and review		
(Day five: 30 minutes)	Quick jazz warm-up.	Explain that jazz is a fusion of African rhythms and movement qualities with Western dance techniques. There are many styles of jazz, from Broadway jazz to funky jazz.
(20 minutes) Have students work in small groups.	Have students practice the combination to be performed for a skills test.	Spot-check to make sure all students know the combination and will be able to perform it for a grade. Observe students as they work together in small groups to keep them focused on the task and provide feedback.
Closure and assessment		
(20 minutes) Ask students to sit with their backs to the mirror to observe their peers performing.	Have students take turns presenting the combination in small groups of four to six.	Have members from each group perform while the other students observe. Ask students to provide general feedback to the members of their group.
(Day six: 30 minutes) Rubric (Teacher assessment)	Have students refine, incorporate critiques, and perform for your evaluation based on the rubric.	
Conclusion of unit		
	Give the students an opportunity to research a particular culture that the unit has introduced. Have them work in small groups to reconstruct a dance from that culture. Give added credit to those who include costumes or bring in a cultural food dish to accompany the presentation.	

Afro-Haitian Movement

Use this script for the introduction, warm-up, and recap sections of this learning experience.

Warm-up: Start with a warm-up in the center, beginning with body isolations. The warm-up can be performed simply, with a more complex foot pattern (step right, touch left, step left, touch right, walk right, left, right, touch left, reverse), or when moving across the floor. On day one, have students start standing center; on day two, add foot pattern; and on day three, have students move across the floor and practice body isolations.

Head

- Move forward (count 1), center (count 1 ½), back (count 2), center (count 2 ½) (stopping cleanly in the center, upright position); then double-time, straight through from front to back.
- Repeat the same pattern, only side right to side left, again stopping in the center position on the 1/2 count, then straight through side to side.
- Repeat the same pattern, only tilting the head (ear to shoulder); tilt right to tilt left, again stopping in the center position on the 1/2 count, then straight through side to side.
- Diamond, front, tilt right, back, tilt left.
- Smooth full circle, right and left (4 or 8 each side if standing still); half circle front; half circle back. If using the foot pattern, half front circle right, half front circle left, and then full circle and one-half ending right; reverse; add the upper torso to the movement, bending the knees. The upper torso should swing in pendulum-like movement.
- Cluck the head forward in a chicken-like fashion.

Shoulders

Circle both back; circle both forward, then alternate; up and down; alternate right and left; repeat the same movement in a triplet pattern. Right shoulder presses forward for 8 counts and then left; alternate right and left shoulders; double-time, then shimmy.

Ribs

Forward, center, back, center; right, center, left, center; front, side, back, side; smooth circle; lift arms in right angles and set them as if on a table top; pump the ribs front and back.

Hips

Keep the knees slightly bent to accommodate movement of the hips. Move right, center, left, center; straight through right to left; front, center, back, center; straight through front to back; front, side, back, side; smooth circle; press the hips side right in plié (sitting in the hip), then press the hip right side high, then the right foot in relevé.

Three Corners

Hit the hips to the front right diagonal (count 1), then back left diagonal (count 1-and), right back diagonal (count 2), hold count 2-and (variation: roll hips to the back), reverse; circle right hip only (8 counts), then left; retrograde to 4 counts each direction, then two, then one; slow half circle forward from side to side, then double time with the accent back; bring the feet together in first position parallel and repeat the hip isolations side to side, and front to back, then front, side, back, side; smooth circles (with the knees in a good demi-plié, the movement will have a more Polynesian feel); double hit, side to side, pull both elbows bent, palms up, to the same side of the hips; place hands on knees (still in demi-plié) and circle the knees 8 counts to the right and then 8 counts to the left; keeping the torso low and forward, mimic picking up the right knee twice, lifting the upper leg toward the chest, then to the left twice. Variation: double time the movement and pound the opposite fist downward, like a hammer.

Isolate each of the fingers. Start by pulling the thumb into the palm of the hand, then have pointer finger close over the thumb, and successively the middle finger, ring finger, and pinkie finger; reverse the procedure, opening the thumb and turning the palm upward and opening each finger in the same pattern; start slowly, then perform in 5/8. Perform each hand separately and then together. Feel the upper body and back respond to the wave-like motion of the hands. Perform the same foot pattern above, lifting the right knee twice and then the left knee twice.

Bounce in demi-plié in First position parallel for 8 counts, open right foot to parallel Second position and bounce for 8 counts, close right foot back into parallel First position, and then open left foot to parallel Second position. Retrograde counts to 4, 2, then 1. On the single counts, bend the torso forward and open the elbows to the sides when the feet are in Second position; bring the elbows into the chest when the feet are together in First position. Hold the hands in fists.

Start again in parallel First position and bounce in demi-plié for 8 counts. Step forward with the right foot into parallel Fourth position. Bring the right foot back to parallel First and bounce for 8 counts, then reverse with the left foot. Again, retrograde the counts from 8s to 4s, 2s, and then 1 count in each position. On the single counts, press the hips forward right diagonal when the right foot is forward and the left hip forward left diagonal when the left foot is forward. Have students add their own arm movements.

Start again in parallel First position and bounce in demi-plié for 8 counts. Step back with the right foot into parallel Fourth position. Bring the right foot back to parallel First, bounce for 8 counts, and then reverse with the left foot. Again, retrograde the counts from 8s to 4s, 2s, and then 1 count in each position. On the single counts, lean the torso forward. Allow both arms to swing to the back.

Variations: (1) When right foot is back, twist torso to the right; the right arm will swing back and the left hand touches the sternum. Reverse to the left. (2) Circle both arms down and back in a 360-degree circle as the head drops to the back. (3) When leg is back, reach both arms forward; when legs are in parallel First, place palms of hands on top of thighs. (4) When legs are back, palms of hands touch chest; when in parallel First, palms touch the floor.

Teaching Cues for Warm-up

"Today, we are starting a unit on African dance and African–based movement. We will also talk about the African slave trade and the spread of African-based dance movements as the slaves entered the Americas and the Caribbean region."

We will discuss how West African movement patterns mimic everyday life, animals, and life-cycle rituals.

We also will discuss the qualities of African and African-derived dance: percussive, explosive, polyrhythmic, and syncopated. The knees are always bent and buoyant, and the torso leans slightly forward. Body isolations are frequently used to allow the body to engage in poly-rhythms. The isolated movements are kept separate from the rest of the body. Movements should be clean, sharp, and evident to the onlooker.

Recap of Lesson, Cool-Down

Start in turned-out Second position. As you grand plié, drop the arms down to low Fifth position and reach outward toward Second and upward to high Fifth. Breathe in through the nose. Allow the arms to cross overhead as you straighten the legs and then press the palms downward. Blow air out the mouth. The arms will again cross at the bottom to repeat.

Variation: Start with the arms in low Fifth. Turn the palms upward, flat. Pull the palms upward to the breast, breathe in through the nose. Turn the palms down, flat. Press downward toward the pelvis. Blow air out of the mouth.

Return to turned-out Second position. Take a flat back over (8 counts), drop to hang over in the center, hands on the floor (8 counts), lunge on right leg (8 counts), lunge left (8 counts), grande plié in Second, heels down, hands still on the floor; then stretch the legs three times, place the hands against the knees, and press backward to enhance the outward movement; place elbows against the knees and continue to press back; place hands behind the ankles and deepen the plié, grasp the ankles and straighten the legs, pull the chest close to the thighs, and look for the ceiling between the legs; walk the toes and heels inward to parallel First, demi-plié, and pull the tail bone toward heels. Slowly roll up, one vertebra at a time, stacking each vertebra in proper alignment.

REVIEW AND INTRODUCTION OF NEW MATERIAL (DAY TWO)   Present the following excerpt from "A Survey of Haitian Voudun Ritual Dance."

> In 1492 Columbus discovered the island of Hispaniola, now the Dominican Republic and Haiti. As the indigenous population died out from disease and slavery, the New World began to import African slaves. As the slaves reached the shores of the island, occupied by the Spanish, they were baptized Catholic. Many slaves ran away into the mountains and set up communities of Maroons. In the mountains they found rem-nants of the indigenous Indians, the Arawaks. Through their common hatred of the slave master, they founded a new religion, based in dance, Voudou. It continues to be part of the Haitian culture. Each deity in Haitian religion has specific steps, drum rhythms and song to supplicate them and bring about positive change.

Two well-known Haitian dances are the *Yanvalou* and *Congo*. The *Yanvalou* is a dance of supplication in honor of Agogue (Agwe), the deity of the sea, and Damballah, the snake god of fertility. In the execution of this dance the worshipers try to mime the undulating movement of a snake and waves of the sea by moving gracefully, forward and back, their shoulders and the upper part of the body. The participants are often dressed in white. . . . (Henry Frank, "A Survey of Haitian Voudun Ritual Dance," 1983, *Caribe* [Double Issue, Vol. 2, No. 1 and 2])

It is important that the knees are kept in a deep plié, parallel, at all times, as the beauty of the movement is to see how low one can go, to almost a crouched or squat position. The back is performing what is commonly known as a body roll taught by tilting the head back on the "and" count, leading with the chest over beginning on the "one" count until the torso touches the thighs, and dropping the head on the "four-and" count. To reverse the action going upward, the movement begins at the base of the spine and rolls upward, vertebra by vertebra on four counts and again the head lifting on the "four-and" count to repeat the whole process again. Once the dancer has taken his/her body roll to a low point, he/she may stay in the low squat position, the back now rather flat, and roll the shoulder backward, together on four counts of the right shoulder and then four counts of the left shoulder. Each shoulder roll is executed on one-quarter note. The shoulder rolling also serves the purpose of bringing the body back to a more upright position to start the body rolls over. A variation on the *Yanvalou* is to travel side to side with a toes-in, toes-out movement, (similar to a Charleston step), while heels stay flat on the ground, the torso contracts and releases (the ribs isolating backward and forward). The arms are extended to the sides, Second position, palms facing forward. The arms and the hands perform a wave-like motion, and the whole body sways to the movement. A third variation on the *Yanvalou* involves the torso swinging side to side, knees bent in plié, arms again in Second position. The torso would swing right for two counts, left for two counts, then circle back to the right, up and over in a high release, drop to the left and finish back to the right on count eight. The movement is then reversed. Another variation is to writhe and roll on the floor, alternately contracting and opening to full length as if possessed by *Damballah*, the serpent deity.

The Congo is performed in honor of *Erzulie*, the mother goddess in the Haitian pantheon visually represented by the Virgin Mary.

> The Congo rite is the intermediary between Rada and Petro rites. Congo dance is in honor of all Congo deities. This dance symbolizes beauty and love. There are many types of Congo dances. In secular presentation the Congo dancers use shiny and multi-colored outfits. (Henry Frank, "A Survey of Haitian Voudun Ritual Dance," 1983, *Caribe* [Double Issue, Vol. 2, No. 1 and 2], p. 40).

When Erzulie, a dancer, performs the Congo, she uses the movement seductively to show off her beauty and entice her gentlemen followers (Dunham Summer Intensive, 1991, Haitian instructor, Louinis). She swings her skirt similar to movements in the Mexican zapateago, with percussive, pounding feet. Her hips sway, and there is much twirling, usually a three-quarter paddle turn with the torso curved and spiraled in the direction of the turn. Another turn is to jump into Second position, plié, pick up the right leg into a parallel attitude, and spin to the right as in an en dedante pirouette in ballet. The turn is then reversed to the left.

A simple Congo step is to perform the paddle step four times on the right and then four times on the left. Add "airplane" arms, palms flexed. When on the right foot, arms "zoom" to the right, left arm high, right arm low. When on the left foot, arms "zoom" to the left, left arm low, right arm high. The floor pattern is a half circle to the right on the right foot, and half circle left when on the left foot.

Variations: (1) When on the right foot, lean the torso to the right and fall sideways, torso facing the front wall. Both arms circle from back to front, palms flexed. Flip the torso to the back wall while switching to left foot. Torso will lean to the left, fall sideways to the left as arms circle backward, and end facing the side wall. (2) Travel side to side (4 right, 4 left) with the paddle step. When on the right foot, the left hip will press upward on each downbeat. When on the left foot, the right hip will press upward four times with each left step. Hands can be in fists on the hips; if wearing a skirt, hold the skirt at the edges and shake vertically in opposition.

When doing the original Congo step described previously and holding the skirt at the edge, jump out to Second position, (right, left), lift the skirt, then jump feet together into parallel First position, plié (right, left), and pull skirt behind bottom. Add a little shake to your bottom. Execute this movement traveling forward.

REVIEW AND INTRODUCTION OF NEW MATERIAL (DAY TWO): TEACHING CUES   Talk about the Atlantic slave route and how the majority of slaves ended up in South America (primarily Brazil), in the Caribbean (especially Haiti, a particularly large importer of slaves), and finally in the southern United States. Explain how in each of these new settings, the slaves adapted their indigenous dance forms to suit their new environment. Many times slaves from various ethnic groups needed to find a common language to communicate. Some of the time, the master's religion was forced upon them. On U.S plantations, slaves needed to practice their religions in the secret of darkness, in the woods at night. All of these elements were incorporated into the dance.

Introduce the lesson: "We will learn some of these dances that honor the specific deities of love, water, and the serpent, and the fiery dances of the powerful, political deities."

CULMINATING MULTIDISCIPLINARY PROJECT ON AFRICAN AND AFRICAN DIASPORA DANCE   This culminating exercise includes both an oral presentation and a written project. Divide students into groups of three or four for this project.

1. Each group will choose one country or ethnic group of a country. Students are encouraged to use their own ethnic or cultural backgrounds or the languages they may be taking at school.

2. Once a country or ethnic group is chosen, the group will decide who will be responsible for specific areas of both the written material and oral presentation: history of the country and its indigenous people; colonization of the country and its effects on indigenous art forms; indigenous religious practices versus those practiced today; and climate, natural resources, economics, government, and politics. Extra credit would include providing posters, maps, props, costumes, or food.

3. Each member of the group will research their section and prepare a one- to two-page report with at least two references. The report should be typed and stored on a disc

so that each section can be compiled into a final report, with a separate title page and reference page (please use an acceptable format for the reference page).

4. The group will then find music, photos, videos, or primary resources to help construct a sample dance from their selected ethnic group or country.

5. The final presentation will consist of the group's oral report—extracted from the written report—a presentation of the dance, and a teaching session when the group will teach the dance and its floor patterning to the rest of the class.

6. The typed report is to be turned in at the conclusion of the presentation (use 12-point font and double space the report).

7. This multidisciplinary project will be graded in the following way:

- Oral presentation: 25 percent
- Written paper: 25 percent
- Presentation of dance material: 25 percent
- Teaching of dance material: 25 percent

OPTIONAL   Bring in a professional African dance teacher or group for a lecture, demonstration, or performance.

EXTENSIONS OR MODIFICATIONS   Have students write research papers on one of the dancers listed later in this exercise who has conducted extensive research in African and African Diaspora dance.

TECHNOLOGY CONNECTION   Students can consult documentaries of various cultures on videotapes and conduct Internet research on various cultures.

ACCOMMODATION OR DIFFERENTIATION IDEAS   Conduct research on a famous dancer in another culture. See how his or her training differs from or is similar to that of a ballet dancer.

Texts

- K. Welsh-Asante, ed., *African Dance: An Artistic, Historical, and Philosophical Inquiry*, 1997, Trenton, NJ: Africa World Press.
- J. M. Chernoff, *African Rhythms, African Sensibilities*, 1981, Chicago: University of Chicago Press.
- A. Djoniba Mouflet, *Joneeba! The African Dance Workout*, 2001, Canada: Hatherleigh Press.
- Darlene Hopson and Derek Hopson, *Juba This and Juba That: 100 African-American Games for Children*, 2001, New York: Fireside (Simon & Schuster).
- C. Williams, *Cotton Needs Pickin'*, 1928. The sheet music and recorded music may be found on the Internet.

EVERYDAY LIVING (LIFETIME WELLNESS) CONNECTIONS   African dance connects specific rites to the different cycles of life. These dances are generally performed in the village center for a village ceremony to celebrate aspects and rituals of life. Usually, there is not a clear distinction between performer and onlooker. Most of these dances can be performed late into life.

RESEARCH OPPORTUNITIES   Select a professional dancer who has done extensive research on African dance; research the individual's work and contributions.

Katherine Dunham	Asadata Dafora
Pearl Primus	Kimati Dinizula
Charles Williams	Jean Leon Destine
Chuck Davis	Percival Borde

Rubric for Hip-Hop Combination

1 to 3 points	4 to 6 points	7 to 10 points	Points awarded
Talking, laughing, or chewing gum	Not laughing, talking, or chewing gum, but not well focused	Focused with good facial expression	
Movements are sloppy and not well executed	Movements are synchronized but not executed clearly	Movements are clean and synchronized	
Group does not make any new formations	Group changes formations one or two times	Group members change their relationships to each other at least three times	
Uses no level changes; movements are performed facing front	Uses few level changes or few facing changes	Incorporates level changes and new facings	
Contains none to few qualities of African movements (e.g., isolations, explosiveness, polyrhythms, athleticism)	Contains some qualities of African movements (e.g., isolations, explosiveness, polyrhythms, athleticism)	Contains the qualities of African movements (e.g., isolations, explosiveness, polyrhythms, athleticism)	
		Total points (possible: 50)	

From National Dance Association, 2010, *Implementing the national dance education standards* (Champaign, IL: Human Kinetics).

Flying Lindy Hop Swing Dance

The goal of this learning experience is to expose students to swing dance in general, and the Lindy Hop in particular. Discuss how swing dance is an American art form, as it originated in the United States during the 1920s. This learning experience may be accomplished in several sessions of varying length over approximately five days, based on 45- to 90-minute sessions (see the following table for teacher instructions).

GRADE LEVEL   Grades 9 to 12

MATERIALS, EQUIPMENT, SPACE NEEDED

- Music
- Stereo
- DVD player or other music source
- Music selections may include "Popping Daddy Strut," "Zoot Suit Riot," "For Dancers Only: Lindy Hop Compilation," or any 8 count swing music at 150 to 180 beats per minute. Videos may include *Malcolm X*, *A Day at the Races*, *Hellzapoppin*, *Swing Kids*, and *Dance Black America*.

NATIONAL STANDARDS ADDRESSED

Content Standard 1. Identifies and demonstrates movement elements and skills in performing dance (Benchmarks: Body a, c; Relationships a, b; Advanced b)

Content Standard 4. Applies and demonstrates critical and creative thinking skills in dance (Benchmarks: a, d; Advanced a, b)

Content Standard 5. Demonstrates and understands dance in various cultures and historical periods (Benchmarks: a, c; Advanced a)

Content Standard 6. Makes connections between dance and healthful living (Benchmark: d)

GOAL   To introduce students to swing dance, swing rhythms, and the history of swing dance in America.

OBJECTIVES   As a result of participating in this learning experience, students will

1. perform the Flying Lindy Hop with no assistance from the teacher. [Psychomotor]
2. recall the history of the Harlem Lindy Hop on the written exam with 85 percent accuracy. [Cognitive]
3. identify the steps of the Flying Lindy Hop. [Cognitive]
4. work collaboratively with a partner. [Affective]

VOCABULARY

Open position	Swing out
Face-off position	Pivot

OPTIONAL   Bring costumes from home (e.g., poodle skirt, cardigan sweater, neck scarf, zoot suit).

EXTENSIONS OR MODIFICATIONS   Conduct research on the history of the Lindy Hop. Write a short paper or give an oral presentation.

TEACHER INSTRUCTIONS FOR FLYING LINDY HOP SWING DANCE

Management	Teaching process	Teaching points and cues
Warm-up and introduction to swing		
(Day one: 15 minutes) Ask students to work as partners.	Play suggested music for the warm-up. This will be a follow-the-leader activity. Have students form a circle and follow your lead: • Start by tapping the foot, keeping the beat of the music. • Move on to clapping hands or snapping fingers; this should occur on the even counts of 2, 4, 6, and 8. • Now choose any movement; keep the beat. • Go around the circle. Let students take turns leading a movement with the others following. • Demonstrate the Flying Lindy Hop. Use a 1, 2, 3, hold, 5, 6, 7, hold pattern. • Talk about the history of this dance.	Share a brief history with the class. Tell students that, "In the late 1920s to the mid-1940s, the Lindy Hop was breaking out in dancehalls across the USA, but it was in the Savoy Ballroom in Harlem, which held 4,000 people, where it caught everyone's attention. As people danced to the big bands, it was a young man by the name of Frankie 'Musclehead' Manning who created the first air steps in 1935. The Lindy Hop is the original style of swing dance. It combined elements of jazz dance with some earlier African dances. The Lindy Hop has soared across the United States. You can catch some of the moves in various movies, including *A Day at the Races* and *Hellzapoppin*. Lindy Hoppers still dance in clubs, particularly in the larger cities like New York, St. Louis, Chicago, Atlanta, and Los Angeles. Swing is the one enduring dance form that originated in America. More details can be found in a number of books or on the Internet. You will use the Internet to do some research about the history of the Lindy Hop, write a short paper, and then discuss your findings in class."
	Teach students both the female and male roles. (1) Open position: Man and woman face each other about 3 feet (1 m) apart with a standard swing hand hold as follows. • The man's left arm is held out about 2 feet (.6 m) from his body with his left hand at the woman's waist height, thumb up and fingers curled in. • The woman's right arm is held out in a similar position, with her right hand palm down, fingers curled in, and placed in the man's hand. • The hand should form interlocking hooks, using the whole of the fingers, not just the fingertips. Do not use the thumbs and do not grasp the other's hand. • There should be a slight amount of back pressure through the joined hands so that the women can feel any forward or backward movement of the man.	We will now learn the basic dance positions.

Management	Teaching process	Teaching points and cues
Warm-up and introduction to swing (continued)		
	(2) Face-off position: Man and woman face each other with hands still held similar to that described previously. • The man's right hand is on the woman's back at her shoulder blade just below her armpit. The man's right arm should be fully extended with the woman's back resting in the cup of his right hand. • The woman's left hand is on top of the man's right shoulder. • There should be some back pressure so that the man's right hand is keeping them from falling apart.	
(25 minutes) Have students stay in partners to practice the dance.	Man: Count 1. Rock-step strongly onto the left foot behind the body and swing the right arm back and down as in bowling. This should put tension into the hand hold so the man can start to lead the woman forward. Count 2. Recover with weight onto right foot, which has not moved much from its original position. Start bringing the right arm up and out to get ready to catch woman. By this time, the tension developed in count 1 should be relieved as the woman springs forward. Count 3. The left foot is planted in front of the right and turned 90 degrees to the right as the man starts rotating clockwise to keep facing the woman, who is pivoting 180 degrees around. The man's right hand should catch the woman's back as they approach the face-off position. Count 4. Hold as man keeps rotating clockwise. Partners should end up in the face-off position, 180 degrees from original position. There should be backward pressure of the woman's hand into the man's right hand as he absorbs the momentum of the woman's forward movement. Count 5. Man steps back with right foot, pulling woman forward and past his right side as he turns slightly with her. Man removes his right hand from behind the woman's back once the woman has started moving past him. The woman's momentum has now been redirected to send her back where she came from. Count 6. Man recovers onto left foot and rotates 90 degrees clockwise as the woman goes by. Count 7. Right foot steps back behind left as man continues clockwise turn to keep facing woman. Count 8. Hold as man prepares for rock step to repeat the figure. This should bring the partners back to original starting position.	Explain that the basic Lindy Hop pattern is called a swing out. It uses 8 beats of music and is therefore called an 8-count figure. Partners start off in an open but facing position, come together, and then separate again as they rotate around each other 360 degrees. It is a high-energy form of swing that makes use of each partner's momentum. It should be danced in a slightly circular motion, not slotted as in West Coast Swing.

~ continued

Teacher Instructions for Flying Lindy Hop Swing Dance ~ *continued*

Management	Teaching process	Teaching points and cues
Warm-up and introduction to swing (continued)		
	Woman: Count 1. Woman steps onto the right foot, which may be slightly forward as she is being pulled forward. For styling, the woman may wave her left hand up over her head. Count 2. Step strongly forward on the left foot. Count 3. Woman steps strongly forward onto right foot and starts clockwise pivot to place her back into man's right hand. Bring left hand down and gently rest on man's right shoulder. Count 4. Hold and continue a pivot to face-off position 180 degrees from original position. Count 5. Step forward on left foot as man pulls the woman past his right side. Count 6. Step forward on right foot (clockwise at 90 degrees to other foot) so woman can continue to face the man. Count 7. Step forward on the left foot, bringing it 45 degrees to right foot. Count 8. Hold and continue a pivot to end in the original starting position. Prepare to repeat figure.	
(Day two: 40 minutes) Have students pair up along a line or circle to practice the Charleston combination.	Play suggested music for warm-up. The follow-the-leader activity can be a simplified version of Charleston kicks or other simple movements. Demonstrate Flying Lindy Hop. Teach steps 1 to 4 (one step at a time). Stop at the hold.	Introduce Charleston warm-up. Explain that this is a simplified version of Charleston kicks, which helps develop the basic rhythm and step pattern of the Flying Lindy. Women can do the same footwork as described for the man. Better yet, she can do mirror image footwork (just interchange left and right foot below). This will allow the couple to do the Charleston kick side by side with the man's right arm around the woman's waist and the woman's left hand on the man's right shoulder.
	Man: Count 1. Rock back on left foot by stepping back with left. Count 2. Recover to right foot, which has not moved from original position. Count 3. Step forward onto left foot. Count 4. Hold. Count 5. Kick right foot forward and down. Keep foot pointed so that bottom of the foot does not show. Count 6. Bring right foot back and next to left foot but do not step onto it. Count 7. Step back onto right foot. Count 8. Hold.	Circulate and watch each pair. Correct holds. Rotate partners.
	Variation (especially for man): On rock step of count 1, place left foot as far back as possible while keeping weight on right foot. This requires you to bend down low. Pretend you are picking up a quarter off the floor. This is a good movement to use to get the original styling of the Lindy Hop rock step.	

Management	Teaching process	Teaching points and cues
Review and introduction of new material		
(Day three: 40 minutes) Have students pair up along a line or a circle with a lead and follow.	Play suggested music for warm-up. The follow-the-leader activity can be a simplified version of the Charleston kicks. Demonstrate Flying Lindy Hop. Review steps 1 through 4. Teach steps 5 through 8 (one step at a time). Stop at hold. Have students complete steps 1 through 8. Have students try the steps to music for a few minutes.	Circulate and watch each pair. Correct. Rotate partners.
(Day four: 30 minutes)	Warm up to music. If students know the "Electric Slide," use that dance set to swing music as a warm-up. Whatever you choose to do, keep the beat of the music. Review steps 1 through 8. Have students complete the full 8 counts several times in a row to music.	Talk briefly about the history of the Harlem Lindy Hop.
(10 minutes) Discuss theory and historical analysis.		Discuss the role of men who danced the Lindy Hop, just as it is acceptable today for men to dance hip-hop. Remind students that hip-hop is a reflection of today's youth in society, just as the Lindy Hop was a reflection of the 1940s. Students will submit papers on their historical research about the Lindy Hop.
Conclusion of project		
(Day five: 30 minutes)	Use a short warm-up. Have students practice the Lindy Hop to the beat of the music.	Explain that keeping the beat of the music is the most important thing in this dance form. At this point, staying on the beat is the goal. Evaluate each couple using the evaluation sheet on page 297.
(15 minutes)		Hold a class discussion about highlights of the research papers.

TECHNOLOGY CONNECTION   Have students bring videos to class that demonstrate swing dance or the Lindy Hop.

ACCOMMODATION OR DIFFERENTIATION IDEAS   Have students call various recreation clubs or dance studios to see if anyone offers swing dance or Lindy Hop. Arrange a field trip to the studio or invite another instructor to conduct a swing class.

TEXTS
- D. Penner and S. Morris, *The Swing Book*, 1999, New York: Back Bay Books.
- Jeff Allen, *Quick Start to Swing: An Easy to Follow Guide for Swing Dancing, Beginner Through Expert*, 2000, Providence, RI: QQS Publications.
- V. Vale and M. Wallace, *Swing: The New Renaissance*, 1998, San Francisco: Re/Search Publications.
- F. Manning, *Ambassador of Lindy Hop*, 2007, Philadelphia, PA: Temple University Press.

EVERYDAY LIVING (LIFETIME WELLNESS) CONNECTIONS   Swing dance is a social dance form that can be performed late into life. Students can wear pedometers or heart rate monitors to track steps or heart rates while dancing.

RESEARCH OPPORTUNITIES   Students can select one of the following professional dancers and conduct research on his or her contributions.

Fred Astaire

Gene Kelly

Frankie "Musclehead" Manning

Alfred "Pepsi" Bethel

Leon James

Al Minns

Sandra Gibson

Willamae Ricker

Mura Dehn

Ruthie Rheingold and Harry Rosenberg

"Shorty" George Snowden

Leroy "Stretch" Jones

Teacher Evaluation Sheet: Flying Lindy Hop Swing Dance

Student's name _____

Skill	Always (7 to 10)	Sometimes (4 to 6)	Never (1 to 3)	
Active learner Pays attention Shows interest in the lesson				
Class participation Shows interest in learning the skill Comes to class ready to participate				
Individual performance level: shows improvement Attempts activity Creative Enthusiastic Stays on beat or rhythm Shows coordination Knows the moves Completes activity successfully				
Performance as a pair Works well together Shows enthusiasm regarding activity Stays on beat or rhythm Shows knowledge of the moves Executes skills properly				
			Total points (possible: 20)	

From National Dance Association, 2010, *Implementing the national dance education standards* (Champaign, IL: Human Kinetics).

Summary

Becoming an effective teacher is an art. The classroom is a stage where teachers must play many roles: scholar, people manager, disciplinarian, negotiator, technician, public relations specialist, and nurturer. Even though the task of teaching may be awkward at first, a good educator makes it look easy. The ease comes from studying diverse content fields, practicing a variety of physical and arts skills, reading about educational theory and teaching methodology, understanding human development, building relationships, and developing a sense of humor. Teaching is a facilitative process where students are guided and challenged to reach their full potential. *Implementing the National Dance Education Standards* is designed to help teachers in their journey to be artists in education as well as in the dance field.

All the chapters in part II were designed to help both novice and experienced dance teachers advance along the continuum to master educator. Chapters 8 to 11 provide easy access to background information on learner characteristics by domain (i.e., psychomotor, cognitive, and affective) for students in grades pre-K through 12. Recommendations are included for designing learning strategies to address specific learner characteristics. The chapters also provide an overview of benchmarks by grade level for student learning based on the seven national dance standards. The sample learning experiences provided are based on the identified learner characteristics, the national dance standards, and the grade-level benchmarks. Using these sample learning experiences can serve as a foundation to help plan lessons that promote a variety of dance experiences at each grade level. The learning experiences also offer an organizational template that may be used to plan other lessons. Overall, this book is a reference text to help dance teachers become better at the art of teaching.

appendix

Benchmarks for the National Dance Education Standards

The following set of tables describes each National Dance Education Standard and its corresponding benchmarks. The suggested outcomes are usually sequenced within each item by grade levels: prekindergarten to grade 2, 3 to 5, 6 to 8, and 9 to 12. However, each teacher will determine an appropriate sequence based on the knowledge, experience, and ability of the student. These standards and benchmarks propose the parameters for dance and are offered as a resource for all who are responsible for dance education.

Similar benchmarks for each standard are arranged left to right in tables so that they represent a sequential progression from prekindergarten to grade 12. There are targeted outcomes for the exit grades of the four designated levels of education: grades 2, 5, 8, and 12. An empty cell within a table indicates that a benchmark appearing at a higher grade level may not be appropriate to assess at younger ages or lower grade levels. However, students may begin learning or developing skills at earlier grades that would lead to success with these benchmarks. A table cell with an arrow represents continued focus on a particular benchmark at higher grade levels. The expectation is continuous learning and that students at the higher grade levels will demonstrate increased levels of refinement in their skills or more in-depth content knowledge, enabling them to reach developmentally appropriate outcomes.

Content Standard 1. Identifies and demonstrates movement elements and skills in performing dance
The student . . .

Grades pre-K to 2	Grades 3 to 5	Grades 6 to 8	Grades 9 to 12
BODY			
a. identifies body parts correctly (e.g., shoulder, elbow, knees, skull, ribcage, forearm, ball of the foot, and spine)	a. recalls anatomical names for major and minor bones and muscles (e.g., phalanges, femur, biceps, quadriceps, gluteus maximus)	a. describes the role that muscles play in the development of strength, flexibility, endurance, and balance	a. analyzes the relationship between a balanced musculoskeletal system and optimal performance (e.g., how muscles work in pairs, benefits of cross training, and functions of body levers)
b. demonstrates simple nonlocomotor (axial) movements (e.g., bend, twist, stretch, and swing)	b. creates combinations of locomotor and axial movements in a repeatable sequence of five or more movements	b. demonstrates basic movement skills and describes the underlying principles (e.g., alignment, balance, initiation of movement, articulation of isolated body parts, weight shift, elevation and landing, and fall and recovery)	b. applies appropriate skeletal alignment (i.e., relationship of the skeleton to the line of gravity and the base of support), body-part articulation, strength, flexibility, agility, and coordination in locomotor and nonlocomotor (axial) movements
c. demonstrates simple locomotor movements (e.g., walk, run, jump, hop, leap, slide, gallop, and skip)	c. demonstrates more complex locomotor movements (e.g., schottische, polka, two-step, and grapevine)	c. identifies and demonstrates basic dance steps, positions, and patterns of dance from two different styles or traditions (e.g., ballet, modern, jazz, square, line, folk, tap, social, and indigenous dance forms)	c. identifies and demonstrates complex steps and patterns from various dance styles (e.g., dances of a particular performer, choreographer, or time period) and traditions (e.g., dances of Bharatanatyam, noh, or folk dances of indigenous people)
d. demonstrates a variety of shapes (e.g., wide, narrow, rounded, twisted, and linear)	d. demonstrates complex shapes, including asymmetrical and symmetrical	d. recalls and reproduces movement sequences either teacher or student designed	d. recalls and reproduces extended movement and rhythmic sequences (i.e., 2 to 3 minutes)
SPACE			
a. demonstrates movement in both personal (self-) and general space	➡	a. improvises, choreographs, or performs in varied settings (e.g., studio, proscenium stage, theater-in-the-round, television, gymnasium, outdoors)	➡
b. demonstrates high, middle, and low levels	➡	b. travels through space using a pattern drawn on paper or displayed on a computer screen	b. creates choreographic phrases that incorporate movements at high, middle, and low levels
c. demonstrates basic directions (e.g., forward, backward, sideways, upward, and downward)	c. demonstrates more complex directions (e.g., right and left, diagonal, and turning)	c. travels through space using self-generated patterns on paper or on a computer screen	➡

Grades pre-K to 2	Grades 3 to 5	Grades 6 to 8	Grades 9 to 12
SPACE (*continued*)			
d. demonstrates movement pathways (e.g., straight, curved, and zigzag)	d. creates movement patterns that combine two or more pathways	→	→
	e. demonstrates changes in range of movement (e.g., large, small, distal, and core actions)	→	→
	f. performs spatial elements used with locomotor and nonlocomotor movements (e.g., skipping forward on a curved pathway)	f. uses appropriate movement terminology and dance and anatomical vocabulary to describe the actions and movement elements observed in a dance	f. analyzes how the meaning of movement changes depending on the dancers' location and facing position on the stage (e.g., upstage right, center, or downstage left)
RELATIONSHIPS			
a. demonstrates the ability to dance alone, with a partner, or with a prop	a. demonstrates the ability to dance alone, with a partner, and in a small group with or without props	a. demonstrates the ability to perform dances with groups of varying sizes	a. demonstrates the ability to dance within classroom groups of varying sizes—with or without props
b. demonstrates basic movement relationships (e.g., around, apart, next to, between, over and under) with people, body parts, and objects	b. demonstrates spatial and temporal relationships (e.g., leading and following, mirroring, or matching)	b. demonstrates partner skills: using complimentary shapes, using contrasting movements, taking and supporting weights, and counting phrases to maintain unison (e.g., counting in canon and understanding counts of the phrasing)	b. demonstrates knowledge of group choreography using a variety of spatial and temporal relationships
		c. demonstrates kinesthetic awareness, concentration, and focus in performing dance movements	c. displays personal presence in formal and informal performance settings (e.g., confident presentation of body and energy to communicate movement and meaning to an audience, performance quality, positive sense of involvement)
TIME			
a. demonstrates accuracy in moving to a steady musical beat	→	→	→
b. demonstrates accuracy in changes in tempo	b. recalls and accurately demonstrates both even and uneven rhythms and accents at varying tempos	b. translates a complex rhythmic pattern from the auditory sounds to the movement patterns (e.g., syncopation and polyrhythms)	b. arranges various complex rhythmic elements in dance sequences and choreography (e.g., duple and triple meters, irregular time signatures such as 5/4 and 9/8)

~ continued

	Grades pre-K to 2	Grades 3 to 5	Grades 6 to 8	Grades 9 to 12
EFFORT				
a.	demonstrates light and strong force	a. demonstrates a variety of movement qualities appropriately (e.g., punch, press, flick, float, glide, dab, wring, slash, sustained, percussive, vibratory)	a. demonstrates a broader range of dynamics (movement qualities) during improvised and choreographed works (e.g., sustained, swinging, percussive, collapsing, and vibratory)	➡
b.	demonstrates starting and stopping with control	b. demonstrates bound and free-flow movements	b. creates and performs combinations and variations with a broad range of dynamics (e.g., sustained, percussive, vibratory, swinging, pausing, or no action on beats)	➡

	Grades pre-K to 2	Grades 3 to 5	Grades 6 to 8	**ADVANCED**
				a. demonstrates a high level of consistency and reliability in performing technical skills
				b. demonstrates technical skills with artistic expression, demonstrating clarity, musicality, and stylistic nuance
				c. evaluates own technique and makes self-corrections

Content Standard 2. Understands choreographic principles, processes, and structures
The student . . .

	Grades pre-K to 2	Grades 3 to 5	Grades 6 to 8	Grades 9 to 12
a.	uses improvisation to discover and invent solutions to simple movement assignments	a. uses improvisation to discover and compose solutions to small-group movement assignments	➡	➡
b.	improvises, creates, and performs dances based on personal ideas or concepts from other sources (e.g., stories, pictures, poetry, emotions, verbs, found objects, artifacts, or technology)	➡	➡	➡
c.	creates a basic sequence with a beginning, middle, and end while alone or with a partner	c. cooperates with a partner or in a small group to create a dance sequence with a beginning, middle, and end	c. cooperates within a small group to create dances demonstrating choreographic principles such as contrast and transition	c. choreographs a duet or small group dance using a variety of choreographic principles, processes, and structures (forms)

Grades pre-K to 2	Grades 3 to 5	Grades 6 to 8	Grades 9 to 12
d. identifies the parts of a movement sequence or dance (e.g., beginning, middle, and end)	d. identifies the structure of the dance (e.g., AB, ABA, or canon)	d. identifies the choreographic structure (e.g., call and response, theme and variations, narrative) and choreographic principles used (contrasts, transitions, unity, and variety) in a movement study or dance	d. demonstrates understanding of choreographic structures (e.g., retrograde or palindrome, theme and variation, rondo, canon, or contemporary forms selected by the student)
e. creates and repeats a dance phrase with and without rhythmic accompaniment	e. creates a dance phrase, accurately repeats it, then varies it (e.g., making changes in the time, space, or effort)	e. demonstrates the process of reordering (i.e., specific movements or movement phrases that are separated from their original order and restructured in a different sequence) and chance (i.e., movements that are specifically chosen and defined but randomly structured) to create a dance or movement phrase	➜
		f. cooperates with a partner to demonstrate the following skills in a visually interesting way: creating contrasting and complementary shapes, taking and supporting weight	➜
		g. cooperates with a partner or small group to produce an original work involving technology-based tools	g. designs a multimedia presentation to accompany a dance (e.g., PowerPoint, camera, video, iPod)
			ADVANCED
			a. demonstrates further development and refinement of the proficient skills to create a small group dance with coherence and aesthetic unity
			b. explains accurately how a choreographer manipulated and developed the basic movement content within a dance production
			c. operates a complex technology system for a dance production (e.g., lighting or sound)

~ continued

Content Standard 3. Understands dance as a way to create and communicate meaning
The student . . .

Grades pre-K to 2	Grades 3 to 5	Grades 6 to 8	Grades 9 to 12
a. observes and discusses how dance is different from other forms of human movement (e.g., sports, everyday gestures)	➡	a. compares and contrasts different styles of dance (e.g., high-kick routine, folk dance, ballroom, hip-hop)	a. formulates and answers questions about how movement choices are used to communicate abstract ideas and themes in dance (e.g., celebration, isolation, relationships, poverty, the environment)
b. discusses in small or large groups interpretations and reactions to a dance (e.g., listening, speaking, or writing)	➡	b. explains how personal experiences influence the interpretation of a dance (e.g., journal writing, class discussion)	➡
c. presents dances to peers and discusses the meanings	c. creates a dance that communicates topics of personal significance	➡	c. presents a dance that communicates a social theme (e.g., contemporary, historical, or cultural)
d. demonstrates appropriate audience behavior in formal and informal performance situations (e.g., respect for performers, applause at the end, and constructive feedback)	➡	d. demonstrates appropriate audience behavior and etiquette in formal and informal performance situations and explains how audiences and venues affect choreography	➡
	e. demonstrates and describes the difference between exaggerated movement and pedestrian movement (e.g., taking a movement that is familiar and changing it in range, dynamics, or quality)	e. demonstrates and describes the different meanings evoked by specific body language, shapes, and movement choices (e.g., low, round shape: fear or repose; high, angular shape: defiance or power; symmetrical shape: harmony)	➡
	f. explains how accompaniment choice (e.g., sound, music, spoken text) can affect the meaning of a dance	f. explains how accompaniment, lighting, technology, and costuming can contribute to the meaning of a dance	➡
	g. practices safe, legal, and responsible use of technology and digital information	g. practices cultural and social etiquette related to technology (e.g., does not post harmful or inappropriate material, does not reveal personal information, follows school policy)	g. describes and practices legal and ethical behavior with digital information (e.g., publishes photographs only with permission, follows copyright and fair use guidelines, provides complete citations from electronic media)
		h. researches a theme using a Web site or media to create a short dance study	➡

Grades pre-K to 2	Grades 3 to 5	Grades 6 to 8	Grades 9 to 12
			ADVANCED
			a. analyzes opinions concerning ways that a dance creates and conveys meaning from a variety of perspectives (e.g., audience, performer, creator, critic, historical context, use of technology)
			b. compares and contrasts how meaning is communicated in two personally choreographed works
			c. analyzes the impact of technology on the archival management of dance works (i.e., the preservation and access to artistic works)

Content Standard 4. Applies and demonstrates critical and creative thinking skills in dance
The student . . .

Grades pre-K to 2	Grades 3 to 5	Grades 6 to 8	Grades 9 to 12
a. chooses a favorite solution to a given movement problem and tells the reasons for that choice	a. creates and demonstrates multiple solutions to teacher-designed movement problems; chooses the most interesting solution and discusses the reason for that choice	➡	a. creates a dance and revises it over time, articulating the reasons for artistic decisions and what was lost and gained by those decisions
b. observes two dances and discusses how they are similar and different in terms of one element of dance (e.g., space, shape, level, and pathway)	b. compares and contrasts movement elements (e.g., body, space, effort, relationships) in two dance compositions	➡	b. formulates and answers aesthetic questions about a particular dance (e.g., What is it that makes the dance unique? What changes to the dance will create a new concept?)
c. discusses opinions about dances with peers in supportive and positive ways	➡	➡	➡
		d. identifies aesthetic criteria for evaluating dance (e.g., originality, visual and emotional impact, variety, transition, contrast, skill of performers)	d. establishes a set of aesthetic criteria (e.g., transition, variety, contrast, repetition, sequence, structure, balance), and applies it in evaluating personal work and that of others
			e. explains how skills developed in dance are applicable to a variety of careers

~ continued

Grades pre-K to 2	Grades 3 to 5	Grades 6 to 8	Grades 9 to 12
			ADVANCED
			a. analyzes the style of a choreographer or cultural form and creates a dance in that style
			b. analyzes issues of ethnicity, gender, society, economic class, age, or physical condition in relation to dance or dance careers

Content Standard 5. Demonstrates and understands dance in various cultures and historical periods
The student . . .

Grades pre-K to 2	Grades 3 to 5	Grades 6 to 8	Grades 9 to 12
a. performs folk and social dances from various cultures	a. performs more complex culturally based folk and social dances with patterns (e.g., steps, formations, tempos, rhythms, and relationships)	a. performs folk, square, social, theatrical, and contemporary dances demonstrating awareness of various cultures and time periods	a. creates a dance study demonstrating elements from a cultural dance (e.g., symbolic gestures, weightedness, posture, partnering, rhythms)
b. recalls the cultural significance of a folk dance (customs, special meaning, location; e.g., the Shoemaker Dance is from Denmark and is about making shoes)	b. describes the differences and similarities between folk dances of more than one culture (e.g., purpose, gesture, style, function)	b. describes the aesthetic qualities and traditions of more than one culture	b. describes the function of a particular dance within the society where the dance was or is performed (explains such things as religious or secular implications and cultural phenomena)
c. names places, situations, and occasions where dance is seen or experienced (e.g., parades, festivals, theaters, weddings, movies, birthday parties, television)	c. answers questions concerning dance in a particular culture and time period (e.g., who, what, where, when, why, and how)	c. researches and explains how technology and social change have influenced the structure of dance in entertainment, movies, or the recording industry	c. uses technology to research cultural or historical perspectives surrounding the career of at least one professional in dance, choreography, or production
			ADVANCED
			a. performs in an informal or formal setting a dance from a selected resource (e.g., video, guest artist, family member, clubs, performance groups, dance society) and describes the cultural or historical context
			b. choreographs a dance reflective of elements within a specific culture (e.g., history, spiritual beliefs, food, music, dress, family structure, artwork)

Content Standard 6. Makes connections between dance and healthful living
The student . . .

Grades pre-K to 2	Grades 3 to 5	Grades 6 to 8	Grades 9 to 12
a. states that dancing helps keep heart, bones, and brain healthy and strong	a. identifies two or more ways that dance is beneficial to health (e.g., flexibility, muscular strength, aerobic endurance)	a. describes how dance is a lifelong healthful physical activity (e.g., aids in weight management, helps prevent diabetes and osteoporosis, and promotes a strong cardiovascular system)	a. develops and implements a personal plan addressing health needs and issues to include regular healthy eating, flexibility, muscular strength, and endurance
b. explains that dancing strengthens muscles	b. explains how and why warming up helps a dancer perform effectively and prevent injury	b. describes and demonstrates three or four safe warm-up practices that relate to personal needs (e.g., hyperextended knees, swaybacks, rounded shoulders, or lack of abdominal tone)	b. designs a personal warm-up based on safe movement practices for a specific dance genre (ballet, modern, cultural dance, hip-hop)
c. identifies two important things that a dancer can do to keep healthy (e.g., appropriate sleep, good nutrition practices, warm-ups, stretching)	➡	c. explains the importance of good nutrition in achieving peak performance	c. explains findings from research on a personal health concern or a dance-related injury
d. demonstrates safe movement in personal and general space	d. describes the difference between safe and unsafe ways of moving (e.g., knees bent on landing, static and dynamic stretching, protecting head and neck when falling and rolling)	d. applies safe movement practices in both technique and choreography (e.g., plié: knees over toes; relevé: alignment of ankle, knee, and hip; balance: vertical alignment of spine)	d. explains how life choices affect a dancer's abilities and longevity (e.g., tobacco, drugs, alcohol, overtraining, overstretching, lack of sleep, eating disorders, emotional balance)
e. recognizes the joy of dance as a lifetime activity to celebrate culture and community events	➡	➡	➡

			ADVANCED
			a. discusses challenges facing career-directed performers in maintaining healthy lifestyles
			b. researches and explains potential dance genres that can be performed by older adults, individuals with disabilities, and others with unique abilities

~ continued

Content Standard 7. Makes connections between dance and other disciplines
The student . . .

Grades pre-K to 2	Grades 3 to 5	Grades 6 to 8	Grades 9 to 12
a. discusses ways dancers and athletes are alike and different	a. describes places, times, or events where dance occurs today (e.g., television, movies, family celebrations, religious ceremonies, community events, festivals)	a. creates a project (e.g., aural, visual, oral, kinetic, or technological) that reveals similarities and differences between dance and another art form (e.g., tone, color, symmetry, dynamics)	a. creates a dance study demonstrating connections between dance and another discipline
b. recognizes that emotions are expressed in dance and other art forms (e.g., dancing in response to music, literature, and the visual arts)	b. recognizes that similar themes, ideas, and concepts are expressed in dance and other art forms (e.g., loyalty, courage, jealousy, affection, hope)	→	b. analyzes characteristics of works in various art forms that share similar subject matter, historical periods, or cultural context
c. identifies common forms used in the various arts (e.g., pathway, rhythm, patterns)	c. cites examples of how similar elements are used in dance and in another art form (e.g., balance, design, contrast, texture)	→	→
d. creates a short dance sequence that reflects a concept from another discipline (e.g., action words, geometric shapes, workers in community, flowers growing)	d. creates a dance that reflects a concept from another discipline (e.g., language arts, math, science, social studies, or health)	→	d. identifies significant changes that occurred in dance as a result of technology, science, and history
e. draws a picture to explain a dance previously observed or performed	e. interprets through dance an idea taken from another medium (e.g., visual arts, music, video, poetry, history)	→	→
			f. uses a different art form to express an interpretation of a dance that students have observed or performed (e.g., drawing, poetry, musical composition, prose, technology)
			g. demonstrates how technology can be used to reinforce, enhance, or alter the dance idea in an interdisciplinary project
			ADVANCED
			a. creates an interdisciplinary project based on a student-identified theme
			b. integrates technology into a group-generated interdisciplinary project

glossary

AB—A two-part compositional (or choreographic) form with an A theme (or phrase) and a B theme (or phrase). Each part is a distinct, self-contained section that shares a specific character or quality (such as the same tempo, movement quality, or style).

ABA—A three-part compositional (or choreographic) form in which the second section contrasts with the first section. The third section is a restatement of the first section in a condensed, abbreviated, or extended form.

accent—An emphasis on a musical beat or movement that is stressed within a series of beats or movements.

alignment (or body alignment)—The relationship of the skeleton to the body's line of gravity to its base of support. It is the proper, functional posture for dance and other body movement.

axial movement—Any movement that is anchored to one spot by a body part using only the space available in any direction without losing the initial contact. Movement is organized around the axis of the body rather than designed for travel from one location to another. It also is known as nonlocomotor movement.

balance—An even distribution of weight so that stability is achieved.

ballistic stretch—A flexibility movement that uses bouncing and jerking motions at an extreme range of motion.

beat—The (usually) even, steady, underlying pulse in music.

choreographer—A person who composes a sequence of steps and movements for a dance performance.

choreographic structure—Specific compositional principles (and forms) that help to create dances, such as AB, ABA, rondo, canon, story-based forms, or visual design.

choreography—The art of creating and arranging sequences of steps or movements of dancers.

core—The muscular and skeletal structures in the center of the body that include the abdomen, spine, and pelvis.

creative dance—Use of the body to communicate one's inner thoughts and feelings in a nonthreatening environment. The process engages the whole person physically, intellectually, and emotionally while involving critical thinking, problem solving, and decision making.

dance movement—An organized change in the location, place, or position of the body or some of its parts using time, force, and space and that also possesses an expressive and aesthetic quality.

dance phrase—A short sequence of related movements that has a sense of rhythmic connectedness.

distal—A term that describes a body part or location away from the center of the body (or other points of attachment).

downstage—The part of a stage that is at the front of the performing area, the closest to the audience.

dynamics—The expressive content of human movement, sometimes called qualities or efforts. It describes the force or energy of movement.

effort (sometimes called dynamics)—The system for understanding the qualities and characteristics of movement as they relate to the inner intention of the person moving or dancing.

even rhythm—A strong, regular, repeated pattern of sound or movement.

folk dance—A traditional dance developed among the common people of a nation or region and generally passed from generation to generation.

footwork—The manner in which a person moves his or her feet in a movement sequence or dance.

force—The energy attributed to an action or movement.

genre—A style or category of dance having a particular form, content, or technique, such as ballet, modern dance, jazz, tap, hip-hop, square dance (and other call dances), or traditional dance.

improvisation—The process of spontaneously creating movement that ranges from free-form to highly structured. Because movements are not preplanned, they involve an element of chance.

indigenous—Originating and living or occurring naturally in a particular area or environment.

isolation—Moving one body part without moving any other part.

Laban movement analysis—A study of Rudolf Laban's theories regarding the interrelationships of the body, effort, shape, and space in dance.

locomotor—A movement that travels from place to place and is usually identified by transferring weight from foot to foot. Some basic locomotor steps are the walk, run, leap, hop, and jump and the irregular, rhythmic combinations of the skip (walk and hop), slide (sideward walk and leap), and gallop (forward and backward walk and leap).

movement quality—The identifying attribute created by the release, follow-through, and termination of energy and is critical to making movement become dance. Typical terms denoting movement qualities include sustained, swinging, percussive, collapse, and vibratory, and such movement combinations as gliding, floating, flicking, dabbing, punching, slashing, pressing, and wringing.

nonlocomotor—A movement that stays in one place. See axial movement.

palindrome—A choreographic structure used with a phrase or longer sequence of movement where the phrase is first performed proceeding from movements one to two to three and so on. When the last movement of the phrase is completed, the phrase is retrograded from the penultimate movement to the first movement. A commonly used example in prose is "Able was I ere I saw Elba." In this example, the letters are the same forward to the *r* in *ere* as they are backward to the *a*.

phrase—A brief sequence of related movements that has a sense of rhythmic completion.

polyrhythm—Has multiple patterns of sound or movement occurring simultaneously.

prop—For dance, may be a costume, supply, instrument, or implement that enhances rather than detracts from dance movement and learning (e.g., scarves, percussion instruments, balls, wands, hoops, stretch fabric, elastic ropes, furniture, media projections).

proscenium—The part of a stage in front of the curtain; it can also be the arch framing the opening between the stage and the auditorium.

relationship—The way in which two or more people or things are connected, such as through movement, sound, or props.

reordering—A choreographic process in which known and defined elements (such as specific movements or movement phrases) are separated from their original relationship and restructured in a different pattern.

retrograde—Reversing (in order) a prepared movement sequence.

rhythm—The regular recurrence of patterns of movement in dance or patterns of sound in music.

rondo—A dance or musical form with a recurring leading theme, such as a choreographic pattern in which sequence A is the primary movement phrase that is constantly repeated while other, different sequences (B, C, and D) are interspersed.

round (or canon)—A group dance structure consisting of two or more regularly occurring patterns or phrases. When performing the dance patterns, dancers perform all parts while starting at different points in the pattern. A comparable musical comparison uses the song "Row, Row, Row Your Boat."

space—An unoccupied area. It is the area in which and through which a person moves.

spacing—The process of arranging the body (or bodies) within space. It may involve helping young children learn how to control their bodies within and through space or helping older students choreograph dances that use performance areas effectively.

static stretch—The process of increasing joint or muscle flexibility where a position is held steady for a designated period of time at an extreme range of motion. The muscle being stretched is lengthened slowly by staying in a fairly comfortable position for 15 to 30 (or more) seconds. When the feeling of stretch subsides, the person stretching can move into a deeper stretch position.

stillness—Not moving; remaining in a state of deep, quiet calm.

stretching—The process of elongating muscles to increase the range of motion of a joint and to prevent or decrease injury.

study (as in dance study)—The exploration of an idea through the creation of a short dance that has a clear beginning, middle, end, and a sense of wholeness.

style—A distinctive manner of moving. It is the characteristic way dance is created or performed that identifies the movement related to a particular performer, choreographer, or period in time.

syncopation—The shift of accents to rhythmic beats that are normally not accented. Beats that usually are strong beats become weak, and those that are usually weak beats become stronger.

tempo—The rate of speed or pace of movement or music.

theme and variation—A compositional structure where a dance phrase (or section) is created, and subsequent dance phrases (or sections) are variations of the original theme.

time—The rhythmic pattern or tempo of movement or music.

transition—The way a movement phrase connects to subsequent movement phrases.

uneven rhythm—Often seen in variations of or combinations of movements using skips, slides, or gallops.

upstage—The part of a stage that is toward the back of the performing area, the farthest away from the audience.

references and suggested readings

Alabama Department of Education. (1998). *Alabama dance standards.* Alabama Department of Education. http://alex.state.al.us/browseallStand.php.

Anderson, L. W., & Krathwohl, D. (Eds.). (2001). *A taxonomy for learning, teaching and assessing: A revision of Bloom's taxonomy of educational objectives.* New York: Addison Wesley Longman.

Anderson, L.W., & Sosniak, L.A. (Eds.). (1994). *Bloom's taxonomy: A forty-year retrospective. Ninety-third yearbook of the National Society for the Study of Education.* Chicago: University of Chicago Press.

Arizona Department of Education. (2006). *Arizona dance standards.* Arizona Department of Education. www.azed.gov/standards/arts/revised/Dance.pdf.

Arts Education Partnership. (2002). *Critical links: Learning in the arts and student academic and social development.* Washington, DC: Arts Education Partnership.

Arts Education Partnership. (2003). *Creating quality integrated and interdisciplinary arts programs.* Washington, DC: Arts Education Partnership.

Arts Education Partnership. (2005). *Third space: When learning matters.* Washington, DC: Arts Education Partnership.

Bailey, R. A., & Burton, E. C. (1982). *The dynamic self: Activities to enhance infant development.* St. Louis, MO: C. V. Mosby Company.

Baines, L. (2008). *Teacher's guide to multisensory learning.* Alexandria, VA: Association for Supervision and Curriculum Development.

Bennett, J. P., & Riemer, P. C. (2006). *Rhythmic activities and dance.* Champaign, IL: Human Kinetics.

Blank, M., & Berg, A. (2006). *All together now: Sharing responsibility for the whole child.* Alexandria, VA: Association for Supervision and Curriculum Development.

Block, B. A. (2008). Using iPods in Dance Pedagogy. *Journal of Physical Education, Recreation and Dance, 79*(7), 25–28.

Bloom, B. S. (Ed.). (1956). *Taxonomy of educational objectives: The classifications of educational goals, handbook 1: Cognitive domain.* New York: David McKay.

Boyd, D., & Bee, H. (2006). *Lifespan development* (4th ed.). New York: Pearson-Allyn & Bacon.

Brighton, K. (2007). *Coming of age: The education and development of young adolescents.* Westerville, OH: National Middle School Association.

Brookhart, S. M. (2008). *How to give effective feedback to your students.* Alexandria, VA: Association for Supervision and Curriculum Development.

Burnaford, G., Aprill, A., & Weiss, C. (2002). *Renaissance in the classroom: Arts integration and meaningful learning.* Mahwah, NJ: Lawrence Erlbaum Associates.

Burnaford, G., Brown, S., Dougherty, J., & McLaughlin, H. J. (2007). *Arts integration frameworks, research & practice.* Washington, DC: Arts Education Partnership.

Caldwell, C. (2001). *Dance and dancers' injuries.* Fishbourne, Chichester, Great Britain: Corpus Publishing.

Carr, J. F., & Harris, D. E. (2001). *Succeeding with standards: Linking curriculum, assessment, and action.* Alexandria, VA: Association for Supervision and Curriculum Development.

Cherry, C. (1975). *Creative play for the developing child: Early lifehood education through play.* Belmont, CA: Fearon Pitman.

Clark, D. (2007). Classroom management challenges in the dance class. *Journal of Physical Education, Recreation and Dance, 78*(2), 19–24.

Clark, S. (2006). Moving and seeing: Photographing dance. *Journal of Physical Education, Recreation and Dance, 77*(2), 33–40.

Computer Ethics Institute. (1992). The ten commandments of computer ethics. Computer Professionals for Society Responsibility. http://cpsr.org/issues/ethics/cei.

Cone, T. P., & Cone, S. (2005). *Assessment series—assessing dance in elementary physical education.* Reston, VA: National Association of Sport and Physical Education.

Cone, T. P., & Cone, S. (2007). Dance education: Dual or dueling identities. *Journal of Physical Education, Recreation and Dance, 78*(1), 6–7, 13.

Consortium of National Arts Education Associations. (1994). *National standards for arts education: What every young American should know and be able to do in the arts.* Reston, VA: Music Educators National Conference.

Consortium of National Arts Education Associations. (2002). *Authentic connections: Interdisciplinary work in the arts.* Reston, VA: National Arts Education Association.

Cote, P. (2006). The power of dance in society and education: Lessons learned from tradition and innovation. *Journal of Physical Education, Recreation and Dance, 77*(5), 24–31, 45–46.

Cromwell, S. (1999). Laptops change curriculum—and students. *Education World.* www.education-world.com/a_curr/curr178.shtml.

Dance History Coalition. (2009). *Statement of best practices in fair use of dance-related materials.* Washington, DC: Dance History Coalition.

Danielson, C. (2002). *Enhancing student achievement: A framework for school improvement.* Alexandria, VA: Association for Supervision and Curriculum Development.

Dimondstein, G. (1971). *Children dance in the classroom.* New York: Macmillan Company.

Enghauser, R. (2007). Developing listening bodies in the dance technique class. *Journal of Physical Education, Recreation and Dance, 78*(6), 33–37, 54.

Enghauser, R. G. (2008). Teaching modern dance: A conceptual approach. *Journal of Physical Education, Recreation and Dance, 79*(8), 36–42.

Erlauer, L. (2003). *The brain-compatible classroom: Using what we know about learning to improve teaching.* Alexandria, VA: Association for Supervision and Curriculum Development.

Fineberg, C. (2004). *Creating islands of excellence: Arts education as a partner in school reform.* Portsmouth, NH: Heinemann.

Fisher, D., & Frey, N. (2007). *Checking for understanding: Formative assessment techniques for your classroom.* Alexandria, VA: Association for Supervision and Curriculum Development.

Fiske, E. D. (Ed.). (1999). *Champions of change: The impact of arts on learning.* Washington, DC: Arts Education Partnership.

Gabbei, R., & Clemmens, H. (2005). Creative movement from children's storybooks: Going beyond pantomime. *Journal of Physical Education, Recreation and Dance, 76*(9), 32–37.

Gallahue, D. L., & Donnelly, F. C. (2003). *Developmental physical education for all children* (4th ed.). Champaign, IL: Human Kinetics.

Garner, B. K. (2007). *Getting to got it! Helping struggling students learn how to learn.* Alexandria, VA: Association for Supervision and Curriculum Development.

Gilbert, A. G. (2000). *Creative dance for all ages.* Reston, VA: National Dance Association.

Gilbert, A. G. (2006). *Brain-compatible dance education.* Reston, VA: National Dance Association.

Given, B. K. (2002). *Teaching to the brain's natural learning systems.* Alexandria, VA: Association for Supervision and Curriculum Development.

Griner, B., Hernandez, B. M., Strickland, G., & Boatwright, D. (2006). Achieving the perfect body: Nutritional behaviors of nonprofessional, regional female dancers. *Journal of Physical Education, Recreation and Dance, 77*(9), 40–45, 51.

Hanna, J. L. (1999). *Partnering dance and education.* Champaign, IL: Human Kinetics.

Harrow, A. (1972). *A taxonomy of psychomotor domain: A guide for developing behavioral objectives.* New York: David McKay.

H'Doubler, M. N. (1957). *Dance: A creative art experience.* Madison: University of Wisconsin Press.

Hearn, C. P., & Crabtree, K. E. (2008). Preserving our legacy for future generations of educators. *Journal of Physical Education, Recreation and Dance, 79*(4), 18–23.

Hellison, D. R. (1985). *Goals and strategies for teaching physical education.* Champaign, IL: Human Kinetics.

Hernandez, B. M., & Meyer, F. A. (Eds.). (2002). *Dance: What is it? Why is it important?* Reston, VA: National Dance Association.

Hernandez, B. M., & Strickland, G. (2005). School health and safety standards for dance in physical education. *Journal of Physical Education, Recreation and Dance, 76*(4), 20–25.

Hodgkinson, H. (2006). *The whole child in a fractured world.* Alexandria, VA: Association for Supervision and Curriculum Development.

Humphrey, D. (1959). *The art of making dances.* New York: Grove Press.

Instruction–Technology. (n.d.) www.henrico.k12.va.us/administration/instruction/technology/technology.html.

Interstate New Teacher Assessment and Support Consortium (INTASC). (2001). *New model standards for licensing classroom teachers and specialists in the arts.* Washington, DC: Council of Chief State School Officers.

Jacobs, H. H. (2004). *Getting results with curriculum mapping.* Alexandria, VA: Association for Supervision and Curriculum Development.

Jain, S., & Brown, D. R. (2001). Cultural dance: An opportunity to encourage physical activity and health in communities. *American Journal of Health Education, 32*(4), 216–222.

Jensen, E. (1998). *Teaching with the brain in mind.* Alexandria, VA: Association for Supervision and Curriculum Development.

Jensen, E. (2001). *Arts with the brain in mind*. Alexandria, VA: Association for Supervision and Curriculum Development.

Jewett, A. E., & Bain, L. L. (1985). *The curriculum process in physical education*. Dubuque, IA: W. C. Brown.

Jobling, A., Virji-Babul, N., & Nichols, D. (2006). Children with Down syndrome: Discovering the joy of movement. *Journal of Physical Education, Recreation and Dance, 77*(6), 34–38, 53–54.

Joint Committee on National Health Standards (2nd ed.). (2007). *National health education standards*. Atlanta, GA: American Cancer Society.

Joyce, B., & Showers, B. (2002). *Student achievement through staff development*. Alexandria, VA: Association for Supervision and Curriculum Development.

Kassing G., & Jay, D. (1998). *Teaching beginning ballet technique*. Champaign, IL: Human Kinetics.

Kassing, G., & Jay, D. (2003). *Dance teaching methods and curriculum design*. Champaign, IL: Human Kinetics.

Kassing, G., & Mortensen, L. (1982). Critiquing student performances in ballet. *Dance Research Journal, 16*.

Kaufmann, K. A. (2006). *Inclusive creative movement and dance*. Champaign, IL: Human Kinetics.

Kennedy Center Alliance for Arts Education. (2000). *The arts beyond the school day: Extending the power*. Washington, DC: Kennedy Center for the Performing Arts.

Kleinman, I. (2009). *Complete physical education plans for grades 5–12* (2nd ed.). Champaign, IL: Human Kinetics.

Knowles, T., & Brown, D. F. (2000). *What every middle school teacher should know*. Westerville, OH: National Middle School Association.

Kogan, S. (2004). *Step by step: A complete movement education curriculum* (2nd ed.). Champaign, IL: Human Kinetics.

Krathwohl, D. R., Boom, B. S., & Bertram, B. M. (1973). *Taxonomy of educational objectives, the classification of educational goals: Handbook II: Affective domain*. New York: David McKay.

Laban, R. (1975). *Modern educational dance* (3rd ed.). London, Great Britain: MacDonald & Davis.

Langton, T. W. (2007). Applying Laban's movement framework in elementary physical education. *Journal of Physical Education, Recreation and Dance, 78*(1), 17–24, 39, 53.

LaPointe-Crump, J. (2006). Dance movement and spirit: Issues in the dance education curriculum. *Journal of Physical Education, Recreation and Dance, 77*(5), 3–4, 12.

Levy, F., Ranjbar, A., & Dean, C. H. (2006). Dance movement as a way to help children affected by war. *Journal of Physical Education, Recreation and Dance, 77*(5), 12, 69.

Littky, D., & Grabelle, S. (2004). *The big picture: Education is everybody's business*. Alexandria, VA: Association for Supervision and Curriculum Development.

Louisiana Department of Education. (2003). *Louisiana Arts Content Standards*. Louisiana Department of Education. www.louisianaschools.net/lde/uploads/3308.pdf.

Louisiana Department of Education. (February, 2004). *Standards, assessments, and accountability: Louisiana content standards*. Louisiana Department of Education. www.louisianaschools.net/lde/saa/1222.html.

Martens-Bloomfield, E. (2000, May 1). A laptop for every kid. *Time*. www.time.com/time/magazine/article/0,9171,996807,00.html? iid=chix-sphere.

Marzano, R. J. (2000). *Transforming classroom grading*. Alexandria, VA: Association for Supervision and Curriculum Development.

Marzano, R. J. (2003). *What works in schools: Translating research into action*. Alexandria, VA: Association for Supervision and Curriculum Development.

Marzano, R. J. (2007). *The art and science of teaching*. Alexandria, VA: Association for Supervision and Curriculum Development.

Marzano, R. J., Marzano, J. S., & Pickering, D. J. (2003). *Classroom management that works: Research-based strategies for every teacher*. Alexandria, VA: Association for Supervision and Curriculum Development.

McCutchen, B. P. (2006). *Teaching dance as arts in education*. Champaign, IL: Human Kinetics.

McDevitt, T. M., & Ormrod, J. E. (2004). *Child development: Educating and working with children and adolescents* (2nd ed.). Upper Saddle River, NJ: Pearson Education.

Mertens, S. B., Anfara, V. A., & Caskey, M. M. (2007). *The young adolescent and the middle school*. Westerville, OH: National Middle School Association.

Mohnson, B. S. (2008). *Teaching middle school physical education* (3rd ed.). Champaign, IL: Human Kinetics.

Moss, S. (2006). Embodying the spirits: Puppets in the dance studio. *Journal of Physical Education, Recreation and Dance, 77*(7), 31–34.

Musmon, M., Welsh, K., Heath, F-L., Minton, S., Laverty, M. A., Maeshiba, N., et. al. (2008). Dance specialists around the world—a living history. *Journal of Physical Education, Recreation and Dance, 79*(4), 24–32.

National Arts Education Consortium. (2000). *Transforming education through the arts challenge*. Columbus, OH: National Arts Education Consortium.

National Association of Schools of Dance. (2008). *National association of schools of dance handbook 2007–2008* (2nd ed.). Reston, VA: National Association of Schools of Dance.

National Association for Sport and Physical Education. (2002). *Active start: A statement of physical activity guidelines for children birth to five years.* Reston, VA: National Association for Sport and Physical Education.

National Association for Sport and Physical Education. (2004). *Moving into the future: National standards for physical education* (2nd ed.). Reston, VA: National Association for Sport and Physical Education.

National Association for Sport and Physical Education. (n.d.). *Appropriate practices in movement programs for young children 3–5.* Reston, VA: National Association for Sport and Physical Education.

National Educational Technology Standards for Students. (2007). www.iste.org/Content/Navigation-Menu/NETS/ForStudents/2007Standards/NETS_for_Students_2007.htm.

National Middle School Association. (2003). *This we believe: Successful schools for young adolescents.* Westerville, OH: National Middle School Association.

New Jersey Department of Education. (1998). *New Jersey visual and performing arts curriculum framework.* New Jersey Department of Education. www.state.nj.us/education/frameworks/arts/arts.pdf.

Nine Middle-Level Educators. (2006). *Essential questions—with answers—for middle level teachers.* Westerville, OH: National Middle School Association.

Office of Special Education and Rehabilitative Services. (2008). *Annual report to Congress on the implementation of the Individuals with Disabilities Education Act.* Washington, DC: U.S. Department of Education.

Oliver, W. (2008). Dance is for all ages. *Journal of Physical Education, Recreation and Dance, 79*(4), 6–8, 56.

Oliver, W. (Ed.). (2009). *Dance and culture: An introductory reader.* Reston, VA: National Dance Association.

Olivera, A. E. (2008). Cultural dance and health: A review of the literature. *American Journal of Health Education, 39*(6), 353–359.

O'Shea, M. R. (2005). *From standards to success.* Alexandria, VA: Association for Supervision and Curriculum Development.

Overby, L. Y., Post, B. C., & Newman, D. (2005). *Interdisciplinary learning through dance: 101 movements.* Champaign, IL: Human Kinetics.

Owen, A. (n.d.). *Irving independent school district laptop program.* Office of Technology Education, U.S. Department of Education. www.ed.gov/about/offices/list/os/technology/plan/2004/site/stories/edlite-irving.html.

Penrod, J. W. (2005). Dancing with technology. *Journal of Physical Education, Recreation and Dance, 75*(1), 6–7, 56.

Pollock, J. E. (2007). *Improving student learning one teacher at a time.* Alexandria, VA: Association for Supervision and Curriculum Development.

Rothstein-Fisch, C., & Trumbull, E. (2008). *Managing diverse classrooms: How to build on students' cultural strengths.* Alexandria, VA: Association for Supervision and Curriculum Development.

Ruppert, S. S. (2006). *Critical evidence: How the arts benefit student achievement.* Washington, DC: National Assembly of State Arts Organizations.

Scheff, H., Sprague, M., & McGreevy-Nichols, S. (2005). *Experiencing dance: From student to dance artist.* Champaign, IL: Human Kinetics.

Schmitz, N. (2007). Using video to productively engage learners. In Y. Inoue (Ed.), *Technology and diversity in higher education* (pp. 233–247). Hershey, PA: Idea Group.

Segal, M., & Adcock, D. (1998). *Your child at play two to three years: Growing up language and the imagination* (2nd ed.). New York: Newmarket Press.

Sharp, S. (2007, October 23). Study: Middle school laptop program leads to writing improvements. *Boston Globe.* www.boston.com/news/education/k_12/articles/2007/10/23/study_middle_school_laptop_program_leads_to_writing_improvements.

Sherrill, C. (2004). *Adapted physical activity, recreation, and sport: Crossdisciplinary and lifespan* (6th ed.). New York: McGraw-Hill.

Silvernail, D. L., & Gritter, A. K. (n.d.) *Maine's middle school laptop program: Creating better writers.* Research Brief. Maine Education Policy Research Institute, University of Southern Maine. www.usm.maine.edu/cepare/Impact_on_Student_Writing_Brief.pdf.

Simkins, M., Cole, K, Tavalin, F., & Means, B. (2002). *Increasing student learning through multimedia projects.* Alexandria, VA: Association for Supervision and Curriculum Development.

Simpson, E. J. (1972). *The classification of educational objectives in the psychomotor domain.* Washington, DC: Gryphon House.

Sousa, D. A. (2006). *How the brain learns* (3rd ed.). Thousand Oaks, CA: Corwin Press.

Spencer, J. (2009). *Everyone's invited: Interactive strategies that engage young adolescents.* Westerville, OH: National Middle School Association.

Sprenter, M. (2005). *How to teach so students remember.* Alexandria, VA: Association for Supervision and Curriculum Development.

Stevens, R., Cherry, G., & Fournier, J. (January, 2002). *Video traces: rich media annotations for teaching and learning.* Computer Supported Collaborative Learning 2002 Conference: Boulder, CO.

Stronge, J. H. (2002). *Qualities of effective teachers.* Alexandria, VA: Association for Supervision and Curriculum Development.

Sullo, B. (2007). *Activating the desire to learn.* Alexandria, VA: Association for Supervision and Curriculum Development.

The Task Force on Children's Learning and The Arts: Birth to Age Eight. (1998). *Young children and the arts: Making creative connections.* Washington, DC: Arts Education Partnership.

Thornburg, D. (2002). *The new basics: Education and the future of work in the telematic age.* Alexandria, VA: Association for Supervision and Curriculum Development.

Tomlinson, C. A. (1999). *The differentiated classroom: Responding to the need of all learners.* Alexandria, VA: Association for Supervision and Curriculum Development.

Tomlinson, C. A., & McTighe, J. (2006). *Integrating differentiated instruction and understanding by design.* Alexandria, VA: Association for Supervision and Curriculum Development.

Voice of America. (2005, October 20). *Arizona high school chooses laptops over textbooks.* newsVOAcom. www.voanews.com/english/archive/2005-10/2005-10-20-voa65.cfm?CFID=74688462&CFTOKEN=18290446.

Ward, S. (2008). Health and the power of dance. *Journal of Physical Education, Recreation and Dance, 79*(4), 33–36.

Wiggins, G. (1990). *The case for authentic assessment: Practical assessment, research and evaluation.* http://PAREonline.net/getvn.asp?v=2&n=2.

Wiggens, G. (1999). Foreword. In D. Lazear (Ed.), *Multiple intelligence approaches to assessment: Solving the assessment conundrum* (p. ix). Tucson, AZ: Zephyr Press.

Wiggins, G., & McTighe, J. (1998). *Understanding by design.* Alexandria, VA: Association for Supervision and Curriculum Development.

Willis, J. (2007). The neuroscience of joyful education. *Educational Leadership, 64.* www.ascd.org/publications/educational_leadership/summer07/vol64/num09/The_Neuroscience_of_Joyful_Education.aspx.

Winnick, J. P. (Ed.). (2000). *Adapted physical education and sport.* Champaign, IL: Human Kinetics.

Wisconsin Department of Public Instruction. (1997). *Model academic standards for dance.* www.dpi.state.wi.us/standards/pdf/dance.pdf.

Wolf, P. (2001). *Brain matters: Translating research into classroom practice.* Alexandria, VA: Association for Supervision and Curriculum Development.

Wright, J. P. (1996). *Social dance instruction: Steps to success.* Champaign, IL: Human Kinetics.

about the national dance association

National Dance Association is an association of the American Alliance for Health, Physical Education, Recreation and Dance (AAHPERD) and is the leading not-for-profit organization of professional educators addressing crucial issues in dance education. NDA strives to cultivate and promote excellence in dance programming. As a part of these initiatives, NDA conducts workshops and conferences across the United States, advocates for quality dance programs at all levels, and publishes state-of-the-art materials. NDA services also reach international markets; some publications are translated into four languages.

Association membership includes professionals in a variety of dance disciplines and at all educational levels as well as students in higher education. During its long history, NDA has served as a resource for federal and state agencies and arts and education organizations. The National Endowment for the Arts, Harkness Foundation for Dance, Capezio BalletMakers, the United States Department of Education, and the National Endowment for the Humanities have supported NDA projects.

about the editor

Fran Anthony Meyer, PhD, CHES, is an educational consultant in Fredericksburg, Virginia. For 19 years she taught dance, health, and physical education to students from preschool through eighth grade as well as to students of various ages with disabilities. She worked with teachers to plan and implement elementary and middle school arts programs. Meyer worked with the local schools and parks and recreation department to establish FREDANCO (boys' and girls' performing companies).

Meyer has served as a curriculum writer and a frequent workshop and in-service facilitator at the local, state, national, and international levels; as the founder and director of a state children's dance festival; and as dance editor for the *Virginia Journal.* As a consultant to the Virginia Department of Education, Meyer served on task forces to develop state standards, write dance curriculum and assessment items for grades K through 12, and develop lessons for talented and gifted students in dance. She served as a planning team member and workshop facilitator for the Virginia Fine Arts Leadership Conference for 10 years as well as an adjudicator for the Governor's Schools for Arts Education and the Virginia Fine Arts Scholarship Awards.

Meyer served as dance vice-president and later as president of the Southern District AAHPERD and as president of National Dance Association (NDA), and she is currently NDA's representative to the AAHPERD Board of Governors.

Meyer has received numerous awards, including the VAHPERD Honor and Pioneer Awards, the Distinguished Service to the Community Award from Virginia Commonwealth University, Leaders Who Make a Difference Award from Longwood University, the NASPE Distinguished Leadership in Physical Education Award, and the NDA Presidential Citation Award. Meyer also is recognized as a fellow in the North American Society for Health, Physical Education, Recreation, Sport and Dance.

CD User Instructions

System Requirements

You can use this CD-ROM on either a Windows-based PC or a Macintosh computer.

Windows

- IBM PC compatible with Pentium processor
- Windows 98/2000/XP/Vista
- Adobe Reader 8.0
- Microsoft Office PowerPoint 2003 or higher
- 4x CD-ROM drive

Macintosh

- Power Mac recommended
- System 10.4 or higher
- Adobe Reader
- Microsoft Office PowerPoint 2004 for MAC or higher
- 4x CD-ROM drive

User Instructions

Windows

1. Insert the *Implementing the National Dance Education Standards* CD-ROM. (Note: The CD-ROM must be present in the drive at all times.)
2. Select the "My Computer" icon from the desktop.
3. Select the CD-ROM drive.
4. Open the file you wish to view. See the "00Start.pdf" file for a list of the contents.

Macintosh

1. Insert the *Implementing the National Dance Education Standards* CD-ROM. (Note: The CD-ROM must be present in the drive at all times.)
2. Double-click the CD icon located on the desktop.
3. Open the file you wish to view. See the "00Start" file for a list of the contents.

For customer support, contact Technical Support:

Phone: 217-351-5076 Monday through Friday (excluding holidays) between 7:00 a.m. and 7:00 p.m. (CST).

Fax: 217-351-2674

E-mail: support@hkusa.com